THE BORDER GUIDE

The Ultimate Guide to Living, Working, and Investing across the Border

Robert Keats, CFP® (US), CFP™ (CDA), RFP (CDA), MSFP

Self-Counsel Press
(a division of)
International Self-Counsel Press Ltd.
USA Canada

Self-Counsel Press acknowledges the financial support of the Government of Canada through the Canada Book Fund (CBF) for our publishing activities.

Printed in Canada.
Seventh edition: 2004; Reprinted: 2004
Tenth edition: 2009; Reprinted: 2010, 2012
Eleventh edition: 2016

Library and Archives Canada Cataloguing in Publication

Keats, Robert, author

The border guide : the ultimate guide to living, working, and investing in the United States / Robert Keats. — Eleventh edition.

(Cross-border series)
Issued in print and electronic formats.
ISBN 978-1-77040-248-5 (paperback).—ISBN 978-1-77040-859-3 (kindle).—ISBN 978-1-77040-858-6 (epub)

1. Canadians—United States—Finance, Personal. 2. Investments, Canadian—United States. 3. Finance, Personal—United States. 4. Canadians—Legal status, laws, etc—United States. 5. Taxation—Law and legislation—Canada. 6. Taxation—Law and legislation—United States. I. Keats, Robert. Border guide. II. Title. III. Series: Cross-border series

HG179.K42 2015   332.024008911073   C2015-905105-3
C2015-905106-1

Self-Counsel Press
(a division of)
International Self-Counsel Press Ltd.

Bellingham, WA
USA

North Vancouver, BC
Canada

Contents

Notice

Laws are constantly changing. Every effort is made to keep this publication as current as possible. However, the author, the publisher, and the vendor of this book make no representation or warranties about the outcome or the use to which the information in this book is put and are not assuming any liability for any claims, losses, or damages arising out of the use of this book. The reader should not rely on the author or the publisher of this book for any professional advice. Please be sure that you have the most recent edition.

This book is dedicated to my late father and mother,
Gordon Keats (1922–1992) and Anne Keats (1924–2006).
May they rest in peace with our heavenly Father.
Dad and Mom, I miss you.

Acknowledgments

No man is an island. This book in its 11 editions would not have been possible without the assistance of many people. I have been blessed with a lovely family — my wife, Barbara; my children, Sarah, Daniel, Carl, and Rebekah; and my grandchildren Daniel, Colton, Addison, and Ricky who have been my inspiration. My only regret in writing this book was the time I had to spend away from them all.

The research required to prepare any book of this scope is enormous, even under ideal circumstances. Taking highly technical topics such as immigration, tax planning, and estate planning between Canada and the United States, and presenting them in a format that is both logical and readable, have been formidable tasks. I would like to acknowledge Dale Walters, my partner of more than 20 years, for assistance in editing and providing a great deal of research.

I thank the other many professional employees at Keats, Connelly and Associates, LLC for their encouragement and suggestions to keep *The Border Guide* current and valuable to its readers.

I would also like to thank all of you who read previous editions of this book for your positive comments and enthusiastic support. My final and biggest thank-you goes to all of our cross-border Canadian and American clients. Without their interest and encouragement, I would never have been in a position to enjoy such a wonderful career and assist so many people living the most amazing cross-border lifestyle.

Introduction

Because our social and cultural institutions are so similar, many Americans and Canadians feel completely at home on either side of our two nations' border. Many incorrectly assume that the laws governing investment, taxation, and immigration are the same as well. Unfortunately, this can lead to some unpleasant surprises, particularly when conducting basic financial transactions such as buying or selling real estate. The North American Free Trade Agreement (NAFTA), the demographic push of baby boomers adopting a cross-border lifestyle or retiring in large numbers to the US Sunbelt, the affordable US real estate, and the relatively lower cost of living and the taxes in the US has only served to fuel the fires of cross-border commerce. Many Canadians migrate to the Sunbelt seeking respite from harsh winters, and many Americans migrate to Canada for the pleasant summers.

The Border Guide is specifically written for both Canadians and Americans, regardless of which kind of cross-border lifestyle they are choosing to live across the 49th parallel. This, the 11th edition of *The Border Guide*, has been updated and rewritten to allow readers to live the most amazing cross-border lifestyle possible. It is a particularly great resource for Canadians who are considering some form of permanent or seasonal residency in the United States, or who have resided there for employment or other reasons and are contemplating returning to Canada. It will also prove extremely useful for US citizens living in, investing in, or moving to Canada, or those who are married to Canadians. It will be of particular value to Canadians who intend to invest or do business in the United States, even if their financial curiosity is limited to an occasional shopping trip or vacation. Whatever your interest, the information contained in these pages will help you to transact your cross-border business affairs with competence and confidence. It is the only step-by-step guide for people who want to understand and take advantage of American and Canadian tax, financial, and medical institutions. It will also show you how to avoid many of the common pitfalls of having assets and spending extended periods of time in both countries.

Chapters 1 through 7 deal primarily with Canadians visiting and investing in the US, and Chapters 8 to 11 address Canadians moving and immigrating to the US. Although many of the issues discussed in these chapters are not relevant to Americans immigrating to or investing in Canada, Americans face many similar cross-border issues when they move north. I therefore recommend that American readers review these chapters, paying particular attention to the concerns of US citizens and green card holders living in Canada, and the differences in both income and estate taxation between Canada and the United States. Chapters 10 and 11 discuss the residency status of new or returning immigrants to Canada and certain Canadian tax regulations that apply to Americans who invest in Canada. To get the full picture, both of these chapters should be read by Americans moving to Canada for the first time. Chapters 14 to 16 address investment, social benefits, medical coverage, estate tax, and issues relating to small business ownership for cross-border residents. Check also the download kit, which includes detailed information on the role of a cross-border financial planning professional in helping you get the most benefits from living or investing across the Canada/US border.

To prevent this book from becoming a dry technical manual that is factually accurate but functionally useless, I have presented my ideas in a nontechnical fashion. Certain concepts have been simplified for readability. Sound professional advice is recommended for applying any of the ideas or techniques detailed in this guide. Please be aware that tax and other rules are constantly changing, which can make some of this information outdated the minute the book reaches the shelves. Please rely on your advisors as well as the resources mentioned in the download kit at www.self-counsel.com/updates/borderguide/16kit.htm to keep current on all of these issues as well as to check for possible future updates to *The Border Guide*.

At the end of many of the chapters I have included some typical questions from readers, along with my responses, to illustrate and broaden the concepts presented. The majority of these questions were posed by readers of my numerous newspaper and magazine columns and articles, or by readers of a previous edition of *The Border Guide*. Most were looking for advice relating to their own specific problems or situations, but I hope that my responses will help to answer your questions as well.

The Swinging Door 1

Creating the Most Amazing Cross-Border Lifestyle

The ideal cross-border lifestyle is best portrayed as your own virtual private swinging door on the Canada/US border. The door allows you to go through in either direction whenever you want, for whatever time period you want, free from worry of either Canadian or US immigration or tax authorities. Plus, this swinging door would give you fully paid access to both US and Canadian medical systems for the rest of your life.

This book will endeavor to get each and every reader as close to his or her own private swinging door as possible under individual circumstances.

When I was a young boy living in Hudson Bay, in northern Saskatchewan, we had a swinging door between the kitchen and dining room. I remember how much fun it was as a five- or six-year-old to be able to run through that door in either direction, chasing my brothers at full speed and not having to worry about opening the door. We did have to be careful to make sure nobody was coming through the door in the opposite direction, but it was a great convenience that made our small house with its two-hole outhouse (a very cold proposition in the long Saskatchewan winters) a little bit more livable. The swinging door and its ease of movement back and forth stuck in my mind and helped me create a system to assist the many Canadians and Americans who enjoy a cross-border lifestyle and do not wish to encounter the hassles of worrying about immigration issues, tax issues, medical insurance concerns, and the amount of time they can spend in each other's countries.

In the chapters of this book I will cover all the necessary details that one needs to put together to construct a virtual swinging door that will allow an amazing, worry-free lifestyle. *The Border Guide* will provide you the answers for the new ability to move back and forth between Canada and the US while eliminating or minimizing potential obstacles, so you can enjoy the cross-border lifestyle to its fullest.

CHOOSE YOUR CROSS-BORDER LIFESTYLE

In my many years' experience dealing with individuals and couples attempting to live a cross-border lifestyle, I have found that there are three basic categories of cross-border lifestyles that people fall into or desire:

- The Vacationer: The casual, short-term visitors looking to get a break, such as Canadians wanting a break from Canadian winters by using their vacation time to enjoy the warmth of the Hawaiian beaches or some other US Sunbelt state. Generally, these individuals are still working full time and often bring children with them; they may or may not return to the same area every year and likely have not yet purchased a residence in the US.
- The Snowbird: The regular, longer-term visitors who wish to spend the majority of the winter in the US Sunbelt and limit their stay to less than six months per calendar year. They are generally retired or semi-retired with the flexibility to be away from their home bases for long periods of time, and to return periodically for family events during the winter. The majority of these people would have either an RV of some form, a long-term lease, or own a US permanent vacation property in their Sunbelt area of choice.
- The Settler: Those committed to settling into a full-time cross-border lifestyle for the long haul, including tax relief from high Canadian income taxes. They live in the US the majority of the time and decide that there is no reason to go back to Canada, other than for short visits on special occasions and/or for a few months during the summer. Settlers are generally retired or have their businesses running at a level where they are no longer required to work day-to-day. They frequently purchase a substantial US residence and downsize or sell their Canadian homes. They will normally receive a large tax advantage by changing their official tax residence from Canada to the US. They obtain some form of year-round immigration status in the US, for example, a green card, which is the US legal permanent residence status.

Refer to Chapter 9 for more details with respect to income tax savings when adopting a Settler lifestyle in the US.

Regardless of which of the three categories you fall into, being prepared by building your own virtual Swinging Door can eliminate any potential obstacles and create the most amazing cross-border lifestyle. By putting in place the private Swinging Door that will protect the cross-border lifestyle you choose you can avoid all the problems one hears about visitors to the US or Canada who were not prepared and had their vacations ruined. Some have even been banned from visiting the US for a period of several years. I will refer to the three categories as described above throughout the book so please remember which category applies to your desired cross-border lifestyle in order for you to focus on the parts of the book that apply to the specific category that applies to you.

AN INTRODUCTION TO PERSONAL CROSS-BORDER FINANCIAL PLANNING

After many years of providing cross-border financial planning services, I have come to the conclusion that the US is the best tax haven for Canadians and is likely to remain so for the foreseeable future. The same tax advantages that are available to Canadians by going to a remote island in the middle of nowhere can be had by driving across the US border. Ninety percent of Canada's population is located within a few hours of the US border, so the United States is a very accessible tax haven. In addition, Canadians are familiar with US cities, modes of transportation, the primary language, and other cultural similarities.

The economic and tax environment of the US and Canada has grown in breadth and complexity over the past few decades; along with it, the need for comprehensive personal cross-border financial planning analysis. The intent of such planning is to capitalize on the most satisfactory mix of savings plans, insurance coverage, investment vehicles, tax strategies, retirement plans, and estate-planning techniques available in each country. These cross-border planning opportunities can reap great financial rewards for you and your heirs.

Cross-border financial planning analysis encompasses all the basic individual financial planning requirements of both Canada and the US in the areas of net worth, cash flow, risk management, retirement goals, taxation, estate planning, and investments. It analyzes each area according to your situation, then weighs options; completes timely currency conversions; factors in your immigration status; examines applicable tax treaty rules; and develops a road map for you to follow to achieve your financial goals with maximum income, safety, and tax savings.

One of the major difficulties inherent in cross-border financial planning is that the rules change depending on immigration status and on which direction the cross-border movement is going. For example, a Vacationer or Snowbird to the United States who marries a US resident dramatically alters his or her financial planning options, and new cross-border financial planning analysis becomes necessary in order to take advantage of new opportunities and avoid any costly mistakes. In addition, performing a seemingly simple task (such as purchasing a home in the US) can affect a person's tax status with respect to both income tax and estate tax in the US. The effects are mostly positive if you understand what to do with this changing status and plan appropriately. A Vacationer or Snowbird from Canada has to follow different sets of tax and immigration rules than a Settler with a US visa or green card. Planning issues for each status category are discussed in detail in subsequent chapters.

THE FREQUENT TRAVELER STATUS

Most people are familiar with frequent flyer programs and frequent stay rewards programs. Those with the highest status in their programs get the best perks. To live the most amazing cross-border lifestyle, I have developed what I call frequent Canada/US border crossing program statuses to help readers of *The Border Guide* more easily understand what is necessary to get the most benefits. Here are the categories rated by the ease of crossing the 49th parallel anytime by any transportation mode:

- **Platinum:** Those that are dual US/Canadian citizens are in the highest category. They cannot be denied access from either country even if they have a criminal record. Individuals in this category can spend 365 days or 0 days annually and work in either country anytime they want for the rest of their lives. If they make the effort to get a NEXUS card (explained later in this chapter), I would consider them Platinum Plus.
- **Gold:** Canadian citizens with a US green card, which is legal permanent residence status in the US. Their status is similar to that of the Platinum travelers with the exception that there are restrictions on continuing to maintain a green card, such as continuing to maintain a US residence and following basic morals and laws by avoiding anything more serious than things like traffic tickets. Those in this category with a NEXUS card are Gold Plus.
- **Silver:** Canadians with a non-immigrant visa which allows multiple entries to the US along with the ability to live and work in the US for 365 days a year if they desire. In Chapter 8, I summarize these potential different non-immigrant visas, each with their own qualifications and expiration dates. Silver Plus are those at this level with a NEXUS card.
- **Bronze:** These are Canadians in the Vacationer or visitor category with no visa to remain in the US other than the standard six-month

visitor's arrangement between Canada and the US. Those with a NEXUS card are Bronze Plus.

The goal for some people will be to have the Platinum level of frequent traveler status as they can truly live totally amazing cross-border lifestyles without any hassles or concerns whatsoever with respect to immigration or border-crossing issues, unless they are importing or exporting goods. Those with the Settler lifestyle should generally fall into Platinum, Gold, and to a limited extent, the Silver frequent traveler status level so they can also have some extremely beneficial tax reduction opportunities, which I will cover later in the book.

HOW LONG CAN CANADIANS REMAIN IN THE US? IMPORTANT NEW RULES

There have been many new rules implemented over the last couple of years jointly by Canadian Border Services Agency (CBSA) and US Customs and Border Protection (CBP) that have greatly affected Canadians attempting to live the cross-border lifestyle. In fact, a lot of what you might have remembered in the past is no longer applicable and outright wrong; it might get you in trouble, or conversely new rules may create opportunities for better and smoother border crossings. This section of this chapter is critical in understanding the new rules to use them to your advantage.

CANADIANS DO NOT REQUIRE A VISA TO ENTER THE US

To provide the most accurate picture of what the immigration rules mean, with respect to who can enter the US and for how long, I have gone directly to the proverbial horse's mouth to provide two very significant quotes for Canadians traveling to the US. This should help Canadians focus on what really matters when crossing the border rather than worry about all of the rumors and confusing hype surrounding Canadians entering the US. The first quote is directly from the Canadian US Embassy's website (canada.usembassy.gov, accessed January 2016): "Canadian citizens do not require a visa to enter the United States directly from Canada for the purposes of visiting or studying."

This statement could not be clearer or broken down to a more simple format but it is very important that Canadians understand that the US and Canada do have a special relationship to allow each other's citizens to enter the other's country easily and without formal paperwork. The next quote is directly from the US Customs and Border Protection (CBP) website, addressed specifically to Canadians:

"The burden of proof that the Canadian citizen is not an intended immigrant [plans to make the US their primary residence] is always on the applicant. There is no set period of time Canadians must wait to re-enter the US after the end of their stay, but if it appears to the CBP Officer that the person applying for entry is spending more time overall in the US than in Canada, it will be up to the traveler to prove to the officer that they are not de-facto US residents. One of the ways to do this is to demonstrate significant ties to their home country, including proof of employment, residency, etc." ("Canadian Citizens/Residents/Landed Immigrants entering the U.S.", cbp.gov, accessed February 2016).

Regardless of what anybody tells you, whether it be the border officials themselves, friends, relatives, accountants, or attorneys, it is these two simple quotes that are the basis for understanding how to create your swinging door on the Canada-US border regardless of whether you are a Vacationer, Snowbird, or Settler. Using these two quotes along with the following summary of suggested recommendations will allow you smooth travels back and forth across the 49th parallel whenever you need to travel:

- Know the US visitor rule (generally never spend more than 6 months at a time in the US, or more time in the US than Canada in the previous 12 months). Settlers can ignore this rule.
- Subscribe to NEXUS, Global Entry, TSA Pre or similar trusted traveler programs and never breach the trust; work towards the Platinum Plus frequent border crossing status.
- Avoid the red flags of the border crossing (the red flags are covered later in this chapter).
- Know and follow any rules with respect to bringing goods across the border.
- Understand and follow any IRS income tax rules that may apply to you.
- Always travel with your Border Kit/proof of your status (see what should be included in your Border Kit later in this chapter).
- Ignore the rumor mill.

VISITOR RULES APPLIED

Starting in mid-2014, the United States Citizenship and Immigration Service through their Customs and Border Protection (CBP) personnel (the people you actually meet when you're clearing customs to enter US), have started to implement new policies that affect Canadians. These new procedures are important to understand, since ease of crossing the border is vital to that amazing cross-border lifestyle. Unfortunately these rules are being implemented inconsistently and create substantial confusion. I will attempt to clarify some of the issues as much as possible but please keep in mind CBP is a large government organization that is very bureaucratic, and it is difficult to consistently get the correct information to act upon appropriately. Settlers can ignore this section as it deals strictly with those in the Visitor and Snowbird lifestyle categories.

The first point of confusion is how long a Canadian can stay in the US as a Vacationer or Snowbird. The rules as applied in the past have always been that a Canadian would get six months to visit the US from the date of entry into the country and although this is technically not changed I will explain a few ways that have made it appear as if it has changed. If the Canadian left the US and returned at a later date, the six month clock was reset to that current date of the entry, not at all affected by any previous border entry. Traditionally, Canadians did not have their passports stamped unless it was a simple date-of-entry type stamp and they were not required to have paper I-94 cards (an I-94 card is simply a small card or a dated passport stamp issued by USCIS Indicating a B-2 visitor/tourist visa has been granted, it is inserted into the passport of the visitor and it indicates the date of entry and the expiration of their visitor's time in the US). As noted earlier in this chapter Canadians do not require a visa to visit the US, so this attempt by the USCIS to require Canadians to have B-2 visitors visas and I-94 cards or date stamps indicates to me the struggle the US immigration people are having with dealing with the tradition of free travel between Canada and the US. This simply means more rules with less flexibility and a greater need for diligence on the part of Canadian Vacationers and Snowbirds to the US to build their own swinging doors to achieve as close to the Platinum level of cross-border travel status they can.

To provide a bit of necessary background information, all US visitors, other than Canadians, have needed to have an I-94 card in their passport as proof of their B-2 visitor visa, however the procedure was changed in May 2013 to an automatic electronic authorization for the I-94 combined with a simple B-2 visa passport stamp, included with the visa expiration date in the passport of the visitor. The typical visitor from one of the countries that has a visa waiver program with the US is only allowed a 90-day visa to visit the US before he or she is forced to leave or apply for an extension. This new procedure is only for those countries that are on a visa waiver program with the US which includes most European countries and other major democratic countries around the world.

Canada, because of its special status with the US is technically not part of this visa waiver program and as noted above has a special relationship. The automatic I-94 authorizations for this new program for the visa waiver countries are created electronically from the passenger manifests from airlines and cruise lines submitted to USCIS in advance of the respective flight or cruise. What this has meant to Canadians, primarily flying to the US, is they are frequently getting this B-2 visa stamp in their passports with the infamous expiration date that tells them when they need to get out of the US.

This creates many concerns and brings up many questions. The first concern is that it is not consistently applied throughout all the ports of entry into the US or even amongst the US CBP personnel themselves. This policy, if it is applied at all, appears to be only at airports and seaports. Does this mean those crossing the border at the land points of entry are under a different set of rules? Not really, it just adds to the confusion. Consequently, it is difficult to advise people what to do since US CBP personnel seem to be confused themselves as to how to apply these new procedures to Canadians with their special 180-day visitor time limit. Another major concern is that what happens to a Canadian who has a date stamped B-2 visa in his or her passport who returns to Canada for a short period of time then returns to the US. Does he or she get a new stamp upon re-entry or is the date on the initial B-2 stamp in the passport still the governing date that the visitor needs to be concerned with in order to not overstay legal time in the US?

THE 30-DAY RULE

Those visitors to the US from the typical visa-waiver countries who get their automatic 90-day visitor's visas under this new electronic format with the B-2 visa stamp in their passport can leave the US and visit Canada or Mexico for up to 30 days without having to qualify for or apply for a new visitor's B-2 visa. However, the 30 days they are out of the US does not increase the length of the B-2 visa stamped in their passport. In other words they have a total of 90 days to visit the US and if they use 30 days of it to visit Canada or Mexico, that is up to them, but they do not get an additional 30 days in the US. Even though Canada is not part of this visa waiver program this 30-day rule applies to, in many circumstances, the US CBP border personnel are applying this rule to them at airports. Consequently, if a Canadian visitor were to return to Canada for, say, two weeks at Christmas, does he or she need to subtract two weeks from the total 6-month stay in the US or is he or she allowed to stay in the US 6 months out of the last 12? Would that change if he or she actually had the B-2 visa stamp with expiration date in the passport? Similarly, what happens if the Canadian stays out of the US for 30 days at Christmastime and returns to the US; does he or she get a new 6-month authorization to stay in the US or how do the CBP personnel calculate the time he or she can stay in the US from their latest date of entry? Is this different whether the person flies or drives across the border? Unfortunately, the answer to all these questions is subjective and depends a great deal on the US CBP person you meet when you're entering the US. This person can range from being very pleasant and professional to being quite curt and outright nasty. Personnel could be very experienced or it could be their first day on the job, yet it is their demeanor and interpretation of the rules and the procedures that govern your experience crossing the border. They could stamp your passport, not stamp your passport, decide to allow you to stay 30 days, 90 days, 180 days, ban you from entering on that trip or for up to five years; whatever they determine based on their interpretation of the facts presented. By the power granted to them by the USCIS rules, they are the judge, jury, and executioner. Your recourse to their decision as to what they do or not do for you is very limited.

The Canadian Snowbird Association wrote to USCIS to attempt to clarify this 30-day rule and they got a letter saying that yes it does apply to Canadians. However, besides the CSA not asking the right questions in their letter to the USCIS, there is no explanation or backup to why it might apply to Canadians who do not even require a visa to visit the US. Nor does it make any sense for Canadians who live near the border and cross to the US for shopping or entertainment weekly or more often throughout the year. In addition, the rules are not applied consistently throughout the entire US port of entry CBP system; in fact those that use a NEXUS card to enter and leave the US apparently never get this rule applied. I think asking the CBP whether this 30-day rule applies is like a Canadian writing to the CRA and asking them if the Canadian *Income Tax Act* applies to them; the answer is always going to be yes.

There is plenty of controversy and confusion with respect to how it is determined, as a Canadian visitor whether you have the legal right to visit the US for 180 days out of every 12 months, or 180 days from the date of last entry, and then how this is affected by the number of entries and exits back and forth during any given time period. It used to be fairly clear; six months from the date of your most recent entry. However, now with computers tracking you in and out of the US and airplane manifests being submitted to USCIS prior to your departure from Canada or when leaving the US after a visit, along with myriad new rules, it is less clear. Some CBT personnel look at your travel record and decide you have spent too much time in the US in the recent past and they decide to limit your stay on this visit to a certain fixed time such as 30 days, perhaps much less time than you were hoping to spend in the US on that particular visit. Yet, others will welcome you for another full six-month stay as a visitor without hesitation on the same exact facts. The question is how do you know the correct amount of time a visitor can spend? The answer is you don't, but you do have a lot of control over your experience. If you follow the recommendations in this book it will help you build that virtual swinging door that will make your travels back and forth across the US border much easier and with the results you desire.

We've covered a lot of ground and it gets very confusing so here is a summary of the key points.

SUMMARY OF THE FACTS

- Canadians and Americans have a special relationship that allows them easy access as visitors to each other's countries, a special visitor status.
- No paper visa or prior approval visa is required for Canadians to travel as visitors to the US for up to six months or 180 days at a time. You just go to the border and present yourself with proper identification and enter the US.
- A B-2 visa status is the *de facto* automatic status granted to Canadians who are Vacationers or Snowbirds to the US, or a B-1 visa for those conducting business in the US.
- The 30-day rule that applies to those visitors to the US from a visa waiver country when they want to leave the US to visit Canada or Mexico for up to 30 days does not apply to Canadians on the B-2 visitor status. However, certain CBP personnel have been known to apply this rule to Canadians so Canadian visitors to the US must be aware of it, be prepared to deal with it, and avoid circumstances where it could cause problems for them.
- For Canadians who do get their passports stamped by a CBP official with the B-2 visa (not just a normal entry date stamp), with the expiration date included, it is important that they respect that expiration date and have proof they were back in Canada on the date of expiration of the visa on the stamp in their passport.

Although the stamping of Canadian passports with the date that the Canadian visitor must exit the US is not consistently applied throughout ports of entry to the US, it appears primarily in the Canadian airports that have US customs officials that are applying this procedure. The vehicle border crossings to the US still are not following this procedure at time of writing. No NEXUS travelers, according to my research, have yet ever had the 30-day rule apply to them.

Although there is no official rule as to how many 180-day visiting periods Canadians can start in the US by leaving and then re-entering, it is generally understood that they should spend less than 180 days out of every 365 rolling calendar days.

Canadian Border Services Agency (CBSA) and US Customs and Border Protection (CBP) can and do share information on a regular basis. More and more of this information is online and accessible to the customs officials at the border. In the fall of 2015 the Canadian federal government issued a statement that they were now going to use the information from tracking Canadians going back and forth across the border to reduce or eliminate certain benefits like Employment Insurance, certain tax credits, and qualification for Canadian Old Age Security. The government warns Canadians that they are using this information if you look at the fine print on the customs form that you complete when you enter Canada. Both the US and Canadian governments face challenging privacy violations by using this information so it may not ever actually be able to be used in the manner in which the governments would like.

Consequently, understand that both the CBSA and the CBP are getting better at this tracking so you can make the assumption that either now or in the future they will have every single time you have crossed the border in either direction on their computer systems exactly to the time, date, and mode of travel. All travelers can now go to the CBP website, (cbp.gov) under I-94 arrival/departure history, obtain a complete travel history each and every time they have crossed the Canada/US border in either direction for up to the past five years. However, please note, even after a couple of years of allowing travelers to access these records the Canadian and US immigration information-sharing program has not been very accurate. Many travelers find the information unreliable and many entrances or exits to and from are missed entirely, especially land crossings in the more remote areas. It is always best to keep your own records as you could be denied entry to the US because of inaccurate history in your CBP records. The Canada Border Services Agency can also supply entrance and exit travel records but they are certainly not available online and must be applied for under the *Access to Information and Privacy Act* which takes about 30 days to complete.

EFFORTLESS BORDER CROSSINGS

Regardless of your category, the Vacationer, Snowbird, Settler, or even if you are a Business Traveler, these pointers will help you make your border crossings in either direction fast, smooth, and stress-free.

1. Enroll in any of the trusted traveler programs such as NEXUS, Global Entry, and CANPASS (NEXUS is recommended; currently you get a free registration for Global Entry when you are a NEXUS member). These programs are all pre-clearance for both customs and immigration and they prove to Canadian and US border professionals that you are a trusted traveler, and you do not need to be screened to the same level as the other 90 percent of the travelers trying to cross the border at the same time as you. These programs can be easily applied for online, they are relatively low cost, and they will save time because they allow you to bypass long lineups. Once you are on these programs it is extremely important that you keep your trusted traveler program abreast of any changes in address or other information such as a new passport number. You are required to have a perfect record with both Canadian and US customs and immigration to get on and maintain these programs as they are zero tolerance. I am a member of the NEXUS program and on a recent trip through the very busy Toronto Pearson Airport from Washington DC; it took less than ten minutes total time from leaving the aircraft to the time I was at the curb getting into my cab and I did not have to say one single word to any Canadian customs official; how smooth is that? This is certainly the Platinum Plus status, as other travelers on the same flight who did not have NEXUS probably spent 30 minutes or more in line at Canadian customs.
2. Do not attempt to travel on a passport that has fewer than six months to its expiration date. Canadian passports can now be renewed for up to 10 years at a time, I recommend you use this new option as it will save you money, hassles, and time.
3. Body language is extremely important; border professionals are trained to look for signs in a person's behavior to determine who to examine or question more closely. Act cool, confident, and professional at all times in any custom/immigration area.
4. When speaking to a customs professional, speak in a normal tone of voice, do not talk down to him or her, or have any anger or frustration in your voice. Answer questions without hesitation,

simply and accurately. Rehearse mentally the answers to all of the standard questions customs and immigration persons normally will ask such as: what is the purpose of your visit, what is the length of your visit, where will you be staying in the country?

5. Have any documents that may be requested by the border professional easily accessible and if you are bringing goods across the border that you purchased make sure you know exactly where those items are and the receipts for the purchase are.
6. Know the dollar limits of any amount of goods that applicable custom rules allow you to bring with you duty free, and be prepared to pay duty as required if you are over these limits, and don't try to hide or not declare any goods you have purchased.
7. Do not try to enter the US with any fruits, nuts, or meats of any kind including prepackaged ones.
8. Always carry a Border Kit to prove what you are saying when entering the country. Read about the Border Kit in this chapter.
9. Keep a travel log with you to track each time and mode of transportation that you crossed the border for at least the past 12 months or more and be able to produce it easily. It is also useful to back up this log with boarding passes or actual flight itineraries. If border computers are wrong or inaccurate, it is up to you to provide the proof needed to correct or dispute them; the respective governments will not do this voluntarily.
10. If traveling with a spouse, have one spouse do the talking and the other spouse do the document management or production as required. If you're traveling with children, either bribe them or threaten them within an inch of their life to say nothing to any border professional unless specifically addressed, and no fooling around or joking with brothers and sisters while waiting in line.
11. Smile and be pleasant, and bite your tongue, regardless of how nasty or unprofessional the customs or immigration official is being or how tired you are from a long flight.
12. If you are a business visitor going to be doing work in the US for your Canadian company, state so to the immigration professional at the inspection window, do not say you're coming for a vacation just because it is easier and you have done that many times before. Have a letter from the company (even if it is your own company) that states the purpose of your work in the US and the

length of time you are likely to need to do your job, and confirm the fact that you will be paid only from the Canadian company while working in the US.

13. Next time you cross the border take a few extra blank customs forms with you to fill out at home in advance of your next trip when you are in a relaxed environment. Make sure you fill the customs forms for all family members correctly before you get to the customs window for inspection. Please note that if you have a Global Entry/NEXUS trusted traveler program you no longer have to fill out forms as you answer the required questions on the kiosk terminal that scans your fingerprints.
14. When traveling with a spouse or companion with a different immigration status than you for the country you are entering it is normally best to go through customs and immigration separately or even take separate flights. For example, if you were traveling from Canada to the US with your spouse who is a US citizen and you are simply a visitor to the US it is normally best to travel separately or at the very least don't clear customs at the same time. See Red Flags when Crossing the Border later in this chapter.
15. If you are frequent traveler and make multiple entrances and return visits back and forth across the Canada/US border as a Canadian citizen, consider getting some form of immigration status with the US that allows multiple entries such as an investor visa, a green card, or even becoming a dual US citizen. Having one of these visas can elevate your cross-border travel status to as high as Platinum Plus. Getting visas, green cards, and becoming a dual citizen is covered in detail in Chapter 8.
16. When you are traveling to the US by vehicle, make sure the vehicle you are driving is registered to you or at least somebody who's traveling with you and that the vehicle is licensed in the province and the exact address at which you live. Clean out your trunk of items such as your hunting rifle, tools, and other items that may cause an inspecting officer to ask embarrassing questions. When in the US as a visitor from Canada, be very careful when you need to make a quick trip, for example, from Palm Springs to Vancouver and you fly to Seattle and rent a car to drive up to Vancouver and then try to return to the US in that same vehicle. See Red Flags when Crossing the Border later in this chapter.
17. Use modern technology to make your travel safer and easier. Use one of the many free applications for your smartphone or tablet

or just basic secure Internet drop boxes (a secure place on the web where you can store or share personal documents) so that you can access important documents instantly while traveling. In these drop boxes, keep copies of your passports, visas, wills, powers of attorney, doctor/prescription phone numbers, and details of charge card information. Don't be technology deficient; if my 3-year-old grandson and my 95-year-old client can efficiently operate an iPad, anyone can learn. They are great devices, as easy to use as most remote controls.

18. Do not travel to the US on one-way tickets or tickets that you purchased for cash immediately before the flight is to leave. These are red flags as discussed later in this chapter.
19. Declare all monetary instruments or cash that totals more than $10,000 in the currency of the country in which you're arriving; better still don't travel with that much cash or valuables/jewelry in your possession.
20. Be aware that many foreign-made (from a US-perspective) medications are not FDA-approved, and you cannot bring them into the US; check with a US pharmacist ahead of time if you are unsure. Also, when traveling to the US, bring only the amount of medication you'll need during the trip in its original container.

These pointers give you a solid foundation for the start of building your virtual swinging door to that amazing cross-border lifestyle you desire. If you follow all of these pointers consistently and avoid the red flags noted later in this chapter you will alleviate 95 percent of all cross-border travel hassles. The other 5 percent are things that are beyond your control, for example who you get at the customs/immigration inspection window and what kind of mood he or she is in.

THE BORDER KIT

The Border Kit is, very simply, proof that you are not intending to take up permanent residence in the US without obtaining proper visas or authorizations to do so. It is your obligation to provide this proof, not the customs person's responsibility to attempt to look it up or check for other sources of information pertaining to you. Officials only use the information they have on hand to support what you are saying and if you have nothing to support what you are saying with respect to your intentions when entering the US they automatically assume you are intending to do something illegal. By carrying the information below you will always have proof of your intentions on you at all times —

- most recent phone, electricity, and other utility bills,
- most recent property tax notice if you own, or rental agreement if you rent,
- most recent Canadian tax return and non-resident IRS forms filed, such as Form 8840 or 1040NR (see Chapter 4),
- valid provincial driver's licence and medicare card,
- proof of employment if still employed (e.g., latest pay stub),
- Canadian vehicle registrations if driving or return plane tickets if flying,
- a travel log of every time you have crossed the border in either direction including times, dates, and modes of transportation, boarding passes, and itineraries to back up your records, and
- charge card statements showing recent purchases.

Don't carry any items that may indicate US residency, such as a US driver's licence, US mail, anything relating to US property you own, none of those business cards where you have a Canadian address on one side of the card and a US address on the other, US bank credit cards, etc.

Although carrying this Border Kit may be a pain, Murphy's Law of travel means that if you have the kit in your possession when you enter the United States, you likely won't be asked to produce proof of Canadian residence; the first time you travel without it, you may be refused entry until you can provide proof of your Canadian residence and your intention to return to Canada.

RED FLAGS WHEN CROSSING THE BORDER

In addition to carrying a Border Kit, you can make cross-border travel in either direction much less stressful if you avoid the red flags that immigrations and customs officers are constantly on the lookout for. Some of these red flags are —

- traveling without a valid passport or approved equivalent identification (also, traveling on a passport that is about to expire or is likely to expire during the six-month visitor visa status is grounds for refused entry to the US),
- traveling on a one-way ticket,
- traveling on a ticket that was purchased for cash and/or immediately before a flight,

- traveling with US immigration documents such as a completed green card or visa application ready for filing once you get across the border,
- entering the country as a visitor yet having documents in your possession that suggest you may be conducting business in the US,
- owning rental property in the US and carrying any information that might indicate you are actually working in or on the rental properties, fixing them up, or collecting rent; this may be an indication you are working in the US without authorization to do so,
- traveling in a vehicle that is not registered to you or any other person in the vehicle,
- traveling in a vehicle registered to you in a country in which you have no legal immigration status, for example, a Canadian winter visitor in the US attempting to drive a Florida-registered car into Canada and then back into the US again,
- traveling with a spouse or other companion who has a different immigration status than you do in the country you are attempting to enter, for example, a US citizen or green card holder traveling to the US with a Canadian companion who has no legal status in the US and is attempting to enter the US as a visitor,
- traveling to the US after just marrying a US citizen in Canada or alternatively entering the US with definite plans to get married to a US citizen or resident while visiting the US,
- attempting to cross the border under the influence of alcohol or drugs,
- having a common name (although having a common name is not your fault, your identity may be confused with many others whose names are similar and who are on a terrorist watch list, for example. You may mitigate this concern by having your passport or other forms of identification spell out your entire name. For example, use John Albert Smith rather than John A. Smith and be very diligent in avoiding any other of the red flags noted above),
- having different names or variations of your name on your plane ticket and passport such that the two documents do not match perfectly, or
- traveling with someone who has potentially one or more of the red flags noted above.

IMMIGRATION RULES ARE NOT TAX RULES, AND VICE VERSA

So far we have focused entirely on the immigration rules when crossing back and forth across the US-Canada border and how to use these rules in your favor to make your crossing as effortless as possible. However, to maintain your virtual swinging door's ability to allow you to go back and forth with ease, it is extremely important to understand that there are entirely different sets of rules with respect to taxation of residents and non-residents of the US alike, and, the same for Canada and its residents and non-residents. A great deal of confusion comes into play when Canadians attempt to merge tax rules with immigration rules rather than keep them entirely separate, as they were designed and intended. Immigration rules are enforced by the US Customs and Immigration Service (USCIS), tax rules are enforced by the Internal Revenue Service (IRS), entirely separate branches of the US government which operate without any collaboration or coordination of their separate sets of rules. Few things cause more confusion and controversy among visitors to the United States than how long they can legally remain in the country without breaking any rules when tax and immigration rules are attempted to be applied together. One key thing to remember to help one separate tax rules from immigration rules is that the tax rules apply regardless of immigration status in the US; in fact you can be 100 percent illegal in the US and the tax rules still apply to you 100 percent (see Chapter 2).

In other words, the IRS doesn't care whether you have violated any immigration rules, they apply their rules separately and will collect taxes regardless where you fall under immigration rules. There are several chapters in *The Border Guide* that discuss immigration and tax rules to show that they are different and are applied under different circumstances to visitors to the US. (For Americans visiting or moving to Canada, see Chapter 13.) The source of this confusion is primarily the fact that there are multiple sets of rules governed by various government agencies that deal with tax residency.

Border Guide readers are encouraged to participate in a cross-border Q&A through the new Cross-Border Forum. After registering, you can easily post questions about the contents of this book. Questions will be moderated and/or answered by a cross-border financial planning professional. You can also post comments or create discussions with other *Border Guide* readers to share experiences and swap cross-border financial planning tips. To post a question or comment, go to keatsconnelly.com and click on the title Cross-Border Forum tab at the top of the first page.

CROSS-BORDER Q&A

THE 30-DAY RULE: MYTH OR FACT?

I was told by some snowbird friends that the US is considering a new law that snowbirds who return to Canada for less than one month would be considered not to have left and so their time spent here would become contiguous; i.e., if they spent October through April here in Canada, going back to the US for just three-week increments every other month, they would be deemed to have stayed for the entire six months. Do you know anything about that?

— Peter V. Phoenix, AZ

This is a rumor that has been circulating and recirculating. As with most rumors, there is a small bit of truth in what is being said but it is being misconstrued by almost everyone. Certainly, there is no new rule, only a few US border officers applying an old law differently than they have in the past. Canada has a special arrangement with the US. Canadians automatically get six months' visitor time in the US from their latest date of entry; technically no visa is required to start any six-month stay as a visitor to the US. Most other countries have more structured visa waiver programs and therefore when their citizens come to the US as visitors with a visitor's visa identified by a US Customs and Immigration Service I-94 electronic authorization or passport stamp (visitors from a visa waiver country are generally allowed to visit the US for up to 90 days at a time). When a visa waiver person is in the US and decides to, for example, go from Arizona to Mexico for part of their US trip, the time of the trip they go to Mexico does not extend their US visitor's visa, so the number of days out of the US on a side trip is subtracted from the 90 days originally authorized. Therefore, if they had a 90-day visitor's visa to the US and decide to go to Mexico 30 days, they would have to either return to the US before the 30 days was up or if the Mexico side trip was to take them beyond their 90-day visa end date on the US I-94 stamp, they would need to apply for a new visitor's visa from outside of the country at their country's consulate in Mexico. In addition, if they spend more than 30 days out of the country on their US I-94 Visa, they must apply for a new visa before they can return to the US, hence this is where the 30-day rule originated. Some US border agents are wrongly interpreting this requirement, and not extending the Canadians' six-month visitor visa when they leave the country for less than approximately 30 days. However, since Canadians are not subject to this visa waiver program this 30-day rule doesn't make any sense as no visa is issued normally. It is only a few misguided US border customs officers that interpret these rules as applying to Canadians and actually issued I-94 visitors cards or stamps in passports. If Canadians understand the rule, it's actually quite easy to get around, even though they technically should never have to get around it since it doesn't apply to them. The easiest way to avoid having this 30-day rule applied incorrectly to a Canadian to is to just travel back and forth via the NEXUS program, eliminating most potential concerns.

This is all subject to the interpretation of the people at the border, and as everyone well knows they do not do this very consistently throughout all of the staff and border crossings. Canadians just need to be aware that this can be an issue with the wrong border agent and if they get their US visit shortened they have no choice but to follow what the border person is imposing on them as officials do have the authorization to apply the rules on the spot without challenge.

As of July 1, 2014 Canada and the US have agreed to share information from all the entrances and exits from their respective countries so that each side will have exactly the number of days their citizens spend in each country on their computers at the border. Those flying by air will be automatically checked and recorded according to the airline manifests, and those crossing the land borders will have their passports scanned going both directions. Even though this recording of each border crossing will be a bit of a hassle, it will certainly help those Canadian snowbirds who have been honest with tracking their time in the US.

The bottom line is this mythical 30-day rule should not be a concern for Canadians, because of the no visa requirement for Canadians visiting the US for up to to six months from the date of each entrance to the US.

CROSSING THE BORDER WITH MINOR CONVICTIONS OR ADMISSION OF ILLEGAL DRUG USE

With marijuana being legalized in several US states and perhaps soon, Canadian provinces, what effect does this have for those of us crossing the border into the US?

— MP, Vancouver, BC

This is a short but interesting question and it is extremely important to understand that if you tell a US border official you have eaten a pot brownie or smoked a joint, even though it may have been legal where you were when you did this, your ability to freely enter the United States will go up in smoke. The US, at the federal level (which governs immigration), still considers marijuana an illegal substance. Any use of it, especially by non-US citizens, can have them banned permanently from entering the US. You do not need a drug conviction to be turned away for drug crimes under the US Immigration and Nationality Act, as anything drug-related is typically a crime involving moral turpitude. Even if you are a US green card holder living in a state where marijuana is legal for recreational use, you still could lose your green card next time you cross the border if you admit you used marijuana in any fashion.

Any Canadian who has a of drug conviction, even though it may be very minor, totally pardoned, or a very long time ago, must apply for a visa waiver that will let him or her cross into the US. A visa waiver takes about six months to get so it needs to be applied for well in advance. Lately, with the US and Canadian immigration people sharing records and getting historical legal data into the computers, convictions are showing up that have long been forgotten and getting individuals banned at the border. If you have any kind of drug conviction, get a waiver before your records catch up to you on your next border crossing.

What if a border agent asks if you've ever smoked a joint? Say you have never been convicted if that is the truth; certainly don't lie as that is fraud which may have worse consequences. The border agent has no way to tell whether or not you've actually tried pot or any other drug unless you have been foolish enough to post or discuss it on any social media.

US RESIDENCY HAS MANY OBLIGATIONS REQUIRING CAREFUL FINANCIAL PLANNING

I am writing to you on behalf of my aunt who is a citizen and resident of Canada. For a number of years she was a United States resident with a green card that was reissued to her. Is she eligible to stay in the United States for more than six months? Six months only is required by Canada, but will having a green card entitle her to a longer stay?

— R.J., Glendale, Arizona

If your aunt has a current, valid green card, she is able to stay in the United States for as long as she likes. The green card confers legal permanent residence status. There are many US tax obligations of green card holders that your aunt needs to get in compliance with if she wishes to keep the green card. A good cross-border financial planner will be able to review her situation and make appropriate recommendations on taxes, medical coverage, investments, and estate planning. She does need professional help, as there are some complex issues to address.

SICK RELATIVE NOT ENOUGH TO JUSTIFY VISITS

I am a Canadian citizen living in Toronto. For the past three years I have spent some months with my sister in Ormond Beach, FL. Last year her husband passed away, and this year she has had a couple of bouts of illness and she should no longer live alone. She can't afford a retirement home. Three years ago we filed a petition for my immigration to the United States, but have been told that there is a 10- to 15-year wait for a visa. I phoned USCIS recently and learned that their "six months in the United States" is six months per visit, so that theoretically I could go home for a few days every six months and stay here indefinitely otherwise. Actually I am going home February 11 to 28. So technically, I could stay to the end of August.

But the IRS is another matter. I worked in the United States for 26 years before returning to Canada to retire. Had I known then that I could get dual citizenship I would have done so. I now receive Social Security, income from small annuities from which 15 percent non-resident tax is deducted, and a little from an IRA. I also have US Medicare Parts A and B. I file a T1 General in Canada and a 1040NR in the United States, which gives me a small refund. I have never filed a Closer Connection form, but will probably have to do so for this year. My Canadian income is limited to OAS and interest from about $120,000 in investments.

I talked with an IRS representative recently, and he suggested that I might be better off filing as a US resident and staying on the six-month basis. But how does that affect my Canadian connections? Of course, OAS would be taxed, but Social Security would not. I own a condo in Canada and am buying a life-lease apartment there, so I do not want to stay here indefinitely. However, a few months more next year would be helpful. Can I do it without running afoul of the USCIS, IRS, or Canadian authorities?

— F.R.B., Ormond Beach, Florida

Dealing first with the USCIS, you are technically correct that you can renew your six-month visitor's status by leaving the country and re-entering for another six months. However, every time you enter the United States, you must be prepared to justify why you are asking for a visitor status when in fact your intentions are other than those of a temporary visitor. Any time you enter the United States and tell the USCIS officials you are doing one thing, when in fact you are acting to the contrary, is an illegal entry. Therefore, they can deny you entry if they have suspicions or evidence indicating that your intention is different from what you have told them. I recommend you talk to an immigration attorney about other visa alternatives.

In addition, if you enter as a visitor and stay longer than 183 days, you have technically overstayed your visa and have become an illegal alien. With the new USCIS requirements for checking in and out of the US, overstaying a visa will be easily tracked and you could be denied re-entry by the USCIS for five years or more.

With respect to the IRS, if you spend more than 183 days in a calendar year in the United States, you are considered a tax resident and are required to file a US tax return on your world income. You then have to rely on the Canada/US Tax Treaty to ensure you are not double-taxed on income sourced in one country but taxable by both countries. Canada will not recognize you as a resident of the United States until you are legally able to live there; therefore, you would likely have to file tax returns in both countries on a continual basis.

There is irony in the fact that complying with the IRS rules by filing required tax returns gives the USCIS clearly documented proof you are acting like a resident of the US when you are not legally allowed to do so.

Keeping the Tax Man away from Your Swinging Door 2

The first chapter, "The Swinging Door," covered in very great detail all of the immigration rules that apply to US/Canada cross-border travel. However, it was noted that it is essential to separate immigration rules which dictate how much time Canadian visitors can spend in the US from tax rules that have no bearing on the number of days you can or cannot spend in the US.

To hear that tax rules have no bearing on how much time you spend in the US will come as a shock or surprise to most people. It is very important to understand when building your virtual swinging door that the IRS rules only apply to filing requirements, not to how much time you can spend or not spend in the US. The bottom line is that the IRS does not care whether you are in the country perfectly legally or illegally. It gets very muddled and confusing when newspapers, friends, relatives, and talking heads try to combine US immigration rules with tax rules because the immigration rules tell you how much time you can spend or what type of visa you need to be legally in the US, whereas the tax rules only tell you if, when, and how to file IRS forms or returns. In addition to these IRS filing rules, there are two other areas that have a bearing on and add to the confusion. Those are US estate taxes and the provincial medicare out of country rules. I will explain these additional rules to ensure that you understand them to the extent that you can live an amazing cross-border lifestyle with your own virtual swinging door at the border.

IRS TAX FILING RULES FOR VACATIONERS, SNOWBIRDS, AND SETTLERS

After many years of providing cross-border financial planning services between Canada and the US, I have come to the conclusion that the

US is the best tax haven for Canadians and is likely to remain so for the foreseeable future. The same tax advantages that are available to Canadians by going to a remote island in the middle of nowhere can be had by driving across the US border. This means that most of the effects that the IRS would have on anybody living the amazing cross-border lifestyle would be positive, particularly for those who wish to live the Settler lifestyle; in other words tax reduction, not greater or extra taxes at all.

There is certainly a fear of the IRS that most Canadians have developed over a long period of time mostly through the media and unknowledgeable and untrained Canadian advisors. After working for several decades with both Canada Revenue Agency and the Internal Revenue Service under many difficult and challenging circumstances, I say the fear of the IRS is completely unjustified, relatively speaking. Both the CRA and the IRS have their issues with being large, often unresponsive government bureaucracies, however I find the IRS much better at resolving taxpayer concerns and the US Taxpayer Bill of Rights has much more meat to it than the CRA Bill of Rights. For example, whereas the CRA demands collection of taxes even though the taxpayer has not had an opportunity to dispute a tax notice or assessment, the IRS waits until they hear the taxpayer out through a detailed process outlined in the US Taxpayer Bill of Rights before they start tax collection. The CRA, with this collection attitude, has often shut down businesses, even though their auditors may be completely off base because they demand payment of taxes that the business does not have the cash to pay and will seize assets and bank accounts when a taxpayer appeals process is barely begun. Also, when you fight the CRA it not only takes longer and is more expensive but you can almost never recover your legal costs even if you are correct (I believe the CRA often drags out challenges by taxpayers in the hopes that the taxpayers will run out of money and be forced to settle even if the taxpayer has a good case against the CRA). The US courts regularly award costs to taxpayers when the IRS has been proven wrong.

As noted in Chapter 1, there are no IRS rules that tell you how much time you can or cannot spend in the US legally. The rules I am outlining here and will provide much more detail on in Chapter 4 are strictly time- or transaction-related filing requirements:

- US citizens and green card holders must file annual US individual tax forms, Form 1040, annually regardless of how much time they spend in the US.
- Individuals spending under 120 days a calendar year in the US have no annual filing requirements with the IRS.

- Those spending between 120 and 182 days consistently year after year in the US may be considered by the IRS to be US taxpayers, unless they file a Closer Connection declaration, Form 8840. This possibility of being considered a US taxpayer is explained more thoroughly in Chapter 4 under the Substantial Presence Test. This possibility of the IRS considering you a taxpayer does not mean that you will have to pay US taxes or be subject to US penalties, it is only more of a disclosure requirement that you are spending this much time in the US. The IRS wants you to show them where in the world you are paying your taxes which would be in most cases Canada; in other words they want to see your cards to see what hand you are dealing. This would apply to most Snowbirds.
- If you spend more than 183 days in any calendar year in the US you are considered a person who has a filing requirement to at least file the IRS non-resident tax return, Form 1040NR. The 1040NR can be filed with all zeros in conjunction with the Closer Connection Form 8840 to show the IRS you have no US-sourced income and are paying your taxes in Canada. Again, this is only a filing requirement and does not mean you will have US taxes to pay, the IRS just wants to know where you live and where you pay taxes so that they can understand that you are not required to pay any taxes in the US under both domestic and the Canada/US Tax Treaty rules. This would apply to Snowbirds who are consistently maxing out the number of days they spend in the US under the immigration rules noted in Chapter 1 or to some Settlers making the transition to become US taxpayers.
- Canadians in any of the above four cross-border lifestyle time-in-the-US categories are always protected by a very good and very solid tax treaty, the Canada/US Tax Treaty. The benefits of this Treaty are detailed in Chapter 4, but the bottom line here is that the Treaty is always a trump card which prevents the IRS from taxing Canadians on income sourced in Canada without providing exemptions, deductions, and foreign tax credits, to reduce or eliminate US taxes payable (even for US citizens and green card holders).
- Regardless of whether a Canadian spends zero days in the US in any particular calendar year and conducts business transactions like selling or renting a piece of real estate, he or she is required to file the IRS form 1040NR to reconcile with the IRS if there was any tax due on the sale or rental of the property. See Chapter 4 under Who Must File Tax Returns in the US?

Note that the number of days present in the United States need not be consecutive and that for individuals the IRS rules are always on the calendar year whereas the USCIS immigration rules apply normally for periods of time that can start and end on any particular date of issue of a visa or entry/exit to or from the US. An individual can be deemed a resident of the United States for tax purposes even though he or she may not have any right to remain in the country under immigration rules. Thus a person may become subject to income tax in the United States on his/her world income without having the right to remain legally within its borders for more than six months as a visitor (see Chapter 4 and Chapter 8).

One of the major difficulties inherent in cross-border financial planning techniques is that the applicable rules can change depending on immigration status and on which direction the cross-border movement is going. For example, a Vacationer or Snowbird to the US who marries a US resident dramatically alters his or her financial planning options, and a new cross-border financial planning analysis becomes necessary in order to take advantage of new opportunities and avoid any costly mistakes. A person who is your typical Vacationer/Snowbird from Canada has to follow different sets of tax and immigration rules than a person with a US visa or green card. All the important planning issues for each respective status category are discussed in detail in subsequent chapters.

THE US ESTATE TAX RULES FOR VACATIONERS AND SNOWBIRDS

What US estate tax is and how it applies to non-residents is covered in detail in Chapter 5 and for US residents/citizens/green card holders in Chapter 11. Unlike income tax and immigration, there is no clear set of rules of residency for estate taxes. Residency is based on a series of facts and circumstances. Some of the factors that determine residency or "domicile" for estate tax purposes are the relative size and nature of your permanent homes in Canada and the US; the amount of time spent in each country; your immigration status in the United States; written declarations on such documents as wills or tax returns; the locations of your significant assets and important papers; and your personal, family, and business connections. Generally, Canadians who are clearly Vacationers or Snowbirds to the United States, who have no US green cards and whose intents are to routinely return to Canada each year, could not be considered to have given up domicile in Canada, and would not be subject to American estate tax on their worldwide assets. Court cases in which the IRS has challenged a Canadian winter visitor's estate by attempting to tax worldwide assets of the deceased have failed. The IRS has been unsuccessful in these cases, because the deceased must have shown a clear intent to give up one domicile for another. A 2003 US Internal Revenue Service (IRS) ruling stated that a Canadian living in the US on an L-1 visa (see Chapter 8 for details on how an L-1 visa works) could be considered domiciled in the US for estate-tax purposes, even though the L-1 visa would expire after a maximum of seven years and the Canadian would have had to move back to Canada. This ruling appears to be a liberal extension of these domicile rules and creates a situation similar to the income tax rules, where you may be considered a resident of the US for income tax purposes without receiving any legal immigration status to allow you to stay in the US. Visitors to the US may still be subject to the non-resident estate tax on their assets located in the US. This will be explained in greater detail in Chapter 5, however, to put most people's minds at ease, those individuals who have worldwide estates worth less than $5.45 million USD or couples with combined estates of less than $10.9 million USD will generally never have to worry about paying US estate taxes (see Chapter 11).

PROVINCIAL MEDICARE RULES

Provincial medicare rules are unique because they act in direct opposition to the tax and immigration residency rules, by stipulating that you will not receive provincial medicare if you are away from your home province for longer than a specified period of time. I discuss these Canadian rules here because they often add to the confusion about how much time Vacationers or Snowbirds can or cannot spend in the US.

As of January 1, 2016, the NWT and all provinces with the exception of PEI will allow residents to be out of the country up to seven months a year and still remain current on their provincial health care plans.

Newfoundland allows its residents to stay out of province for up to 8 months in 12 before they lose coverage. Your eligibility for provincial medicare coverage depends on the amount of time you spend out of province, which often includes the time you spend in other provinces as well as out of the country. However, pressure from traveling Canadians has convinced most provinces to not count travel in other Canadian provinces. This has pretty much eliminated most people's concerns with losing their provincial medicare while they are enjoying travel in the US, around the world, or within Canada outside of their residential provinces. In most provinces, once you've lost medicare you have to wait three months as a returning resident to reinstate your coverage. Alberta, New Brunswick, and PEI are exceptions. They have no waiting period for coverage to start for returning residents from outside of Canada.

For those moving to the US, your provincial medical coverage generally ceases within 30 days of leaving Canada. In some provinces it ceases at the end of the month in which you leave. Check with your local medical office and plan accordingly so you don't have any gaps in your coverage.

We are often asked, "How does a particular government department responsible for enforcing any of the above rules know how much time you are spending out of your province?" The fact of the matter is that they do not necessarily know, or need to know. Instead, they pass the burden of proof on to you by asking you to declare, under penalty of perjury, that the facts you present regarding your travel itinerary are true. They will obviously also want proof of your travels, such as airline tickets or charge card statements. You should also remember that we live in a computer age in which information is easily stored, retrieved and shared by various government agencies and government-owned corporations.

WHERE TO LIVE OR WINTER IN THE US

The nature of cross-border financial planning and your ability to live the amazing cross-border lifestyle will often be determined by the US state in which you choose to reside or vacation. This guide is not meant to provide you with a travel brochure about which Sunbelt state is the best, but it examines some of the major tax implications of the most popular Sunbelt states: Arizona, California, and Florida. In Appendix B, we will provide tax rates and other technical data on these and another popular state, Hawaii. The reasons that Arizona, California, and Florida are popular with Canadians can be summarized in a collection of comments from long-time residents or visitors to one or more of these three states.

ARIZONA

Offers the most sunshine of almost any populated area in North America. Expect clear skies nearly 85 percent of the time, and an annual rainfall of 6 inches (15 cm) in the desert southwest. Winter daytime temperatures range from 65° to 85°F (18° to 30°C) in the Phoenix and Tucson areas.

- Great for people with arthritis because of the dry climate. Not so good for allergy sufferers, since something is always in bloom.
- Golfers' paradise. There are more than 250 golf courses in the Phoenix area alone that are open 365 days a year.
- Geographically diverse state, from the Grand Canyon to high mountains to the Sonoran desert. There is decent snow skiing in northern parts of the state during winter at elevations in excess of

10,000 feet, and plenty of year-round water sports on the numerous man-made reservoirs and lakes. Arizona has the most boats per capita of any state in the US.

- Arizona has a relatively kind tax regime. In a 2015 in-depth national survey of all 50 states for the 10 Best States to Live In for Low Taxes completed by Kiplinger, Arizona scored in the top seven considering all forms of taxes combined, including state income, sales, and property taxes. Arizona is a very tax-friendly state to Canadians, and if you take into consideration the special tax credits for Canadian taxes paid, Arizona would likely have been rated in the top three on the Kiplinger survey had the survey included Canadian issues.
- The most frequently mentioned drawback about Arizona is that if you choose to stay in the Phoenix area during the summer, you can face average daily high temperatures of over 100°F (38°C). In spite of these high summer temperatures, in recent years, I have found many more Canadians choosing to spend summers in Arizona or the Palm Desert because the heat is easy to deal with when you have air-conditioned homes and cars, but the weather is still otherwise close to perfect, particularly in the early mornings and evenings. Popular retirement communities such as Prescott, in the central part of the state, offer peak temperatures 20° lower than the lower deserts around Phoenix with four distinct seasons (although snow is rare) and an ambience not unlike that of a small town in New England.
- Arizona has nearly fully recovered from the great recession of 2008–2009 with one of the lowest unemployment rates in the country, with plenty of new growth opportunities for permanent or part-time employment in all areas of the economy. Several large Canadian companies have chosen to invest heavily in the Arizona infrastructure creating over 150,000 jobs for Arizonans. There are about 350 Canadian companies doing business in Arizona and there are approximately 1 million Vacationers, Snowbirds, or Settlers traveling to Arizona every year.
- Several airlines now have daily nonstop flights from most major Canadian cities, particularly during the winter months when Canada's Westjet schedules numerous daily flights through Phoenix Sky Harbor Airport. American Airlines has daily nonstops from Phoenix to Vancouver, Calgary, and Edmonton year-round.

CALIFORNIA

- Plenty of sun and ocean. Temperatures vary considerably from the coast to the inland desert, with the coastal areas having less extreme temperature changes because of the moderating effect of the Pacific Ocean. The Palm Springs area has a climate almost identical to that of southern Arizona.
- Major man made and natural tourist attractions abound, such as Disneyland, Hollywood, Yosemite, and Big Sur.
- The ocean provides plenty of recreational opportunities.
- A geographically diverse state, from the miles of spectacular coastline to mountains, farmland, vineyards, and desert.
- The major drawback of this state is its population, which is greater than all of Canada's. In the past decade, it has also seen more than its fair share of earthquakes, floods, mudslides, and wildfires. California is also noted for its high cost of living and relatively high taxes.
- California scored in the top 10 on the 2015 Kiplinger survey, however it was the wrong top 10; California is in the top 10 least tax-friendly states in the US. It is also not very tax-friendly to Canadians who have assets and income from Canada. It does not offer tax credits to its residents for taxes paid to any Canadian province or the federal government and also taxes Canadian RRSPs annually on any interest dividends or capital gains earned inside of the RRSP plan.
- For those seeking employment in the computer industry, Silicon Valley (near San Francisco), remains a worldwide innovative computer technology center and is headquarters to one of the largest companies in the world, Apple, and also many other technology companies such as Google, Facebook, Twitter, and LinkedIn.
- California is easy to fly to from any city in Canada, particularly through LAX, one of the largest airports in the world, and is easily accessible by car from Vancouver and Calgary. WestJet has many nonstop flights during the winter months to Palm Springs from many western Canadian cities.

FLORIDA

- Very mild climate with a minimal difference between winter and summer temperatures, 70° to 90°F (20° to 32°C) on average. Expect plenty of rain year-round and high humidity during summer.
- Provides two surprisingly different coasts: the Atlantic and the Gulf. Each has miles of beautiful beaches, islands, and keys, and all the year-round water sports that go with them.
- Like California, it has major man-made tourist attractions such as Disney World, Universal Studios, and Kennedy Space Center.
- Florida has no personal income tax; in spite of this it did not make Kiplinger's 2015 10 Best States to Live In for Low Taxes in the US, primarily due to its very high property taxes, sales taxes, gasoline taxes, etc. In addition, Canadians get no homestead exemptions on any property they own in Florida until they become full-time Florida residents.
- It's easy to drive to Florida from Ontario, Quebec, and the Maritimes. There are five major airports in Florida with multiple daily flights from most major Canadian cities.
- Florida offers the most services for Canadians. It has several radio and TV stations broadcasting Canadian news in both French and English and a good distribution of Canadian daily newspapers. Several major Canadian banks have branches throughout Florida.
- The major complaints about Florida seem to be that it is getting too crowded and that it has a hurricane season. With respect to the hurricanes, it is important to note that the US Federal Emergency Management Agency (FEMA) does not provide any aid to seasonal residents who are not US citizens.

Nevada, Washington, New York, Texas, and Hawaii are other popular states with Canadians. Nevada placed just after Arizona in Kiplinger's 10 Best States Live In for Low Taxes; Washington and Texas have no personal state income tax so are close to the top 10, but New York and Hawaii are in, along with California, the list of 10 Least Tax-Friendly States in the US.

POPULAR CROSS-BORDER MISCONCEPTIONS

One of the primary purposes of this book is to dispel many of the popular misconceptions Canadians have about living, visiting, and investing in the United States. Some of the more common misconceptions are:

- You lose money changing Canadian dollars to US dollars! No, there is no loss in exchanging one currency for another, other than the commissions you pay as a transaction cost. You don't make a profit changing US dollars to Canadian dollars either. See Chapter 3 for a more complete explanation of this popular misconception. Another misconception dealing with currency exchange is that banks are the best places do a currency exchange. Chapter 3 outlines best methods to obtain the best possible exchange rates changing Canadian funds to US funds or vice versa possibly saving you hundreds or thousands of dollars.
- Canada has no estate or inheritance taxes! Wrong: Canada's deemed disposition tax on RRSPs or RRIFs and appreciated property can be as high as 60 percent. Many provinces also levy significant probate or estate administration fees. For a combined husband and wife estate of less than $16 million, Canadian estate taxes are most often much higher than those in the US. Less than 1 percent of the population in either Canada or the US would have estates greater than this amount. See Chapters 5 and 11 for further details on this tax.
- The Canada/US Tax Treaty eliminates the US non-resident estate taxes! No; some high-net-worth Canadians are actually worse off under this new treaty, but many are unaffected by the new rules. These rules are much more complex than the old rules, so a new level of understanding is required to determine if you are any better off. See Chapter 5 for the real scoop.
- RRSPs, RRIFs, and other registered plans can be left alone if you move to the US! Leaving your RRSPs in Canada when you move to the United States can create many potentially costly tax problems as well as numerous complicated annual IRS tax reporting filings, and you may miss opportunities to withdraw them at no or very low tax rates. Chapter 10 will discuss how to remove your RRSPs and other registered plans at very low or even no net income tax, once you have taken up residence in the United States.
- Canadian exit tax or deemed disposition tax is too high for you to leave Canada. This misconception is frequently perpetuated by Canadian accountants, financial planners, and other advisors who emphasize this exit tax as an obstacle rather than as a great planning vehicle that could actually reduce taxes. The CRA does impose a deemed disposition tax when exiting Canada to go live in another country. However, this tax is not an additional tax; it

is tax one would normally pay if the appreciated asset were sold. The CRA allows you to defer any tax that might be due upon exit from Canada to the date the asset is actually sold. The CRA may require collateral for this tax deferment, but you pay no interest on any tax due, so you get the equivalent of an interest-free loan. In addition, as noted in Chapter 8 and Chapter 11, proper planning before you leave Canada can help you avoid this tax altogether on a net basis.

- You will earn lower rates of interest investing in the United States! Although interest rates paid by banks in both Canada and the US vary greatly with supply and demand dictated by the marketplace and with this long sustained current low interest rate environment, neither US or Canadian banks are paying any significant interest on any money market or short-term investments. There are a few countries in the world like Switzerland where the interest rate is negative so in other words investors have to pay the bank to keep the money on deposit. However, overall diversified investment portfolios earn about the same rate of return for a similar level of risk in both Canada and the United States. Chapters 7 and 14 provide further insight into this misconception.
- The IRS with its US tax rules dictates how much time you can spend in the US as a Vacationer or Snowbird. This is completely wrong; the IRS really does not care at all whether you are in the country for one or 365 days or even if you are in the country illegally. They just want to collect taxes that are due on US-sourced income. Note the discussion earlier in this chapter and Chapter 4.
- You can rely on your longtime Canadian advisor to provide you with the planning necessary for you to build your virtual Swinging Door on the Canada/US border and live an amazing cross-border lifestyle. Although most Canadian advisors are very knowledgeable on Canadian affairs there are very few that have the formal education, experience, and abilities to provide cross-border planning merging Canadian rules with US rules to give you a cross-border lifestyle that works best for you and often they can be a deterrent for you to get to your goals accomplished. This and the remaining chapters throughout this book will help you determine what type of advisors to use and where to find them.
- You need to fear the IRS and do anything that you can to avoid them. This is unjustified and misguided; the IRS, like the CRA,

at times can be very difficult to deal with. However, for those that are not attempting to deliberately break any tax filing rules the IRS is positively easier to deal with than the CRA and has a much better Bill of Rights protecting US taxpayers. In addition, the IRS will provide Canadians lower tax rates on just about any kind of income they may have; pensions, interests, dividends, capital gains, and employment income. Chapter 4 and Chapter 9 will show this in much more detail.

- Wills are all you need for a complete estate plan! Wills are very necessary, but there are more effective estate-planning vehicles, such as living trusts and living wills, that may provide for lower estate settlement costs and better estate management. See Chapters 5 and 11 for further explanation.
- Investing in the United States means you must file US tax returns! No — there are a large number of investments you can put money into in the United States that are exempt from taxes and any filing or reporting requirements. Chapter 7 lists the investments that are exempt from US taxes for non-residents.
- You can't be a citizen of Canada and the United States at the same time! Wrong — dual citizenship is possible and has been for over 20 years. Chapter 8 explains dual citizenship status.
- You lose your CPP/QPP and OAS by moving to the United States! No, you keep all these benefits, and in reality you will likely keep much more of your Canada Pension Plan/Quebec Pension Plan and Old Age Security after taxes once you have become a resident taxpayer of the United States. Chapter 9 provides the calculations to show you some of the tax savings available on CPP/QPP and OAS when a Canadian moves to the United States. You will not be subject to the OAS clawback if you are a US resident, regardless of your level of income. You can also double dip and qualify to receive CPP/QPP, OAS, and US Social Security payments with good cross-border planning. See Chapter 14 for more details.
- Medical insurance is too expensive in the United States! Some US health insurance is expensive; however, those under 65 can obtain very good coverage with high deductibles for less than $400 per month for up to a $2-million limit of coverage, depending on an absence of pre-existing conditions, age, and other factors. With the new Affordable Care Act in the US, any Canadian who moves to the US on virtually any kind of visa or green card regardless of

pre-existing conditions will be eligible for full US medical coverage at any age at a cost, much less than Canadian travel insurance in most cases but particularly for those living in the US past the age of 70 right up into their 80s and 90s. Those over 65 are usually also eligible for US Medicare at no or reasonable costs. Chapters 6 and 14 provide further details for those needing health insurance in the United States.

- Investments in the United States are riskier than in Canada! No, the same rules of prudent investing apply in both countries. Because there are more investment choices in the United States, there can be greater opportunity to choose an inappropriate investment. However, this greater selection also allows prudent investors to find a greater number of safe investments in the United States at lower costs, which can actually help lower risk. In addition, the US regulatory environment is much more consumer protective with stiffer fines and jail sentences for those trying to rip off the public through investment scams.

The Value of a Buck 3

How to Beat the Exchange Rate Blues

Regular Vacationers and Snowbirds who plan annual migrations to the Sunbelt often exhibit symptoms of confusion, helplessness, and insomnia just prior to leaving the country. This highly contagious phenomenon is known as the Exchange Rate Blues. A general feeling of malaise develops when the soon-to-be-departed snowbirds begin calling banks, searching the Internet, poring over the financial pages of the newspaper, or listening to the talking heads on financial TV. This is done in an often futile attempt to pick the best possible moment to convert their hard-earned Canadian dollars into US currency. Questions like "should I wait until___________?" (fill in the blank with an appropriate response such as "tomorrow," "next week," or "until the exchange rate goes up another cent," etc.), feverishly run through the minds of travelers infected with the Exchange Rate Blues. Finally, the deal is struck and the currency exchanged, but the very next day the Exchange Rate Blues continue when new symptoms known as the "I should haves" appear. "I should have waited until ___________" (again fill in the blank with the appropriate response, such as "the exchange rate improved" if the dollar went up, or if it went the other way, "I should have exchanged more"). It's funny that when the dollar is trading around 65 or 75 cents US, we'd give our right arm to exchange at 100 cents, but if or when the dollar reaches that level again we still want to hold off for a better rate.

I have spoken to thousands of Canadians in the US, and every one of them, including myself, has suffered from the Exchange Rate Blues. Most start feeling the symptoms just before a large amount of dollars need to be exchanged. Americans visiting Canada don't seem to get caught up in the Exchange Rate Blues; it's as if they are inoculated against it regardless of where the dollar is trading.

ELIMINATING THE EXCHANGE RATE BLUES

Most people wouldn't dream of becoming currency speculators to earn money for their retirement because of the great risks involved in such an activity. Going through the ritual guessing game of which way the Canadian dollar is going to go is precisely that: currency speculation. In fact, currency speculation is the root cause of the Exchange Rate Blues, a feeling very similar to that which novice commodity traders have every time they make a trade or that gamblers have when they place a bet.

How do you avoid currency speculation and cure the Exchange Rate Blues? The answer is very simple for those planning to live the most amazing cross-border lifestyle in the United States in their retirement, but most people will ignore it until it is too late: Place enough income-producing assets and savings in US-dollar-generating investments long before retirement even begins. For those business owners who have most of their savings tied up in their businesses who are selling the business to retire it is important to invest some or all of the proceeds to produce the income to protect the cross-border lifestyle they choose. These savings, if accumulated and invested faithfully, should produce income sufficient to safely cover expenses during stays in the US or to pay for travel to other parts of the world (see Chapter 7 for assistance with investing in the US). A reliable Canadian study found that nearly half the Canadians who need to make a conversion from Canadian to US dollars wait until less than 24 hours before they actually need US funds, leaving them at the mercy of whatever exchange rate the bank might give them at that particular time. What these people are doing is currency speculation, even though they would turn down an investment advisor who recommended they speculate in currencies because of the risks involved.

When the Canadian dollar reached par with the US dollar in 2007 after several decades below par, there was great rejoicing by most Canadians. However, true to its volatile nature the Canadian dollar fell precipitously to as low as $0.76 in early 2008, struggled back to the $0.80 level in early 2009, and by spring 2010 it was back up to par again. With the dollar at around par in 2010 and real estate prices still in the dumps in the US as a result of the recession, buying opportunities for Canadians in US real estate were once-in-a-lifetime opportunities to secure US accommodation for a wonderful cross-border lifestyle with a home in both Canada and the US. Those who bought during that period remain very happy with their purchases. The Sunbelt states were the hardest hit in real estate and most areas still have not seen real estate prices rise above the post-2007 levels, leaving US purchases for that second home still a relatively good bargain. In spite of the less favorable currency exchange, particularly comparing prices say in Phoenix or Tampa with those in Vancouver or Toronto, you can get a new, single-family home, with a pool, on a golf course, still for substantially less than you can buy a smaller house with no amenities in either of these Canadian cities.

For those Canadians wishing to secure a low cost but very fulfilling cross-border lifestyle, it would be a mistake to assume that the exchange rates of the Canadian dollar relative to the US dollar are going to stay the same or get better in the future. By some measures, the Canadian dollar is sometimes amongst the most overvalued of the major currencies. Unlike bonds and stocks, currencies are difficult to model, so valuation can be extremely elusive. Economists often use purchasing power parity, or PPP, which holds that in the long run, currencies move to equalize the price of a basket of traded goods. The Organization for Economic Cooperation and Development (OECD) estimates that the PPP for the Canadian dollar when it was around parity with the US dollar in 2014 was a little above $0.79, representing about a 25 percent difference from where it was trading at that time. I spoke to many Canadians early in 2014 who were waiting for the Canadian dollar to get back up to $1.10 before they were going to exchange the opposite of what this OECD indicator was showing. Those that took our advice to heed this warning were well rewarded. The OECD, using their PPP in the late 1990s and in early 2000 when the dollar was undervalued, (as low as $0.62 USD), indicated that the Canadian dollar PPP was in the low $0.80 range, this at least gives some comfort that the OECD purchasing power parity method of determining currency values is relatively decent at predicting longer-term trends. The latest OECD purchasing power parity with the Canadian dollar indicates it should be slightly higher, towards $0.80, than its current trading level of $0.70 as this edition goes to print so at least that is good news that hopefully the Canadian dollar will not fall precipitously lower.

With all of the recent financial turmoil in the world, it may be difficult to use this indicator for purchasing power parity amongst the currencies until the world economies stabilize. The key risk is not whether the Canadian dollar goes up in value, but if it will pull back down to previous levels, such as those from a few years back when the dollar was trading in the low $0.60s when this made it extremely expensive to spend Canadian dollars in the US, and many Canadians had to give up their US Sunbelt vacations or at least shorten them dramatically.

If all or most of your savings are wrapped up in your RRSPs, the Canadian foreign content rules (which allow up to 100 percent of your RRSP to be invested in foreign investments), now provide you the opportunity to receive the US-dollar income needed for your retirement from inside your RRSP. Don't ignore or put off this advice because it sounds so basic: Simplicity is a key ingredient in a successful retirement plan. With the nearly 40 years of experience I have had in retirement planning, I have seen far too many people get hurt and have their retirement goals fall short of expectations quite unnecessarily, simply because they failed to implement this very important strategy. Since the Canadian dollar has recently been trading at about the average over 35 years, now might be a great time for those who have not yet implemented this strategy to do so. Protect yourself from a potentially falling Canadian dollar while you have the opportunity. There is little risk if the dollar continues to go up, but there is substantial risk if it heads south again. A very simple example of how this would have worked over the past year is that had one taken $100,000 CAD of RRSPs and bought a US-dollar term deposit, even though it probably would've paid a meager 2 or 3 percent interest, in Canadian dollar terms that would have meant close to a 25 percent positive return for the year of 2014. This is because of the drop in the Canadian dollar, when everybody else was losing more than that amount because of the bad economic conditions.

This advice is simply a variation on the time-honored tradition of not putting all your eggs in one basket. By following this advice you will be diversified against currency risk and hedged against rapid fluctuations in either currency. You'll also save the many hundreds or even thousands of dollars in commissions that financial institutions build into their exchange rates. These commissions are particularly high when small sums are exchanged. To determine the rate of commission you pay on currency exchanges, compare the rate listed in the financial section of the newspaper with that posted at your bank or at the airport on the same day. The difference can be as high as 10 percent or more.

For those people making a permanent or temporary move to the United States for employment reasons, the Exchange Rate Blues can be avoided by simply biting the bullet and changing all your hard-earned Canadian dollars into one or two large lump sums and then never looking back. After you have been in the United States for a year or more, you will find that the extra quarter- or half-cent better rate you were thinking of holding out for will have absolutely no bearing on your financial success.

HEDGING YOUR BETS

Almost every corporation conducting cross-border commerce practices some form of currency hedging or simply stated, protecting themselves from adverse currency fluctuations. A Canadian airline, for example, knows that next year it needs to pay for that new Boeing 787 Dreamliner it just ordered. It needs to generate more US income from assets or purchase a currency futures contract locking in the current US dollar rate. That ensures that it will enjoy the current exchange rate or better when the jet has to be paid for. Failure to hedge or reduce currency risk exposure in this situation might mean paying millions more for the 787, based solely on fluctuations in the Canadian dollar.

Canadians who seek a cross-border lifestyle in any of the three categories, Vacationer, Snowbird, or Settler, south of the border, or in most other parts of the world for that matter, will require US funds. If you are currently age 65 and want to maximize your time in the sunny south, you'll need at least $270,000 USD in today's dollars to fund 15 years of six-month stays at a spending level of just $3,000 USD per month. If you do not protect yourself or hedge your currency risk as the Canadian airline would, your retirement in the US could end up costing you thousands more, or end your cross-border lifestyle altogether. Figure 3.1 shows the year-end Canadian dollar values, as expressed in US funds, since 1975.

Dollar speculation for the period from 2008 to current may have cost some Canadians, who did not follow this basic advice, a great part of their cross-border lifestyles, since the dollar was devalued more than 25 percent during that period. However, the speculators sometimes looked as if they knew what they were doing for short periods, such as from 1987 to 1991, from 2002 to 2008, or 2009 to 2013. In fact, over the long term, they were losers. I have far too many examples of readers of *The Border Guide* or of clients in our practice who have chosen to speculate that the Canadian dollar would increase or at least stay the same in value, and

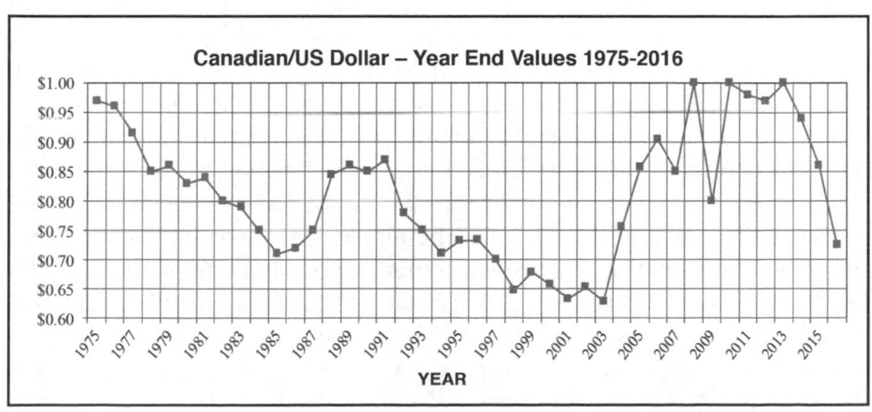

FIGURE 3.1

they left the majority of their investments or cash portfolio in Canadian-dollar denominated accounts.

This speculation and refusal to follow basic cross-border lifestyle protection strategies cost the speculators anywhere from tens of thousands of dollars to millions of dollars lost purchasing power. My advice here is not from the perspective of trying to guess which way the Canadian dollar is going but from the point of view of protecting the chosen cross-border lifestyle which can be afforded currently, ensuring it will be affordable throughout your lifetime. The sad thing about most of the cases where people have either deliberately or unknowingly become currency speculators, is that had the Canadian dollar increased in value and their speculation paid off, their lifestyle would have been affected only marginally. However, now some face cutting back to ensure they don't outlive their money. It is difficult for speculators to understand that the risk is not whether the Canadian exchange rate will go in their favor; the possibility that it may go down is the real risk. Speculating on the Canadian dollar can be profitable if you happen to get lucky. If you want to have a secure retirement though, avoid the Exchange Rate Blues, and avoid becoming a currency speculator by diversifying away from the currency risk well in advance of implementing your chosen cross-border lifestyle.

NO EXCHANGE LOSS IF YOU CONVERT CANADIAN DOLLARS NOW

Investing all or a portion of your savings in the United States or in US-dollar securities in Canada, depending on whether you are going to be a Vacationer, Snowbird, or Settler, is a surefire way to avoid the Exchange Rate Blues and protect yourself from currency risk. How amazing would it be to live your chosen cross-border lifestyle without ever having to worry about the Canada/US exchange rate. Whenever we recommend this strategy, nearly every client says, "How can I exchange my dollars now? I'll take too big a loss." Recently, a well-educated multimillionaire from Vancouver told me (with full conviction, believing his sincere but misaligned statement was true) that he didn't want to move to the US because he couldn't afford to take the hit to his net worth if he converted his assets into US funds. This gentleman, who is looking at choosing the Settler cross-border lifestyle, did not realize that calculating his net worth in another country's currency, in this case in US dollars, does not increase or decrease the value of his net worth one penny. Had he chosen, for example, to value his net worth in Hong Kong dollars, his net worth would have appeared to be about 5 to 6 times more valuable in Hong

Kong dollars when in fact it was still worth exactly the same. Simply put, it makes no difference what currency you decide to evaluate your net worth in at any particular moment in time, it still has the same value or purchasing power. The truth is that there is no loss or gain at the time you convert Canadian dollars to US dollars. It is very simply a fair market value exchange from one measurement to another, just like converting centimeters to inches or celsius to fahrenheit. Net worth value is value regardless of the measuring stick currency you choose. Losses or gains, if there are any, occur prior to any conversion or change in measurement. To illustrate this point, Figure 3.2 shows that $1,000 CAD changed into foreign currency would net you $700 USD, $5,818 Hong Kong dollars, ¥92,475 Japanese yen, or 0.7 oz. of gold.

We'll assume that you paid no commissions and that all exchanges transpired simultaneously.

Would you consider it a gain because you changed $1,000 CAD to $5,818 Hong Kong dollars? Or would you consider yourself hitting a jackpot because your $1,000 CAD bought you more than ¥92,475 Japanese yen? Of course not. Why should you think you have lost money because your $1,000 CAD bought you only $700 USD? Yet it happens all the time, and because the idea is so firmly entrenched, it is difficult to explain to Canadians that they are not losing any value in such an exchange.

Figure 3.2 also illustrates that it doesn't matter what currency you are using. It takes the same relative amount of each currency to purchase the same tangible object such as the 0.7 oz. of gold used in this chart. For gold, you could substitute a week's rent on a US vacation property and the net result would be the same. To further illustrate that there is no loss or gain on currency exchange transactions, run through a full cycle of exchange from $1,000 CAD, to ¥92,475 Japanese yen, to 0.7 oz. of gold, to $700 USD, and back to $1,000 CAD. There is no loss at any time during the currency exchange, since in theory you could go back and forth from the $1,000 CAD to the $700 USD as often as you like (assuming you paid no commissions or markups for the exchanges). Losses or gains occur only if you repeat part of this full cycle of exchange at some other point in time. The relative values of the currencies and the gold will change, but guessing what those relative values will be is pure speculation.

The only loss when exchanging Canadian dollars with US funds is that which is perceived, not real. This misconception comes from Canada's proximity to the US and the fact that both countries call their currency the dollar. At a few times in recent history (approximately 42 years ago, in 2007, 2010 and 2013), one Canadian dollar was worth approximately

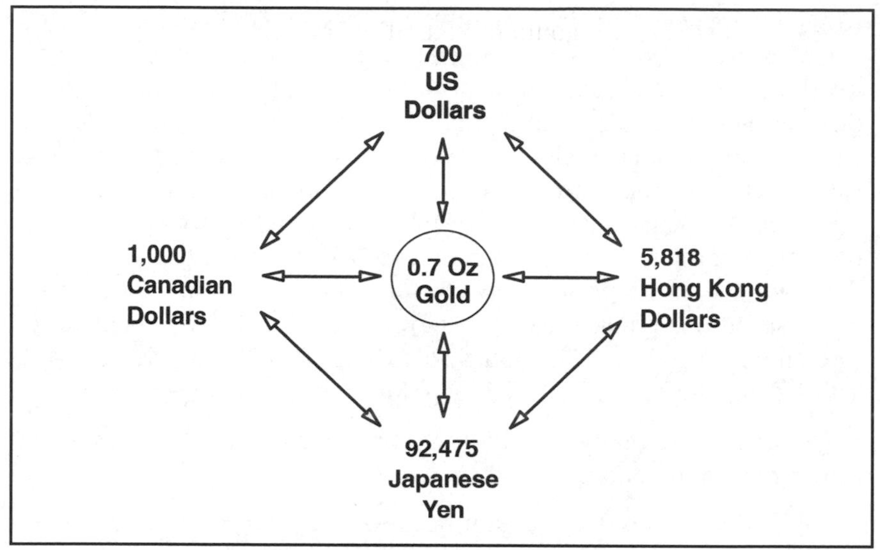

FIGURE 3.2

one US dollar. But there is no law or agreement that says a Canadian dollar must be worth one American dollar, just as there is no law that says one Canadian dollar must equal one Hong Kong dollar. The relationship between the Canadian dollar and the US dollar is market-driven and is every bit as unrestrained as the relative values of the Canadian dollar and the Japanese yen. Had the US called their currency something different, like zlotnays, this perception of loss would likely never have happened.

One final point on the issue of currency exchange and Canadians waiting for the dollar to come back. Currencies should not be confused with stocks or bonds, which tend to be "mean reverting." Mean reverting is the tendency to come back to what might be considered a normal or average value. Large, well-established blue-chip stocks such as IBM exhibit this tendency, so if IBM stock goes down, it normally would come back in value if you waited long enough. However, currencies are not mean reverting and do not display this tendency to revert back to what could be considered a normal value; they are constantly setting new levels without regard to past history. A good example of this is the British pound. After the Second World War, one pound would buy more than $5 USD, whereas now it will buy under $1.50. Is there anyone out there who believes, British or not, that they should wait for the pound to come back to $5 before they do a currency exchange? The wait could be a lifetime or two — perhaps forever — but is that any different for a Canadian waiting for the loonie to go up to $2 USD? Think about it: The real risk for most people is that the loonie may go down further against the US dollar, whereas there is no risk if it goes up. So why are so many people waiting for it to go up regardless of what its current levels do to their exchanges? Even in November of 2007, with the Canadian dollar reaching all-time highs of around over $1.10 against the US dollar, people who felt they needed to protect themselves from a falling Canadian dollar were still waiting for it to go higher before they made their exchanges, meaning they may have missed the chance of a lifetime. If that describes you, remember the earlier discussion regarding becoming a currency speculator: In the short term you may come out okay, but longer term you will inevitably lose out.

WHAT CAN YOU EXPECT IF YOU INVEST IN THE UNITED STATES?

For most periods prior to 2004, interest rates on bank term deposits, GICs, and government bonds in Canada were higher than the same respective rates in the United States. Consequently, Canadians tended to avoid investing in the United States because they felt they could get better returns in Canada. Canadian rates tend to be higher to compensate global investors for a greater risk factor perceived in Canadian currency investments. However, due to current convergent policies of the Bank of Canada and the US Federal Reserve, Canadians can now take advantage of higher interest rates in the United States.

In today's global economy, investments need to be administered as if you are operating a business on a worldwide basis. Since Canada constitutes only approximately 2 to 3 percent of the world's economy, you're not only taking a greater risk, but missing out on growth opportunities by not investing outside of Canada. If the business of your investments is astutely managed and diversified worldwide, you'll earn the same level of profit or income at the same relative risk whether your portfolio is in the United States or Canada, providing your portfolio expenses are the same.

For example, compare a mutual fund in Canada to one in the United States, with the same objectives, restrictions, management, and fee structure; over time, you will see that their returns will also be similar on a percentage basis. The only difference is that one generates Canadian-dollar funds and the other generates US-dollar funds. In fact, most brokerage firms and mutual fund companies in Canada have US-dollar investments that you can use without even leaving Canada. As a result, you do not have to take any reduction in income and can maintain the same level of safety by directing some or all of your investments to the United States. This effectively avoids speculation on the Canadian dollar and will cure the Exchange Rate Blues.

Please note that commissions paid to brokers and the management expense ratios — the fees you pay directly out of the mutual fund to the managers in Canada — are on average twice what they are in the US. The poor market of 2008 and 2009 forced some mutual fund companies to reduce their management expenses, but not by more than they were raised from 2000 to 2003. I have not been convinced by any Canadian brokerage firm or mutual fund company that they need to charge twice the rates of their US counterparts when the cost of doing business in Canada is approximately the same, or even less in some cases. Canadian consumers should be outraged at this and either demand their fund providers lower their rates or bypass them altogether and purchase Exchange Traded Funds (ETFs), which have become very popular with investors. ETFs give Canadians full access to the US and other world markets as well as the same diversified portfolios at a fraction of the cost of mutual funds.

Chapters 7 and 14 provide insight for non-residents and residents respectively, who are investing in the US. Chapter 13 helps Americans who wish to invest in Canada.

AVOIDING US INCOME TAX ON YOUR INVESTMENTS

Investing in the United States as a non-resident can be rewarding and worry-free if you follow the same investment principles you would in Canada, and stick with investments that are exempt from both American income- and estate-tax. There is no substitute for diversification and good management, regardless of your investment objectives. Chapter 7 lists those investments that Canadians can use to produce a steady tax-free US income for US non-residents and non-citizens, while avoiding the non-residents' estate tax discussed in Chapter 5. The fact that these investments are exempt from tax and reporting requirements in the United States does not mean that you do not have to report the income to the Canada Revenue Agency (CRA). A Canadian resident is subject to Canadian tax on world income.

WHERE IS THE BEST PLACE TO EXCHANGE MONEY?

Experienced travelers will tell you that the rate of currency exchange can vary dramatically, depending on the form of your Canadian dollars (cash, check, or traveler's checks) and the facility you use to make the exchange (a bank, ATM, brokerage firm, or airport exchange booth). Whether you are in Canada or the United States will also be a factor in obtaining the best exchange rates. World currency markets dictate exchange rates based on numerous demand factors, but it is primarily commission rates, spreads or markups, and other related charges that vary between exchange rate vendors. Trillions of dollars in currency are exchanged every day around the world so it is a big business, bigger than any other in terms of sheer volume, more than any other commodity or security. On every transaction there is normally a commission that goes to the bank, broker, or trader being asked to buy or sell a certain currency. Regardless of who is facilitating the trade/exchange there is invariably a spread or markup. Before they do the exchange for you they mark up the price from whatever wholesaler or exchange that they got the currency from to sell to you. The spread or markup is usually invisible to you as a consumer as are often the commissions and these costs are just built into the price that you pay for the transaction. There are no regulations that require the banks or exchange brokers to disclose what exactly the transaction is costing you. For that reason they usually take as much as they can get away with, often depending on the knowledge or vulnerability of the consumer. For most banks their currency exchange trading is by far the most profitable product line. Often there are other fees as well that are identified as a transaction or currency exchange fee etc. When you total all of these fees up your cost can range from .01 percent or lower all the way up to 10 percent or more, so obviously you want to be as close to the .01 percent or below as possible. Being a knowledgeable consumer can pay off big in real cash dollars for you.

There is no exact formula that will guarantee you the best exchange rate each time, but the basic guidelines listed below have saved previous readers of *The Border Guide* hundreds and even thousands of dollars in exchange commissions, fees, or markups annually:

- Exchange large sums at one time, whenever possible. The cost of exchanging $1,000 five separate times is roughly twice that of exchanging $5,000 once.
- When exchanging at a bank, ask for the "spot" rate. This is the special rate, and a generally much more favorable rate, because of the much lower markup or spread than standard posted rates, right from the currency market at that time. Generally this service is available only when exchanging amounts of $5,000 or more or when dealing with good currency exchange brokers.
- Avoid using Canadian cash for the exchange. Commission rates on cash can go over 10 percent, particularly if you are outside

Canada. Wire transfers, checks, and traveler's checks generally attract the best rates. Personal checks only work at a bank where you are known.

- Shop around. Go to at least three institutions and tell each vendor the exact amount you want to exchange and the form of Canadian dollars you plan to use in the exchange. Exchange rates vary widely from institution to institution and change constantly throughout the day. If you are going to use a bank, include both US and Canadian banks and at least one foreign currency exchange broker in your survey. You may get some pleasant surprises if you do.
- Use foreign exchange brokers. Some even guarantee that they will beat the bank rate every time. I have found that most foreign exchange brokers exchange Canadian dollars for US dollars at far better rates than any bank or stock brokerage firm. They also won't try to sell you something that you may not want or need. The good ones are easy to work with regardless of where you are, including the US, through their toll-free numbers and websites. See Dealing with Foreign Exchange Brokers, the next section.
- If you have a relationship with a brokerage firm, you can generally exchange money with them at no or very low commissions or price markups. They are, of course, hoping you will invest the money through them and will often attempt to sell investments to you whether you are looking or not!
- If you're in a major gambling center such as Las Vegas, casinos often tend to offer excellent exchange rates. They may frown upon it, however, if you do not stop to gamble with some of your newly acquired US currency.
- Credit card companies may offer what they call "preferred exchange rates" when you use their cards to purchase foreign goods. However, these preferred exchange rates still may not be very good for the consumer. Credit card companies generally charge 2 to 3 percent currency exchange fees as well as transaction fees for some foreign purchases. They also charge exorbitant interest rates if you are not back in Canada or have not made other arrangements to pay the bill when it's due. All the major Canadian banks now issue US-dollar credit cards, which means you pay your bill in US funds. If you have followed our advice on how to live the most amazing cross-border lifestyle by ensuring you have plenty of US-dollar income, you can pay your US-dollar credit card with some

of those US dollars. You can also negotiate a better rate through an exchange broker at the time you make the payment. Using a US-dollar charge card in conjunction with a currency exchange broker is a much better solution than being at the mercy of the issuing bank to set its own exchange rate for a Canadian-dollar charge card for US purchases. Using a Canadian-dollar charge card in the US means paying additional fees and getting hit with a poorer exchange rate on each transaction.

DEALING WITH FOREIGN EXCHANGE BROKERS

Foreign exchange brokers are well established in Canada. They have been made possible by deregulation, which took away the banks' near monopoly on currency exchange. Banks do not really like this competition since their currency exchange departments tend to be among their most profitable areas. So if you ask your local bank manager about dealing with these brokers, don't expect too many favorable comments.

Foreign exchange brokers have done a lot to eliminate the air of mystery and poor service associated with exchanging currency. They provide ordinary customers with the same level of service that banks usually reserve for very large clients, and at a much lower cost — even lower than the special promotions and preferred rates that many banks offer their private banking clients. Foreign exchange brokers can give you real-time dollars (or other currencies), exchange quotes from world currency markets at any time. Once you've established a working relationship you can deal with them from anywhere in Canada or the US using their toll-free numbers or websites. You could be in Florida, your Canadian dollars could be in a bank account in Calgary, and the currency broker could be in Vancouver. Yet, you could still exchange any amount and have the US cash wired to your Florida bank on the same or very next business day.

One valuable service exchange brokers provide that banks do not is the ability to use standing orders. That means you can set the rate you want your money exchanged at, and if the exchange rate reaches your stated price, your transaction is processed automatically. For example, if the Canadian dollar was trading on the market at $0.70 USD and you had $5,000 CAD to exchange, your standing order might look like this: "Exchange my $5,000 CAD when the Canadian-dollar rate hits $0.71 USD." This standing order can be placed overnight or on weekends to be traded on other world exchanges, such as the Tokyo Exchange.

In certain circumstances you may wish to buy what is, in effect, an insurance policy to hedge against a falling Canadian dollar (when the funds you wish to exchange will not be available for a period of time because they may be locked in a GIC, and you are waiting, for example, to close a US house purchase). A good currency broker can help you through the ins and outs of this relatively complex transaction to ensure that you understand how it works and the limitations of these hedging contracts.

The majority of foreign exchange companies in Canada are well capitalized and professionally managed. However, since this is a new financial industry and foreign exchange companies are not regulated like banks or stock brokerage firms, consumers planning to use them need to investigate who they are dealing with and what guidelines they should follow to protect themselves. The following guidelines will help *Border Guide* readers take advantage of the better exchange rates offered by foreign exchange brokers without being taken advantage of:

- Know who you are dealing with. Ask for referrals of the exchange brokers and their company from other customers. Ask for financial data on the company and a banking report from the bank(s) the company uses to facilitate its transactions. Determine how long the company has been in business and how many offices and employees they have. In general, the longer they have been in business and the larger they are, the safer they will be to use.
- When dealing directly over the counter at a local foreign exchange broker, request that the broker have a US-dollar bank draft prepared in advance for you to exchange directly with your Canadian-dollar draft or check in the applicable amounts.
- When dealing over the phone with foreign exchange brokers, and they are wiring US funds to a third party such as a bank or brokerage firm, have the brokers wire the US funds in trust to the third party if possible. You can confirm that the money has been released before you pay for the US funds.
- Don't forget to use some of the exchange techniques we have discussed in this chapter, such as exchanging large amounts at one time, and getting more than one quote.

PREFERRED CURRENCY EXCHANGE

With the extremely large volume of currency exchanged annually by readers of *The Border Guide* and my cross-border planning firm, Keats-Connelly and Associates LLC (KC), we have negotiated and created what we believe is the best and fairest currency exchange program in North America. By going to the KeatsConnelly website, keatsconnelly.com, and clicking on Preferred Currency Exchange under Resources, all readers of *The Border Guide* can access this program at no cost. This currency exchange program was negotiated with MTFX, a currency exchange firm headquartered in North Toronto. MTFX has been in business more than 20 years and on our website it gives, live up-to-the-minute currency rates with the spread/markups listed and also the exact cost based on the amount you need to exchange. This is a good basis for you when you are getting quotes from other currency exchange facilitators like the banks. As noted, banks are reluctant to give the consumer the full disclosure on their markups or spreads and their commissions/fees they are charging you but when you can see them on this table through the KC website you might be able to convince the bank or other exchange brokers into giving you the same disclosures. If they refuse to provide it perhaps just tell them you are taking your business elsewhere and hopefully eventually they will get the message. On the KC website, MTFX provides their toll-free number and website information, and a personal contact person responsible for working directly with you, however to negotiate exchange rates let MTFX know that you are using the KC website or are a *Border Guide* reader.

Other popular travel websites such as the Canadian Snowbird Association (snowbirds.org), offer a preferred exchange rate through their Snowbird Currency Exchange program. However, the CSA does not disclose the fact that they are earning a large commission on each transaction nor do they disclose the spreads/markups members are paying even though they are usually providing better exchange rates than the banks. Through the preferred currency exchange on the KC website, neither KC nor anyone affiliated with the company receives any commissions or kickbacks whatsoever; this is a free service with full disclosure to all readers of *The Border Guide*, their friends and relatives, and KC clients, as a complimentary but extremely valuable service that puts more money in the pockets of Canadians wishing to live that amazing cross-border lifestyle.

The Taxman Cometh 4

Cross-Border Tax Planning

Cross-border financial planning tax analyses can be very beneficial for all those who undertake them diligently, and very costly to those who choose to ignore them or try to do it without professional help. The key points, in order to live the most amazing cross-border lifestyle and to provide the best return on your investment of time and money, come in the areas of income tax and non-resident estate-tax planning. This chapter deals with the income tax issues. Chapter 5 delves into non-resident estate issues.

TAXING VACATIONERS AND SNOWBIRDS

Vacationers and Snowbirds are considered non-residents, or non-resident aliens, as the US tax and immigration publications like to refer to them; they are generally taxed on their US-sourced income only. Income from US sources includes interest on bonds, notes, and other interest-bearing obligations; all wages for services performed in the United States; dividends; rents; royalties; and the gains from sale of US property. The Canada/US Tax Treaty sets forth the withholding rates, if any, on these sources of income (see Figure 9.9 in Chapter 9).

The treaty withholding rate is 0 percent on US-sourced interest. To receive the treaty benefit and be exempt from the withholding tax that US banks and similar institutions may implement, the IRS requires that the non-resident file an IRS Form W-8BEN (Certificate of Foreign Status of Beneficial Owner for United States Tax Withholding, see Figure 4.6 later in this chapter) with the payer of the interest. Form W-8BEN entitles you to this withholding exemption. Persons filing any type of US tax return or form, with the exception of Form W-8BEN and Form 8840, Figure 4.2, must use IRS Form W-7 (Application for IRS Individual Taxpayer Identification Number, see Figure 4.5), to apply for an Individual Taxpayer Identification Number (ITIN). The ITIN is similar to a Social Insurance Number or Social Security Number and is used to track payer and payee income tax reporting, as well as expedite non-resident income tax filings. You are not required to have an ITIN for completing form W-8BEN and Form 8840, but if you have one (or a Social Security Number) use it when you complete these forms. Most banks keep a good supply of W-7 and W-8BEN forms, and they can also be obtained free in electronically fillable formats from any IRS office or the IRS website: irs.gov.

Non-residents earning dividends in the United States will face a 15 percent withholding rate, reduced from 30 percent by the Canada/US Tax Treaty. Canadians will have to file the IRS Form W-8BEN to ensure that they get the treaty rate of withholding, rather than the regular rate.

By properly filing a Form W-8BEN with your bank and brokers, they will be prevented from filing certain tax slips that would normally require you to file US tax returns with the IRS.

Canadian non-resident Vacationers or Snowbirds collecting rent from the US have two options: either pay a flat 30 percent withholding tax on the gross rent, or file a non-resident tax return (Form 1040NR, see Figure 4.3). With the 1040NR you can elect to be taxed as a business in the US and net expenses against the rent, and then pay regular tax rates on the net rental income at the applicable rate. Depending in which US state the property is located, all of the states that have state specific income tax require a non-resident state income tax form be used to report rental income from non-residents. Most Canadians with rental income will find they will pay less tax, and perhaps no tax at all, if they file a US return rather than opt for 30 percent withholding. Even if you clearly made no profit from your rental property and paid no withholding tax on your gross rent, you must still file a Form 1040NR, unless you enjoy playing Russian roulette with the IRS. IRS regulations have been enacted that will disallow any rental expenses 16 months after the normal filing deadline of June 15 each year if there was no return filed. If the IRS catches up with you for failure to file, you will be forced to pay the 30 percent flat withholding tax and penalties on the gross rent collected. When no returns have been filed on the rental income, the IRS may go back indefinitely and ask for back taxes, penalties, and interest for the entire period you have rented out the property, which could be many years. In addition, failure to file and take mandatory depreciation could result in your paying substantially higher taxes when you eventually sell the property, even if you have to sell it at a loss. In other words, it is best to file a timely 1040NR each year you have any rental income or expenses. The chickens come to roost, in the tax sense, when a rental property is sold and the annual tax returns have not been filed or have been filed inaccurately as the sale will not close until the IRS clears the escrow company from withholding a portion of the sale proceeds, until they get proof the taxes due have been paid as required.

Canadians selling personal use (i.e., not rental or investment property) real estate in the United States will be exempt from federal withholding tax if the property is valued at less than $300,000, and if the buyers are going to occupy the home for their own personal use. Otherwise, the federal withholding rate is 10 percent up to a property value of $1 million and 15 percent above that level, whether or not there will be any profit on the sale. Applications to reduce or eliminate the required withholding tax can be made, in advance to the closing of the sale, to the IRS if there is only a small gain or a loss on the sale of the property. This application for reduced withholding should be made to the IRS a minimum of six weeks prior to the closing of the real estate sale by filing IRS Form 8288 (Application for Withholding Certificate for Dispositions by Foreign Persons of US Real Estate Property Interests). If the seller does not have an Individual Taxpayer Identification Number (ITIN) or US Social Security Number (SSN), they will have to apply for the ITIN using Form W-7 (see Figure 4.5) and include it with the Form 8288 submission. The IRS now requires a copy of the signed agreement by the buyer and the seller of the property before they will accept the form W-7 and Form 8288 to reduce any withholding or issue the ITIN. Frequently the application to reduce the withholding takes longer than the agreed-to closing date by the buyer and seller. In that case, normally what will happen is the escrow or title company responsible for the transaction will withhold the tax and keep it in an escrow account once they have proof that the paperwork has been filed with the IRS to refund to the seller once the IRS has processed the paperwork.

It is important that an exemption from withholding tax is not confused with an exemption from tax, as tax is often due even when withholding tax is not. The gross amount of the sale transaction is reported by the buyer or the buyer's agent, most often the escrow or title company facilitating the transaction, to the IRS on Form 1099-S. The reconciliation details of any net gains or losses must always be reported to the IRS on Form 1040NR by the seller, for the year of the sale. If there is further tax to be paid on a gain, it will be paid with this return. Likewise, if there is a refund of any withholding tax due, this is the mechanism for applying for it. There are several cross-border tax and accounting firms that sellers can hire to process all this paperwork and it is recommend. For a few hundred dollars it will save a lot of aggravation time and taxes; look for the resources in the Appendix E of this book for some contact information for a qualified professional firm to assist with these filings.

If the state in which the property is being sold has a state income tax, there are normally state withholding requirements on top of the federal withholding requirements. Check with the local state tax authorities well in advance of the closing date of your property or use a professional services firm so you know exactly what the requirements are, and so the closing is not delayed because of state withholding taxes.

Just as American visitors to Canada who purchase property in Canada do not qualify for the Canadian principal residence exemption, Canadian Vacationers/Snowbirds with property in the US do not qualify for the $250,000 per person or $500,000 per couple US principal residence exemption unless they make the transition to the Settler lifestyle.

Remember that exemptions, reductions in withholding tax, and filings from US tax on any of the aforementioned income do not mean the income is exempt from Canadian taxation. Any sale or transfer of US property must always be reported to the Canada Revenue Agency on the individual's T1s for the year of the transaction regardless of whether there are gains or not. For Canadians who purchased their US real estate when their dollar was at or above par and are deciding to sell, currently will likely have a large currency gain to pay tax on with CRA even though in terms of US dollars and with the US filings there may be no gain at all.

Canadian residents are taxed on their world income and must report these US earnings annually to the Canada Revenue Agency, whether exempt from a US perspective or not. You will generally receive a credit on your Canadian return for any taxes paid to the US (to the extent allowed by CRA and Canada/US Tax Treaty rules). It is important to ensure any withholding is done according to the Canada/US Tax Treaty. The CRA only allows credits on a Canadian return to the amount specified by the treaty. Excess withholding won't be credited and will be lost unless attempts are made to recover it; a difficult job at best. Most Canadians investing to produce US income will have no US withholding tax to pay or tax returns to file if they use the exempt investments mentioned in Chapter 3, and explained in detail in Chapter 4. Canadian non-residents will discover under what circumstances and when they must or should file a non-resident tax return (Form 1040NR) with the IRS.

DUAL CITIZENS AND GREEN CARD HOLDERS RESIDENT IN CANADA

Canada taxes its citizens on their world income only when they are residents of Canada. The United States taxes its citizens, permanent resident aliens/green card holders on their world income, with certain exclusions, regardless of where they reside in the world.

Many Canadians obtained US green cards years ago, perhaps through business, marriage, or family connections. Some never used these green cards, while others might have used them but moved back to Canada without formally giving up their green card status. Chapter 8 deals with the immigration implications of Canadians in this situation. From a tax standpoint, the IRS considers all green card holders legal permanent residents of the US and views them as subject to the same filing requirements as anyone else with resident status. That is, they must file annual tax returns in the US on their world income. There can be numerous tax advantages to paying taxes in the US rather than Canada. These are covered later in this chapter and in Chapter 9. However, Canadians in this situation need to determine whether they should officially abandon their green cards or use them to their best advantage. In other words, they need to come out of the closet about having a green card. The best way to make the final decision about what to do in this situation is to complete a full cross-border financial planning analysis that addresses every issue, with the goal of getting the best of both the Canadian and US systems and choosing the cross-border lifestyle they wish to follow. If you are in possession of a green card and you do nothing and continue to sit in the woods trying to stay under the radar, you may inevitably end up getting the worst of both systems, instead of the best. If you have had your green card for more than eight years, you may be subject to the same income tax and estate tax rules as expatriate US citizens discussed later in this chapter. As noted in Chapter 2, US Customs and Border Protection and the Canadian Border Services Agency share information and are constantly updating their computer systems. I believe all green card holders will eventually be logged into the system regardless of how long ago they obtained a green card if they still have it in their possession. Unless they take positive action now, a very unpleasant surprise may be waiting in the future when these closet green card holders are entering the US and the border computers now show that green card still outstanding.

Canadians who were born in the United States or obtained US citizenship from another source (see Chapter 8's sections on derivative citizenship and dual citizenship), and who are also naturalized Canadian citizens, are dual citizens of Canada and the United States. Dual citizens living in Canada are in a similar situation, tax-wise, to the green card holders described above. They need to file annual tax returns in both countries on their world income. These dual citizens residing in Canada need to determine as soon as possible whether they should officially abandon their US citizenship or use it to their best advantage. Our advice here is the same: Complete a cross-border financial planning analysis that positions your dual citizenship to obtain the best tax advantages between Canada and the United States and the chosen cross-border lifestyle. This planning can easily save you thousands or even hundreds of thousands of dollars in taxes. Chapters 9, 10, and 14 will show you what many of your options are.

VOLUNTARY DISCLOSURE

Canadian residents holding US green cards, US citizens, dual citizens, and derivative US citizens who have not been filing US annual tax returns on their world income, have one key option to come out of the closet and get back on the correct US filing rolls without penalty. Over the past decade, the IRS has implemented several voluntary disclosure programs for foreign and domestic non filers each with their own specific set of rules of who qualifies for the disclosure program and what penalties the taxpayer might face. Some of the tax penalties started as high as 25 percent of the value of all foreign accounts not reported. The penalty could go as high as 50 percent with interest if the IRS found that the underreporting was deliberate. However, in 2014 the IRS decided that perhaps they could get more people back on the filing rolls by introducing a new program that, providing an individual qualifies, could put him or her back in the favorable light of the IRS without any penalties.

This new voluntary disclosure program is called the Streamlined Foreign Offshore Procedure (there is also a domestic version of this program). The criteria to qualify for this streamlined procedure are:

- Meet the non-resident requirements as defined by the IRS.
- For each of the most recent three years, file the delinquent or amended returns (US citizens must file IRS Form 1040, green card holders who are considered Canadian residents under the treaty tiebreaker rules explained later in this chapter, may file the non-resident IRS Form 1040NR along with their treaty disclosure Form 8833) together with all of the other informational returns such as IRS Forms 3520, 5471, 8891, and Form 8938.
- For each of the most recent six years file any delinquent foreign bank account or investment account reporting forms, and Financial Crimes Enforcement Network, FinCen Form 114.
- The full amount of tax and interest due in connection with these findings must be remitted with the delinquent or amended returns.

- Complete and sign a statement certifying that you are eligible for the Streamlined Foreign Offshore Procedure and that all required foreign reporting forms have been filed and that the failure to file tax returns resulted from non-willful conduct.
- File all future returns and stay in compliance with foreign reporting requirements starting with subsequent years immediately after filing the three years' returns under this procedure.

Even though meeting all of the above criteria will take some time and effort, this is by far the most generous voluntary disclosure program that the IRS has made available and it should be taken advantage of by anyone that has not been filing or not been filing correctly while living outside of the US with US citizenship or green card status. Being able to get back in the IRS's good graces without late filing penalties, underpayment penalties, and failure to file reporting form penalties (when one looks at what the penalties could be without this streamlined procedure, as high as 50 percent annually), is an unexpected gift from the IRS. In addition, previous voluntary disclosure forms have required six years of past returns whereas this program only requires three. Unfortunately, the IRS may change or eliminate this program at any time so it is difficult to let people know how much time they have to take advantage of this program. My recommendation is that they do it as soon as possible.

Sitting in the woods as a green card holder, or living in Canada as a US citizen hoping no one will find out, is clearly the worst of all possible strategies. By hiding, you are effectively giving the IRS control of your financial life or your final estate's future. As noted in Chapter 2, the IRS is very reasonable to deal with for those who follow the rules and pay taxes as required, but has a system of severe penalties for those that either deliberately or through ignorance did not comply with their rules. Without taking advantage of this current program the IRS may raise its head unexpectedly at any time, as many in this situation have found out, and huge taxes and penalties may be assessed well after there was opportunity to zero them out by using the Streamlined Foreign Offshore Procedure, and by completing a cross-border financial planning analysis to best optimize future cross-border tax reduction strategies. If the IRS gets to you before you do your voluntary disclosure you will feel the full impact of all penalties and interest that could have been avoided. The information sharing amongst various government agencies explained in Chapter 1 with the US Customs and Border Protection and the Canadian Border Services Agency integrated computer systems, and the new agreements amongst Canadian and US banks reporting to each other's governments when citizens of one country has a bank or investment account in the other, will continue to make those trying to stay under the radar of the IRS more difficult. If, lately, you have attempted to open up a new Canadian bank or brokerage account you will inevitably be asked by the Canadian institution whether you are a US citizen or taxpayer, under penalty of perjury if you give a false answer. Often, US citizens or green card holders in Canada who are not in compliance with the IRS are found out only after their deaths, when their executors find they must either pay the tax and penalties, or face perjury charges or other sanctions. This is not a pleasant position for any executor to be put in, and beneficiaries get mightily upset when they see a good portion or even all of their inheritance evaporate before their eyes in favor of the IRS.

The requirement to file US tax returns and report world income in the United States does not necessarily mean that there will be taxes due to the US on income earned in Canada. There are exemptions such as the earned income exclusion of $101,300 USD, and the maximum ancillary housing costs exclusion of $13,576, providing the earned income was not US-sourced. When one fails to file in a timely fashion, the IRS can deny these exclusions entirely. In addition to this employment income exemption, the Canada/US Tax Treaty allows foreign tax credits for taxes paid in Canada to be used on the US return for the same income. Since Canadian tax rates have been significantly higher than US rates in recent years, the foreign tax credits from taxes paid in Canada usually cover any US taxes due. However, there are certain circumstances under which US taxes can become due on income that would not be taxed if the taxpayer or US citizen was filing only in Canada. For example, the IRS taxes RRSPs very differently than Canada and can unexpectedly create taxable income in the US while the Canadian income tax is still deferred until withdrawal (see Chapter 10, the section named Withdraw Your RRSP Tax Free on a Net After-Tax Basis for more detailed information on how the US taxes RRSPs), these people would pay tax to the US at the standard rate with no offsetting Canadian credit available (since no Canadian tax would be owing on the RRSP income unless there were actual withdrawals from the RRSP). A similar problem can arise when a Canadian resident or US citizen takes advantage of the small-business capital gains exemption, as there would be no Canadian tax due, but the IRS would require taxes also be paid on the entire capital gain including the exemption portion of the business sale. In addition, Canadian principal residence exemptions work differently than the US principal residence exemption, so consequently, sales of principal residences may be taxed on the Canadian return and not on the US, or vice versa.

US citizens in Canada who are taking dividends from their closely held Canadian corporations in an attempt to zero out or reduce personal Canadian tax with the dividend tax credit, could also find themselves paying US taxes on the dividends received. Similarly, income earned and held inside the closely controlled private corporation in Canada can be taxed by the IRS as if the income was earned personally by the taxpayer, with no tax credit for taxes paid by the corporation (this topic is discussed in more detail in Chapter 13). One can correctly surmise that IRS regulations requiring US citizens to file annual returns, in light of the differences in tax rules between Canada and the US, is extremely complex and can provide some very unpleasant surprises. The streamlined foreign voluntary procedure can be of great advantage to US citizens who want to get back into the good graces of the IRS and avoid penalties. They may also want to use this voluntary disclosure to prevent the IRS from scrutinizing financial transactions prior to the three years of required returns, which otherwise could have required the payment of large tax amounts.

It is highly recommended that US citizens and green card holders in Canada seek regular cross-border tax advice to avoid unnecessary tax, and should construct a plan that takes best advantage of the US and Canadian tax systems and avoid common pitfalls. Proper planning from a knowledgeable cross-border financial planning professional can turn these apparent tax problems into great tax-saving opportunities. In general, US citizens and green card holders living in Canada are going to be hit with the worst of both the Canadian and US tax systems if they remain full-time residents of Canada for the rest of their lives. If they have no intention of returning to the United States for any reason, including winter vacations, they may want to seriously consider renouncing their US citizenship, but only after taking into consideration the new expatriation rules explained in the next section. Likewise for green card holders, they should abandon their green cards through a formal process by completing USCIS Form I-407 or a letter stating the intent to abandon legal permanent resident status together with the green card attached, by giving the form/letter to any USCIS or US consular officer/office. It should be clearly noted though, expatriation does not relieve the taxpayer of any taxes, interest, or penalties accrued up to the date of expatriation; these can only be dealt with by actually doing return filing with the IRS for a minimum of five complete years. This step should be taken only after they have addressed all of their options in a comprehensive cross-border financial planning analysis as well as understood some possible concerns with travel to or through the US after expatriation.

US TAX LEGISLATION CONCERNING EXPATRIATION FROM THE US

The US has had rules concerning expatriation since 1995. These expatriation rules have been modified three times, with the most recent change June 17, 2008. The most recent changes to these rules made them easier to follow and enforce by the IRS, but for the first time in recent US tax history, created an exit tax and an inheritance tax in the US upon expatriation or termination of residency. For the purposes of these rules, expatriation refers to a person who relinquishes his or her US citizenship or renounces his or her permanent resident status or green card, after holding it for at least 8 of the last 15 years. The person conducting the expatriation will be subject to the latest rules and will be considered a "covered expatriate" if he or she meets the following criteria —

- the individual had an average annual income tax liability over the preceding five years before the date of expatriation or termination of residency that was greater than $161,000, as of 2016 tax year adjusted for inflation;
- the individual's net worth is $2 million or more, including interests in certain trusts, on the date of expatriation or termination of residency; or
- the individual fails to certify on IRS Form 8854 and provide evidence of compliance with US federal tax obligations for the five years preceding the date of expatriation or termination of residency.

No relinquishment of citizenship or termination of lawful permanent residency will be effective for federal tax purposes until such person gives notice of an expatriating act or termination of residency to the Secretary of State for relinquishment of citizenship, or the Secretary of Homeland Security for relinquishment of a green card. The expatriated person must file a statement with the IRS by completing IRS Form 8854, Initial and Annual Expatriation Statement. There are severe penalties for failure to file Form 8854 starting at $10,000.

The expatriation tax, but not the Form 8854 filing requirement, does not apply to persons meeting the above tests for covered expatriates if they became dual citizens at birth and continue to be dual citizens to the date of expatriation and meet further additional tests as follows —

- they are taxed as residents of the other country at the date of expatriation, or

- they have not been US income tax residents for more than 10 of the last 15 years.

Covered expatriates pay tax on capital gains on the deemed disposition of their worldwide assets at the time of expatriation. This capital gains tax is very similar to the deemed disposition tax Canadians have been subjected to by the CRA when they exit Canada to take up residency in another country. A basic exemption on the first $693,000 USD (2016, indexed for inflation) of capital gains is provided to covered expatriates. The capital gains tax on the deemed disposition can be deferred on any asset until it is sold or until death if security is provided and applicable interest is paid on the taxes due.

Covered expatriates face an additional tax on income from a deemed withdrawal from IRAs, 401(k)s, and other similar qualified retirement plans based on the value of these plans the day before expatriation. Deferred compensation plans are also included in income in the year of expatriation, but the expatriate's employer can elect not to have a deemed disposition. To do this they must file an election with the IRS guaranteeing that when an actual distribution is made, 30 percent of the deferred compensation plan will be withheld and forwarded to the US government. Careful planning with a cross-border financial planning professional is highly recommended in situations with deferred plans in order to determine when it is best to take actual distributions versus deemed distributions to avoid double taxation. Matching foreign tax credits is a complex and time-consuming process, as it also needs to take into consideration early withdrawal penalties on US IRAs and qualified plans for those under the age of 59½. Covered expatriates who have contributed to Canadian RRSPs may find that under IRS code section 72(w), their RRSPs are also subject to this deemed distribution on expatriation with no offsetting foreign tax credits available. This could result in a double tax on the RRSPs totaling up to as much as 90 percent (39.6 percent US tax on top of any Canadian federal and provincial income taxes, averaging around 50 percent).

A special transfer tax on gifts and bequests made by the covered expatriate for the rest of their lives or at death is mandated under these expatriation rules. This means that any gifts to any US resident or citizen exceeding an annual exclusion of $14,000 USD and any payments to a US resident beneficiary from an estate of the deceased covered expatriate are subject to the maximum US estate tax rate, currently 40 percent. This special transfer tax is in fact an inheritance tax that is paid by the US beneficiaries with no exemptions available whatsoever. Covered expatriates who are beneficiaries of a US trust are subject to 30 percent withholding taxes on any distributions they receive from these US trusts.

After the date of expatriation, given that the covered expatriate has fulfilled all of the requirements noted above, the expatriate will be treated for all income tax purposes as a non-resident of the US (he or she is still subject to the gift and inheritance tax rules noted in the previous paragraph). In effect, he or she would be treated just like any Canadian citizen visiting or wintering in the US. Consequently, the remainder of this chapter and subsequent chapters describing when non-residents must file US returns and when they are subject to other US income tax rules will apply to covered expatriates as well.

There is a provision in US immigration law (referred to as the Reed Amendment) that allows the federal government to deny an expatriate admission into the United States. This law has never been enforced and many experts believe that it is unenforceable as currently enacted. However, the law may be amended, and there is a risk the US could deny an expatriate the right to re-enter. The IRS does make public a quarterly list of those US citizens who have expatriated during that previous quarter.

US Customs and Border Protection personnel have been known to refuse expatriates entrance. As you recall from Chapter 1, CBP personnel have the power of judge, jury, and executioner with respect to refusing individuals from entering. Some of these personnel resent Americans giving up their US citizenship and can either give the expatriate a hard time or refuse entry into the US, even though technically the expatriate has done everything according to the law. Although this resentment is fortunately not widespread it does happen, as many of the CBP are very patriotic and consider giving up US citizenship a very unpatriotic act.

In summary, any US citizen or long term US resident/green card holder should seriously consider options with the assistance of an experienced cross-border financial planner before expatriating. There may be other options. For example, a US citizen retaining citizenship who is likely to have US beneficiaries may be far better off keeping US citizenship and having available the $5.45 million USD individual standard estate tax exemption, without any of the deemed disposition requirements.

NON-RESIDENT TO RESIDENT IN THE US FOR INCOME TAX PURPOSES

Canadians who are Vacationers and regularly spend less than four cumulative months per calendar year in the US do not have to worry about becoming residents of the United States for tax purposes. They will be free of any filing requirements unless they are in one of the situations listed later in this chapter.

You may recall from the discussions in Chapters 1 and 2 that different sets of rules apply to those living in the cross-border lifestyle as to who is tracking their time in the US and for what purpose. Since the IRS only deals with filing tax returns and does not really care how many days you spend in the US from an immigration perspective, there is a possibility of being considered a US resident for tax purposes and yet having no right to remain legally in the United States as an immigrant. This section will examine the tax rules that make this apparent contradiction possible, whether you have a US visa or not.

THE SUBSTANTIAL PRESENCE TEST

Vacationers and Snowbirds are considered residents of the US for tax purposes if they meet the Substantial Presence Test. They satisfy this test if they have been in the United States for at least 183 days during a three-calendar-year period that includes the current year. The current year is the particular tax year for which the Vacationer/Snowbird is determining a resident status. For purposes of the Substantial Presence Test, a visitor will be treated as present in the United States on any day that he or she is physically present in the country at any time during the day. This would include any cross-border trip you make to the United States being counted as a full day, even if you were present in the country for only a few hours. Note that the days present in the United States need not be consecutive but are cumulative throughout each calendar year.

Each day of presence in the first preceding year is counted as one-third of a day, and each day of presence in the second preceding year is counted as one-sixth of a day. For example, Figure 4.1 illustrates the results of these calculations for a winter visitor who spends four months in the United States Sunbelt, plus a few shopping days in the adjoining border town. Even though this winter visitor never came close to spending six months in the United States in any one year, he or she can still be deemed to have spent 187 days in the current year, and is therefore a US resident for tax purposes under the Substantial Presence Test. It is important to note that being considered a resident of the US for tax purposes is not the catastrophic scenario that it is led to be by Canadian newspapers and advisors; there are some very simple things that will be explained in this chapter and subsequent chapters of *The Border Guide.* Follow basic filing requirements to keep the IRS happy as well as be able to take advantage of their rules to reduce Canadian taxes significantly.

THE SUBSTANTIAL PRESENCE TEST	
Number of days present this year	124 x 1 = 124
Number of days present last year	124 x 1/3 = 42
Number of days present previous to the last year	124 x 1/6 = 21
Total days deemed present in the current year	187

FIGURE 4.1

In computing the days of presence in the United States under this rule, there are exceptions that certain days are not considered days of presence. These include any days that an individual is prevented from leaving the United States because of a medical condition that arose while the visitor was in the country.

If an individual is not physically present for more than 30 days during the actual current year, the Substantial Presence Test will not apply even if the three-year total is 183 or more days.

As an example: John, a Snowbird, was physically present in the United States for 52 days in 2016, 300 days in 2015, and 186 days in 2014. John meets the 31-day requirement for the current year, the year 2016 in this example. He also meets the 183-day requirement ((186/6=31 days in 2014) + (300/3=100 days in 2015) + 52 days in current year of 2016= 183 total days by IRS formula in 2016). As a result of this Substantial Presence Test formula, John is considered a resident of the US for tax purposes by the IRS for 2016.

Another example: Barbara was physically present in the United States on 120 days in each of the years 2016, 2015, and 2014. The full 120 days count for 2016; 40 days or one third the days count for 2015 (120/3); and 20 days or one sixth of the days count for 2014 (120/6). Since the total for the three years (180) is less than 183, Barbara would not be considered a resident in 2016 under the Substantial Presence Test. However, if Barbara were to decide to take the 2- or 3-day trip to visit, shop, or go to Las Vegas anytime she was back in Canada, those extra days would put her over under this substantial presence test.

Over many years, thousands of Canadians living the cross-border lifestyle as Vacationers or Snowbirds consistently plan their US stays under the 120 days, as Barbara in the above example, just to avoid a very simple statement to the IRS that takes about 10 minutes to complete. They are letting a simple procedure run their lives even though they would much rather spend more time out of the Canadian winters in the US Sunbelt because of an unfounded fear that the IRS is going to get them. The next section lets you know how simple it is to complete a statement that if you are not completing is giving you unnecessary fear and a much shorter winter vacation or time in the US than you otherwise might desire. This is definitely a letting the tail wag the dog type of scenario.

THE CLOSER CONNECTION EXCEPTION

Vacationers or Snowbirds who meet the Substantial Presence Test and their three-year total days under the formula exceed 182 days may still be considered non-residents and be exempt from US income tax on their world income for the current year by very simply letting the IRS know they have a close connection to Canada and maintain a "tax home" there.

The way the IRS asks non-residents let them know they have a closer connection for tax purposes to Canada is by letting them complete IRS Form 8840 (The Closer Connection Exception Statement, see Figure 4.2) or Form 1040NR (the non-resident Tax Return, see Figure 4.3) by June 15 of each year for the previous calendar year. If an individual goes over 183 days in the current year, in spite of the Substantial Presence Test formula, he or she needs to file the form 1040NR and attach Form 8840 to this non-resident tax return otherwise just Form 8840 needs to be filed. Filing Form 8840 is easy, it takes about 30 minutes the first time and about 10 minutes each time after that because the information seldom changes other than the date. There are fewer than 30 very basic questions and the majority of them are yes/no checkboxes, and it is only a little bit longer than the customs forms one completes every time you fly into or out of the US. Filing Form 8840 in a timely manner keeps the IRS informed and happy and protects one from myriad tax rules that could have adverse effects if applied to a Canadian retroactively. For those wishing to live the amazing cross-border lifestyle there is comfort and peace of mind knowing that there will be no hassles coming from the IRS because they have shown a closer connection to Canada, so for this reason alone I recommend the Closer Connection Exception form be completed and a copy of the filed Form 8840 be included in your Border Kit.

Higher net-worth Canadians who are deemed US residents for tax purposes under the Substantial Presence Test may want to take an additional precaution and file Form 8840 together with a timely-filed Form 1040NR (the US Non-Resident Tax Return, see Figure 4.3). If you have a high six-figure RRSP or larger, have a large or complicated Canadian business structure, have done a Canadian estate freeze, use Canadian dividends as your chief source of income, or any combination of these situations, and regularly spend more than four months a year in the US, I would consider you to be a bigger target of an IRS challenge to your being a non-resident of the US (but not necessarily at higher risk of audit). I would encourage those who may be these bigger targets to file the Form 1040NR, even though it is not technically required. The reason for this is that the Form 8840 filing by itself does not trigger any statute of limitation protection, so in theory the IRS could challenge the veracity of the form even though you filed it many years previously. However, if you file Form 1040NR with Form 8840 attached, in a timely fashion and with the appropriate treaty election, the IRS has only three years to challenge the contents of the return and the Form 8840 or they will be statute barred from doing so (unless they can prove fraud was involved).

On many occasions of late US Customs and Border Protection officials have requested a copy of the most recently filed Form 8840 of regular Canadian visitors to the US in order to prove that they are indeed only visitors, and were following IRS rules so therefore my recommendation is to ensure that a copy of the latest filed Form 8840 be a prominent part of your Border Kit that you have in your possession each time you enter the US as a Vacationer or Snowbird. Most Settlers will not need to complete Form 8840 because they normally would be filing tax returns as US residents and Canadian non-residents.

WHAT IS THE CANADA/US TAX TREATY?

One of the most important documents for the protection of a Canadian's financial assets in the United States is the Canada/US Tax Treaty. Most Canadians are unaware of its existence and the benefits that it gives them. Even though tax planning is an important part of cross-border planning, few financial advisors on either side of the Canada-US border have ever cracked the cover of this treaty on behalf of their clients. They tend to focus instead on the tax rules of their own individual countries.

Canada and the United States signed their first full tax treaty in 1942, with amendments in 1950, 1956, 1966, 1980, and 1995. The most recent amendment was initiated in 2000 and completed in 2007. This latest amendment, called the Fifth Protocol, was fully ratified December 15, 2008. Some of the new provisions in the Fifth Protocol are retroactive to 2000. Other provisions were not fully effective until 2011. In general the Protocol is effective for tax years beginning on or after January 1, 2009.

The tax treaty is the most important business treaty for both Canada and the United States. Millions of Canadians and Americans are affected

Form **8840** | **Closer Connection Exception Statement for Aliens** | OMB No. 1545-0074

► Attach to Form 1040NR or Form 1040NR-EZ.
► Information about Form 8840 and its instructions is at *www.irs.gov/form8840*.
For the year January 1—December 31, 2015, or other tax year beginning , 2015, and ending , 20 .

Department of the Treasury
Internal Revenue Service

2015
Attachment Sequence No. **101**

Your first name and initial	Last name	Your U.S. taxpayer identification number, if any

Fill in your addresses only if you are filing this form by itself and not with your U.S. tax return	Address in country of residence	Address in the United States

Part I General Information

1 Type of U.S. visa (for example, F, J, M, etc.) and date you entered the United States ►

2 Of what country or countries were you a citizen during the tax year?

3 What country or countries issued you a passport?

4 Enter your passport number(s) ►

5 Enter the number of days you were present in the United States during:
2015 ______ 2014 ______ 2013 ______ .

6 During 2015, did you apply for, or take other affirmative steps to apply for, lawful permanent resident status in the United States or have an application pending to change your status to that of a lawful permanent resident of the United States (see instructions)? . . . ☐ Yes ☐ No

Part II Closer Connection to One Foreign Country

7 Where was your tax home during 2015?

8 Enter the name of the foreign country to which you had a closer connection than to the United States during 2015 ►

Next, complete Part IV.

Part III Closer Connection to Two Foreign Countries

9 Where was your tax home on January 1, 2015?

10 After changing your tax home from its location on January 1, 2015, where was your tax home for the remainder of 2015?

11 Did you have a closer connection to each foreign country listed on lines 9 and 10 than to the United States for the period during which you maintained a tax home in that foreign country? . . . ☐ Yes ☐ No
If "No," attach an explanation.

12 Were you subject to tax as a resident under the internal laws of **(a)** either of the countries listed on lines 9 and 10 during all of 2015 or **(b)** both of the countries listed on lines 9 and 10 for the period during which you maintained a tax home in each country? . . . ☐ Yes ☐ No

13 Have you filed or will you file tax returns for 2015 in the countries listed on lines 9 and 10? . . . ☐ Yes ☐ No
If "Yes" to either line 12 or line 13, attach verification.
If "No" to either line 12 or line 13, please explain ►

Next, complete Part IV.

For Paperwork Reduction Act Notice, see page 4. Cat. No. 15829P Form **8840** (2015)

FIGURE 4.2

by this agreement, and as long as Canada and the United States continue as each other's major trading partners, its impact will only increase.

The Canada/US Tax Treaty attempts to accomplish the same goals as any tax treaty: the prevention of tax measures that may discourage trade and investment, reaching a common ground on the taxation of non-residents to avoid double taxation on the same income, and to protect the domestic treasury. To a large extent, the Canada/US Tax Treaty has accomplished these goals, as long as one plans.

Form 8840 (2015) Page 2

Part IV Significant Contacts With Foreign Country or Countries in 2015

14 Where was your regular or principal permanent home located during 2015 (see instructions)?

15 If you had more than one permanent home available to you at all times during 2015, list the location of each and explain ▶

16 Where was your family located?

17 Where was your automobile(s) located?

18 Where was your automobile(s) registered?

19 Where were your personal belongings, furniture, etc., located?

20 Where was the bank(s) with which you conducted your routine personal banking activities located?

a ______ c ______

b ______ d ______

21 Did you conduct business activities in a location other than your tax home? ☐ Yes ☐ No
If "Yes," where?

22a Where was your driver's license issued?

b If you hold a second driver's license, where was it issued?

23 Where were you registered to vote?

24 When completing official documents, forms, etc., what country do you list as your residence?

25 Have you ever completed:

a Form W-8BEN or any other W-8 form (relating to foreign status)? ☐ Yes ☐ No

b Form W-9, Request for Taxpayer Identification Number and Certification? ☐ Yes ☐ No

c Form 1078, Certificate of Alien Claiming Residence in the United States? ☐ Yes ☐ No

d Any other U.S. official forms? If "Yes," indicate the form(s) ▶ ☐ Yes ☐ No

26 In what country or countries did you keep your personal, financial, and legal documents?

27 From what country or countries did you derive the majority of your 2015 income?

28 Did you have any income from U.S. sources? ☐ Yes ☐ No
If "Yes," what type?

29 In what country or countries were your investments located (see instructions)?

30 Did you qualify for any type of "national" health plan sponsored by a foreign government? ☐ Yes ☐ No
If "Yes," in what country?
If "No," please explain ▶

If you have any other information to substantiate your closer connection to a country other than the United States or you wish to explain in more detail any of your responses to lines 14 through 30, attach a statement to this form.

Sign here only if you are filing this form by itself and not with your U.S. tax return — Under penalties of perjury, I declare that I have examined this form and the accompanying attachments, and to the best of my knowledge and belief, they are true, correct, and complete.

▶ Your signature ▶ Date

Form **8840** (2015)

FIGURE 4.2 — Continued

The two countries negotiated an estate tax article that was added to the existing treaty in 1995. For some people this will resolve the potentially high non-resident estate tax and/or capital gains tax that Canadians face if they hold US real estate and stocks. This is covered in greater detail in Chapter 5.

Up until 1996, Canadian winter visitors were able to use the Canada/US Tax Treaty protection by default, without having to make any filings or declarations. Current regulations now require that formal statements be filed with the IRS, forcing Canadians who spend four to six months in the US to become more aware of the treaty and how it can help them if they do not wish to be taxed on their world income in both countries.

Form **1040NR** Department of the Treasury Internal Revenue Service

U.S. Nonresident Alien Income Tax Return

▶ **Information about Form 1040NR and its separate instructions is at *www.irs.gov/form1040nr*.**

For the year January 1–December 31, 2015, or other tax year beginning , 2015, and ending , 20

OMB No. 1545-0074

2015

Please print or type

Your first name and initial	Last name	**Identifying number (see instructions)**
Present home address (number, street, and apt. no., or rural route). If you have a P.O. box, see instructions.		Check if: ☐ Individual ☐ Estate or Trust
City, town or post office, state, and ZIP code. If you have a foreign address, also complete spaces below (see instructions).		
Foreign country name	Foreign province/state/county	Foreign postal code

Filing Status

Check only one box.

1 ☐ Single resident of Canada or Mexico or single U.S. national
2 ☐ Other single nonresident alien
3 ☐ Married resident of Canada or Mexico or married U.S. national
4 ☐ Married resident of South Korea
5 ☐ Other married nonresident alien
6 ☐ Qualifying widow(er) with dependent child (see instructions)

If you checked box 3 or 4 above, enter the information below.

(i) Spouse's first name and initial	(ii) Spouse's last name	(iii) Spouse's identifying number

Exemptions

7a ☐ **Yourself.** If someone can claim you as a dependent, **do not** check box 7a
b ☐ **Spouse.** Check box 7b only if you checked box 3 or 4 above **and** your spouse **did not** have any U.S. gross income

Boxes checked on 7a and 7b ____
No. of children on 7c who:
• lived with you ____
• did not live with you due to divorce or separation (see instructions) ____
Dependents on 7c not entered above ____

c **Dependents:** (see instructions)

If more than four dependents, see instructions.

(1) First name Last name	(2) Dependent's identifying number	(3) Dependent's relationship to you	(4) ✔ if qualifying child for child tax credit (see instr.)
			☐
			☐
			☐
			☐

d Total number of exemptions claimed . . . **Add numbers on lines above** ▶ ☐

Income Effectively Connected With U.S. Trade/Business

Attach Form(s) W-2, 1042-S, SSA-1042S, RRB-1042S, and 8288-A here. Also attach Form(s) 1099-R if tax was withheld.

Line	Description		Amount
8	Wages, salaries, tips, etc. Attach Form(s) W-2		8
9a	**Taxable** interest		9a
b	**Tax-exempt** interest. **Do not** include on line 9a	9b	
10a	Ordinary dividends		10a
b	Qualified dividends (see instructions)	10b	
11	Taxable refunds, credits, or offsets of state and local income taxes (see instructions)		11
12	Scholarship and fellowship grants. Attach Form(s) 1042-S or required statement (see instructions)		12
13	Business income or (loss). Attach Schedule C or C-EZ (Form 1040)		13
14	Capital gain or (loss). Attach Schedule D (Form 1040) if required. If not required, check here ☐		14
15	Other gains or (losses). Attach Form 4797		15
16a	IRA distributions 16a	16b Taxable amount (see instructions)	16b
17a	Pensions and annuities 17a	17b Taxable amount (see instructions)	17b
18	Rental real estate, royalties, partnerships, trusts, etc. Attach Schedule E (Form 1040)		18
19	Farm income or (loss). Attach Schedule F (Form 1040)		19
20	Unemployment compensation		20
21	Other income. List type and amount (see instructions)		21
22	Total income exempt by a treaty from page 5, Schedule OI, Item L (1)(e)	22	
23	Combine the amounts in the far right column for lines 8 through 21. This is your **total effectively connected income** ▶		23

Adjusted Gross Income

Line	Description		Amount
24	Educator expenses (see instructions)	24	
25	Health savings account deduction. Attach Form 8889	25	
26	Moving expenses. Attach Form 3903	26	
27	Deductible part of self-employment tax. Attach Schedule SE (Form 1040)	27	
28	Self-employed SEP, SIMPLE, and qualified plans	28	
29	Self-employed health insurance deduction (see instructions)	29	
30	Penalty on early withdrawal of savings	30	
31	Scholarship and fellowship grants excluded	31	
32	IRA deduction (see instructions)	32	
33	Student loan interest deduction (see instructions)	33	
34	Domestic production activities deduction. Attach Form 8903	34	
35	Add lines 24 through 34		35
36	Subtract line 35 from line 23. This is your **adjusted gross income** ▶		36

For Disclosure, Privacy Act, and Paperwork Reduction Act Notice, see instructions. Cat. No. 11364D Form **1040NR** (2015)

FIGURE 4.3

Form 1040NR (2015) Page 2

Section	Line	Description	Box	Amount	Line	Amount
Tax and Credits	37	Amount from line 36 (adjusted gross income)			37	
	38	**Itemized deductions** from page 3, Schedule A, line 15			38	
	39	Subtract line 38 from line 37			39	
	40	Exemptions (see instructions)			40	
	41	**Taxable income.** Subtract line 40 from line 39. If line 40 is more than line 39, enter -0-			41	
	42	**Tax** (see instructions). Check if any tax is from: a ☐ Form(s) 8814 b ☐ Form 4972			42	
	43	**Alternative minimum tax** (see instructions). Attach Form 6251			43	
	44	Excess advance premium tax credit repayment. Attach Form 8962			44	
	45	Add lines 42, 43, and 44 ▶			45	
	46	Foreign tax credit. Attach Form 1116 if required	46			
	47	Credit for child and dependent care expenses. Attach Form 2441	47			
	48	Retirement savings contributions credit. Attach Form 8880	48			
	49	Child tax credit. Attach Schedule 8812, if required	49			
	50	Residential energy credits. Attach Form 5695	50			
	51	Other credits from Form: a ☐ 3800 b ☐ 8801 c ☐ ______	51			
	52	Add lines 46 through 51. These are your **total credits**			52	
	53	Subtract line 52 from line 45. If line 52 is more than line 45, enter -0- ▶			53	
Other Taxes	54	Tax on income not effectively connected with a U.S. trade or business from page 4, Schedule NEC, line 15			54	
	55	Self-employment tax. Attach Schedule SE (Form 1040)			55	
	56	Unreported social security and Medicare tax from Form: a ☐ 4137 b ☐ 8919			56	
	57	Additional tax on IRAs, other qualified retirement plans, etc. Attach Form 5329 if required			57	
	58	Transportation tax (see instructions)			58	
	59a	Household employment taxes from Schedule H (Form 1040)			59a	
	b	First-time homebuyer credit repayment. Attach Form 5405 if required			59b	
	60	Taxes from: a ☐ Form 8959 b ☐ Instructions; enter code(s) ______			60	
	61	Add lines 53 through 60. This is your **total tax** ▶			61	
Payments	62	Federal income tax withheld from:				
	a	Form(s) W-2 and 1099	62a			
	b	Form(s) 8805	62b			
	c	Form(s) 8288-A	62c			
	d	Form(s) 1042-S	62d			
	63	2015 estimated tax payments and amount applied from 2014 return	63			
	64	Additional child tax credit. Attach Schedule 8812	64			
	65	Net premium tax credit. Attach Form 8962	65			
	66	Amount paid with request for extension to file (see instructions)	66			
	67	Excess social security and tier 1 RRTA tax withheld (see instructions)	67			
	68	Credit for federal tax paid on fuels. Attach Form 4136	68			
	69	Credits from Form: a ☐ 2439 b ■ Reserved c ☐ 8885 d ☐ ______	69			
	70	Credit for amount paid with Form 1040-C	70			
	71	Add lines 62a through 70. These are your **total payments** ▶			71	
Refund Direct deposit? See instructions.	72	If line 71 is more than line 61, subtract line 61 from line 71. This is the amount you **overpaid**			72	
	73a	Amount of line 72 you want **refunded to you.** If Form 8888 is attached, check here . ▶ ☐			73a	
	b	Routing number ▶ c Type: ☐ Checking ☐ Savings				
	d	Account number				
	e	If you want your refund check mailed to an address outside the United States not shown on page 1, enter it here.				
	74	Amount of line 72 you want **applied to your 2016 estimated tax** ▶	74			
Amount You Owe	75	**Amount you owe.** Subtract line 71 from line 61. For details on how to pay, see instructions ▶			75	
	76	Estimated tax penalty (see instructions)	76			

Third Party Designee Do you want to allow another person to discuss this return with the IRS (see instructions)? ☐ **Yes.** Complete below. ☐ **No**

Designee's name ▶ Phone no. ▶ Personal identification number (PIN) ▶

Sign Here Under penalties of perjury, I declare that I have examined this return and accompanying schedules and statements, and to the best of my knowledge and belief, they are true, correct, and complete. Declaration of preparer (other than taxpayer) is based on all information of which preparer has any knowledge.

Keep a copy of this return for your records.

Your signature	Date	Your occupation in the United States	If the IRS sent you an Identity Protection PIN, enter it here (see inst.)
▶			

Paid Preparer Use Only

Print/Type preparer's name	Preparer's signature	Date	Check ☐ if self-employed	PTIN
Firm's name ▶		Firm's EIN ▶		
Firm's address ▶		Phone no.		

Form **1040NR** (2015)

FIGURE 4.3 — Continued

Form 1040NR (2015) Page 3

Schedule A—Itemized Deductions (see instructions) 07

Section	Line	Description		
Taxes You Paid	1	State and local income taxes		1
Gifts to U.S. Charities		**Caution:** If you made a gift and received a benefit in return, see instructions.		
	2	Gifts by cash or check. If you made any gift of $250 or more, see instructions	2	
	3	Other than by cash or check. If you made any gift of $250 or more, see instructions. You **must** attach Form 8283 if the amount of your deduction is over $500	3	
	4	Carryover from prior year	4	
	5	Add lines 2 through 4		5
Casualty and Theft Losses	6	Casualty or theft loss(es). Attach Form 4684. See instructions		6
Job Expenses and Certain Miscellaneous Deductions	7	Unreimbursed employee expenses—job travel, union dues, job education, etc. You **must** attach Form 2106 or Form 2106-EZ if required. See instructions ▶	7	
	8	Tax preparation fees	8	
	9	Other expenses. See instructions for expenses to deduct here. List type and amount ▶	9	
	10	Add lines 7 through 9	10	
	11	Enter the amount from Form 1040NR, line 37 [11]		
	12	Multiply line 11 by 2% (0.02)	12	
	13	Subtract line 12 from line 10. If line 12 is more than line 10, enter -0-		13
Other Miscellaneous Deductions	14	Other—see instructions for expenses to deduct here. List type and amount ▶		14
Total Itemized Deductions	15	Is Form 1040NR, line 37, over the amount shown below for the filing status box you checked on page 1 of Form 1040NR: • $309,900 if you checked box 6, • $258,250 if you checked box 1 or 2, or • $154,950 if you checked box 3, 4, or 5? ☐ **No.** Your deduction is not limited. Add the amounts in the far right column for lines 1 through 14. Also enter this amount on Form 1040NR, line 38. ☐ **Yes.** Your deduction may be limited. See the Itemized Deductions Worksheet in the instructions to figure the amount to enter here and on Form 1040NR, line 38.		15

Form **1040NR** (2015)

FIGURE 4.3 — Continued

The Canada/US Tax Treaty is one of the most important tools used in cross-border financial planning analyses for two key reasons:

- The terms of the treaty take precedence over almost all the Canadian *Income Tax Act* (ITA) rules in Canada and the Internal Revenue Code (IRC) rules in the US. It is an important card to play when doing cross-border planning.
- The terms of the treaty seldom change. The Canada/US Tax Treaty has been amended only six times in its more than 72-year history and can be relied on to a much greater degree for long-term planning than either the ITA or the IRC (which are subject to constant revision without notice and are affected by annual budgets, bipartisan politics, and election campaigns). In fact, since the major treaty negotiations of 1989, the IRS has changed the US domestic tax rules an estimated 15,000 times and CRA has probably made an equal number of changes to Canadian rules. The latest change, the Fifth Protocol (as noted above), took nearly ten years for the two countries to complete.

Take a look at Figure 4.4 for an illustration of how the treaty is structured.

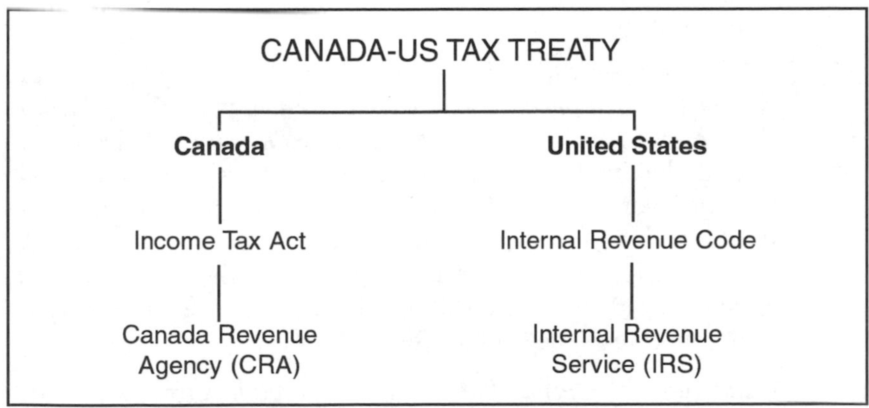

FIGURE 4.4

TAX TREATY PROTECTION FOR US NON-RESIDENTS AND RESIDENTS

One of the foremost roles of the Canada/US Tax Treaty is its tiebreaker rules for determination of residency. These rules prevent an individual from being taxed as a resident of Canada and of the United States at the same time, on world income. These rules are the very important tools in the cross-border lifestyle toolbox that allow tremendous flexibility and tax savings particularly for those Canadians choosing the Settler lifestyle. Technically speaking, the treaty states that an individual is only required to pay tax on their world income in either Canada or the US, but not both. By following these four tiebreaker rules and passing just one of the tests clearly in favor of one or the other country, the taxpayer will be protected from having to face two complete sets of tax rules at the same time. The tiebreaker rules in Article IV of the Canada/US Tax Treaty are outlined here, along with comments to explain them:

1. *The individual shall be deemed a resident of the country in which he or she has a permanent home available.* If a permanent home is available in both countries, or neither, an individual is deemed to be a resident in the country that is closer to his or her personal and economic relations (center of vital interests). Generally, a permanent home is any accommodation that is considered permanent. The home may be rented or owned. It is considered permanent where it is available for the individual's use throughout the year. A person's center of vital interests would be objectively determined and would be based upon familial, social, occupational, political, and cultural activities. Economic relations are also considered, and are generally linked with the locality of the main source income.

2. *If the country in which the individual has a center of vital interests cannot be determined, he or she shall be determined a resident of the country in which he or she has an habitual abode.* What constitutes an habitual abode requires an evaluation of the individual's lifestyle over a sufficient length of time. In most circumstances the length of time spent in one country over any other may be determinative. Also, the transient nature of the stay may be examined, e.g., living at a vacation cabin at a lake versus at a typical year-round residence in the city.

3. *If the individual has an habitual abode in both countries or in neither country, he or she shall be deemed a resident of the country of which he or she is a citizen.* The immigration status is very important; for example, if one had a permanent residence status, that would most definitely be considered. Ultimately, citizenship is the final determination.

4. *If the individual is a citizen of both countries (generally the most recent citizenship obtained will be considered the primary citizenship barring other dominant factors) or of neither of them, then competent*

authorities of the contracting countries shall settle the question by mutual agreement. The competent authorities will consider all the facts and circumstances applying to the individual with respect to all relevant tiebreaker rules to determine the residency of the individual. The competent authorities are committees of individuals from both Canada and the US who sit down and examine the facts before making a determination. This process should be avoided at all costs. It is lengthy and heart-wrenching. It is difficult to determine in advance what the outcome may be. Starting in 2009, as a result of the new Fifth Protocol to Canada/US Tax Treaty, this competent authority system of determination of residency has been greatly improved. Now, if the competent authorities cannot come to agreement within two years, the individual may force the competent authorities into binding arbitration. This greatly limits the amount of time an individual has to wait for the competent authority's determination.

The Canada/US Tax Treaty affords all Canadian Vacationers and Snowbirds a great deal of latitude from filing in the United States and paying taxes on income not sourced there. This treaty protection is even available if the Canadian forgets or neglects to file the Closer Connection Exception, Form 8840, as discussed in the previous section. In addition, income that is effectively sourced in the United States is generally prevented from being double-taxed (once in the United States and again in Canada). The treaty accomplishes this in three key ways:

1. **Foreign Tax Credits:** The treaty allows for a system of credits so that tax paid to one country on specified income will be allowed as a full credit against any tax due on that same income in the country of residence. For example, a non-resident who earns a taxable rental income in the United States files and pays tax as required by the IRS. The tax paid to the IRS after netting income and expenses on Form 1040NR is converted to Canadian funds and is used on the Canadian return as a full credit. This reduces or eliminates Canadian taxes due to the CRA on that same rental income, adjusted for Canadian depreciation and rental expense rules. The CRA limits these credits to the amount of the stated Canada/US Tax Treaty withholding rates on any specific taxable income source, regardless of what foreign tax was actually paid.
2. **Exemptions:** The Canada/US Tax Treaty provides certain exemptions from filing or reporting income of a non-resident in the United States that would otherwise be taxable by the IRS. The

Substantial Presence Test, without any treaty protection, would apply to a large number of Canadian winter visitors who regularly spend four to six months each year in the US. Under the Canada/US Tax Treaty, there is an exemption from the Substantial Presence Test for those Canadians who, without the treaty protection, would be required to report their world income in the United States under the terms of this test. IRS rules implemented in the 1992 tax year require Canadians who are using the Canada/US Tax Treaty as protection from the Substantial Presence Test to file a Closer Connection Exception Statement (IRS Form 8840, see Figure 4.2) and/or Form 1040NR (Figure 4.3) declaring they are treaty-exempt. Simply put, the IRS wants to know what you want with your chosen cross-border lifestyle from a tax perspective and since they know tax treaties take precedence over their domestic rules they just want to know when you are or when you are not using treaty provisions to reduce or eliminate taxes.

3. **Withholding Rates:** Provisions in the treaty establish the maximum amount of withholding tax either country can take on various forms of income earned within that country from residents of the other country. These withholding tax rates, updated to the 2009 provisions of the Fifth Protocol to Canada/US Tax Treaty, are detailed in Chapter 9 in Figure 9.9. The provisions for maximum withholding rates prove very useful when doing cross-border financial planning, as you will see in Chapters 9, 10, and 14.

CANADA AND THE US DO EXCHANGE TAXPAYER INFORMATION

The exchange-of-information capabilities between Canada and the United States, as provided for in the Canada/US Tax Treaty, often trap those who do not report income earned in one country to the other country, where applicable. Computer-sharing of interest, dividends, and real estate sales income information is completed on a routine basis between the CRA and the IRS, in both directions. Financial institutions in either Canada or the US are to report an individual's information banking or investment income information for citizens or residents of the other country. For example, a US citizen and/or US resident with an investment brokerage account in Canada will have investment income as reported on CRA T3, T4, or T5 income slips, converted to US funds and placed onto the equivalent IRS investment income reporting Form 1099 notification slip, then issue it to the IRS and the US taxpayer to include and pay taxes on a US tax return. The vice versa of this information-sharing program is also true, and other words a US financial institution will report on a Canadian taxpayer to the CRA on income earned in a US investment account. This cross-border sharing of tax information is not just a Canada and US phenomenon, most every country in the world that are members of the Organization of Economic Cooperation and Development (OECD) have signed agreements to report on foreigners who have business or investments in their respective countries to the taxpayers' home countries in an attempt to prevent taxpayers worldwide from trying to hide taxable income from their home countries.

Canadian and US tax authorities can, at any time, ask for and obtain a complete tax profile of most anyone they choose who lives in the other country. The current Canada/US Tax Treaty contains provisions to enforce the tax judgment from one country in the other through the facilities of the local taxing authorities. Additional, recent agreements outside of the treaty between Canada and the US also can force withholding taxes be taken and forwarded to the IRS or the CRA for their taxable residents from the other country. The days of taxpayers being able to hide cash and investments in other countries around the world, including the tax havens, are pretty well ended with all of these multilateral agreements to catch taxpayers failing to report all of their worldwide income to their respective home countries of residence or citizenship.

WHO MUST FILE TAX RETURNS IN THE US?

This section illustrates the situations and types of income that legally require a non-resident Vacationer or Snowbird to file a tax return in the United States. They, as non-residents, must file a return under the following circumstances:

- The sale of any US real property requires that the seller file IRS Form 1040NR (the non-resident tax return) before June 15 following the year of the sale. If the property was held jointly, each of the joint owners must file separate Form 1040NRs to report their respective shares of the property sale. Form 1040NR must be filed whether or not there was any gain or withholding tax collected on the sale. There are no exceptions to this rule. The buyer or the buyer's agent in the transaction is required to report to the IRS that he or she paid funds to the seller with proper withholding or they actually may be responsible to the IRS for any taxes due on the transaction.

- Any non-resident who regularly spends four to six months per year in the United States is deemed a resident under the Substantial Presence Test as described earlier in this chapter unless he or she files Form 8840 (the Closer Connection Exception statement, see Figure 4.2) by June 15 every year. Many Canadians unnecessarily fret about whether or not they should complete this Form 8840 when it is by far the simplest and most effective way prevent the IRS from interfering with the most amazing cross-border lifestyle. As the Nike ads say, "just do it"; in all my years of dealing with many thousands of readers of *The Border Guide* and clients, not one single Canadian that I am aware of has ever been harmed or even hassled by the IRS by filing The Closer Connection Exception form, whereas the same cannot be stated for those that chose not to file or were unaware of the filing requirement.
- A Canadian who spends more than 182 days in the United States any particular calendar year is considered a resident for tax purposes for that year and must file a US tax return (Form 1040 or Form 1040NR) declaring all world income. A Canadian spending this much time in the US is not eligible to file Form 8840 by itself and must attach it to Form 1040NR. The treaty tiebreaker rules where they apply will generally prevent world income from being taxed in the United States, and it will help to eliminate most, if not all of the taxes due to the IRS. Canadians in this situation or wishing to spend more time in the US for their cross-border lifestyles should review Chapter 8 on immigration, and consider becoming Settlers through obtaining permanent residency in the United States so that they may take full advantage of the lower US tax rates as outlined in a later section of this chapter. When counting the days of residency, remember to include cross-border shopping days in the US, not just time spent vacationing in the Sunbelt.
- Any non-resident who collects rental income from any owned property in the United States, including his or her own personal-use home, must file Form 1040NR by the required deadline of June 15 the year after the income was derived (unless the lessee is withholding the 30 percent non-resident withholding tax on the gross rental income).
- Any non-resident who carries on a business of any form in the US must also file Form 1040NR regardless of whether that business is profitable. This requirement applies even though the person may not have any legal immigration status to work in the US.

- If a non-resident has had withholding tax withheld incorrectly or at an improper rate, he or she must file Form 1040NR for the year in which the error occurred to obtain a refund. Be sure to keep all the reporting slips that any withholding entity must provide. Generally, these would be 1042S, 1099, or 8288A slips, which are similar to Canadian T4s, T5s, or NR4s.
- Lottery and certain gambling winnings are considered taxable income in the United States and are subject to a non-resident withholding tax of 30 percent. If you hit a jackpot in Las Vegas, this filing method could make you an even bigger winner by giving you some or all of your withholding tax back. Planning tip for gamblers: Keep detailed daily records of both wins and losses, as the losses can be used to offset tax on winnings providing the winnings and losses are from the same type of gambling, e.g the blackjack tables, on the same day. Without good records, however, the IRS will not allow this offset of losses against winnings, as is now allowed under the latest amendment to the Canada/US Tax Treaty.
- A descendant's estate trustee/executor must file IRS Form 706NA after the death of a non-resident who has a US taxable estate of more than $60,000 (within nine months of the death). See Chapter 5 to determine the taxable estate of a non resident. Also, if the estate is going to take a treaty benefit from the Canada/US Tax Treaty, a regular Form 706NA (the US Estate Tax Return) that fully discloses the treaty benefits requested must be filed.
- Any non-resident who gives a gift of taxable US property worth more than $14,000 total in one year to any single person, or worth $147,000 (inflation adjusted) in one year to a spouse, is subject to US gift tax and must file IRS Form 709 (the US Gift Tax Return) to pay any taxes due (by April 15, after the year end in which the gift was made). The gift tax rates are equal to the estate tax rates. Be aware of unintentional gifts such as putting a son, daughter, or spouse on title to your residence located in the US. See Chapter 5 for a more complete discussion of gift taxes.
- The US Department of Commerce requires certain foreign investment filings. The rules require an initial filing when the investment is first made, Form BE-13, and then an annual filing, Form BE-15, and then a special filing every fifth year, Form BE-12. Unfortunately the definition of foreign investment for this purpose includes Canadians purchasing rental real estate in the US. However, if your investment is the purchase of US real

estate held only for your personal use or a small business with consolidated assets less than $3 million and less than 200 acres of US land, you can instead file a simple two-page Exemption Claim on Department Of Commerce Form BE-13 Supplement C. The initial filings are required 30 days after the purchase with no apparent extensions available. The fine for failure to file these forms when due is a minimum of $2,500 and a maximum of $25,000. The forms and detailed instructions for these Department of Commerce filings can be found on their website: www.bea.gov.

HOW AND WHEN TO APPLY FOR A US SOCIAL SECURITY OR TAX ID NUMBER

Generally speaking, Canadians do not need a US taxpayer identification number, commonly known as a Social Security Number (SSN) or Individual Taxpayer Identification Number (ITIN). However, you are required to have at least an ITIN if you are going to sell a US home or conduct any other financial transaction in the United States, including filing or claiming exemptions on US tax returns/forms. SSNs and ITINs look alike, but ITINs are for those non-US persons who have no visa, green card, or other employment-type immigration status in the United States. SSNs must be obtained by all US visa holders who plan on working in the US.

Those who have obtained SSNs in the past may continue to use them, but it is quite incorrect for Canadians under any circumstances to provide their Canadian Social Insurance Number (SIN) to any US entity for any reason. Doing so is not only illegal from the standpoint of providing a false SSN, but it throws the IRS computers for a loop. Your SIN may be the same as some innocent American's SSN or there may be no record of it at all in IRS files! When you open a bank or brokerage account ask for IRS Form W-8BEN (Certificate of Foreign Status, see Figure 4.6 later in this chapter), which will satisfy any legal tax reporting requirements.

There is no real disadvantage to having an American SSN/ITIN unless having another number to keep track of bothers you. Many Canadians unnecessarily fear an SSN/ITIN, thinking that the IRS is going to come after them for some reason; as noted in earlier chapters you need not fear the IRS as long as you file and pay taxes as required. An SSN/ITIN is not only required for the circumstances noted above, but it can also be a convenience to you in certain financial transactions, such as filing tax returns, opening bank accounts, or selling property. Having an ITIN may also be to a person's advantage, as it will provide assurance that the IRS has properly recorded certain facts that could be helpful in the future, such as tax losses that are permitted to be offset against future profits. In fact, the IRS will now refuse to accept tax returns without an ITIN or Social Security number and will hold refunds or delay return processing for those who have failed to supply an SSN/ITIN for themselves or any dependents for which they are claiming deductions or exemptions.

To obtain your own ITIN, you will need to complete IRS Form W-7 (see Figure 4.5) and attach the required pieces of identification, or if you do not want to enclose copies of actual IDs you must have copies certified to be accepted. The Form W-7 can be filed with the tax return being filed providing the copies of any required identification are examined and certified by an approved IRS person or firm. Your number will normally be provided four to six weeks after filing the form. The IRS has stopped issuing ITINs unless you can prove, via a tax return/form filing, that you need one. It is important to apply for the ITIN with the W-7 as soon as possible if you are attempting to sell your US property; you can generally send in the W-7 application as soon as you have a signed contract on your property and you bring all of the required documents to the approved firm to examine and certify your identification documents. Because of the timing and the procedures involved it is easy to make mistakes so I recommend that you get professional assistance with filing for your ITIN; for a few hundred dollars it will be done professionally and in a timely fashion so that large withholding amounts can be either eliminated or refunded quickly. Starting with the year 2016, anyone who has an ITIN who has not used it to file any IRS form for five years will lose the ITIN and have to reapply if they ever need it again. Consequently, since it is very difficult process to get an ITIN it is recommended that if you have an ITIN you use it to file regular non-resident returns, Form 1040NR, the Closer Connection Exception Form 8840, or other forms filed directly with the IRS periodically, but certainly at least every four years.

When Vacationers or Snowbirds open accounts with banks or brokerage firms, they are required to complete Form W-8BEN (Certificate of Foreign Status, see Figure 4.6) if a non-resident, or Form W-9 (Request for Taxpayer Identification Number and Certification, see Figure 4.7) if a US Settler/resident taxpayer, a US citizen, or a green card holder. Even though these forms are not filed with the IRS at any time, banks or brokerage companies cannot open accounts without them, and must keep them on file and update them periodically. Do not be alarmed if every year or two you are asked to re-sign these documents to verify your status with that institution.

Form **W-7**
(Rev. August 2013)
Department of the Treasury
Internal Revenue Service

Application for IRS Individual Taxpayer Identification Number

▶ **For use by individuals who are not U.S. citizens or permanent residents.**
▶ **See instructions.**

OMB No. 1545-0074

FOR IRS USE ONLY

An IRS individual taxpayer identification number (ITIN) is for federal tax purposes only.

Before you begin:

- ***Do not submit*** *this form if you have, or are eligible to get, a U.S. social security number (SSN).*
- *Getting an ITIN does not change your immigration status or your right to work in the United States and does not make you eligible for the earned income credit.*

Reason you are submitting Form W-7. Read the instructions for the box you check. **Caution:** If you check box **b, c, d, e, f,** or **g, you must file a tax return with Form W-7 unless you meet one of the exceptions** (see instructions).

a ☐ Nonresident alien required to get ITIN to claim tax treaty benefit
b ☐ Nonresident alien filing a U.S. tax return
c ☐ U.S. resident alien **(based on days present in the United States)** filing a U.S. tax return
d ☐ Dependent of U.S. citizen/resident alien } Enter name and SSN/ITIN of U.S. citizen/resident alien (see instructions) ▶
e ☐ Spouse of U.S. citizen/resident alien
f ☐ Nonresident alien student, professor, or researcher filing a U.S. tax return or claiming an exception
g ☐ Dependent/spouse of a nonresident alien holding a U.S. visa
h ☐ Other (see instructions) ▶
Additional information for **a** and **f**: Enter treaty country ▶ and treaty article number ▶

Name (see instructions)	**1a** First name	Middle name	Last name
Name at birth if different . . ▶	**1b** First name	Middle name	Last name
Applicant's mailing address	**2** Street address, apartment number, or rural route number. **If you have a P.O. box, see separate instructions.**		
	City or town, state or province, and country. Include ZIP code or postal code where appropriate.		
Foreign (non-U.S.) address (if different from above) (see instructions)	**3** Street address, apartment number, or rural route number. **Do not use a P.O. box number.**		
	City or town, state or province, and country. Include ZIP code or postal code where appropriate.		
Birth information	**4** Date of birth (month / day / year)	Country of birth	City and state or province (optional) **5** ☐ Male ☐ Female
Other information	**6a** Country(ies) of citizenship	**6b** Foreign tax I.D. number (if any)	**6c** Type of U.S. visa (if any), number, and expiration date

6d Identification document(s) submitted (see instructions) ☐ Passport ☐ Driver's license/State I.D.
☐ USCIS documentation ☐ Other
Issued by: No.: Exp. date: / / Date of entry into the United States (MM/DD/YYYY) / /

6e Have you previously received a Internal Revenue Service Number (IRSN) or employer identification number (EIN)?
☐ **No/Do not know.** Skip line 6f.
☐ **Yes.** Complete line 6f. If more than one, list on a sheet and attach to this form (see instructions).

6f Enter: IRSN or EIN ▶ and
Name under which it was issued ▶

6g Name of college/university or company (see instructions)
City and state Length of stay

Sign Here

Under penalties of perjury, I (applicant/delegate/acceptance agent) declare that I have examined this application, including accompanying documentation and statements, and to the best of my knowledge and belief, it is true, correct, and complete. I authorize the IRS to disclose to my acceptance agent returns or return information necessary to resolve matters regarding the assignment of my IRS individual taxpayer identification number (ITIN), including any previously assigned taxpayer identifying number.

Signature of applicant (if delegate, see instructions)	Date (month / day / year) / /	Phone number
Name of delegate, if applicable (type or print)	Delegate's relationship to applicant	☐ Parent ☐ Court-appointed guardian ☐ Power of Attorney

Keep a copy for your records.

Acceptance Agent's Use ONLY

Signature		Date (month / day / year) / /	Phone / Fax
Name and title (type or print)	Name of company	EIN / Office Code	PTIN

For Paperwork Reduction Act Notice, see separate instructions. Cat. No. 10229L Form **W-7** (Rev. 8-2013)

FIGURE 4.5

If you have a US visa or other legal immigration status to work in the US, you can take it to the nearest Social Security Administration office and complete Form SS-5 to obtain an SSN. All residents of the United States are required to have an SSN if they have a visa that allows them to work in the US or an ITIN if they don't have an employment-type visa.

CANADA AND THE UNITED STATES: INCOME TAX COMPARISON

This section is primarily for Vacationers or Snowbirds who want to see if there is any advantage to becoming Settlers and spending more time in the US to take advantage of possibly lower tax rates.

There are two main issues to consider when it comes to the amount of tax you pay: the tax rates, and the income on which those rates are applied (called your taxable income). No comparison between Canadian and American income tax would be complete without considering both factors. Since there are fifty states, ten provinces, and four territories in the US and Canada, a detailed comparison of each state and province is beyond the scope of this book (Appendix B includes the average maximum tax rates from all provinces and the key Sunbelt states). However, we will provide you with a guide to the major cross-border financial planning opportunities, as well as illuminate potential tax minefields that need to be avoided. We will also compare the tax rates of Ontario and Florida, the two locations that generate the most winter-visitor and immigration traffic (Quebec also accounts for a significant number of visitors to Florida). Other provincial and state tax rates will vary somewhat from the Ontario and Florida numbers, but the trends will be the same (see Figure 4.9 which compares Alberta and Arizona tax rates). The states in the United States that have a personal income tax collect their tax on a separate return in the same manner as Quebec has traditionally, and as the other provinces now do if they have decided to levy their taxes as tax on income, rather than a percentage of the federal tax collected.

Figure 4.8 charts the tax rates and income brackets of Ontario and Florida. The rates shown are for the year 2016 and include all provincial and federal surtaxes, the Ontario rates include the 2016 adjustments by the newly elected Canadian government. The Canadian-US dollar exchange rates for the first quarter of 2016 are used where applicable. For the purpose of our comparison, we assume that the Canadian is married to a spouse who has too much income to qualify for the married exemption in Ontario, and that the Florida person is also married and filing jointly with a spouse. As you can see, a Florida taxpayer in the

Form **W-8BEN**
(Rev. February 2014)
Department of the Treasury
Internal Revenue Service

Certificate of Foreign Status of Beneficial Owner for United States Tax Withholding and Reporting (Individuals)

▶ **For use by individuals. Entities must use Form W-8BEN-E.**
▶ **Information about Form W-8BEN and its separate instructions is at *www.irs.gov/formw8ben*.**
▶ **Give this form to the withholding agent or payer. Do not send to the IRS.**

OMB No. 1545-1621

Do NOT use this form if:	**Instead, use Form:**
• You are NOT an individual	W-8BEN-E
• You are a U.S. citizen or other U.S. person, including a resident alien individual	W-9
• You are a beneficial owner claiming that income is effectively connected with the conduct of trade or business within the U.S. (other than personal services)	W-8ECI
• You are a beneficial owner who is receiving compensation for personal services performed in the United States	8233 or W-4
• A person acting as an intermediary	W-8IMY

Part I **Identification of Beneficial Owner** (see instructions)

1 Name of individual who is the beneficial owner

2 Country of citizenship

3 Permanent residence address (street, apt. or suite no., or rural route). **Do not use a P.O. box or in-care-of address.**

City or town, state or province. Include postal code where appropriate.

Country

4 Mailing address (if different from above)

City or town, state or province. Include postal code where appropriate.

Country

5 U.S. taxpayer identification number (SSN or ITIN), if required (see instructions)

6 Foreign tax identifying number (see instructions)

7 Reference number(s) (see instructions)

8 Date of birth (MM-DD-YYYY) (see instructions)

Part II **Claim of Tax Treaty Benefits** (for chapter 3 purposes only) (see instructions)

9 I certify that the beneficial owner is a resident of ________________ within the meaning of the income tax treaty between the United States and that country.

10 **Special rates and conditions** (if applicable—see instructions): The beneficial owner is claiming the provisions of Article ________ of the treaty identified on line 9 above to claim a ________ % rate of withholding on (specify type of income): ________

Explain the reasons the beneficial owner meets the terms of the treaty article: ________

Part III **Certification**

Under penalties of perjury, I declare that I have examined the information on this form and to the best of my knowledge and belief it is true, correct, and complete. I further certify under penalties of perjury that:

- I am the individual that is the beneficial owner (or am authorized to sign for the individual that is the beneficial owner) of all the income to which this form relates or am using this form to document myself as an individual that is an owner or account holder of a foreign financial institution,
- The person named on line 1 of this form is not a U.S. person,
- The income to which this form relates is:
  (a) not effectively connected with the conduct of a trade or business in the United States,
  (b) effectively connected but is not subject to tax under an applicable income tax treaty, or
  (c) the partner's share of a partnership's effectively connected income,
- The person named on line 1 of this form is a resident of the treaty country listed on line 9 of the form (if any) within the meaning of the income tax treaty between the United States and that country, and
- For broker transactions or barter exchanges, the beneficial owner is an exempt foreign person as defined in the instructions.

Furthermore, I authorize this form to be provided to any withholding agent that has control, receipt, or custody of the income of which I am the beneficial owner or any withholding agent that can disburse or make payments of the income of which I am the beneficial owner. **I agree that I will submit a new form within 30 days if any certification made on this form becomes incorrect.**

Sign Here ▶

Signature of beneficial owner (or individual authorized to sign for beneficial owner) — Date (MM-DD-YYYY)

Print name of signer — Capacity in which acting (if form is not signed by beneficial owner)

For Paperwork Reduction Act Notice, see separate instructions. Cat. No. 25047Z Form **W-8BEN** (Rev. 2-2014)

FIGURE 4.6

Form **W-9**
(Rev. December 2014)
Department of the Treasury
Internal Revenue Service

Request for Taxpayer Identification Number and Certification

Give Form to the requester. Do not send to the IRS.

Print or type
See Specific Instructions on page 2.

1 Name (as shown on your income tax return). Name is required on this line; do not leave this line blank.

2 Business name/disregarded entity name, if different from above

3 Check appropriate box for federal tax classification; check only **one** of the following seven boxes:
☐ Individual/sole proprietor or single-member LLC ☐ C Corporation ☐ S Corporation ☐ Partnership ☐ Trust/estate
☐ Limited liability company. Enter the tax classification (C=C corporation, S=S corporation, P=partnership) ▶
Note. For a single-member LLC that is disregarded, do not check LLC; check the appropriate box in the line above for the tax classification of the single-member owner.
☐ Other (see instructions) ▶

4 Exemptions (codes apply only to certain entities, not individuals; see instructions on page 3):
Exempt payee code (if any)
Exemption from FATCA reporting code (if any)
(Applies to accounts maintained outside the U.S.)

5 Address (number, street, and apt. or suite no.)

Requester's name and address (optional)

6 City, state, and ZIP code

7 List account number(s) here (optional)

Part I Taxpayer Identification Number (TIN)

Enter your TIN in the appropriate box. The TIN provided must match the name given on line 1 to avoid backup withholding. For individuals, this is generally your social security number (SSN). However, for a resident alien, sole proprietor, or disregarded entity, see the Part I instructions on page 3. For other entities, it is your employer identification number (EIN). If you do not have a number, see *How to get a TIN* on page 3.

Note. If the account is in more than one name, see the instructions for line 1 and the chart on page 4 for guidelines on whose number to enter.

Social security number

or

Employer identification number

Part II Certification

Under penalties of perjury, I certify that:

1. The number shown on this form is my correct taxpayer identification number (or I am waiting for a number to be issued to me); and
2. I am not subject to backup withholding because: (a) I am exempt from backup withholding, or (b) I have not been notified by the Internal Revenue Service (IRS) that I am subject to backup withholding as a result of a failure to report all interest or dividends, or (c) the IRS has notified me that I am no longer subject to backup withholding; and
3. I am a U.S. citizen or other U.S. person (defined below); and
4. The FATCA code(s) entered on this form (if any) indicating that I am exempt from FATCA reporting is correct.

Certification instructions. You must cross out item 2 above if you have been notified by the IRS that you are currently subject to backup withholding because you have failed to report all interest and dividends on your tax return. For real estate transactions, item 2 does not apply. For mortgage interest paid, acquisition or abandonment of secured property, cancellation of debt, contributions to an individual retirement arrangement (IRA), and generally, payments other than interest and dividends, you are not required to sign the certification, but you must provide your correct TIN. See the instructions on page 3.

Sign Here | **Signature of U.S. person ▶** | **Date ▶**

FIGURE 4.7

highest income bracket has a strong advantage over an Ontario taxpayer who is also in the highest bracket, because the Florida tax rate is approximately 35 percent lower than Ontario's and it takes a much larger income to reach the highest bracket in the United States. With the same income stream, a high-income resident of Ontario (in the income range of $65,000 to $225,000 CAD) would cut his or her highest tax rate by approximately 48 percent if he or she paid taxes in Florida.

Chapter 9 will make direct comparisons using actual cross-border tax situations to provide a more complete picture for those considering becoming Settlers or permanent residents in the United States. Florida has no state income tax, so the rates reflect the actual US federal tax rates.

As previously noted, you must look at taxable income as well as the tax rate to get a complete picture of the total taxes paid. Now we will look at the deductions that reduce your gross income to your taxable income. This list of deductions is by no means a complete summary of all the deductions available in both Canada and the United States, but it does cover major tax deductions that apply to a married couple at or near retirement age.

PERSONAL EXEMPTIONS

Canada has converted the basic personal exemption of $11,474 into a non-refundable federal tax credit of $1,721. The age exemption for those over 65 has been reduced to a tax credit of $1,069, it is reduced for those with income over $35,927, and eliminated when income exceeds $83,427. For a spouse or dependant without income, there are non-refundable credits available of $1,721. The exemptions are all indexed for inflation. The benefits of credits are enhanced by applicable provincial tax rates.

The United States has a standard deduction total of $12,600 for married taxpayers (all numbers referring to US deductions are in US funds). If the taxpayer itemizes certain deductions (as outlined in the next several sections of this chapter) rather than taking the standard deduction, he or she may take a greater total deduction. Add $2,500 to the standard deduction if you and your spouse are older than 65. Add another $4,050 for yourself, your spouse (regardless of his or her income), and each of your dependants, for personal exemptions. The United States is more liberal with their dependant deductions. You may claim adult children, grandchildren, parents, and other close relatives who live with you and for whom you supply over 50 percent of their financial support. The basic personal exemptions are partially phased out for married persons with incomes of between $311,300 and $433,800.

PENSIONS

Canada has converted the $2,000 pension deduction into a non-refundable federal tax credit of $300. Old Age Security is taxed up to 100 percent owing to a clawback on incomes exceeding $73,756.

The United States has no standard pension deduction and allows a tax-free return of contributions to contributory pension plans, making these pensions partially tax-free. US Social Security payments are totally tax-free until a married couple's income exceeds $32,000; if their income is in excess of $32,000, they are taxed on 50 percent of the benefits over this income level up to $44,000. If their income is in excess of $44,000, then the tax is levied at the regular tax rates on 85 percent of these benefits. Those in the top tax brackets will pay a 34 percent maximum tax on Social Security payments.

CANADIAN AND US TAX RATES 2016

CANADA (Ontario)		UNITED STATES (Florida) Married Filing Jointly	
Taxable Income	Tax Rate	Taxable Income	Tax Rate
$41,536 or less	20.05%		
$41,537–$45,282	24.15%	$25,411 or less	10%
$45,283–$73,145	29.65%	$25,412–$103,151	15%
$73,146–$83,075	31.48%	$103,152–$208,082	25%
$83,076–$86,176	33.89%	$208,083–$317,055	28%
$86,177–$90,563	37.91%	$317,056–$566,233	33%
$90,564–$140,388	43.41%	$566,234–$639,658	35%
$140,389–$150,000	46.41%	$639,659 and over	39.6%
$150,001–$200,000	47.97%		
$200,001–$220,000	51.97%		
$220,001 and over	53.53%		

FIGURE 4.8

Canada-US TAX RATES 2016

CANADA (Alberta)		UNITED STATES (Arizona) Married Filing Jointly	
Taxable Income	Tax Rate	Taxable Income	Tax Rate
$45,252 or less	25.0%	$25,411 or less	12.6%
$45,252–$90,563	30.5%	$25,411–$103,151	17.9%
$90,563–$125,000	36.0%	$103,151–$208,082	29.2%
$125,000–$140,388	38.0%	$208,082–$317,055	32.5%
$140,388–$150,000	41.0%	$317,055–$566,233	37.5%
$150,000–$200,000	42.0%	$566,233–$639,658	39.5%
$200,000–$300,000	47.0%	$639,658 and over	44.1%
$300,000 and over	48.0%		

FIGURE 4.9

MORTGAGE INTEREST AND PROPERTY TAXES

In Canada, mortgage interest and property taxes are not generally deductible in any amount. In the US, mortgage interest on as many as two homes is fully deductible as an itemized deduction. The definition of a residence could also include an RV or a yacht. Total mortgages on these residences cannot exceed $1.1 million. Property taxes are deductible regardless of the number of homes involved, even if they are located outside the United States.

PROVINCIAL AND STATE INCOME TAXES

In Canada, provincial taxes cannot be taken as a deduction from federal taxes paid. In the United States, state and municipal taxes are deductible as an itemized deduction. If, for example, Ontario residents were able to deduct their provincial income tax against the federal tax as the IRS allows within the US, the maximum effective tax rate in Ontario would drop from 53.5 to 45 percent.

EARNED INTEREST DEDUCTIONS OR DEFERMENT

In Canada there is no ability to defer interest on investment vehicles such as term deposits, GICs, Canada Savings Bonds, and annuities; this was eliminated for all Canadian taxpayers several years ago. There is no such thing as tax-free interest earnings in Canada other than the new Tax-Free Savings Account (TFSA) as discussed in more detail later in this book.

In the United States, any amount of interest earned on certain municipal bonds is tax-free at the federal and, in most cases, the state level. Interest on US Savings Bonds and most other federal government securities is tax free at the state level. Any amount of interest, dividends, or capital gains can be deferred as long as desired through the use of various forms of deferred annuities.

CAPITAL GAINS DEDUCTIONS

Only 50 percent of actual gains are taxable, making the maximum capital gains tax approximately 26 percent (depending on the province). Persons who own qualified small businesses may obtain $826,176 in capital gains exemptions on the sale of the shares of their companies. All capital gains on the sale of a principal residence in Canada are tax free. On the date of a taxpayer's death, all of his or her capital assets are deemed as sold at fair market value and any capital gains are fully taxed. If there is a surviving spouse, the capital gains can be deferred to that spouse's death.

The United States taxes capital gains at a reduced rate, with a maximum federal rate of 20 percent (the maximum capital gains tax is 0 percent if you are in the first two income tax brackets, as noted in Figure 4.8 and Figure 4.9). There is a capital gains exemption of $250,000 ($500,000 for a married couple) on the sale of a principal residence. In addition, any gains on the sale of investment real estate can be rolled tax-free into a new property of equal or greater value. It should be noted here that these capital gains exemptions are not available to non-residents owning real property in the US. There is no capital gains tax on deemed dispositions at death. Beneficiaries will receive appreciated property with a stepped-up cost basis so they can sell the appreciated property without any income tax owing. However, some assets of larger estates may be subject to estate tax. See Chapters 5 and 10 for more details.

MEDICAL EXPENSES

In Canada, medical expenses that exceed 3 percent of income are converted into a non-refundable federal credit at the 15 percent computation.

In the United States, medical expenses that exceed 10 percent of adjusted gross income are deductible as an itemized deduction.

Premiums paid for health insurance and long-term care insurance are included as a deductible medical expense. US persons who are on high deductible health insurance plans ($4,450 but not more than $6,700) are able to contribute up to $8,150 for a family per year to a Health Savings Account. Contributions to this account are fully deductible against taxable income and are allowed to be invested on a tax-free basis. As long as withdrawals are used for qualified medical expenses, they are tax free.

REGISTERED RETIREMENT PLANS

Canadians with earned income can contribute 18 percent of their last year's earnings to a Registered Retirement Savings Plan (RRSP) each year, to a maximum of $25,370 (indexed for inflation). The 2008 Canadian federal budget, for the first time ever, has created a Tax-Free Savings Account (TFSA) to which Canadians are allowed to contribute $5,000 each year, (the increase to $10,000 for 2015 has been reduced back to $5,500, indexed for inflation, by the newly elected federal government for 2016 and later years). All the earnings created in these accounts (along with the principal) can be withdrawn on a tax-free basis.

Americans with earned income can contribute up to the lesser amount of 100 percent of their income or $5,500 to their own and $5,500 to a spouse's Individual Retirement Account (IRA). You may add $1,000 to each of these contributions for those over the age of 50. There is also a Roth IRA that is subject to the same contribution limits as a regular IRA, but is not deductible from taxable income. The Roth IRA allows US savers to accumulate earnings tax-free inside the plan, and also to withdraw the full plan balance tax free regardless of how much the savings grow.

The new Canadian TFSA was created to mimic the US Roth IRA. The US now has a Roth 401(k) program as an option for those persons contributing to a company-qualified, regular-deductible 401(k) plan. Consequently, the employee can contribute $18,000 (add an additional $6,000 if over the age of 50) annually to a Roth 401(k) plan. Like the Roth IRA, these investments grow tax-free and all earnings can be withdrawn tax-free over the lifetimes of the contributor and any designated beneficiaries. There are numerous other similar qualified plans that can allow contributions of up to 25 percent of income (to a maximum of $47,000 per year, or $53,000 if over 50), depending on your employment status and income levels.

CHARITABLE DONATIONS

In Canada, donations to qualified Canadian charities of amounts not exceeding 75 percent of income are allowed as non-refundable federal credits at the 15 percent computation for the first $200 (and 29 percent for the remainder). Highly appreciated assets donated to a charity, such as shares of privately owned companies or certain kinds of land, can have their entire capital gain eliminated and donation equal to the fair market value taken.

In the United States, donations to qualified charities of amounts not exceeding 50 percent of income are allowed as itemized deductions. Donations of highly appreciated assets provide the taxpayer with a full charitable deduction on the fair market value of the asset, without either the taxpayer or the charity paying any capital gains tax on the transaction.

EDUCATION PLANS

Canadians with children can contribute up to $50,000 lifetime limit for each child under age 18 to a Registered Education Savings Plan (RESP). The income in an RESP is tax-deferred until it is paid to a beneficiary, at which time it is taxed at the full-time student's lower rates. In addition, the Canada Education Savings Grant (CESG) can add 20 percent per year to the RESP contribution with an annual limit of $500 and a lifetime limit of $7,200.

The US has an Education Savings Account, also known as a Cloverdell IRA. You can contribute up to $2,000 per child per year. These accounts accumulate on a tax-deferred basis, like an RESP, but can be taken out tax-free if used for qualified education expenses. There are refundable tax credits for tuition to encourage low-income persons to attend college. All states have programs called 529 College Savings Plans through which parents or grandparents can contribute up to $320,000 depending on the state sponsoring the plan, and all income earned in the plan is tax-free if the proceeds are used for qualified college expenses. These 529 plans are considerably more flexible than RESPs.

STOCK OPTIONS

Canada allows for a deduction equal to 50 percent of the money portion on the exercise of stock options and the sale of underlying shares. The new federal government, elected in the fall of 2015, has stated that they will reduce the amount taxed at 50 percent to $100,000 and the balance will be taxed at full rates, or they may eliminate this 50 percent benefit altogether.

The United States has Incentive Stock Options (ISO), which allow unlimited deferral of tax upon the exercise of the stock options, providing the options meet all the IRS criteria to qualify as ISOs. The stocks purchased from the exercise of the ISOs must be held for a minimum of one year to receive the 15 percent long-term capital gains tax treatment. Non-qualified stock options are taxed upon exercise at ordinary tax rates.

MISCELLANEOUS DEDUCTIONS

In Canada, union and professional dues, safety deposit box fees, interest on funds borrowed for investment purposes, and fees for investment advice are deductible expenses.

In the United States, tax preparation fees*, vehicle licences, property and casualty losses exceeding 10 percent of income, unreimbursed employment expenses*, trustee fees*, certain sales taxes, mortgage interest, property taxes safety deposit box fees*, interest on funds borrowed for investment purposes to the extent of portfolio income, IRA administration fees*, and fees for financial planning or investment advice* are deductible expenses. (*These items are totaled and only the amount that exceeds 2 percent of the individual's adjusted gross income is deductible.)

The net effect of the differentials in tax rates and deductions between Canada and the United States can be best illustrated by example, or by an exact calculation based on your personal situation. Chapter 9 shows some typical cross-border tax situations that will show you how the application of different tax rates to the same income source can result in substantial net tax differences between the two tax systems.

Border Guide readers are encouraged to participate in a cross-border Q&A through the new Cross-Border Forum, which is a platform where, after registering, you can easily post questions about the contents of this book. Questions will be moderated and/or answered by a cross-border financial planning professional in a timely fashion. You can also post comments or create discussions with other Border Guide readers to share experiences and swap cross-border financial planning tips. To post a question or comment, go to keatsconnelly.com and click on the Cross-Border Forum tab at the top of the first page.

CROSS-BORDER Q&A

EDUCATION PLAN FOR A US GRANDCHILD

I have been a subscriber to the MoneySaver *for a number of years, and I'm wondering if you or someone can help me with a current question. My daughter lives in Los Angeles and is expecting her first baby in October. She and her family expect to remain in the US as American citizens, at least for the foreseeable future. As I would like to help with the baby's college education, I am looking for information as to whether there are any education plans to which I could contribute (similar to the RESPs). Or is there some other way to do this and obtain a tax deduction?*

Thank you for any help you can give.

— John B., Whitby, Ontario

Congratulations on your upcoming grandchild. There is an excellent college savings program in California to which you can contribute up to $350,000 USD. The program is called the ScholarShare College Savings Plan, and it is the California version of the federal US Section 529 College Savings Program. I use the California plan for my own children even though I am an Arizona resident, as it has more investment options and lower fees than the AZ 529 Plan. This program is funded with after-tax dollars only, but all interest, dividends, and capital gains are tax-free as long as the funds are used for education purposes (available for most US colleges, and even a majority of key Canadian colleges). Your daughter can control the distribution of the program, and if your new grandchild doesn't go to college, your daughter can transfer the program to another child or close relative, or even to her own grandchildren. Unless you have a US Social Security number, your daughter will need to open the account. She can contact the plan toll free at 1-877-728-4338 or on the web at www.scholarshare.com. Also, just because your daughter is located in California, there is no requirement that you must use the California 529 plan. Most other states have 529 plans as well, some even better than California's. It is a competitive market, so it pays to shop around.

FILINGS FOR PART-TIME WORK IN THE US

I need your help. If I may ask/present my situation: I am going to provide some computer programming services from Toronto for a US client, while residing in Canada, and will probably make $10,000 to $15,000 USD.

The client sent me IRS Form W-8BEN, Certificate of Foreign Status of Beneficial Owner. Is this the right form for me?

I inquired with the IRS (and maybe I'll do it again) regarding how to fill in the form and my understanding is:

Part I: This part is straightforward, except for item 6: do I have to get an ITIN?

Part II: It looks to me as if I have to fill in only 9a (Canada) and possibly 9b, but what about part 10? By IRS telephone instructions, I have to enter article 15 percent and a 30 percent rate! Is that right?

If it is possible for you to respond, I thank you very much in advance.

— Tom R., Toronto, Ontario

If you agree that you are an independent contractor and not an employee of the US company, you are exempt from withholding. However, you will need to provide the US-dollar paying company with Form 8233, Exemption From Withholding on Compensation for Independent Personal Services of a Non-Resident Alien Individual (all forms and instructions are available from the IRS website, www.irs.gov), rather than W-8BEN (see page 1 of Form W-8BEN instructions). The explanation on Form 8233 states that you are performing independent personal services from Canada, with no fixed base in the US, and are exempt from withholding under Article XIV of the Canada/US Tax Treaty. Note that Article XV is for employees or dependent service providers who are exempt from withholding only if payment is less than $10,000 USD. You do need to get an Individual Taxpayer Identification Number (ITIN) to claim treaty benefits by filing a W-7 Form (Application for ITIN).

NO US TAX-DEFERRED ANNUITIES CAN BE USED IN CANADA

Perhaps somebody can help me with the following problem: During my five-year stay in the States I purchased a US Annuity. After coming to Canada, I *paid each year taxes on all the yearly annuity interest although it was tax-free in the USA. Now comes the payout for several years. The interest for these payments is now taxed in the USA. The company ignores my W-8BEN and told me Interest on Annuity payments are not treated like Interest for CDs and withheld 15 percent from the payout with a 1042-S slip. I pay taxes twice now, because tax-payments in Canada are already made. Is there a way to recover the amount withheld ($860) and can I avoid somehow future taxation in the States for three more yearly payments? Is the opinion of the company correct about this? Thank you.*

— Fred A, Waterloo, ON

Your situation is not particularly unusual and it is a good example of where the Canadian rules on deferring interest versus the US rules can create a double tax situation. The double tax arises for exactly the reason you have described in that Canada taxes that the interest annually and the US does not require any tax until the interest is distributed, and if these two separate events do not happen in the same tax year you cannot take a credit for any taxes paid to the US. However, the insurance company should honor your W-8BEN which tells them you are a non-resident of the US and there should be no withholding on the interest earned. This would only be true though if your annuity was an interest-only type annuity and not a variable annuity where there are interest, dividends and capital gains all in one annuity, then the answer they are giving you is correct in that the W-8BEN still does require them to withhold taxes on the income you are taking from the annuity. Your best bet I believe to get back the taxes you have already paid to the US or will pay in the future is to file a US tax return, Form 1040NR, and simply include the 1042-S slip with it as the only income, with the withholding amount, and request a refund. I believe you should have no problem getting a refund of all of the withholding if this return is filed correctly so I do recommend that you use somebody with experience and the proper qualifications for filing US tax returns; you will need a separate 1040NR for each year in which you had this interest earned. The 1040NR should include a statement referring to the Canada/US Tax Treaty that there is no withholding on interest for Canadians with US investments.

CHOOSE TAX FILING WISELY

If you have any information on the following question, I would appreciate receiving it from you. I believe that if all of my income is from Canada, and Canadian income tax rates are higher than American rates, there is no point in filing a US return. That's because a reciprocal agreement between the two countries allows one to deduct the amount paid in Canada from the amount payable in the United States, and the Canadian amount would always be more. I have read a variety of US and Canadian publications on this subject and none of them covers this point.

— Margaret L., Satellite Beach, Florida

You did not state what country you are a resident of and whether you were a US citizen or green card holder. If you are a Canadian resident and not a US citizen or green card holder, you are correct that there is little point in filing a US tax return, unless you had US-sourced income. However, if you are a green card holder or US citizen, there are several important reasons why you should look at filing US tax returns:

1. You are required by law to file US returns when your world income exceeds the total of your standard deduction ($13,050 for 2016) and/or the personal exemptions for yourself and your spouse ($4,050 each for 2016).
2. You may be able to receive an overall reduction in taxes paid by using the Canada/US Tax Treaty to your best advantage, thus getting the lowest tax rate available to you.
3. Proper foreign tax credit planning may help you recover some of the higher taxes paid to Canada on future US returns, since unused foreign tax credits can be carried forward for up to ten years.
4. There are several IRS reporting forms that you are required to file that disclose certain kinds of foreign income, ownership in foreign companies, and foreign investment or bank accounts. Failure to file these disclosure forms may result in penalties exceeding $10,000 per year for each account and form not filed in a timely manner with your US tax return.

There is not a lot of literature that can help you on this matter, but you should consult both the CRA and IRS publications included in Appendix A, as well as other chapters in this book.

REMARRIAGE LEGALITIES NEED ATTENTION

I am a Canadian citizen who winters in Florida. My income comes from my late husband's Canada Pension Plan (CPP), company pension, and some investment income. I am going to be married this spring to an American and we plan to reside in Florida year-round.

I wish to maintain my Canadian citizenship. Do I need to apply for a green card in order to stay in the United States for more than six months each year or will my marriage qualify me for residency? Also, will I pay income tax in Canada or in the United States (my income is all from Canadian sources)? Are there other legal repercussions of which I should be informed? We plan to be married in Canada and will have a prenuptial contract drawn up by my Canadian attorney.

— Shirley L., Lakeland, Florida

For you to reside legally in the United States, your new husband will need to sponsor you for a green card. You do not have to give up your Canadian citizenship to do this, even if you apply later for US citizenship. It will be much easier to obtain a US green card if you get married in the US and have your husband immediately sponsor you for a green card. Otherwise you may have problems entering the US once you are married because the US Customs and Immigration person may prevent you from entering the US as a visitor if your intention is to reside there permanently. A marriage to a US citizen is definitely a red flag that you are no longer a visitor. Since you are no longer a visitor you cannot enter the US unless you already have some other kind of US visa or green card.

Once you no longer reside in Canada on a permanent basis, you do not have to file Canadian tax returns after you file a final exit return. You will report all of your world income on your US return only. You will have to notify the payers of all your Canadian pensions that you are a non-resident. They will then apply 15 percent non-resident withholding tax on your company pension and 0 percent on CPP and OAS. You will get a credit for the withholding tax paid to Canada when you file your US returns, which will likely cover most if not all of any US federal income tax you may have to pay.

There are some other issues, both good and bad, relating to Medicare and estate planning that you should discuss with a cross-border financial planner to make sure you maximize benefits and minimize pitfalls. You should also have your Canadian prenuptial agreement reviewed (or prepared) by a Florida attorney to ensure it will be effective there; it is always better to have those kind of documents prepared in the state of residence where you will be spending the majority of your time.

TAXES ON OWNERSHIP OF A US RACEHORSE

I have a 5 percent interest in a racehorse, racing in the USA. Westpoint Thoroughbreds, who runs the partnership, has advised me I will be sent a K-1. I'm not sure what this is about. Will I be able to use depreciation of the horse's expenses etc., on my Canadian income tax return? I had difficulty finding the correct form.

— John H., Vancouver, BC

Since you are part of what appears to be a US partnership, the K-1 is the tax summary sent to you and the IRS annually, as a report on a limited partner from the managing partner, detailing to you and the IRS your income and expenses for the year. You take this K-1 form and use it to file a US non-resident tax return, Form 1040NR. If you do not have a US taxpayer identification number (ITIN) yet, you need to file IRS Form W-7 when you file your first return to obtain one. The CRA has a similar form for partnerships, Form T5013.

On a US return, you would be able to offset losses against other similar forms of passive income that you may have in the US. If you do not have other income to deduct the losses, you can carry the loss forward until perhaps you win the big race or the horse is sold for a good profit. As far as the Canadian writeoffs go, you are in a gray area as to whether you will be able to deduct the losses against other forms of income under the restricted farm losses. I would recommend that you take your K-1 (when you receive it) and sit down with a Canadian tax accountant to translate it into an equivalent form T5013 to put on your Canadian T1. At that time, they can make a determination as to what will be deductible for you in Canada. In either country you need to prove that the business is not a hobby, otherwise no loss deductions will be allowed (but you will still be taxable on income earned if your horse wins big).

REMARRIAGE LIVING IN CANADA

I am a Canadian living in Ontario. I married a US citizen in May, 2014. She lives in New York City. I have no ties to the US and have submitted the paperwork to sponsor my wife to become a Canadian permanent resident.

My wife and I are both retired and live off of our investment income. After my wife takes up Canadian residence we will have no ties to the US, other than a couple of Roth IRAs which my wife isn't sure how she is supposed to handle.

My wife has questions about how she is supposed to file her US tax returns. Since I do not have (and don't want) an ITIN, does my wife choose Married Filing Separately or Single on her US tax returns? How does she account for me (if needed) on her US tax returns? Must she also file a Canadian tax return even though she does not yet live in Ontario with me or have any Canadian income?

— Wayne B., Toronto, Ontario

Your wife must now file her US tax returns as Married Filing Separately if you do not get a US ITIN (Individual Tax Identification Number). In this filing mode she cannot take an exemption for you because you do not have the ITIN. She will almost always pay higher US taxes on any income in the Married Filing Separate mode, and the Canada Revenue Agency will not require your new wife to pay tax on any earnings from the Roth IRA (these earnings will continue to be tax-free in both Canada and the US under the Treaty). If you get an ITIN she will be able to file Married Filing Jointly and should pay less income tax under this filing option. You may find the ITIN relatively easy to get; it has no negative consequences, but many positive ones.

Your wife does not have to start filing Canadian returns until she has officially taken up Canadian residency. You should look into having her sponsor you for your US permanent resident status/green card, which would require you to file only one tax return in the US and would likely save you both a tremendous amount of income tax, and you may qualify for both US Medicare and Social Security under her spousal benefit if she ever worked on salary at a job for ten years or longer in the US.

JACKPOT WITHHOLDING

During our visit to the United States this past winter my wife won money on a slot machine [in a casino] and from her winnings an amount equal to 30 percent of the winnings was deducted for US federal tax. Is there any way of recovering this amount as she is a Canadian citizen?

— Jack S., London, Ontario

The 30 percent withholding from your wife's winnings is routine for the casinos, as it is required by the IRS. However, if you have good records of how much your wife lost during the same time period and slots in which she had her win, then you can file a US non-resident tax return, Form 1040NR, to offset her gambling winnings with her losses in that same year. She would then be taxable only to the extent her winnings exceeded her losses, if at all. So if she spent more than she won in the on the same machines at the same time, she should get a full refund of the 30 percent withholding tax.

The proof of her losses that the IRS will normally want to see can be charge card records, casino records, chip/token purchase receipts, or just a very good log of money spent on gambling. Your wife needs to file IRS Form 1040NR, with a deadline of June 15 after the end of the year in which she had her big win.

If she does not have a US Social Security number she will need to apply for an Individual Tax Identification Number (ITIN) by completing Form W-7 and attaching it to the return. Without this, the IRS will withhold her refund, if she is entitled to one.

REAL ESTATE EXEMPTIONS

A friend of mine told me his tax accountant advised him that if he and his wife spent six months a year in the United States (they have a home in Sun City West, AZ), up to $300,000 would be exempt from capital gains tax on the sale of their home there. I was reading your tenth edition of The Border Guide *and note the response to a question to the effect that a US taxpayer has an exemption of $250,000. Has this been increased to $300,000 and could this be what my friend's accountant is referring to? I can see from the question and your response that an exception could apply but may not apply where the person has a home in both countries.*

— Henning H., Winnipeg, Manitoba

The $300,000 exemption mentioned by the accountant is only from a 10 percent withholding tax on the sale of a personal residence under certain qualifying circumstances, not from the tax due for non-residents of the United States. You must file a return and report any gains in the year of sale for any property, and pay capital gains taxes at both the state and federal levels, whether or not you were subject to withholding tax. The $250,000 exemption I mentioned in the tenth edition of *The Border Guide* is an actual exemption from tax, but it is only for US resident taxpayers on their principal residence. It has no application to Snowbirds or non-residents of the US. There are no exemptions for non-residents other than if they qualify for not being subject to withholding tax, but this does not affect tax on the sale of their US residences.

TAX-FILING STRATEGY COULD SAVE MONEY

My wife (deceased in August 2014) and I bought a condo in Florida in 2001. We received our green cards as resident aliens in 1998, through my sister in LA, who has been a US citizen since 1971. Since then we have spent six months in Florida and six months in Canada. I elected to file Canadian income tax and also US income tax relative to reciprocal tax laws. All taxes paid to Canada (federal and provincial) were used as a credit on US tax forms, adjusting the income each year for the current exchange.

All of my income, investments, bank accounts, and family are in Canada. We do not own property in Canada as my son has ample room in his residence, and we spend the six months with him. On the US side, I own the condo, with about a $248,000 value.

A year ago a consultant advised me that I have dual resident status. Also, I have been given power of attorney by the State of California to look after my sister's affairs in Los Angeles. She is 98 years of age and ruled not competent to attend to same.

My questions:

1. *What is the situation regarding capital gains?*
2. *Should I sell my condo?*
3. *In effect, it is my principal residence for six months and the only property I own: Isn't your principal residence exempt from capital gains?*
4. *Dual residency in Florida calls for my will to be probated in Florida. I only have a Canadian will. Can that will be probated in both places?*

— Howard S., Ft. Lauderdale, Florida

Your US condo can be both your Canadian principal residence and US principal residence for tax purposes. Any gain on the sale of this residence would not be reportable to CRA. In the US you could use your principal residence exemption of up to $250,000 allowed to all US taxpayers. Consequently, you should not have any tax to pay either country on the sale of your Florida residence. If you hold the condo at your death, it will be income-tax-free in both countries under current rules.

By filing returns both in Canada and the United States as you currently do, you may be paying more tax than necessary. You should look into this with a competent cross-border accountant or planner as there may be some substantial annual income tax savings if you arrange your affairs correctly and file only in the US on your world income.

Your will, if it is a valid Canadian will, is generally usable to settle your Florida affairs. If you have both Canadian and US property, it may be advantageous for you to put all your assets into a US living trust so that your estate is not required to go through probate in either country, saving a great deal of cost and aggravation for your heirs.

BETTER LATE THAN NEVER

I read your informative article "Save on Currency Exchanges" in the newspaper. If possible, I would appreciate an answer to the following questions.

A person born and living in the United States for 25 years moves to Canada 30 years ago, receives Canadian citizenship, still retains his US citizenship, lives and works in Canada all those 30 years but now lives in the United States about five months each year.

If this person decides to purchase property in Arizona and builds a house on that property, are there rules and regulations that he should be aware of before he starts this project? Is this dual citizen required to file his

Canadian income with the IRS even though he had no US income? If so, what is the proper procedure for doing this? Thank you for your assistance.

— Ralph A., Apache Junction, Arizona

As a citizen of both Canada and the United States, you are subject to the tax rules of both countries at the same time. Canadian citizens pay tax on their world income only when they are residents of Canada, whereas US citizens pay tax on their world income regardless of where they are resident. Consequently, you are subject to filing returns in both Canada and the United States unless you leave Canada to become a resident of the United States only.

The requirement to file in the United States is not negated based on the fact that all your income was Canadian-sourced. This requirement to file has always been there ever since you left the United States 30 years ago, so in effect you are quite overdue with your IRS filings. Please remember that just because you were required to file US returns does not mean that you necessarily owe any tax to the IRS. There are certain exemptions and foreign tax credits from taxes paid to Canada for US citizens living outside the United States that can greatly reduce or even eliminate US taxes payable. However, the only way to find out whether you have taxes due is to go back and actually file returns. It is in your best interests to voluntarily disclose information to the IRS as soon as possible, there is a Streamlined Voluntary Disclosure program available from the IRS to help you get back on their good side of filing without penalties.

Getting square with the IRS needs to be your top priority regardless of whether or not you build a place in Arizona. There may be some tax savings in store for you in the future if you file in the United States and leave Canada for tax purposes. There are no particular issues you need to be concerned about in building your new place in the Sunbelt, but you may want to consider using a living trust to hold title to your property so that it does not have to go through probate in Arizona or Canada.

Some of the issues you need to deal with are quite complex and I recommend that you seek assistance from a qualified person knowledgeable in both the applicable Canadian and US matters.

DOES A GREEN CARD HAVE AN EXPIRATION DATE?

My wife and I moved to Florida in 2012 on a permanent basis as retirees. My wife is a US citizen and I have a green card issued in 1973. I do not intend to work. I returned to Canada in 1974, retaining my green card, and filed Canadian income tax returns from 1974 to 2012. I will file a US return for the year 2012, and subsequent years. I will not file a Canadian return. My questions are these:

1. *Is my green card still valid, or do I have to reapply for another one?*
2. *Do I apply in Tampa or do I have to go back to Toronto?*
3. *When I file my US return, am I likely to be asked why I have not filed a return since 1974 and if so, how do I answer? And depending on the answer, will the Internal Revenue Service inform US Citizenship and Immigration Service (USCIS) of my status?*
4. *Will I be able to apply for US citizenship after three years?*

— Edward P., Venice, Florida

1. Since you did not surrender your green card, and it has no expiration date, it is still valid. However, you were supposed to surrender the green card in 1974 when you left the United States.
2. Your best bet is to tread softly with the US Citizenship and Immigration Service for a while, and just start using the green card again each time you cross the border. According to new USCIS rules, you do need to file a USCIS Form I-90 to obtain a new green card with/updated pictures and a ten-year expiration date. Since you have a permanent Florida home, the US Citizenship and Immigration Service will likely not bother you.
3. The Internal Revenue Service may question you, though, about where all your tax returns were filed since 1974. If you hurry you can also take advantage of a Streamlined Voluntary Disclosure program with the IRS that requires you to file the last three years' US returns and six years of foreign reporting forms. You should end up paying no penalties but will have to pay the taxes due, if any, with interest for the three years. Since income taxes were higher in Canada than in the US during this period, the credits from the Canadian tax paid should cover most, if not all, the US taxes due for the three years. The IRS should forgive any taxes that may have been due before the three years.
4. You need three or more continuous years in which you spend over six months a year in the US before applying for US citizenship.

SELLING US LAND

When selling undeveloped real estate in the United States, the titles company will hold back a portion of the proceeds for the IRS.

How can I claim this back? Can I claim it against the capital gains taxes on my Canadian T1 return?

— Tom J., Kingston, Ontario

The US non-resident withholding tax should be 10 percent of the sale price of your property. If you have not yet actually sold the property, you can apply to the IRS for a clearance certificate (use IRS Form 8288) six to eight weeks in advance of the sale, and they will authorize a lower withholding rate, closer to the actual tax due on the capital gains. Regardless of whether or not you get a clearance certificate, you must file a US tax return (Form 1040NR, the non-resident tax return) to report the sale. Form 1040NR is due by June 15th in the year following the sale. It is by filing this form that you obtain any refunds due to over withholding at the time of sale. You will also need to apply for an ITIN (Individual Tax Identification Number) by filing Form W-7 with the IRS. It is best that you get this number as soon as you get the sales contract from the buyer, as this will make things go a lot more smoothly.

Depending on which state the property is located in, there may be additional non-resident withholding tax and state tax returns to file. The net tax that you pay to both the IRS and the applicable state will be a tax credit for Canadian taxes due on your T1 for the capital gains in the same tax year.

You can do all of this on your own if you have the time and patience, but I do recommend that you get professional help — particularly if the transaction is large — as mistakes can be very costly.

EFFECTS OF DUAL CITIZENSHIP

What effects does dual citizenship have on Canadian citizens regarding income tax, etc.?

— Candy O., Tampa, Florida

Although your question is a short one, there are no short answers. There are a large number of tax issues that will need to be addressed if a Canadian becomes a dual citizen, including country of residence, the size of the estate, and the types of income the person is receiving.

Probably the first question you need to address is: Why become a dual citizen? Unless you intend to reside in the United States for more than six months a year and Canada for less than six months a year, you will not likely benefit tax-wise by becoming a dual citizen. You may even expose yourself to some unnecessary tax complications.

Canada taxes its citizens only when they are actual residents of Canada. US citizens are taxed wherever they live in the world, with tax credits allowed against foreign taxes paid by those US citizens in other countries of residence. Consequently, if you become a dual citizen and still intend to reside in Canada, you will be required to file tax returns in both countries on world income. Filing in both countries affords you no tax advantages since you will pay the Canadian tax rate and take a credit for those taxes paid on the US return. Your total tax paid between the two countries under most circumstances will not be any greater, but why complicate your life unnecessarily?

The real tax advantages of dual citizenship come when you become a non-resident of Canada and are no longer subject to Canadian tax rules. Depending on your sources and amounts of income, you can realistically cut your annual income tax bill in half or more.

Under the Canada/US Tax Treaty, you can be a dual citizen and maintain a lifestyle of winters in the Sunbelt and summers in Canada without being subject to taxes in both countries. Consequently, dual citizens can arrange their financial affairs in such a way that they pay tax on their world income only in the US. Once you have completed an exit tax return from Canada, your tax situation becomes much clearer. CPP/QPP and OAS are partially tax free in the United States and are not subject to non-resident withholding tax or OAS clawback by the CRA. Taxes on RRSP and RRIF withdrawals drop to 15 percent or 25 percent, depending on whether they are periodic or lump-sum withdrawals. Canadian dividends and corporate pensions are subject to a non-resident withholding tax of 15 percent. Under the new treaty, interest withholding has been reduced to 10 percent. You can also take advantage of a large variety of tax-free, tax-deferred, or tax-sheltered investment options in the United States to substantially reduce or eliminate any tax on investment income.

The tax advantages of becoming a dual citizen and paying your taxes in the United States need to be greater than the net cost of US Medicare, which is approximately $8,000 USD each year (or less if you qualify for full US Social Security). There are many complex estate-planning issues that should be addressed before making the move to dual citizenship, particularly if you and your spouse's total estate is over $16 million CAD. Over this amount, US estate taxes will have to be taken into account.

Because of the complexity of the issues involved with becoming a dual citizen, I don't recommend you attempt such a move without a written plan completed by a knowledgeable cross-border financial planner. Talking to an attorney or accountant in either or both countries may give you only part of a much larger puzzle and can be confusing, especially if the advisor lacks knowledge of the other country's systems.

TORONTONIAN MARRYING NEW YORKER

I have just finished reading your very helpful book, The Border Guide, *in search of an answer regarding my situation: a Canadian citizen, age 72, I am in a new relationship with a partner living in New York. We were married in October this year. My new wife was 68 in July.*

I have low income. I almost have no savings left.

My questions are as follows:

1. ***Health care:*** *My wife works in a hospital and is also self-employed. She is covered by her workplace medical insurance. She was told I'll be covered by her insurance while we are married as long as she still works for the hospital. She will be covered by US Medicare when she retires. I understand that I have to wait until after one year of marriage to apply to be covered by US Medicare. She plans to work another year so I am covered during the waiting period. Is this necessary and the only way to do it?*
2. ***My stay in the US:*** *What first steps should I take now that we are married? I would like to apply for permanent residency. Do I have to give up Canadian citizenship to become an American citizen? Can I travel during the waiting period?*
3. ***Income:*** *I understand that I will always receive my CPP and OAS. But I will eventually lose my Guaranteed Income Supplement (GIS). You wrote me that I may receive half of my wife's Social Security. Can you confirm this and give me some details? Is this only if she predeceases me?*

— J. K., Toronto, Ontario

Since you have married a US spouse who has qualified for Social Security under her own earnings, you will be eligible for both US Medicare and a Social Security pension (approximately 50 percent of her pension) after one year of marriage. If she predeceases you, you would then be eligible for 100 percent of her Social Security pension, which on average is $2,500 USD per month. This means that you would get a gift from the US of about $1250 USD a month after your first year of marriage. I am sure you will agree this is a very generous wedding gift from US Social Security. If you predecease her, she would be eligible for about 70 percent of your CPP as a widow's benefit. Even though your wife is still going to work for another year, she should still apply for her Social Security now as she is over 66 and will not have her pension reduced even though she has employment earnings. You also will get Medicare Part A at no cost (this is the major part of Medicare) and will have to pay for Part B, like other US residents (about $110 per month). You likely will have to give up your Guaranteed Income Supplement (GIS).

You need to have your new wife sponsor your application for your permanent residence, more commonly called your green card. Since you are already living in New York, you need to apply for your green card and advance parole as soon as possible (which will allow you to leave the US and re-enter while the green card application is in process). The green card will take you over two years to finalize. I recommend that you get some help from an immigration attorney to do this, as it can be a complex process. Once you have had your green card for three years, you can apply to become a dual US/Canadian citizen. Under current rules, you do not have to give up Canadian citizenship at any time during this process.

WITHHOLDING TAX COMPLIANCE ON US RENTAL INCOME

What options are available to Canadian owners/renters in Florida who through ignorance have failed to comply with the 30 percent withholding tax, and who wish to square themselves immediately with the Internal Revenue Service?

— Ed F., Williamsburg, Ontario

Your question is a very good one, as it applies to a situation we run into quite often. Anyone who rents out his or her US property for longer than two weeks per year is subject to taxation on this income in both the United States (under the Internal Revenue Code) and Canada (under the *Income Tax Act*). You must decide which of the two methods explained below is appropriate for you.

The first method has the renter withhold 30 percent of the gross rental income and forward it to the IRS Service Center in Philadelphia, Pennsylvania. The onus is on the renter to withhold the tax (if you are a non-resident landlord), but the IRS will come after both the renter and the landlord if the tax is not paid as required.

The second method is to make an election under Section 871 of the Internal Revenue Code to be taxed as effectively conducting business in the United States. You would then file a Form 1040NR tax return in the United States annually.

On this return, expenses incurred to earn the rent (such as property taxes, utilities, mortgage interest, travel, etc., and allowable personal exemptions) are subtracted as deductions to arrive at a net taxable income for a non-resident.

By filing Form 1040NR for both the current and past years, the non-resident taxpayer will generally pay less tax. Most people in this situation make little or no profit after all expenses have been deducted, and therefore no tax is due. Even if you do have some net rental profit, the tax rate after deducting personal exemptions of $4,050 starts at only 10 percent.

A husband and wife can split this income on separate US returns and both take personal exemptions if the rental property was purchased jointly. It is important to get into compliance as soon as possible and file at least the last three years' returns before the IRS finds you.

The forms for filing a return (the Form 1040NR and the necessary rental income Schedule E) may be found at any IRS office and on the web (at irs.gov), or they may be requested by calling the IRS toll free at 1-800-829-3676. If you do not already have a US Social Security Number or an Individual Taxpayer Identification Number (ITIN), you need to apply for one by completing IRS Form W-7. You must attach it to the first US tax return you file.

There is a statute of limitations (the period of time the IRS has to audit a return) of three years if you have filed a completed Form 1040NR. If you have not filed or you filed without reporting all income, the statute of limitations does not apply, and the IRS can go back as far as they like to collect earlier taxes.

Don't forget to report this income on your Canadian tax return as well; the penalties from Canada Revenue Agency can be as bad or worse than those from the IRS. I recommend that you find someone experienced in cross-border tax filings to assist you, as the process can be complex.

RESIDENCY FOR TAX PURPOSES

Do I need to have a green card or other visa before I am considered a US resident for tax purposes? Are there other regulations that apply to becoming a resident for tax purposes without actually immigrating?

— Oscar G., Sun City, Arizona

Residency for tax purposes does not relate to permanent resident status, but rather to your physical presence within the United States. The following is the general explanation offered by the IRS in its publication on tax obligations of legalized aliens.

If you are in the United States as a lawful permanent resident (with a green card) at any time during the year, you are considered a resident alien for tax purposes and are taxed just like a US citizen. That is, you are taxed on your income from any source throughout the world.

Even if you do not have a green card, you are still treated as a resident alien if you are actually in the United States for enough days during the year. Generally, if you are in the United States for 183 days during that year, you are considered a resident for tax purposes for that year. But you may also be considered a resident for a year if you are in the US for fewer than 183 days during that year, providing you were there for a certain minimum number of days over a three-year period. You do not count the days you were there on a diplomatic, student, or teacher visa. Under the Canada/US Tax Treaty, most Canadian visitors who stay less than the 183 days would not be considered residents of the United States. Consult a tax advisor if you are in doubt about your status.

The more important question is whether you can be taxed in the United States but not in Canada if you do not have any legal immigration status in the United States. The answer to this question will be no in most circumstances, as it is very difficult to convince CRA that you are a non-resident of Canada when you are not a legal resident somewhere else.

SHARING THE WEALTH OF TAX INFORMATION

My wife, a Canadian citizen, sold a condominium in the US in 2012 at a small loss from the original 2005 purchase price. She did not report the sale to CRA due to the loss, although she did report it to the IRS. I obtained an exemption from withholding tax because a loss was incurred. She has just received a letter from CRA requesting copies of the purchase and sale documents and the reason why the disposition was not reported on her 2012 tax return. Is it necessary to report the sale of property in the United States (not principal residence) to CRA when no profit results? Also, if an "equity membership" in a golf club is sold for more than the original cost, is this deemed to be income or profit? Am I required to report it for Canadian tax purposes?

— Don R.C., Naples, Florida

You didn't tell me which country your wife is a resident of for tax purposes.

Judging by the tone of CRA's request, they still consider your wife a Canadian resident. If they are wrong and your wife is a non-resident, you need to provide them with information to prove she has left, such as a US green card, sale of Canadian residence, etc. If she is still a resident of Canada, CRA is correct in their requests. Residents of Canada must report their world income to CRA, including both the sale of the condominium and the golf club membership. Tax could be owing to CRA on the net gain on the sale of these two items, adjusted for Canadian dollars on the difference in exchange rates between the purchase and sale, which could be substantial depending on recent increases in the Canadian dollar.

This is a good example of the CRA and the IRS sharing your tax information as allowed under the Canada/US Tax Treaty.

5 You Still Can't Take It with You

Non-Resident Estate Planning

Canadians have not had to deal with any true inheritance or estate taxes since the capital gains tax was introduced in 1972. The provinces that had an inheritance tax at the time opted out of their own tax programs in favor of collecting the provincial portion of the capital gains tax from the deemed disposition at the death of a taxpayer. However, anyone owning property in Canada needs to be aware of the increasingly heavy-handed taxman encroaching on their estates upon transference to heirs, regardless of which country they permanently reside in or which cross-border lifestyle they may choose; whether Vacationer, Snowbird, or Settler.

The first step in understanding cross-border estate planning is comprehending all the forces of Canadian law that come into play, and the need for estate planning in the first place. It is amazing to me that a recent survey indicated that over 50 percent of the Canadian population do not have wills and do not understand the burden they leave on their families at death. Not having a valid will often results in families splitting up and attorneys taking most or all of the estate that should have rightly gone to the beneficiaries with minimal expense or tax.

Many Canadians are complacent and believe estate or inheritance taxes concern only Americans. However, on joint estates of less than $16 million CAD, the Canadian inheritance or estate tax can be much greater than it is in the US. See Figure 11.1 in Chapter 11 for more details.

The deemed disposition at death of capital assets with capital gains, and retirement programs such as RRSPs and RRIFs, create a substantial tax liability at death. In some cases, these hidden taxes can exceed 60 percent of the value of the of the applicable estate assets. The CRA and the provinces do not call these taxes inheritance taxes, but if it looks like a duck, and walks like a duck …

The province of residence of the deceased collects approximately half of this deemed disposition tax at death. However, several provinces don't seem to be happy with their share of the tax and have implemented new taxes disguised as user or probate fees.

British Columbia led the way by implementing a probate fee, with many other provinces quickly getting in line. The probate fee is a cleverly disguised inheritance tax, since the majority of one's assets go through probate either at time of death, a spouse's death, or both times, hitting the estate twice. Here is a brief summary of the provincial probate fees:

- Newfoundland and Labrador: $60 for the first $1,000 and $6 per $1,000, or 0.6 percent, thereafter with no maximum fee.
- Nova Scotia: $973 for the first $100,000, progressing to $16.45 per $1,000, or 1.645 percent, for estates over $100,000 with no maximum fee. Nova Scotia has a land transfer tax of 1.5 percent determined by each municipality applied to the value of the property transferred.
- Prince Edward Island: $400 for the first $100,000, progressing to $4 per $1000, or 0.4 percent for estates over $100,000 with no maximum fee. Prince Edward Island has a land transfer tax of 1 percent of the property's assessed value.
- New Brunswick: $100 for the first $20,000, then $5 per $1,000, 0.5 percent, with no maximum. New Brunswick has a land transfer tax of the 0.5 percent of the property's fair market value.
- Quebec: This province has a different legal system with no probate or probate fees but does have a $105 will verification fee. Quebec does have a land transfer tax of up to 1.5 percent fair market value of the property at the time of transfer.
- Ontario: $5 per $1,000 for the first $50,000 and $15 per $1,000, 1.5 percent, thereafter with no maximum. Ontario has a land transfer tax maximum of 2 percent of the value of the property being transferred.
- Manitoba: $70 on the first $1000 then $7 per $1,000, 0.7 percent, with no maximum. Manitoba has a land transfer tax of 0.5 percent of the value of the property being transferred.
- Saskatchewan: $7 per $1,000 of estate value subject to probate less balance of any mortgages, with no maximum fee.
- Alberta: $35 for the first $10,000, progressing to a maximum of $525 for estates of $250,000 or more.

- British Columbia: $0 for estates of less than $25,000. For estates between $25,000 and $50,000, there is a fee of $208 and $6 per $1,000. On more than $50,000 the fee is $208 and $14 per $1,000, or 1.4 percent, with no maximum fee. BC also has a land transfer tax of 2 percent when transferring property owned by an estate.

Canadians or Americans who live in one country and own property in the other face additional tax rules, which can leave them exposed to double tax. The double tax arises from Canada's deemed disposition tax stacked on top of the US resident/non-resident estate tax, if applicable. This multiple death tax can total up to 70 percent of the property value in the other country. The 1996 amendment to the Canada/US Tax Treaty goes a long way toward eliminating most of this potential double tax for Canadians and Americans in this situation.

Canadians, particularly those who own property in both the United States and Canada, may be setting their estates up for trouble in the form of high taxes, liquidity problems, and high legal fees, if they ignore current or future inheritance taxes. Use the examples in Figure 5.1 to see what happened to the estates of some well-known people, as measured by estate shrinkage. Estate shrinkage, as the name implies, is simply the amount of the estate consumed by probate fees, legal fees, accounting fees, and estate taxes before the beneficiaries actually inherit it. You can also see that there is a great deal of difference in estate shrinkage between these wealthy deceased persons. Why did Elvis Presley have 73 percent shrinkage while Henry Kaiser, with a much larger estate, had only 2 percent? The answer is simple: estate-planning techniques.

There are a number of planning tools you can use to reduce or eliminate inheritance taxes, regardless of your residency and whether you have property in both Canada and the United States. This chapter provides you with some basic guidelines and directs you to some of the

ESTATE SHRINKAGE

Name	Gross Estate	Net Estate	Shrinkage
John Rockefeller	$26,905,182	$9,780,194	64%
Elvis Presley	$10,165,434	$2,790,799	73%
Walt Disney	$23,004,851	$16,192,908	30%
Henry J. Kaiser, Jr.	$55,910,973	$54,879,958	2%

FIGURE 5.1

most appropriate estate-planning tools for your situation. Remember that attempting to implement an estate plan without the assistance of a financial planning professional who is familiar with both US and Canadian estate-planning techniques, is analogous to reading up on removing your gall bladder and then carrying out the procedure by yourself.

THE US NON-RESIDENT ESTATE TAX

The first thing I would like to do with respect to those who choose a cross-border lifestyle of Vacationer, Snowbird, or Settler is to let them know that US estate taxes, under very recent new IRS rules and the Canada/US Treaty, apply only to a very small part of the population, in fact only the top 1 or 2 percent in terms of net worth. Contrast this with Canada were probably more than 75 percent of Canadians own an RRSP, similar registered plan, or some appreciated asset at their death and therefore are subject to the Canadian estate taxes. Even though you may not be subject to US estate taxes either as a resident or a non-resident it is still important to understand how to utilize available credits and exemptions to your full advantage to ensure that you don't get caught paying taxes because of the lack of understanding of the applicable US domestic or the Treaty rules. Throughout the rest of this chapter I will explain the rules as to where and when they apply and how to take advantage of a little bit of cross-border planning to assist you to enjoy that most amazing cross-border lifestyle without being concerned about having an estate that may span the US and Canada.

US federal estate tax is similar to income tax because of the progressive way it is calculated. There are two main factors that determine the amount of tax paid: first, the tax rate in any given bracket, and second, the amount of the estate that the tax rate applies to. We will deal with each of these issues and then illustrate how they apply with some examples.

THE TAXABLE ESTATE

Estate tax in the United States is technically a transfer tax on property owned at death where the total value of property owned exceeds the exemption amount. If the property is transferred during one's lifetime, it may be subject to a gift tax at the same rates as the estate tax, with some minor exceptions noted later in this chapter. US citizens and Settlers/residents of the US are subject to estate taxes on their worldwide assets, while Vacationers/Snowbirds/non-resident Canadians are subject only to tax on their property either actually or deemed to be situated in the US. The Income Tax Rules and Estate Tax Rules covered in Chapter 2 detail the situations in which Canadians may be considered residents of the United States for estate tax purposes. Estate tax is based on the fair market value (not just the appreciation) of all assets either on or exactly six months after the date of death. The property subject to estate tax for a Canadian who is a Vacationer/Snowbird/non-resident of the United States includes real property located in the United States; personal property normally located in the United States (such as autos, jewellery, boats, RVs, furniture, and artwork); shares of US corporations, regardless of where they were purchased or where they are physically held; and certain bonds and notes issued by US residents and corporations.

Assets normally excluded from the estate of a non-resident include US bank deposits; government and corporate bonds; and shares or notes of non-US corporations. Chapter 7 provides more specific details, under "Exempt Investments," about which investments are exempt from both income tax and estate tax for US non-residents.

The total of all taxable assets noted above, minus any of the exclusions, exempt assets, and certain deductions for estate settlement costs and non-recourse mortgages, equals the taxable estate.

US FEDERAL ESTATE TAX

For Vacationers/Snowbirds/non-residents of the US the non-resident estate tax starts at 24 percent on a taxable estate. Once the non-resident estate tax exemption of $60,000 has been reached, the maximum tax rises to 40 percent for assets over $1 million. The Canada/US Tax Treaty gives Vacationers/Snowbirds/Settlers access to the full resident estate tax exemption of $5,450,000 US (2016, indexed for inflation), on the fair market value of their worldwide estate. This treaty benefit, like all treaty benefits, must be applied for by the deceased estate trustee or executor by filing the proper IRS tax forms discussed in the next several sections of this chapter. Consequently, as noted earlier, most Canadians living the cross-border lifestyle need not be concerned about US estate taxes, particularly when a married couple's family assets need to exceed nearly $11 million US before any US estate tax applies. Refer to Figure 5.2, which illustrates the graduated estate tax rates before any exemptions or exclusions are applied., and Figure 5.3, which illustrates the estate-tax exemptions and maximum tax rates.

DETERMINING US ESTATE TAX EXEMPTION

For US citizens and Settlers/residents of the US, the estate tax exemption is a straightforward $5,450,000 based on the fair market value of their

US ESTATE TAX TABLE 2016
(US Dollars)

Column A	Column B	Column C	Column D
Taxable amount over	Taxable amount not over	Tax on amount in column A	Rate of tax on excess over amount in column A (in %)
US$0	US$10,000	US$0	18%
US$10,000	US$20,000	US$1,800	20%
US$20,000	US$40,000	US$3,800	22%
US$40,000	US$60,000	US$8,200	24%
US$60,000	US$80,000	US$13,000	26%
US$80,000	US$100,000	US$18,200	28%
US$100,000	US$150,000	US$23,800	30%
US$150,000	US$250,000	US$38,800	32%
US$250,000	US$500,000	US$70,800	34%
US$500,000	US$750,000	US$155,800	37%
US$750,000	US$1,000,000	US$248,300	39%
US$1,000,000	No upper limit	US$345,800	40%

FIGURE 5.2

US ESTATE TAX AND EXEMPTIONS

YEAR	EQUIVALENT EXEMPTION	MAXIMUM TAX RATE
2016	$5,450,000	40%
2017	(Est. 5,500,000)	40%

FIGURE 5.3

taxable estate (or $10.9 million for a married couple). The Vacationer/Snowbird/Non-resident exemption is also straightforward but it is only $60,000; when calculating the US non-resident exemption under the Treaty rules, they simply compare the fraction of their total world estate to their US situs estate. Thus the non-resident will get the same percentage of the $5,450,000 USD maximum exemption as the ratio of value of US assets relative to the value of their world assets. As you may have already surmised, to get this higher exemption, non-residents must reveal their worldwide assets to the IRS by filing Form 706-NA (US Estate Tax Return) and be subject to an IRS audit for any of the numbers or statements provided on this return. Since nearly 100 percent of all large estate tax returns in the United States are audited, executors will have this added burden, which could prove to be time-consuming and expensive.

As an example, here's how it would work for a Snowbird/non-resident Canadian who owns US property with a fair market value of $200,000 USD, and has a total net worth (including the US property) of $1 million USD. Under the Treaty, he or she would receive 20 percent or $1,090,000 of the $5,450,000 exemption (calculated by ($200,000/ $1,000,000) X $5,450,000 = $1,090,000). They would not be subject to any US non-resident estate tax since their $200,000 USD property is valued at less than the allowed exemption of $1,090,000 under the Treaty formula. They might still be subject to the Canadian deemed disposition tax at death, or in other words the Canadian estate tax, if the property appreciated in value during the term of ownership before death.

When determining the value of your world estate, you must follow US reporting rules, which can be very different from Canadian rules. A US taxable estate includes such things as the value of life insurance policies that you own on which you are the insured, the full value of Canadian-controlled private corporations which you control or have controlled and in which you still own shares (even if you have sold or given away most of your shares the entire fair market value of the entire Corporation would still be included in your taxable US estate), and the present value of all the future payments you might leave a spouse under the spousal benefit of your pensions. Since most Canadians do own life insurance on their own lives and do have some form of government and private pensions, the value of their world estates (which are calculated to figure the size of their US exemptions under the treaty formula) can be greatly affected. Note that the Treaty does not give Canadian residents with appreciated US property any break from the Canadian deemed disposition tax (Canada's estate tax equivalent) at death. The sole exception is a credit that will now be allowed to offset this tax if any US non-resident estate tax is paid. The Treaty has some other positive Canadian non-resident estate provisions. For example, it adds US stocks to the list of investments that Canadians can make that will be exempt from the non-resident estate tax. This applies only to Canadians whose world estates are less than $1.2 million USD. (See Chapter 7 for a complete list of exempt investments, in addition to this specific US stock exemption.)

Previously, exempt investments included only bonds and treasury bills issued by the US government, bank deposits, life insurance, and corporate bonds. The inclusion of US stocks will enable most Canadians who are non-residents of the United States to freely hold a very diversified portfolio of US stocks, bonds, and mutual funds without being exposed to any non-resident estate tax. Figure 5.5 shows the effects of the Canada/US Tax Treaty formula election. Compare it with Figure 5.4, which was calculated under the current US domestic rules. I am assuming Dorothy has a worldwide estate of $1 million USD, including her Hawaiian villa. Also note in both examples the Canadian deemed disposition tax at death must be calculated and paid to the Canada Revenue Agency regardless of what happens in the US the non-resident estate tax.

Another important provision in the Treaty for those Canadian citizens who are either dual citizens or US residents is the ability to waive the right to roll their estates over to their spouses to defer any estate tax to the second spouse's death. This waiver allows the deceased's estate to take a double exemption equivalent to $10.9 million USD. Consequently, estates of that size can benefit greatly if they are structured correctly to take advantage of this double exemption. Finally, the Treaty allows for an estate of the Canadian to take credit for any tax paid to the US or vice versa so that any double tax where the estate is being taxed in both countries on the same income is pretty well eliminated.

In summary, the options regarding non-resident estate tax in the Canada/US Tax Treaty provide substantial relief for Canadians owning US property, but at the expense of complexity. The estate may incur legal and accounting fees that can be, in some instances, greater than the tax itself without proactive cross-border estate planning professional assistance.

There are a number of estate-planning techniques designed for Canadians to avoid or reduce the effects of this US non-resident estate tax. These techniques will be discussed in the next section.

HOW TO AVOID THE US NON-RESIDENT ESTATE TAX

Each of the following techniques has its individual merits and drawbacks in dealing with the US non-resident estate tax and reducing estate settlement costs for those that have property in both Canada and the US. There is no silver bullet solution for all people in all situations. I will briefly cover the circumstances under which each technique works best and what to watch out for with each option. These options are given as a

**NON-RESIDENT ESTATE TAX
AT CURRENT US DOMESTIC RATES**

Dorothy, a Canadian non-resident of the United States, owns a villa in Hawaii her deceased husband had purchased for her more than 15 years ago. The villa is valued at $300,000 fully furnished, with a small mortgage of $50,000 remaining at a local bank. This property is all she owns in the United States.

Dorothy's taxable estate is $250,000 (the $300,000 value of the villa less the $50,000 non-resources mortgage).

Her estate tax from Figure 5.2 would be $38,800 less her unified credit of $13,000 for a net tax of $25,800 USD before Canada/US Tax Treaty benefits are applied. (See Figure 5.5.)

FIGURE 5.4

**NON-RESIDENT ESTATE TAX
ACCORDING TO THE TREATY RULES**

Dorothy's taxable estate would remain the same as in Figure 5.4 at $250,000 and tax before the non-resident exemption of $38,800. Her new exemption would be:

($250,000 ÷ 1,000,000) x 5,450,000 = $1,362,668

Therefore, the net US estate tax due is:
$250,000 – 1,362,668 = 0

FIGURE 5.5

guide only and any attempt to apply these methods to your own situation should be accomplished with the assistance of a qualified cross-border estate-planning professional. The Canada/US Tax Treaty with its articles on estate tax may make the following strategies less necessary than in the past, since those Canadians with estates of less than $5.45 million USD would likely always qualify for larger non-resident exemptions than the $60,000 under existing US domestic rules (providing they file the US estate tax return and claim Treaty benefits).

BECOME A US RESIDENT OR SETTLER

In a previous section in this chapter, "The US Non-Resident Estate Tax," I mentioned the fact that residents of the United States receive an estate tax equivalent exemption of $5.45 million USD (see Figure 5.3) compared to the non-resident exemption of $60,000 USD (unless the Canada/US Tax Treaty allows for a greater exemption; see the earlier sections of this chapter). A married couple who become US residents would be eligible for a total spousal exemption of $10.9 million USD or about $16 million CAD, which is enough for most Canadians to be fully exempt from paying any estate taxes. Without further estate planning, persons with larger estates could still be subject to tax. There are other implications in becoming a US resident besides estate tax reduction. These ramifications are covered in greater detail in Chapters 8, 9, 10, and 11.

MORTGAGE YOUR US PROPERTY

Examples given in Figures 5.4 and 5.5 illustrate that non-recourse mortgages can be deducted from the taxable estate and only the net equity will be taxable. A non-recourse mortgage is from a lender whose only security is the property itself. If there is a default, the lender cannot go after the borrower's other assets if there is insufficient collateral in the property. Typically, most US mortgages are non-recourse depending on the state, where as in Canada, most are recourse so that the Canadian banks can go after all of your other assets if you default on the mortgage.

One side benefit of taking out a mortgage is that you may be able to deduct the mortgage interest on your Canadian tax return. If you invested the mortgage proceeds in income-producing investments outlined in Chapter 7, you would be able to deduct the interest as interest paid to produce investment income. This could go a long way toward producing US investment income that could protect you from a falling Canadian dollar. For this to work most effectively, the return on your investments must provide a greater return than the cost of your mortgage.

You should also be aware of potential currency risks if you mortgage your property and then take the proceeds back to Canada, since your loan obligation is in US funds. In this situation, a falling Canadian dollar would require larger Canadian-dollar conversions with each payment and the Exchange Rate Blues discussed earlier and would be a continuing concern for the term of the mortgage. A simple example of someone taking out a $100,000 USD mortgage two years ago would now have to pay back roughly $140,000 CAD if he or she had not planned correctly using some of the techniques discussed.

Mortgages advanced through traditional Canadian banks in Canada or non-arm's-length lenders such as controlled Canadian corporations, will not work for this strategy since the debt would not be non-recourse.

There are many US lenders, including subsidiaries of Canadian banks, in the US that can provide non-recourse mortgages at reasonable rates.

JOINT PROPERTY OWNERSHIP WITH CHILDREN

Since each individual non-resident has a $60,000 USD estate tax exemption, and possibly more under the Canada/US Tax Treaty, it sometimes makes sense to place all family members on the title of an existing or new US property. A family of five could combine their exemptions and own a vacation home worth $300,000 USD, and none of them would be subject to a non-resident estate tax. Although this strategy appears to be very simple, it can be fraught with pitfalls. Simply put, joint ownership is not simple regardless of whether it is initiated in Canada or the US.

Much as we may not care to admit it, our children are only human, and they will experience some of the not-so-pleasant things in life such as divorce and bankruptcy. Many unsuspecting parents join the cross-border lifestyle have had to pay off an ex-spouse or a child's creditors so they could keep their own winter vacation homes. Serious family discord can sometimes result in a battle over control of a family-owned property.

If you have considered the drawbacks carefully and still feel this is a suitable technique for you, you should consider several things concerning the actual placement of adult children's names on the property title. If you already own a property and want to place one or more children on the title, there are both Canadian and US tax implications of which to be mindful. First, CRA will consider this transfer subject to capital gains tax on the portion of the property being transferred. From a US standpoint, the IRS will consider the transfer of the American property a gift which may be subject to gift tax. It would be wrong to assume that joint ownership means the same thing in Canada as it does in the US. It is important to get appropriate legal advice in the jurisdiction in which the joint ownership is being conferred on to a spouse or child. A more detailed description of the gift tax appears later in this chapter. If both you and your spouse are not already on title, you can run into some of the same US gift tax problems when adding a spouse to the title.

Sometimes the best method to complete this type of transfer may be to sell a portion of the property to your children, even if you have to loan them the money in Canada at no interest. This way you will avoid the US gift tax, but not the Canadian capital gains tax if the property has appreciated in value. The capital gains tax, if any, could be paid by the recipient children, who are likely getting a pretty good deal anyway.

When using "joint ownership with right of survivorship" on your US property, it is important that you are aware of the fact that the first of the joint owners to die is assumed by the IRS to have contributed the entire capital for the purchase of that particular property. That means that the entire property would be included in the taxable US estate of the first to die unless the executor could provide proof to the IRS that the other joint owners actually contributed to the property purchase.

If you are about to purchase US property, this arrangement is much easier to make at the time of purchase than after the sale is completed. One additional benefit is that the estate will likely avoid probate at the time of both parents' deaths, since a joint ownership with right of survivorship titling of the property with the children will allow the property to pass directly to them without probate after both parents have died.

HAVE AN INSURANCE COMPANY PAY THE TAX

Life insurance benefits from non-resident insured persons are not included in their taxable US estates. The development of no-load life insurance has made this option more practical than ever. Most people who buy life insurance aren't aware that an average of 150 percent of their first year's premiums and 20 percent of the next nine years' premiums go toward agents' commissions, manager overrides, marketing costs, and other related costs. No-load life insurance strips out all of these costs so that you enjoy both lower premiums and cash values equal to your paid premiums, plus interest at fair market rates. No-load life insurance works a lot like a term deposit, yielding slightly higher rates, but has the added benefit of a life insurance death benefit. It can be purchased only through some fee-only financial planners or directly from certain life insurance companies in the United States. You pay a fee for the service of the financial planner, much as you would for hiring any professional, such as an accountant or an attorney, to do a specific job for you.

No commissioned agent should be involved. If you sell your property later, you can generally cash in your policy and walk away with all the premiums, plus a good rate of return.

This method is simple and can be very cost-effective for most couples. Used in combination with the method of establishing appropriate trusts outlined in the next section, it provides a worry-free, easy-to-maintain US estate plan. Most insurance companies would require Canadians to have both a US address and a US Social Security Number or Individual Tax Identification Number for the purchase of the life insurance policy.

ESTABLISH APPROPRIATE TRUSTS

The Canadian spousal trust allows the deemed disposition capital gains tax, ordinarily due at the death of the first spouse, to be deferred until the second spouse's death. In a similar manner, there is also the opportunity to defer US estate tax until the death of the surviving spouse.

The US estate tax deferment is accomplished through the use of a qualified domestic trust (QDOT). This is a very simple trust created either during one's lifetime through a living trust with the QDOT language, through a will, or by the executor of the estate. At the death of the first spouse, the QDOT holds the deceased's share of the US property in trust, under certain IRS guidelines, for the benefit of the surviving spouse for his or her lifetime.

If the QDOT is created under a living trust arrangement, you will achieve the added benefit of avoiding US probate of your estate at either spouse's death, if you have the trust hold all your US property. This is a major side-benefit, as you will avoid the legal and filing costs of probate, which in some states can get as high as 5 percent of the value of the property (not to mention that a probate is a lengthy process and can take years to complete). However, if you are transferring property into the living trust, you may face a deemed disposition tax collected by CRA; check with your cross-border advisor.

A living trust/QDOT designed specifically for Canadian residents, along with a joint and right-of-survivorship title, and a no-load life insurance policy (or a trust in combination with a non-recourse mortgage), may easily be a good solution for coping with the non-resident estate tax. It is very important to use an experienced and qualified cross-border estate planning attorney for drafting any of these documents or providing specific cross-border estate planning advice. These trusts are simple to understand, flexible, economical, easy-to-maintain, and do not operate in any untested or controversial areas of tax law. According to CRA rules, you will need to disclose annually on your Canadian tax return (using Form T1135) that you own foreign property, unless it is used for your personal use only, whether or not it is owned by the trust.

USE EXEMPT US INVESTMENTS

Chapter 7 provides the details of US investments you can use to generate income that is free from both US income and estate tax. Use of these investments will go a long way toward simplifying your estate plan.

Real estate does not fall under the category of exempt investments, so must be dealt with under some of the other estate planning tools.

Remember, exempt investments (unless held in a living trust) could be subject to probate in the US, and all foreign investment and property ownership must be reported to the CRA each year on your tax return.

USE A CANADIAN HOLDING COMPANY

Many Canadians hold US winter homes or similar property by purchasing or transferring the property through a single-purpose Canadian holding company. This is the most complex strategy and was the one most often recommended by lawyers and accountants on both sides of the border. However, in 2005 CRA changed its rules and no longer allows this practice. Those with winter residences already in single-purpose holding companies are grandfathered but no new arrangements of this type will be allowed. From an IRS perspective, owning personal-use real estate inside a corporation was never a good idea and is still not. Corporations must pay capital gains tax at the rate of 35 percent instead of the 15–20 percent personal capital gains rate. In addition, both the IRS and CRA may infer taxable benefits to the shareholders for the personal use of the residence. Those individuals that still do have their US vacation homes in Canadian corporations should seriously consider unwinding this situation to realize better future tax results. One of the trusts noted in an earlier section of this chapter is a far superior alternative than owning your US vacation property through a corporation.

SELL YOUR PROPERTY AND RENT

Selling your property and renting each year may seem a bit drastic, but it can be a very good alternative for some people. It is a simple solution and the only tax consideration may be capital gains tax on the sale of your property. Capital gains taxes in both Canada and the US have a special, lower tax rate than other forms of income and with the current lower Canadian dollar exchange rates a lot of US- owned property has greatly appreciated in terms of Canadian dollars and it may be a good time to lock in these profits, yet keep the funds in US dollars for future lifestyle spending. Review Chapter 4 for the tax rates and filing requirements for non-residents selling real property in the US.

Proceeds from the sale of the home should be put into US tax-exempt investments, to generate US-dollar income to finance future winter stays.

If the death of the property owner is anticipated in the near future, a quick sale to a family member in Canada can be a very smart estate-tax-saving and probate fee reduction move.

ESTATE TAX CONCERNS IN INDIVIDUAL STATES

Several US states do levy their own individual versions of estate taxes on their residents or property located within the state owned by non-residents of that state. Currently, 15 states and the District of Columbia have estate tax and six states have an inheritance tax. These state estate taxes range from 16 to 20 percent, with Washington state being the highest, based on the taxable estate with these states allowing exemptions ranging from $675,000 to the full federal equivalent exemption of $5,450,000. With the exception of Hawaii, all of the US Sunbelt states including California, Arizona, Texas, and Florida do not have any state estate tax so the majority of Canadian Vacationers, Snowbirds, or Settlers will normally have little or no concern with any state related estate taxes. Since states are not party to the Canada/US Tax Treaty, non-resident Canadians that have property in states that have an estate tax such as Washington state and Hawaii may face potential taxes at a state level, with no treaty protection against double taxation and no access to other treaty benefits.

In recent years, several Canadian provinces have separated their provincial income tax systems from the federal system, the way Quebec did years ago, and residents of those provinces must file a separate provincial tax return. As noted above, neither provinces nor states are party to the Canada/US Tax Treaty. Provinces such as British Columbia and Ontario do not allow for foreign tax credits for estate tax purposes. Residents in these provinces would not get any foreign tax credits at the provincial level for US estate taxes paid on the death of the taxpayer. The result would in effect be a double tax. This situation would not have been anticipated in the Canada/US Tax Treaty negotiations that created the new estate tax rules in 1995. Consequently, Canadians and Americans who own property on a cross-border basis need to be acutely aware of the provincial and state estate tax rules where they own property, as well as of the Canadian and US federal rules.

IS YOUR CANADIAN WILL VALID IN THE UNITED STATES?

There are plenty of legitimate concerns among Canadians owning property in the United States about whether their Canadian wills will be valid in the United States at the time of their deaths.

Generally speaking, if your Canadian will has been drafted correctly and is valid in Canada and the province in which it was completed, it will also be valid in the United States. There is no real need to have separately drafted wills for American and Canadian property. There is some merit to having a separate US will drafted in the state you normally reside in under your chosen cross-border lifestyle to simplify the probate process, but having two wills can also create problems, such as when you are trying to convince the courts which one is valid. You will also have to pay for and keep track of two separate wills and your executors will have to find them both and then seek advice on how to use them.

If you do not have a valid will in either country, your estate will be subject to the intestate laws in your place of residence. This creates double work for your appointed executor when there are assets in two separate jurisdictions, such as a Canadian province and a US state. Many people ignore the need for a will or do not look at alternative estate-planning vehicles because they are under one or more misconceptions about wills, joint ownership, and the probate process.

Probate comes from the Latin word meaning "to prove." After a person dies, probate is the process of proving what the deceased person legally owned and how the person wanted his or her property distributed. This proof is accomplished by presenting the will to court for probate. Unfortunately, it isn't always that easy. You may know someone who has been through the frustration and the expense of probate.

To help you better understand wills and the alternatives now available, here are twelve common estate misconceptions that apply whether your assets are in Canada or the US or both:

- **Misconception 1:** Probate costs are low. Wrong! Most personal representatives hire an attorney to help with the paperwork of probate. The laws relating to probate and estate administration are extremely complex for a layperson. So while provincial and state laws allow a personal representative to go through the probate without a lawyer's help, most personal representatives do not want to face this challenge alone and hire a lawyer. Legal fees for even a simple probate taking less than one year can easily reach $5,000 to $10,000 or more. Some states and provinces allow attorneys to charge a percentage of the assets going through probate, rather than their normal hourly rates, regardless of how simple the probate process is. These fees can reach as high as about 5 percent (Florida and California are 3 percent, Arizona is about 0.1 percent) of the value of the assets. Provincial probate fees, depending on the province involved, can add up to 1.5 percent of the value of the estate to the total costs. Total legal fees and other estate administration costs can average from 3 to 10 percent of the total estate value, not including any probate fees, income tax, or death taxes that may also be assessed (depending on the complexity of the probate, the state or province of residence of the deceased, and the property location). Owning property in both the US and Canada increases the complexity of probate.

- **Misconception 2:** Your will and your assets remain private. Sorry! Probate is a matter of public record, so all of your assets and liabilities will be spelled out to the penny in court records. Names of beneficiaries and the amounts of their inheritances are all open to the public. Anyone can go to the court and ask to see your probate file. If you valued your privacy in life, you'd probably find probate uncomfortable and should have your assets owned through the trust which remains private seen only by those authorized by you to see it.
- **Misconception 3:** A will can be probated in just a few weeks. No way! Even with a simple estate, probate can take from ten months to several years. During that time, the deceased person's property must be inventoried, maintained, and appraised. Relatives and beneficiaries must be notified. Creditors must be notified and paid. Income or estate taxes must be paid. Any contested claims or inheritances must be settled. Only then is the property distributed to the beneficiaries.
- **Misconception 4:** A will helps you avoid taxes. Dead wrong! A standard will does nothing to lower your taxes. A properly drafted will, however, may take advantage of certain estate-planning options such as setting up trusts that can save or defer estates taxes. A standard will simply indicates how you want your property distributed and who you want to care for your children.
- **Misconception 5:** A will or a testamentary trust (a trust set up by your will) avoids probate. Not true! By law, all property governed by a will must go through the probate process before it passes to beneficiaries. Some states and provinces, for very small estates (generally less than $50,000), have a simplified or accelerated probate process. The law does not allow minors to inherit bank accounts, stocks and bonds, or real estate. That is why parents often set up a testamentary trust for their children, which holds the property until the children reach the age of majority. But since the testamentary trust is part of the person's will, it still must be probated by the court.
- **Misconception 6:** Joint tenancy is the safest way to own property. Not so! Joint tenancy with right of survivorship exposes each party to the debts of the other. For example, assume you own a home in

joint tenancy with your child. Your child starts a business that goes broke. His or her creditors are chasing, trying to collect the money. The home you own with your child could now be taken away from you to satisfy your child's debts. In addition, as detailed earlier in this chapter, adding joint owners to existing US property can create substantial capital gains taxes in Canada and gift taxes in the US. Also, joint tenancy property must go through probate when the second person dies, or in the event that both people die (in a common accident). As also noted earlier in this chapter, for non-residents owning property jointly in the US, the IRS presumes that the first joint owner to die has the entire property included in his or her taxable estate, unless the executor can prove contributions by the other joint owner or owners — sloppy or inadequate records could mean both higher probate costs and estate taxes.

- **Misconception 7:** Your permanent home and your vacation home can be handled through the same probate. Yes, but only if they are located in the same province or state. If you own a home or property in another province, or in the US, you'll need to open a second probate, which means another lawyer. This usually doubles the probate expense. If you own real estate in a third location, you'll need to open a third probate and hire a third lawyer.
- **Misconception 8:** A will prevents quarrels over assets. Not on your life! Wills are the subject of more lawsuits than any other legal document. Today, it is common for unhappy friends or relatives to contest a will, resulting in higher legal fees and added delays. This is one more reason why the average probate takes from ten months to two years.
- **Misconception 9:** Family members can sell property in the estate to raise money. A fatal mistake! The court freezes the estate's assets until the probate has ended. The court may allow the personal representative to give family members small living allowances, but only up to the amounts allowed by provincial or state law. Permission to pay beneficiaries out of the estate must be granted by the court. Regardless of the outcome, asking the court's permission to sell property increases the legal fees and can take a great deal of time.
- **Misconception 10:** A will from one province is not legal in another or in the US. Untrue! If the will is legal in one province, it is also legal in another, and in the United States. However, if your will contains certain legal language, it can go through probate more

quickly and smoothly. If you want to avoid delays in probate, you might want to have any will that must go through probate reviewed by a lawyer in each province or state in which you own property.

- **Misconception 11:** The cost of planning your estate is only the cost of drawing up your will. Not quite accurate! The cost of any estate plan is both the cost of drawing up the documents and the cost of carrying out the plan. If your will costs $150 in legal fees and the probate costs $5,000, the cost of your estate plan is $5,150. This is a lot more than merely the cost of the will. The will is not only the most common document in our legal system, it is also one of the most expensive.
- **Misconception 12:** You must name your lawyer as your personal representative. No. When you name your lawyer as your personal representative, you are in effect giving him or her your permission to get paid twice — once for acting as your personal representative, and again when he or she acts as your estate's lawyer. You can select anyone you wish to be your personal representative. For convenience's sake, you may want to choose someone who lives in your province or state, as non-resident executors are often required to post bonds before they will be authorized to represent your estate.

LIVING TRUSTS: A SIMPLE SOLUTION TO PROBLEMS WITH WILLS

A living trust is a legal entity formed to hold your property for your benefit while you are alive. After an estate-planning lawyer drafts your living trust, he or she helps transfer your assets into the trust. Property held by a living trust does not go through probate after death.

Here's why: the law says that any property owned when you die must go through probate, with a few exceptions such as joint tenancy property with right of survivorship. When you set up a living trust, property is transferred into the trust and retitled in the name of the trust. So after your death, the property doesn't have to go through probate, because the property is no longer in your name — it's owned by the trust. If you want to manage the trust, name yourself as trust manager or "trustee."

A trust company's involvement is not needed at all. As trustee, you can put property into or take property out of the trust, change the trust, and even revoke the trust, any time you wish. If you want someone to manage the trust for you, you can select a relative, friend, lawyer, bank, or trust company. Normally, both spouses are trustees while either is still living. In the case of death or disability, a successor trustee is named in the trust document, usually the same person who would be your personal representative in your will. While you are living, the operation of the trust provides you with all the same rights to your property, and your personal affairs operate pretty much the same as before the trust was opened.

When you form a living trust you accomplish the following:

- Save your family thousands of dollars in legal fees.
- Save your family months of lengthy court proceedings.
- Keep your family's legal affairs out of court records.
- Protect your family from the dangers of joint tenancy.
- Reduce the likelihood that your wishes will be challenged by unhappy friends and relatives.
- Give your family complete control over the property, because the trust assets are not frozen by the court.
- Avoid added probates for property you own in other provinces or states.
- Provide more efficient management of your estate in the event of death or disability.

As you can see, a living trust can be a very useful tool in cross-border financial planning, particularly when it has the qualified domestic trust provisions mentioned earlier in this chapter (for deferring non-resident estate taxes). Living trusts are a very common estate-planning vehicle in the United States and are routinely recommended by estate planners at all levels. In fact, Canadians wintering in the United States see a continual barrage of advertisements for living trust seminars put on by banks, attorneys, brokerage firms, and financial planners. Some use the living trust as a loss leader to sell other products or services.

A small number of Canadian lawyers and financial planners have started to recognize the benefits of living trusts. For Canadians over 65, CRA is now allowing "alter ego" trusts. These trusts are very similar in both use and design to US living trusts, and they can help people avoid the additional tax reporting that standard Canadian trusts require. Trusts should not be reserved for Americans only. Canadian trusts, like wills, are generally valid in the United States and vice versa. However, if you are going to use your trust to hold property in both Canada and the United States simultaneously, I highly recommend that you use a cross-border financial planning professional to help coordinate legal services such as drafting the documents and transferring the assets, in both your Canadian home province and the US state in which you own property. There may be Canadian tax implications, including land transfer tax, when transferring assets to a trust.

POWER OF ATTORNEY: SHOULD YOU HAVE ONE?

One of the simplest and most useful documents you can add to your estate plan is a power of attorney (POA). This will be of great assistance to you in almost all US states and Canadian provinces.

POAs are very basic documents that give some other person(s) whom you trust the right to transact business or make medical decisions on your behalf if you are physically or mentally unable to do so for yourself. Anyone who has had a spouse or a loved one in this situation may have discovered the long, costly, and frustrating process of going to court to get authorization for a conservatorship or guardianship so they could pay for and implement that person's care. Correctly drafted, a power of attorney should eliminate the need for the conservatorship or guardianship.

To be effective, the POA must be a durable (US terminology) or enduring (Canadian terminology) power of attorney. A durable or enduring POA means that it will be valid even after you become incapacitated, the point at which a non-durable POA would lapse. Please note that any POA, regardless of whether it is durable or not, ceases to be valid the minute the person granting the power of attorney dies.

Many lawyers in Canada and the United States recommend two separate durable POAs, one for general financial needs and one for medical needs. Good estate lawyers will routinely include the proper POAs with the wills and trusts they draft at no extra cost. Have the POAs reviewed and updated regularly (every two to three years) by a lawyer in each of the jurisdictions that they are most likely to be used in, to ensure that they will be valid there if they need to be used. If you have property in more than one province or state, you may have multiple powers of attorney.

Durable or enduring POAs are the kind of documents you hope you never have to use, but when you need them they are invaluable.

WHAT HAPPENS IF YOU DIE IN THE UNITED STATES?

We've covered a lot of ground in this chapter on cross-border estate planning, but what actually happens when a death occurs? How does the IRS find out whether the deceased owned property in the United States?

Whether physical death occurs in Canada or the United States, there is technically no difference with respect to taxes or any other obligations. At the time of your death, either your personal representative (or, if there is a living trust, your successor trustee) has certain responsibilities. This person must do the following:

- Make a separate list of assets in both Canada and the United States and arrange for appraisals of the property.
- Initiate probate, if the deceased did not have a living trust holding his or her assets, in the province(s) or state(s) where he or she owned property.
- Determine what, if any, estate tax or probate fees are due to the IRS and to the state(s) or province(s) at the property's location.
- Arrange for the filing of the final tax returns in Canada and, if necessary, in the United States by the appropriate deadlines.
- Arrange for the filing of the federal and state estate tax returns in the United States if the taxable estate, as defined earlier in this chapter, exceeds $60,000 USD.
- Obtain estate tax clearances for both the IRS and the appropriate state department if property in the United States is to be sold.
- Hire and coordinate the professionals needed to execute all of these responsibilities.

The IRS will normally learn about a death during one or more of the above procedures. The Canadian executor, personal representative, or successor trustee becomes personally liable for any estate tax due if it is not paid correctly from the estate. If there is no specified executor, the tax code states that any person in receipt of a deceased person's property is considered that person's executor, known as a statutory executor. Being an executor can be a very arduous, time-consuming and stressful job so it is extremely important that anyone you ask to be your personal representative or executor understand this and generally what composition and complexity of your estate is and be provided with all the necessary resources to do the job. If the executor is a family member make sure the other siblings, family members, and/or beneficiaries understand the legal and time constraints of going through an estate settlement process and give the executor their full support without complaint.

There is an automatic and conveniently invisible estate tax lien the IRS attaches to all US property of the deceased. These liens, even though they may not appear as being attached directly to the property title, must be satisfied before the property is released. If a personal representative wants to sell the property before the estate is finalized, he or she will be required to obtain federal estate tax clearance and may face withholding taxes of up to 40 percent. The withholding tax may be refunded after the estate is settled by filing the appropriate returns.

The CRA gives the personal representative six months from the date of death or until April 30 in the year following the date of death, whichever is sooner, to file the final Canadian tax return of the deceased and to pay any tax due. The IRS requires that the non-resident estate tax return, Form 706-NA be filed within nine months of the date of death, although they do offer an extension of up to six additional months. Incidentally, estate tax returns are audited at least ten times more often than regular tax returns. The IRS routinely audits nearly 100 percent of all larger estate tax returns because collecting the extra taxes can be lucrative, and since the owner of the assets is deceased it is their last chance to settle any outstanding claims.

WHAT IS A GIFT TAX?

Throughout this chapter we have referred to gift taxes. Most Canadians are not familiar with this terminology, but they hear it mentioned frequently in the United States. Gift taxes are paid by the giver/donor, not the recipient/donee.

The US gift taxes are unified with US estate tax which means that one can transfer up to the estate tax exemption of $5.45 million USD of assets during their lifetime or at death not both. Gift tax applies to a transfer of property during one's lifetime, while estate tax applies to the transfer of property after one's death. The rates for gift taxes are identical to the estate tax rates (provided in Figure 5.2, earlier in this chapter). The lifetime exemption or any portion thereof, if used up through gifting, is not available for use as an estate tax exemption after death. There is no lifetime gift tax exemption for non-residents of the US through the Canada/US Tax Treaty as there is for estate tax.

In addition to the lifetime exemption, there is an annual gift-tax exemption of $14,000 USD of US property per donor, whether resident or non-resident of the United States, to any recipient the giver chooses. For example, a married couple with one child could give $14,000 USD each to the child tax-free each year and not reduce their lifetime estate or gift tax exemption. Non-US residents, non-citizens, and citizens alike are allowed to give an annual tax-free gift of $147,000 USD in property to a non-US citizen spouse. US citizens and residents can gift unlimited amounts of cash or property to a US citizen spouse tax-free at any time without affecting any of their gift or estate tax exemptions.

Canadians are subject to gift tax rules whenever they give or transfer any US real or personal property that would normally be included in the estate of the individual doing the gifting. You should be careful and plan transfers of US property accordingly. As noted earlier, adding children's or spouse's names to the title of US property would be treated as if the property were given as a gift. There are severe penalties for failure to pay this tax, and ignorance of the law will be of no help to you if you are caught; if this happens, the entire value of your property could go to the government in the form of penalties, interest, and taxes, when you were just trying to save a few dollars in probate fees.

CREATING OR RECEIVING A CROSS-BORDER INHERITANCE OR GIFT

Every year I receive numerous inquiries from parents who live in Canada, whose children or other beneficiaries live in the US (or vice versa), and they want to know the tax implications of this situation. I also hear from the children or beneficiaries who want to know what tax obligations they may face if they receive a gift or an inheritance from Canada while they are living in the US, or from the US if they are living in Canada.

Generally speaking, once an estate is settled and all taxes have been paid by the estate representative, the remaining estate can be dispersed to beneficiaries whether they live in Canada or the US without any further tax obligations to either the CRA or the IRS. This general rule also applies to cross-border gifts in either direction as long as the donor has complied with US gift tax rules in the case of a US donor and with respect to the CRA deemed disposition rules for a Canadian donor. Only if the donor (in the case of the gift) or the executor (in the case of an inheritance) has not complied with the gift or estate tax rules of their particular country, are there any tax obligations conferred to the recipients or donees. Both the CRA and the IRS have rules that may require recipients or donees of gifts or inheritances to pay the tax obligations of the donor or the estate, respectively, if the taxes were not paid correctly before the gift or the inheritance was received.

US resident beneficiaries of Canadian estates or recipients of Canadian gifts in excess of $100,000 are required to file IRS Form 3520, Annual Return to Report Transactions with Foreign Trusts and Receipt of Certain Foreign Gifts, due by the normal filing date of April 15th, or including extensions October 15, of your US tax return for the tax year the inheritance or gift was received. Although Form 3520 is strictly a reporting form and no tax is due by filing the form, failure to file Form 3520 comes with substantial penalties ranging from 5 percent of the amount of the gift to 35 percent of the amount of the inheritance. In 2008 the IRS began a campaign to tighten up compliance by US residents for failure to file Form 3520 when required and is aggressively assessing penalties that they used to waive with voluntary late filings. Consequently, prompt filing should not be ignored under any circumstances.

Border Guide readers are encouraged to participate in a cross-border Q&A through the new Cross-Border Forum, which is a platform where, after registering, you can easily post questions about the contents of this book. Questions will be moderated and/or answered by a cross-border financial planning professional in a timely fashion. You can also post comments or create discussions with other Border Guide readers to share experiences and swap cross-border financial planning tips. To post a question or comment, go to keatsconnelly.com and click on the Cross-Border Forum tab at the top of the first page.

CROSS-BORDER Q&A

SEPARATE POWER OF ATTORNEY IN THE UNITED STATES

I have a will and a power of attorney for property in Ontario, Canada. Will these be acceptable in Florida if needed? My property is a condo and a bank account in the United States.

— J.W., Fort Pierce, Florida

Your will, if a valid will in Ontario, would normally be accepted as valid in the state of Florida. Your power of attorney may or may not work in Florida depending on what you want to do with it and what the requirements are at the condo association and the bank. I strongly recommend you draft an additional Florida power of attorney prepared or reviewed by a Florida attorney for use in that state. You should also show the new power of attorney to the condo association and the bank to see if they would act on it if necessary. It is not worth taking the risk that your Ontario power of attorney would not work in Florida when it is needed.

CANADIANS OWNING US STOCKS MAY BE SUBJECT TO US NON-RESIDENT TAX

The following applies to a Canadian citizen and resident, with no real estate holdings in the US.

Upon his death, will his estate be subject to US taxes? The estate includes approximately $150,000 in the stocks of US corporations (e.g., Exxon), and has a world wide value of slightly over $1.5 million. If not subject to US taxes, will his executor be nevertheless required to file documents with the US authorities?

Also, is it correct to assume that Canadian corporate stocks (e.g., Royal Bank of Canada) held in US dollars and traded on the NYSE through a Canadian brokerage account, will not attract US estate taxes whatever their value or the overall estate's value, at the time of the above owner's death? If so, will there nevertheless be reporting requirements to US authorities for the executor?

— Andre M., Ottawa, Ontario

This is a very thoughtful question that many Canadians need to consider when doing their own or any family member's estate planning, as US non-resident estate taxes on shares of US companies are often missed until it is too late.

In a straight technical sense, that person you are referring to is subject to US non-resident estate tax strictly on the US stocks you have mentioned. However, because it appears that the person you are referring to has a worldwide estate of less than $5.45 million USD, he will likely have no US estate tax to pay providing his executor files for the exemption allowed under the Canada/US Tax Treaty. The Canada/US treaty now gives Canadians access to the same worldwide exemption as US residents and citizens, which currently stands at $5.45 million USD. The key here is that the executor must file a US estate tax return with Form 706-NA, declaring a treaty exemption from the IRS that will allow them to receive the larger deduction (otherwise this person would only have a $60,000 USD non-resident deduction under US domestic tax rules). Filing this US estate tax return can be an expensive complication to an estate plan and can be avoided with some simple planning ideas (for example, doing a tax-free rollover of the US stocks to a Canadian holding company or selling them to another family member). The Canadian stocks that are traded on any US exchanges are not included as US estate taxable property for non-residents of the US, but they obviously will be included in the total value of the world wide estate to determine whether the estate goes over the $5.45 million USD exemption limit from the treaty.

As a sidebar to this question, Canadians often ask "How does the US IRS know that the deceased person owned US stocks?"

The short answer is that when someone dies owning US stocks, their executor must go through a US transfer agent to transfer the stocks to the estate or the beneficiaries of the estate. The US transfer agents must ensure that any estate tax has been accounted for before the transfer to the new owners is complete. If the transfer agent fails to do so, they can become responsible to pay the tax due. Therefore, they are very careful not to transfer the stock ownership until they know for sure that the IRS has cleared them to do so. Also, if the executor tries to deliberately get around or fails to comply correctly through ignorance to pay the US estate tax, then he or she takes on the liability for the tax once the IRS catches up with them (and under the Canada/US Tax Treaty, the IRS can come into Canada to collect the taxes and penalties due from the executor or the beneficiaries whichever they can get their hands on first).

DOES A LIVING TRUST SATISFY CRA?

What will happen to my property, in terms of taxation, when I die? According to information I have gathered from attending estate-planning workshops, I could have a living trust. However, I need to know if this would satisfy CRA or the Ontario government. These questions could not be answered by the American financial planners I have asked.

My house and property are located in Arizona, where I would like to live for eight months of the year, instead of the usual six months less a day. How would I apply for resident alien status? My efforts to reach US Immigration by telephone have been thwarted by their computer answering system.

— Morris C., Lake Havasu, Arizona

You are correct in thinking that you should have a living trust as part of your estate plan. You can use this trust to hold both Canadian and US assets. You need to be aware that CRA considers most transfers into a living trust a deemed disposition unless you are over 65 and use a Canadian alter ego trust or are married and create a spousal trust. Consequently, if you have any potential capital gains in the property you are transferring into a non-alter ego/spousal trust, you will be subject to Canadian tax when you complete the transfer. If you are transferring your personal residence, you will have no Canadian tax to pay. Items such as term deposits, GICs, and bank accounts can be transferred in without tax consequences, and the tax on income earned after the transfer can be either paid by the trust or passed on to you individually.

If your trust is set up correctly, it will allow your estate to avoid probate in both Canada and the US. A desirable goal for most people.

Since you are likely to be trustee of your own trust, the trust will be a resident of the same country as you. If you are earning income from assets in a non-alter ego trust, you will be subject to different sets of reporting requirements depending on your residency and that of the trust. If you have Canadian bank term deposits in the trust and you are a resident of Canada, your trust will file Canadian tax returns to report the interest earned. If you passed this interest through to yourself personally, the trust would issue a T3 slip and you would ultimately pay the tax on your personal return. The trust would pay no tax, as the interest earned on the term deposit would be offset by a deduction for the interest paid through to you, but it would still have to file its own return. Alter ego trusts are not considered separate taxpayers by CRA, and all income flows through the trust as if he or she earned it directly. For alter ego trusts, no tax returns, other than a basic reporting form T3, need to be filed with CRA.

It is much simpler if you are a US resident with a US bank deposit. The IRS does not require the trust to report interest earned if you report it on your own personal tax return, which cuts out any unnecessary duplicate reporting. Also, transfers of property into a living trust are not considered deemed dispositions and are allowed without tax consequences.

As far as your chances of immigrating to the US, you will likely need either a business or family sponsor to give you a realistic chance at a green card. Your best option for immigration might be the EB5 legal resident status, often referred to as the "Gold Card," which is simply a green card that requires a qualified investment of $500,000 USD. There are no green card lotteries in the near future that I am aware of in which Canadians will be able to participate.

CAN A CANADIAN RESIDENT GIFT TO THEIR US RESIDENT CHILD WITHOUT INCURRING US GIFT TAX?

If a Canadian citizen living in Canada gives $20,000 to their adult child who lives in the US and is a Canadian citizen, is this gift subject to the US gift tax? The adult child pays US taxes and has a green card.

— Elaine T., Toronto, Ontario

Neither you nor your child in the US is subject to any gift tax on your generous cash gift. To make this comment, I assume that you are Canadian residents and are not US citizens and you were never a US citizen that expatriated, and that the cash is not coming directly from US real estate. US gift tax only applies to US residents or citizens gifting an amount in excess of their annual exclusion of $14,000 USD, or their lifetime exclusion of $5.45 million USD. It can also sometimes apply to Canadians gifting US real estate and if any tax is due it is paid by the donor, not the donee.

WHERE THERE'S A WILL, THERE'S A WAY

I am a Canadian citizen and I own property in Florida. May I legally bequeath this property and money to a relative who lives in Europe? If so, is a will appropriate or is there another way to accomplish this?

— Arne I., St. Petersburg, Florida

You may bequeath your Florida property to a relative in Europe. You can pass on the property via your will, or by forming a simple trust. From the information you've provided, the only real advantage of the trust would be to avoid the expenses of probating your will in Florida. Your executor or representative will have to file a US Estate Tax IRS Form 706-NA and pay any US non-resident estate tax if your US property exceeds the $60,000 exemption (unless the Canada/US Tax Treaty allows for a greater exemption, which can be obtained by filing the US estate tax return Form 706-NA and claiming treaty benefits). The tax, if any, would have to be paid before the property passed to your European beneficiary. If you did not make a provision in your will to pay any US estate tax and/or Canadian deemed disposition tax on this property from other funds in your estate, the Florida property would likely have to be sold to pay the taxes.

CALCULATING THE NEW TREATY EXEMPTION

We are Canadian citizens who are permanent residents of Ontario, but spend about six months in Naples, Florida; we own a condo there.

Could you please advise me of the actual exemption for estate taxes that now applies? You referred to $60,000 USD in the tenth edition of The Border Guide, *but implied that this could end up higher for non-resident aliens.*

— A.E.B., Naples, Florida

Under the 1996 amendment to the Canada/US Tax Treaty, Canadians can now get two major benefits to help them reduce their US non-resident estate tax. The first benefit is that they get a crack at a higher estate tax exemption than the $60,000 you mention in your letter. However, to determine whether you can get this higher exemption you must use a basic formula: US taxable estate, divided by worldwide estate, multiplied by the current US estate tax exemption of $5.45 million USD, equals your non-resident estate tax exemption.

For example, if your condo is worth $250,000 USD (and it is your only US estate taxable property) and your worldwide estate value is the equivalent of $1 million USD, your non-resident exemption would be $250,000 (taxable estate) divided by $1,000,000, (worldwide estate) times the US estate tax exemption of $5,450,000 = $1,362,500 USD. This exemption is available to both spouses, so if you can prove that you each paid for half of the condo (and didn't just put it in joint names), you can each calculate and use your own individual exemptions to reduce or eliminate any US non-resident estate taxes. In general, as you can conclude from the formula, only those Canadians with larger worldwide estates have diminishing benefits and could likely get only the $60,000 minimum exemption, whereas those Canadians with estates of less than $5.45 million USD could get the full exemption and pay no US non-resident estate taxes. In certain circumstances, transfers between spouses can qualify as the equivalent of a double exemption.

The second benefit from the 1996 treaty amendment, is that if you do have to pay US non-resident estate tax, you will get a credit for it against a Canadian deemed disposition of your US property at death. The treaty gives you relief from paying the Canadian deemed disposition tax, which can reach 26 percent of the appreciation on your US property if you are fortunate enough to have bought when property values were low and/or the Canadian dollar was higher than its current value.

Be careful with the formula noted above; it is deceptively simple. There are items that you could never expect to include in your worldwide estate — for example, death benefits from life insurance you own for which you are the insured — and you have to file a US estate tax return (Form 706-NA, Estate Tax Return) to get the exemption over the $60,000 limit, which could subject your entire worldwide estate to IRS audit.

CHANGING TITLE AND US TAX OBLIGATIONS ON FLORIDA PROPERTY

I am a Canadian who lives seven months per year in Ontario and five months in Sarasota. I owned our house in Florida jointly with my husband, who passed away recently. How do I remove his name from any ownership documents? Also, I think my house would sell for $225,000 to $250,000. Please tell me the Florida laws that apply to Canadians.

— Doreen A., Sarasota, Florida

Since you owned your Florida property jointly with right of survivorship and are now the sole owner, you can simply have the title changed at your local county recorder's office. They will require a copy of your deceased husband's death certificate and have you complete a basic form that varies from county to county.

You didn't say whether you had filed IRS Form 706-NA, Non-Resident Estate Tax Return, and took an exemption for the US non-resident estate taxes. This form needs to be filed within nine months of a death unless you received an extension. You would need to prove to the IRS that you paid for your half of the jointly owned property with your own cash. Otherwise, the entire value of the property will be included in your deceased husband's estate. Form 706-NA details how to calculate the non-resident estate tax due.

You would be wise to get an appraisal of the Florida property, including the contents, as of the date of your husband's death. If the value of your deceased husband's share of the US assets exceeds the non-resident estate tax exemption of $60,000 (as it appears it does), you will have to pay tax starting at 26 percent of the amount that exceeds $60,000. Although your filing will be quite simple, I recommend seeking professional help to complete Form 706-NA, as it can be rather intimidating. Remember, if you have taxes due, interest and penalties for late filing will keep accruing, so you should get started as soon as possible. The Canada/US Tax Treaty should allow your deceased husband's estate a greater exemption than the current $60,000 if you file the US Estate Tax Return (Form 706-NA). Ask a cross-border legal professional for an assessment as to whether or not the Treaty will be of benefit to you in this situation. Don't forget about the Canadian deemed disposition tax if your property accrued any capital gains before your husband's death (your deceased husband's cost basis in the property is automatically rolled over to you; however, you can elect to get up a stepped-up basis in the cost basis to fair market value at his death if that is to your advantage).

CANADIAN TAX OBLIGATIONS WHEN SELLING FLORIDA PROPERTY

As a recent widow, I plan on selling my Florida home in the near future, if the real estate market improves. I could use up-to-date information regarding the sale of real estate concerning Florida sales taxes and Canadian capital gain (or loss) taxes. What is the advisability of changing the deed from joint ownership to a family member to avoid paying estate taxes? Is this change made through a Florida lawyer or my lawyer in Ontario?

— Veruca S., Chatham, Ontario

This question is similar to the previous one with respect to US tax obligations and filing requirements for a widow with Florida property. However, since you are intending to sell the property, you must deal with the US non-resident estate obligations as well as US income tax rules once the property is sold. For US purposes, when you sell the property, you actually do get a free US income tax holiday on your husband's share of this property as the IRS gives you a free step-up in cost basis to the fair market value at the date of your husband's death. Consequently, from the US perspective, you would only have US capital gains tax to pay on your portion of the sale proceeds. However, from a Canadian perspective taxable capital gains would be the capital gains tax on both the appreciation of yours and your deceased husband's share of your Florida property as adjusted for the differential in Canadian/US dollar exchange rates from the date of purchase to the date of sale. US income taxes for non-residents are due by June 15 the year following the sale of the property and of course Canadian taxes are due by April 30 year following the sale.

Changing the joint ownership with right of survivorship from your deceased spouse to another family member could cost you a hefty US gift tax if you do it all at once. If you are transferring US property either while you are alive or through your will, you are subject to transfer tax in the form of a US gift or estate tax, respectively. These taxes are levied at the same rates, with the gift tax having a $14,000 annual exclusion and the estate tax a $60,000 once-in-a-lifetime exemption for a non-resident (the Canada/US Tax Treaty allows for a greater estate tax exemption). Consequently, if you transferred the property (worth say $200,000) to a family member, it would be considered a gift of $200,000 and would attract tax on $186,000 (the fair market value of the property of $200,000, minus the $14,000 annual exclusion). The gift tax starts at 26 percent or around $50,000 and must be paid by filing IRS Form 709.

You would probably be much better off selling a share of the residence to the family member and avoiding this potential problem. If the family member has no money, you can loan him or her the funds in Canada and take back a promissory note.

As always, we recommend you seek professional advice before you make any changes. A good US estate-planning attorney in Florida should be able to advise you on your best course of action, but it will be easier for you if you can locate an estate attorney that is permitted to legally practice in both your Canadian province and Florida.

PROBLEMATIC TRANSFER OF US PROPERTY TO DAUGHTER

I acquired a Florida condominium from my mother that cost her $50,000 in 2006 and is now worth $150,000. I am often told that the condo should also be in someone else's name to avoid any complications should I pass away. This practice seems to be commonplace. What are the possible complications? Are the Canadian taxes equivalent to what I would pay on a second *home in Canada? Do I have to pay taxes in the US if I pay them in Canada? I look forward to your response.*

Clarifications:

1. *I acquired the condo from my mother. At first, she transferred it to me, and in return she retained the right of usufruct. Last year, she gave up this right.*
2. *The condo is in my name.*

I think this information would be helpful to many Quebecers who own a home in Florida. Thank you in advance.

— Lise A., Montreal, Quebec

When you acquired the property from your mother, there were tax implications that appear to have been overlooked. Since your mother gave you the property, it would have been considered a deemed disposition for Canadian tax purposes, and she would have needed to pay Canadian income taxes on the increase in value since she originally purchased the property. In the US there would have been no income tax on this transfer, but your mother would have had to pay US gift taxes, which can be as high or higher than the Canadian income tax on gifts of real US property.

The Canadian income taxes need to be calculated based on the difference between what your mother purchased the property for and the fair market value at the time of the transfer to you. The US gift taxes are based on the full, fair market value at the time of transfer, minus the present value of her right to live on the property. When your mother gave up the right to use the property, there would also have been a Canadian taxable deemed disposition and a US gift tax based on the fair market value of her right to use the property. If the Canadian and/or US tax returns have not yet been filed, you are leaving an open back door for CRA or the IRS or both to come after you and/or your mother for the tax and penalties, which could be substantial, possibly up to and beyond the value of the property. Just because it was extremely easy for your mother to transfer the property to you, you should not be complacent in dealing with these complex tax implications since as long as you fail to file the proper returns there is always a hidden but powerful tax lien by the IRS on this property until the proper returns are filed in any taxes due paid.

I recommend that you get some professional cross-border tax help to voluntarily get into compliance with CRA and IRS rules as soon as possible. I realize this isn't good news and sounds really complex, but is better you know now rather than much later, as the longer you leave it, the worse it may become. You are correct in noting that it is common practice to complete these sorts of transfers for various perceived benefits, but as you can see it is a virtual minefield when one is not familiar with all the Canadian and US rules that apply.

Now that the condo is in your name, it is likely best you leave it as such, as trying to just put it someone else's name creates all the same issues as noted above but in reverse with you being subject to the US gift taxes.

Yes, you are somewhat correct that owning a US property has much the same tax consequences as owning a second property in Canada. However, the IRS gets first swing at the income taxes on a sale or rent of US property and any tax you pay to the US is normally a full credit against any Canadian tax on the same property income.

CANADIAN LEAVING INHERITANCE TO US BENEFICIARY

If you leave money to a member of the family in the US when you die, how is that taxed? Is there a set sum for all of the US or is it governed by state rules? Is there any way of making this easier? I would appreciate it if you have any knowledge on this and could help me.

— Charles H., Regina, Saskatchewan

There is no US tax for the US beneficiary on any inherited funds, regardless of the amounts that you leave or the US state that your family member is located in providing you were never a US citizen that expatriated. However, before the funds leave Canada for the US, your executor will need to ensure that all the Canadian tax on your estate has been paid to CRA and the province(s) in question.

You may want to consider the formation of a testamentary trust through your will for your family member in the US. Without a correctly drafted trust, if this person were to die, be sued, or get divorced the day after he or she received the funds from your estate, all or part of the money could go to a creditor. This kind of trust is very practical on amounts over $500,000. Depending on the trustee you choose for the trust, a trust below that amount tends to be a bit expensive to maintain.

Your family member in the US will have to file IRS Form 3520 in the year in which he or she receives the inheritance from you. There is no tax due when submitting Form 3520, but failure to complete it could result in a 35 percent tax penalty on the amount of the inheritance.

IDAHO PROPERTY INADVERTENT GIFT

My husband and I purchased recreational property in Idaho in 1999. In 2002 we added the names of our three adult children to the title of the property. The adjusted cost basis (ACB) was $26,000 CAD at that time. Market value was $35,000 USD to $40,000 USD. Since that time we have made improvements of $54,000 CAD (total ACB $80,000), of which 75 percent has been paid by my husband and me. Market value today is estimated $200,000 to $225,000 USD. If either my husband or I were to die, what would be the tax consequences in Canada and the US? If we were to gift our share of this asset to our children, what would be the tax consequences? Is there a gift exemption in the US? Would there be a Canadian deemed disposition along with the US gift tax and carry-over basis? If we sold the property how would the taxes be handled? Could my husband and I claim this as our personal residence?

— Joan M., Calgary, Alberta

I suspect your situation is much more complicated than you may have imagined, as you have several issues that you appear to have not dealt with, probably primarily because you were not aware of them. I am sure you know, though, that tax departments in Canada and the US don't have any sympathy for those who don't know the rules.

First, you made US taxable gifts to your children at least twice; once when you put their names on the title in 2002, and again when you made improvements without them contributing to the cost (in proportion to their ownership shares). If the value of these respective gifts was less than $14,000 USD to each child from both you and your husband (at the time when they were given), then you have no US gift tax to pay, but you should have filed US gift tax returns to confirm and document all of this with the IRS. For US tax purposes the children carry over your cost basis to themselves, and so at the time of sale they will pay the capital gains tax in proportion to their percentage of ownership (or, in your case, on 20 percent of the gain of what you paid for the property, plus the cost of the improvements). In other words, all five owners would have exactly the same US capital gain to pay tax on when the property is sold. If you still owned the property at the time of your and/or your husband's respective deaths, the one-fifth shares that you and your husband owned would receive a free step-up in basis to fair market value at the time of death, for US tax purposes. If either or both of your worldwide estates are less than $5.45 million USD, your children would have no US non-resident estate tax to pay upon your deaths providing they completed the proper US estate tax return, Form 706-NA.

From a Canadian tax perspective you should have paid deemed disposition taxes when you made the gifts to the children, based on the difference between the gifts' original costs and their fair market values when they were given. The children then get a new basis for Canadian tax purposes, equal to the fair market value at the time they received the gifts. Consequently, you and your husband have a different tax basis for CRA purposes than your children. CRA might want to collect the deemed disposition tax that may have been due back at the time of both of the inadvertent gifts, and you could be charged interest and penalties. At the time of your and your husband's respective deaths, each of your one-fifth shares will go through a deemed disposition and capital gains tax will be due to CRA on the date of death (based on the difference between the cost and the fair market value of your property, upon your deaths).

If you gave your children your two-fifths of the property before your deaths, you would still go through all the same US and Canadian tax issues as when you made the original gifts (as noted earlier).

My recommendations would depend on whether your children are likely or unlikely to use the property after you and your husband are gone or no longer able to travel. If they are unlikely to use it, it would probably be best to sell the property before your deaths, and take credits under the Canada/US Tax Treaty for taxes paid to the US on each of your five respective Canadian tax returns. One final complication is that the State of Idaho will also tax the gifts, the estate, and/or the gains on any sale according to their own rules for these kinds of situations.

As you can see, this all gets very complicated. I strongly recommend that you get professional help whenever putting your children on a US property title or whenever you are going to sell US property. This is not a do-it-yourself procedure.

Doctor in the House 6

Getting the Most from Out-of-Country Medical Coverage

One of the most perplexing matters for Canadians choosing any of the three amazing cross-border lifestyles — Vacationers, Snowbird, or Settler — in the United States is medical insurance. Americans moving to Canada can, after a 90-day wait (in most provinces; New Brunswick now has no waiting period), simply join the provincial medical system. There appears to be an endless squeeze in both Canada and the US between medical services provided and the costs of those services. This squeeze guarantees that the areas of travel insurance and medical insurance are complex and constantly changing.

The last thing people need to worry about when they travel is becoming ill or suffering an accident. Unfortunately, sickness and accidents respect neither your travel itinerary nor your socioeconomic status. A medical emergency can happen anywhere, at anytime, and to anyone!

Any unforeseen expense is important to today's traveller, and you will want to be protected no matter how great or small the potential loss. Minor problems, such as the loss of luggage, can be a traumatic experience for many travellers, ruining their holidays or business trips. However, a catastrophic illness or an accident outside Canada can turn a relaxing trip into a financial nightmare.

For Vacationers and Snowbirds, the Canadian insurance industry has now consolidated into about a dozen committed and professional companies, offering 20 to 30 plans. Current provincial medical coverage for Canadians while outside of Canada is listed in Figure 6.1 along with phone numbers and websites you can consult for more information.

Many travellers are unaware of the need for adequate travel insurance or they hope they will never need it. While provincial health and hospital programs may provide adequate benefits at home, a Canadian in trouble outside the country may discover the provincial plan covers only a small portion of the actual medical expenses. As illustrated in Figure 6.1, provincial plans vary considerably with respect to the amounts paid outside Canada. Prince Edward Island was the first province to reimburse travellers at provincial rates of reimbursement, and currently still pays the most for out-of-country medical services. A few provinces have followed suit under pressure from their residents, but still no provinces have matched Prince Edward Island's reimbursement schedule for out-of-province travelers. Most provinces pay out-of-province hospital bills, at around $100 per day. This is only a small fraction of what hospitalization actually costs, especially in the US, where medical expenses may easily exceed $2,000 per day. In most US hospitals, $100 a day would barely get you a parking spot, a bed pan, or a couple of aspirins. Canadians should be aware that in many parts of the world, physicians and hospitals do not follow the Canadian system of billing, where the daily room charge is all-inclusive and covers most services and treatments. Many hospitals outside Canada charge a fee for room and board, and then charge for every procedure, examination/consultation, and bandage they use. In the past, the Ontario Health Insurance Plan and other provincial plans have not only reduced the portion of these costs that they pay, but they have also made it more difficult to collect reimbursement. More people had to rely on their travel insurance for the entire medical bill, emphasizing the need to obtain travel insurance before you leave Canada.

Travellers who purchase token medical insurance plans may discover that the plans they purchased are inadequate or do not cover them when they need hospital and medical treatment. Your bargain medical insurance may be instead a simple trip cancellation or flight accident insurance policy. Many of you have heard stories of Canadians who were forced to mortgage their property or worse in order to pay for US medical expenses. The purchase of proper travel insurance not only reduces financial risk, but provides peace of mind as well.

Many Vacationers or Snowbirds purchase travel protection as a supplement to their provincial medical plans before heading south for the winter. The typical insurance plan has an expiration date of less than six months although with most provinces allowing Canadians to be out of province for up to seven months, extended policies are relatively easy to obtain. Premiums have become quite costly, and a typical married couple aged 65 can expect to pay between $4,000 and $6,000 for a six-month policy, depending on the company and deductible chosen. Numerous travel insurance plans are available through travel agencies, insurance companies, the Canadian Automobile Association, the Canadian Snowbird Association, the Canadian Association of Retired Persons, and premium credit cards. The types of coverage and premiums can also vary widely.

PROVINCIAL HEALTH INSURANCE PLANS
HOSPITAL BENEFITS OUTSIDE CANADA

- **British Columbia** 800-663-7867; www.gov.bc.ca/health: $75/day as well as a small payment by the B.C. Medical Services Plan for services rendered in the emergency room before admission.
- **Alberta** (780) 427-1432; www.health.alberta.ca: $100/day.
- **Saskatchewan** (306) 787-0146; www.health.gov.sk.ca: $100/day, outpatient — $50/day.
- **Manitoba** 800-392-1207, ext. 7303; www.gov.mb.ca/health: 1 to 100 beds — $280/day; 101 to 500 beds — $356/day; 501 or more beds — $570/day; pays the greater of 75% or per diem in the case of referrals only.
- **Ontario** 866-532-3161; www.health.gov.on.ca: $400/day for "high level" care; $200/day for outpatient care.
- **Quebec** 800-561-9749; www.ramq.gouv.qc.ca/index_en.shtml: $100/day, including surgery in a day hospital.
- **Prince Edward Island** (902) 368-6130; www.gov.pe.ca/health: $959/day regardless of bed capacity.
- **New Brunswick** (506) 457-4800; www.gnb.ca/0051: $100/day; higher rate possible but requires prior approval.
- **Nova Scotia** 800-387-6665; www.gov.ns.ca/health: $525/day for hospital bill and 50% for ancillary charges such as X-ray and lab bills.
- **Newfoundland** and Labrador 800-563-1557; www.health.gov.nl.ca: $350/day maximum.

All provinces cover medical expenses outside Canada to 100 percent of the provincial level.

FIGURE 6.1

Most plans have benefit limits of $2 million to $5 million for covered medical expenses, although some plans have no dollar limitations on benefits. Terms may range from 24 hours to a maximum of one year. Premiums are based on the age of the travellers — usually with categories for those over age 65 and those age 65 or younger — and may also depend on the number of people in a party. Nearly all carriers require you to purchase your coverage before you leave Canada. Don't assume that the association in which you are a member has the best medical plan for you. More often than not, you will get better coverage through a travel insurance broker, who can give you quotes from many companies as well as provide you with information on the claims-paying experience. Many associations change underwriters every year, so claims paying can vary greatly from year to year. Several associations tend to make the sale of travel insurance a key source of annual income, so they may tend to pressure members into thinking they must get the travel insurance from them even when they know there are better policies elsewhere. Here are some places to start: kanetix.ca, caa.ca, carp.ca, and snowbirds.org.

Not all policies are alike, and you often need to work through a maze of costly options to ensure coverage for all major travel hazards. Here are some pointers to help you through that maze:

- You get what you pay for. Buying the lowest premium may get you inadequate coverage. However, just because a plan is expensive doesn't mean it won't have gaps in its coverage. Premiums alone should not be the sole criterion for purchasing travel insurance.
- For Canadians with reasons to return to Canada one or more times during a visit to the US, tagging up with a multiple trip annual plan can result in substantial savings verus a single-trip plan. A 30- or 60-day multiple trip plan compared with a 120-day single trip plan can reduce premiums by 50 percent or more.
- Look for a policy that covers all of the expenses that your provincial plan does not, with no limitations on standard doctors' fees or daily hospital expenses.
- Check the upper limit of the policy. A few policies have total benefit limitations as low as $25,000, so you'll have to pay any costs beyond that amount that your provincial plan doesn't cover. Even a brief emergency stay in a US hospital can exceed this limit. Claims paid by travel insurance companies for hospital stays in the US have been over $750,000 (for claims such as heart bypass operations with complications). So as long as your upper coverage limit is higher than this amount, you should be okay.
- Choose the highest deductible available from an insurance carrier. Canadians are conditioned to think they must have no out-of-pocket expenses regardless of how small the claim. Since small claims are relatively expensive to process, you'll pay through the nose for a low or no-deductible policy. You'll pocket big savings by sharing a small amount of risk. Particularly on higher premium policies, choosing deductibles up to $10,000 can reduce premiums by close to 50 percent.

- Review the "exclusions" clause of your policy very carefully. Many policies will exclude coverage for any prior medical condition or pre-existing condition, as insurance companies like to call them, which means any condition that has been treated by a doctor within the past year (or some other specified time period). If you had a bypass operation several years ago and have an annual checkup by your doctor, any hospital stays that are even remotely related to your heart may not be covered.
- If you have a pre-existing medical condition, look for a policy that will at least provide you with emergency coverage for that illness up to a specified dollar amount. If you are uncertain how your pre-existing condition will be covered, call the underwriting department of the company and ask to be medically underwritten so that your conditions and the coverage will be spelled out in advance, eliminating surprises. Be absolutely clear and honest about any conditions or treatment you have had or are currently having, and do not be tempted not to mention a pre-existing condition when signing up for travel insurance. A five-minute telephone call may save you thousands of dollars. Be very leery of insurance companies that don't complete some form of medical underwriting using detailed questioning in their applications. These companies are the most likely to decline claims related to pre-existing conditions, as they try to do their underwriting after a claim is made. On the surface, such plans may appear to be easy to qualify for, but you may be denied coverage later. There is definitely an inverse relation between the difficulty and detail required in the application form and the number of claims paid — the harder it is to get through the detailed application, the more likely your claim will be paid once you are accepted for coverage.
- Talk with friends and other travellers who have made a claim through the insurance carrier you are considering, to see whether they were treated fairly and if their claims were paid on time.
- Don't expect miracles from insurance companies when submitting claims. Most will pay only according to the letter of the policy and have highly structured claims systems to prevent fraud. Some companies pay only after the provincial plans have paid their portion of the claim. Only British Columbia, Ontario, and Quebec allow insurers to bill them directly on your behalf. With payments from Ontario and some other provinces running many months behind, payment from private carriers will, as a consequence, also be slow.

The better travel insurance carriers will pay your claims quickly, without waiting for provincial plans to pay up.

- Look for a few of the better travel insurance carriers that have set up claims-paying offices and have negotiated payment schedules with hospitals in the more heavily populated winter visitor areas in the US. This will often mean much faster claims processing. Instead of you paying the hospital and waiting months for reimbursement, you pay nothing and the carrier pays the hospital directly. This valuable service is worth asking for when shopping for travel insurance.
- Some provinces have reduced the repatriation allowance for Canadians returning to Canada for further medical treatment. It currently costs about $15,000 to fly a patient back to his or her home province from the Sunbelt. Check your policy to see whether you are covered for the portion your provincial plan won't pick up.
- Look for a plan that has a toll-free or collect emergency assistance telephone number manned by the insurance carrier itself, not by a third party. It can be very reassuring to have a 24-hour hotline that you can call if you need assistance or wish to verify coverages. Often hospitals will call this line for you and establish any necessary liaison between you and your insurance provider.
- Most companies have early-bird rates if you purchase your insurance well in advance of traveling. For example, major carriers will give you last year's rates before the new season's rate increases if you purchase before mid-August for upcoming winter travel. Rate increases for many years have been in the 10 percent range or higher, so these early-bird savings can be significant. When purchasing policies in advance, be aware of your obligation to notify the insurance company if your medical condition changes prior to your designated travel date in your policy.
- Be aware that most travel insurance companies operate with age bands so depending on what age band you are coming up against, waiting to purchase a policy after your birthdate may be costly. For example, purchasing a policy at age 64 versus age 65 or at age 69 versus age 70 can result in more than 30 percent in savings.
- Travel insurance tends to include coverage for things that may not be useful or important to you at all. For example, trip cancellation or lost baggage coverage may add as much as 25 percent to your travel insurance premium, yet if you're driving your car down to

your vacation home in Florida, this coverage does you absolutely no good. Shop for policies that don't have these kind of whistles and bells that add unnecessary costs to your insurance.

- Finally, review the policy's cancellation procedures. Many policies are canceled automatically the minute you use them if you don't return immediately to Canada after the treatment. For example, say you went to an emergency room when you thought you might be having a heart attack and it turned out to be indigestion. If you wanted to stay the rest of the winter in the Sunbelt like you had originally planned, you might find your insurance company canceling your policy automatically and leaving you without coverage for the remainder of your stay.

MEDICAL COVERAGE FOR THE MOST AMAZING CROSS-BORDER LIFESTYLE

Without your health, nothing else matters! This phrase was said to me by a client, who passed away more than 25 years ago, and it has sat on my desk as a reminder that one's health should never be taken for granted and it is important to get things fixed with your body when they are broken, by the best professionals you can find. So whether you are a Vacationer, Snowbird, or Settler, finding the best medical coverage for any kind of a cross-border lifestyle is extremely important. Over my many years of doing medical insurance planning for individuals in all three of these cross-border lifestyles I have found that when medical stuff happens those individuals that have the most flexibility, a large choice of doctors, specialists, or hospitals, and access to immediate medical services without waiting or lineups are the ones that not only have better lifestyles, less pain and suffering, but also more often than not, longer lifetimes. Because they have gotten medical attention immediately when they needed it and with the best services they can live the quality cross-border lifestyle they desire.

How does this happen when particularly Vacationers or Snowbirds who have access only to their Canadian system in the area in which they live, with long waits to see their primary doctor or specialists, to get tests or required surgeries, and then also have to pay for travel insurance to cover emergency coverage when outside of their home provinces? Settlers often use these travel plans as their best option but normally they will get full US coverage as residents as noted in the next section of this chapter.

My recommendation for perhaps the best life-saving medical coverage to achieve this very important part of the most amazing cross-border lifestyle is rather than purchasing travel insurance they purchase comprehensive, year-round medical insurance coverage. These policies cover individuals 24/7/365 for the doctors, hospitals, and other medical services anywhere in the world so they have complete freedom to go wherever's best to get timely quality medical services. These worldwide policies, even though they cover you 365 days a year, are not that expensive compared with the price of travel insurance, which only covers emergencies for specified shorter trips outside of the home Canadian province. These policies will certainly replace travel insurance and actually can replace your provincial Canadian provided medical coverage, particularly in those provinces that demand you pay a premium for your Canadian coverage as many provinces have decided to charge over the last several years in an attempt to offset rising costs. In 2015, Ontario, for example, introduced a 3 percent levy on income over $100,000 including a $100 deductible and a $6.11 co-pay for its OHIP member drug coverage; for those over 65 that used to be free. Alberta, in the same year, has increased monthly premiums to most everyone significantly for the same reasons.

I've already talked about the cost of travel insurance in the previous section of this chapter and where and how to shop for it, This year-round comprehensive worldwide medical insurance coverage is available through a network of brokers that can place policies with different insurers around the world. If you choose a high deductible plan, which I certainly do recommend, the annual cost for a 65-year-old individual with no pre-existing conditions is around the same monthly cost as one of the better travel insurance policies, particularly if you choose a high deductible policy. The premiums, as with travel insurance, vary greatly with deductibles and the company chosen, but a recent informal review of the rates shows a 60- to 64-year-old individual can get coverage with the highest deductible for less than $4,000 USD annually.

Once you are on these policies you generally are guaranteed to be able to renew them annually regardless of medical conditions up to age 75 or 80 depending on the insurance companies. Contrast this guaranteed renewability with travel insurance where there are no guarantees that the policy will be or can be renewed at all; and the travel insurance only goes for generally a maximum of six months before you must get a completely new policy and go through medical underwriting again (when you could be refused coverage entirely).

Although these worldwide policies give full coverage and can be renewed in the US, they must be purchased while you are a resident outside of the US. In the next section there is a referral call number and email of a very reliable insurance agent who handles these policies and has done so for readers of *The Border Guide* and many of my clients for more than 25 years.

How nice would it be for your cross-border lifestyle if you needed a hip replacement and you could choose the hospital, have a private room in that hospital, get the latest surgery techniques from the best available surgeons, and schedule the surgery for a time that is convenient for you and your family, not just the doctor and the hospital as is normally the case in Canada? As you are most likely familiar with the Canadian medical system, besides extensive waiting lists to see doctors, specialist referrals, then tests, then surgery, etc. You may be waiting months, or longer, in pain when you could just hop on a plane and go down to the Mayo Clinic and be fully recovered before you even see a surgeon in most Canadian cities. We've had several clients over the years do this and it works incredibly well to enhance their cross-border lifestyles and lets them take advantage of the best of the Canadian and the US medical systems.

INSURANCE FOR CANADIANS MOVING TO THE UNITED STATES

There are a great many myths about Canadians finding effective and affordable medical insurance when they take up permanent residence in the United States. I have prepared plans for Canadians for a number of years and have successfully discredited most of these myths. We have been able to develop a variety of alternatives that ensure Canadians receive the best of both medical systems.

With the passing into law of the controversial US government-run US medical insurance, the Affordable Care Act in March 2010, president Obama has provided a very important benefit to Canadians wishing to move to the US. This benefit was not specifically intended for Canadians but Canadians who legally immigrate to the US will be able to get access to "affordable" health insurance regardless of any pre-existing conditions or age. Canadian Vacationers or Snowbirds who decide to become Settlers and immigrate to the US have immediate access to medical insurance coverage. So far it has worked very well for Canadians even with several pre-existing conditions, and we've had clients get access to it well over the age of 80 with premiums in the \$500–\$1000 range monthly, even when they are no longer eligible for Canadian travel insurance. This is extremely valuable for living the cross-border lifestyle because for most Canadians, once they reach 80 and have any kind of pre-existing condition, (and just about everyone has something at that age), there are virtually no options available for travel insurance.

I recently had a conversation with my 87-year-old uncle who very much enjoyed a regular Snowbird lifestyle to the US for over 30 years, but now has had to cease his cross-border lifestyle because he just cannot get any Canadian travel insurance for himself and his wife. He said he feels trapped in Canada, particularly when it's 40 below in January in Saskatchewan, where he lives. There are lots of options with deductibles and companies that offer these plans, so it can be confusing to figure out which option is be best for you.

Canadians and Americans like to constantly debate which country's medical system is best. My nearly 40 years' experience in this area has taught me that you can never answer this question unless you can determine when, where, and what medical assistance you will need in advance. Of course, this is the million-dollar question, because if you knew when, where, and what illness you were going to have, you could shop the medical purveyors in advance in either country to get the best care. However, this is equivalent to trying to plan your spending in retirement so that the last cheque you write on the day you die bounces. By combining the best benefits from both countries and planning so you can easily access both countries' medical systems, you can obtain the best protection with maximum flexibility that meets your chosen cross-border lifestyle. Many Canadians currently enjoying Vacationer or Snowbird lifestyles may wish to become Settlers just to access the full US medical system through this new opportunity created by the Affordable Care Act. (Review Chapter 8 for possible visa or green card opportunities to assist those who desire the Settler lifestyle.)

Canadians over 65 who have resided in the United States legally for at least five years, or who are US citizens, are eligible for complete US Medicare regardless of any pre-existing conditions. The cost is approximately $600 USD per month each, or $110 USD per month each if you or your spouse has contributed at least the minimum amount to US Social Security programs on US employment earnings. (See Chapter 15 for more information about qualifying for US Social Security.) There are also numerous private insurance carriers that provide Medicare supplements to fill any gaps in US Medicare coverage. If you do not qualify or are waiting to qualify for US Medicare and are over 65, the Act policies or the worldwide health insurance policies are available to provide coverage until fully qualified for US Medicare.

A good health insurance broker knowledgeable about both US and Canadian health issues can be of great assistance to those who are considering living in the US.

We have used a very good broker for the past 25 years who has helped Vacationers, Snowbirds, and Settlers get full US medical coverage in even the most difficult of situations. Through working with us to solve cross-border health insurance issues, he has become as close to an expert as you will be able to find in this unique area. His name is Bill Norgaard, of Norgaard Insurance Services, and you can reach him toll-free from Canada and the US at 1-877-679-7900, or email bknorgaard@qwest.net.

Those heading to the US for employment will generally have excellent medical coverage available from most large employers' group plans.

WHAT HAPPENS IF YOU GET SICK IN THE UNITED STATES?

Contrary to what you might have been led to believe by some Canadian media, you will not be left to die in the streets because you do not have large buckets of cash when you arrive in the emergency room of a US hospital. It is the law in every state that you cannot be turned away from an emergency medical facility because of your ability to pay for your emergency treatment.

If you are a Vacationer or Snowbird using a travel insurance company with an emergency assistance line, your first call should be to them as soon as possible after entering the hospital.

If you are unable to make the call, instruct someone else to do it for you. Usually the hospital will have trained personnel to deal directly with the insurance company for you, since they have a vested interest in getting paid. The travel insurance company can be invaluable in providing you with reassurance, finding medical specialists, or just getting you home in the shortest possible time.

If you do not have travel insurance, contact your provincial medicare office during business hours at the first possible moment. It won't be quite as easy as contacting a private insurance provider with a 24-hour hotline, but you should receive some valuable assistance nonetheless.

Be careful not to overdo it with medical treatment that can be deferred until you return to Canada, unless you have purchased one of the year-round, full-coverage policies discussed earlier in this chapter. Out-of-province travel medical insurance will not cover elective procedures, so you could be doing it at your own expense. Once again, if you are not sure what is or isn't covered, call the emergency assistance line and confirm the treatments that will be covered.

If your condition has stabilized and your doctors agree that you are well enough to travel, your insurance company and/or the provincial medicare services will make arrangements to have you flown back to Canada for follow-up treatment. The insurance company will normally make arrangements for loved ones and your car to return to Canada.

Generally, you are exempt from any adverse consequences from the IRS or United States Immigration if your stay in the United States has to be extended beyond normal limits for medical reasons, and as noted in Chapter 2 your extended stay days in the US because of a medical condition that occured while you are in the US are not counted in your Substantial Presence Test when you file your IRS Form 8840.

Border Guide readers are encouraged to participate in cross-border Q&A through the new *The Cross-Border Forum,* which is a platform where you can easily post questions about the contents of this book, which will be answered by a cross-border financial planning professional in a timely fashion. You can also post comments or create discussions with other *Border Guide* readers to share experiences and swap cross-border financial planning tips. To post a question or comment, go to keatsconnelly.com and click on the *Cross-Border Forum* tab.

CROSS-BORDER Q&A

SOME CAN MAKE USE OF BOTH OHIP AND US MEDICARE

My wife and I are US citizens by birth and have resided in Ontario for 18 years, with landed immigrant status. By virtue of our residency and my working prior to retirement, we enjoy full benefits of several senior programs, including OHIP and the Ontario Drug Benefit Plan.

Since retirement, we have been spending our winters in Florida. Each year we purchased out-of-country supplemental health insurance. Two years ago, as these premiums began escalating, we reinstated our US Medicare insurance, both Parts A and B. My reasoning at that time was that while in the States, Medicare would be our primary insurance provider, with OHIP as the supplemental coverage. I then confirmed that this was a valid approach, first by asking Medicare, followed by the questions to OHIP. Medicare advised that primary coverage would be forthcoming at the time of need, the same as for any US citizen with the same coverage; however, they could not respond to the supplemental coverage from OHIP.

The OHIP office I spoke to advised that, indeed, it is a valid plan. The routine would be to obtain duplicate originals of all bills, so that after submitting them to Medicare and receiving reimbursement, the second set of originals, along with documentation showing Medicare reimbursement, would be submitted to OHIP. OHIP would then determine their allowable share of the costs and reimburse accordingly.

My question is this: Have you had any information from correspondents that would indicate problems with this arrangement? If not, it might be helpful for others in like circumstances to look into. We do pay a small penalty for not having taken Part B at age 65, but it's negligible compared to buying supplemental insurance on the Ontario market!

— Lee F., Port Huron, Michigan

Your Medicare strategy is a sound one that gives you full access to both the US and Canadian medical systems any time you need them. Since US Medicare has no rules requiring you to be present in the US for a certain time period each year, you only have to ensure you follow OHIP rules and are residents of Ontario without being out of province more than seven months each year. It is economically wiser to use US Medicare supplemented by OHIP instead of OHIP supplemented by travel insurance, as 12 months at $110 per month for US Medicare is a lot less than 6 months of travel insurance, and provides you much better coverage. As US citizens living in Canada, please don't forget to file your annual US tax returns as required by the IRS.

HEALTH COSTS OFTEN RAISE US COST OF LIVING

My concern is whether it is affordable for dual citizens to live here year-round. As you know, medical costs are covered in Ontario by OHIP. I have never paid toward medical coverage in the United States.

— L.M.A., Lauderhill, Florida

US Medicare, available to all US citizens and legal permanent residents (of at least five years) after the age of 65, does cost approximately $600 per month if you have never paid into the US Social Security system. With the required 40 quarters of US Social Security credits, the cost of US Medicare drops to approximately $110 per month for Part B only, with Part A provided at no cost. However, HMOs (Health Maintenance Organizations) usually do not charge extra and are contracted to provide you with complete medical coverage for only the premium you are paying to Medicare, plus small fees for doctor visits and drugs. US Medicare does not provide for long-term care beyond 100 days, so private insurance should be obtained for this, which can add $200 to $400 per month in premiums. Long-term care insurance should be purchased regardless of whether you are a Canadian or US resident, so this cost is not really an extra expense of US residency. Insurance premiums can be a deductible expense for those US filers who itemize their deductions.

Even though OHIP appears to be free, it is not. It is paid for by income tax, employer health tax, and other tax revenues. Those looking to live in the United States need to understand exactly what they are paying for in Canada and just how much it is costing them. You should calculate whether the US taxes you'd pay at your income level would drop sufficiently to produce a net savings, after accounting for increased US medical expenses. Generally speaking, if you have not paid enough US Social Security to receive Medicare Part A at no additional cost, lower US income taxes will not be sufficient to cover the medical costs, unless your annual income is more than $70,000 (for you, and if applicable, a spouse). With Medicare Part A paid for, the income tax advantage falls to those couples with about $50,000 total taxable income per year. Cost is only one of the factors that should be considered with respect to this medical coverage, since as a US citizen you would have access to any US medical facility with facilities and specialists that may not be available in Canada under OHIP, or there may be a long wait time.

RESIDENT ALIENS MAY FIND MEDICARE PROBLEMS

I am a Canadian citizen, 72 years of age, with resident alien status and a Social Security Number in the United States. I have tried and failed to get Medicare. I pay my taxes in Canada and return to Ontario for the mandatory period to retain OHIP. My son is a US citizen, and for what it is worth, a commander in the US Navy. I have no family or relatives in Canada; he was the one who sponsored me. I am in good health, but the problem could arise that I would become incapacitated. There is no one to care for me in Canada, and my family worries about this. Is there any point in discussing this with OHIP? I am prepared to continue paying my taxes in Canada and fulfill any criteria that may be necessary.

— P.M.S., St. Augustine, Florida

You did not say how long you have held your resident alien status, more commonly called a green card. If you have had your green card for at least five years, you are entitled to apply for and receive US Medicare since you are over 65. Assuming you qualify for US Medicare, you would have to pay the full premium of approximately $600 per month. You didn't say whether you were ever employed in the US, or have a spouse who was employed there. Those who contributed to Social Security through wage deductions, or whose spouse contributed, pay only approximately $110 per month for both parts of US Medicare. A Medicare supplement is generally also recommended, which can cost you another $100 to $200 per month, depending on the company and extent of coverage taken. A Health Maintenance Organization (HMO) that contracts with Medicare can provide the supplemental coverage at no additional monthly cost.

US Medicare does not cover long-term nursing care, so if you are going to give up OHIP, you should purchase insurance from a wide choice of private insurance companies to cover this potential risk. You can buy this now whether or not you have US Medicare.

If the cost of US Medicare with supplemental and long-term care insurance is less than the savings in income tax and annual travel insurance premiums, you will come out ahead financially by moving to the United States. Aside from not having to file returns in Ontario, you will also achieve your goal of being close to your family in the United States.

There is no provision in OHIP to allow for persons in your situation.

If you haven't had your green card for five years, there are many insurers available to you under the Affordable Care Act, until you have spent the qualifying amount of time in the US.

RESIDENT ALIENS MAY NEED HOSPITAL INDEMNITY INSURANCE

I am under the impression that in order to use your advice, the planning has to start sometime before the actual date of leaving Canada. Is this correct?

My wife and I are quite happy with our present situation of living six months each in the US and Canada. If for financial or medical reasons we had to choose one place, it would be Florida. But we want to be prepared.

I can get fairly good medical-only coverage through my former place of employment. Is it possible to obtain hospital-only coverage down here? Our ages are 73 and 72.

— John W., Fort Pierce, Florida

Yes, there are several good companies with hospital indemnity-type policies for anywhere from $100 per day to several thousand dollars per day for hospital stays; premiums can be quite reasonable. Also, check with the American Association of Retired Persons (AARP), 1-800-424-3410 or online at www.aarp.com. Most policies of this kind cannot be applied for after age 75, so don't wait much longer to start your planning with a knowledgeable cross-border financial planning practitioner before you leave Canada. If you need some help locating an insurance company for this coverage, give us a call and we can put you in touch with a broker.

SNOWBIRD MUST QUALIFY FOR US SOCIAL SECURITY, MEDICARE

I am a Canadian, age 56, spending my first year as a "Snowbird." I hope to spend five to six months in Florida each winter. I would appreciate your answers to the following:

1. *In the 1980s I worked in the United States and have earned 35 credits of Social Security benefits. I understand 40 credits are required to receive retirement and Medicare benefits. Can my work life in Canada contribute to my US credits? Can I receive Social Security benefits from the United States and also from Canada? I worked full time in Canada from 1990 to 2010.*
2. *If I need to work longer in the US to qualify for benefits, I hope to be able to do so. I no longer have a green card, but for the Social Security benefits it may be worth the effort to apply. Can you comment? My son (age 25), born in Canada, has an American father. Will his dual citizenship make my application for a green card any easier?*

I appreciate any information you can give me.

— J.L., Cocoa Beach, Florida

1. Since you already have 35 quarters of credit for US Social Security, you may, as early as age 62, use the Canada-US Social Security totalization agreement (a Social Security treaty between the two countries) to apply for a reduced Social Security pension. However, the totalization agreement does not include US Medicare, so you would be required to obtain the full 40 quarters of credit to qualify for free Part A Medicare at age 65. However, since you do have more than 30 quarters of credits, you do qualify for a one-third reduction in the standard Part A premium of $450.
2. In order to get your final five quarters for a full Social Security pension and Medicare, you could work in the US for a year plus one quarter. To work you will need to get another green card. Your son can sponsor you for one without a long waiting period providing he tells US Customs and Immigration Service that it is his intention to live in the US currently or in the near future.

You may have another angle for a full Social Security pension and Medicare. If you were married to your ex-husband for more than ten years and he qualified for Social Security, you can get a benefit of half of the amount he is entitled to receive, plus Medicare. This benefit would not affect the amount he would receive, so you should have no problem getting it if he qualifies. Also, 50 percent of his benefit could actually be more than 100 percent of your reduced benefit.

DOES A CANADIAN SPOUSE RECEIVE MEDICARE?

I live on the Maine-New Brunswick border. My fiancée lives on the New Brunswick side. We spend most of our time together and winter in Florida. We would like to get married and live in the United States.

However, my fiancée has MS and depends on the New Brunswick government for medication and medical services. Would she receive Medicare help here in the United States if we were to get married? Could she use the same hospital and doctors if Medicare were to help? I'm 59, disabled, and on Medicare.

— Joe C., St. Agatha, Maine

Your fiancée can become eligible for US Medicare. However, the following requirements must be met first: She must be 65 or over, you must have been married for at least one year, and you must sponsor her for a green card. This assumes that you would also be over 65 and on US Medicare at the time you apply for your fiancée's coverage which means you may have a five or six year wait to get your future wife fully covered in US. Your fiancée would need a good Medicare supplement to ensure complete coverage of hospitals, doctors, and medicine. It is unlikely she will be able to use the same doctors she has now if she is on Medicare. This coverage is generally only for expenses incurred in the United States, so she would need to establish new relationships with US doctors near your Florida home. US Medicare Part D can usually provide the medication your wife will need at little cost or no cost; alternatively she could be covered entirely with an insurance policy under the Affordable Care Act.

Take the Money and Run 7

An Investor's Guide to the United States

The Canadian dollar has been fraught with uncertainty for most of the past three decades. At the turn of the century, it had declined to record low levels against its US counterpart, and then in early 2003 decided to rocket over 50 percent very briefly to the high 110 cent range by 2007. Then, in late 2008, it fell to $0.76, virtually in lock step with the price of oil and back to par with the US dollar in early 2010 as oil reached near $100 per barrel. In 2015 and 16 as the price of oil fell below $30 a barrel the Canadian dollar followed relatively closely into the low/high 60 cent range. Few experts had predicted such a significant increase in the value of the Canadian dollar in so few months followed by such quick decreases. The major reasons for the dollar's volatility are as varied as the number of economists you can find to talk about it, but common themes are that the US dollar also fluctuated greatly against other major currencies, there were wide variations in the price of oil and other commodities, and Canada's ability to largely sidestep the 2008/2009 great recession in the real estate market. Currently the Canadian dollar is performing reasonably well against the Euro but the US dollar, for various reasons, has been the strongest currency in the world leaving most currencies' measurements against it appearing weak.

Since the Canadian economy relies heavily on exports of commodities, in particular oil and gas, the Canadian dollar has recently been dubbed the "Petro" dollar. Consequently, the Canadian dollar is subject to a great deal of volatility since the price of its commodities vary greatly with world economics and demand. The real truth is that no one really knows which way the Canadian dollar will head. At best, experts can only somewhat consistently predict the general direction of short-term trends.

Since the Canadian dollar continues to be subject to wide swings in relative value against the US dollar, you may want to take a good, hard look at investment opportunities across the border, particularly if you are attempting to set up the most amazing cross-border lifestyle as a Vacationer, Snowbird, or Settler. With the Canadian dollar around 40-year averages, this may be the time to use the Canadian dollar to shore up your US-dollar investments before it falls again below its long-term averages.

THE INVESTMENT OPTIONS

Canadians often lack the confidence to invest across the border. They may opt for putting available US funds into US currency savings accounts at their local Canadian banks, where they'll earn a meager 0.5 percent interest. By doing this they also give up the security of Canadian Deposit Insurance Corporation (CDIC) insurance. Contrary to what some bank employees may tell you, no Canadian bank or trust company offers CDIC insurance on any US-dollar account.

This chapter is intended to help Canadians take advantage of US investment opportunities, while minimizing or eliminating any adverse income tax and non-resident estate tax consequences. Chapter 3 discussed the need to protect yourself against a fluctuating Canadian dollar and how to obtain the fairest rate of exchange. Now I will focus directly on the major investment options in the US, in the context of the income and estate tax implications for Canadians who have chosen to live a cross-border lifestyle. Chapter 14 helps Canadians who become Settlers/ residents of the US with many of the investment options in the US.

CERTIFICATES OF DEPOSIT

Term deposits, or guaranteed investment certificates (GICs), as they are known in Canada, are called Certificates of Deposit (CDs) in the United States. CDs are issued by most US banks, trust companies or credit unions.

Interest on CDs is guaranteed. Rates currently range from .05 percent to 2 percent, depending on term selected. CDs are insured by a government agency, the Federal Deposit Insurance Corporation (FDIC), for up to $250,000 USD per bank and account holder. The FDIC is similar to the Canadian Deposit Insurance Corporation (CDIC). However, the CDIC's insurance limit is $100,000 CAD or about $70,000 USD.

By filing an Internal Revenue Service (IRS) Form W-8BEN, Canadian non-residents who invest in CDs or other similar accounts are totally exempt from paying US income and non-resident estate taxes.

Unlike most Canadian GICs, funds invested in CDs are not normally locked in and are fairly liquid. However, if you withdraw principal before a CD matures, you may be penalized and could lose one to six months' interest earnings. Currently, with the higher rates available in the US, it is a great time for Canadians to obtain an additional 0.5 or 1 percent interest on their fixed deposits by investing in US CDs.

MUTUAL FUNDS AND EXCHANGE TRADED FUNDS

Mutual funds are diversified portfolios of professionally managed investments of any variety, or mixes of stocks and bonds. Also known as investment funds, they are very similar in both Canada and the US. However, the mutual fund investor in the United States has a much broader choice, with more than 10,000 funds currently available. That should be more than adequate to suit any investment objectives with any level of risk.

Some US-dollar mutual funds are available through your Canadian broker or advisor, provided you do not mind paying higher commissions and higher annual expenses on the US-dollar funds available in Canada.

Many mutual funds in the US have been purchased through a typical broker/investment salesperson and have commission levels around 4 percent or less. Many are available to the investor at no sales cost on either purchase or liquidation. These are known as no-load funds. True US no-load funds will not have any sales charges at all, either on the sale or after the sale in the form of trail commissions paid annually to a broker or salesperson. The Canadian definition of no-load funds is much more liberal, and has relatively inadequate fee disclosure rules than what the US Securities and Exchange Commission permits for investors in the US; Canada allows for very large commissions, very high expense ratios, and trail commissions paid to brokers and agents. When investing in mutual funds, read the detailed version of the prospectus before you invest and be aware of all the fees payable at the time of purchase, upon withdrawal, and on an annual ongoing basis. There is great diversity in how individual funds charge fees, so careful shopping can save you a great deal of money. Canadian mutual funds on average charge fees typically in the 2 to 3 percent range per year while US funds are typically half that with some good index funds available for less than .05 percent per year.

Finally, through consumer pressure, Canadians are going to get a much fairer shake on how, when, where and how much the investment industry charges fees to the investing public. On July 15, 2016, the final implementation of the Client Relationship Model (Phase 2), "CRM 2," by all Canadian provincial and federal regulators force all investment dealers and portfolio managers to provide an annual summary of all charges incurred by the investor. The summary must include all trail commissions, referral fees, and other compensation received by the dealer that relates to the client's account. Even though it seems logical that Canadian financial institutions should have been providing this information to their investors voluntarily, these new rules will force a much better disclosure to allow Canadians the ability to choose their investments much more wisely. It is my belief that once Canadians see the outrageous amount of fees and commissions charged they will become much better financial consumers and these costs across the board will become much reduced and much more competitive, allowing Canadians a similar access to what US investors have had for decades. It is also my personal opinion that these new disclosure rules for CRM 2 do not go far enough because most all of the broker dealers and portfolio managers are owned by or affiliated with the six major Canadian banks, which creates many areas where the banks take fees and other expenses from their investors that are not part of the CRM 2. Types of major things the banks still do not wish investors to know and are still not required to disclose under CRM 2 are such things as spreads or markups on securities they sell to the public; the fees they collect from underwriting stocks and bonds that they sell to investors; profits on loans they receive from companies they are selling to you; foreign exchange fees as noted in Chapter 3; profits/fees on checking, savings and money market accounts they earn from investors, and the list goes on. These undisclosed fees can be extremely high to the investor and very profitable to the bank, for example the markup or spread on a bond that you might buy from the bank owned brokerage firm could easily be as high as 5 percent and nowhere would you see where the bank collected this markup. Consequently, on the purchase of $100,000 of bonds a fee as high as $5,000 (in addition to the commissions that would be disclosed) could be charged without the investor knowing about it. If there were full disclosure on these kinds of fees it would allow a Canadian investor to either decide to pay the 5 percent or shop the market to see whether somebody else could sell the same bond for 1 percent or a flat fee like $100, as is often easily negotiated by US investors. A side note to this disclosure discussion, there are few firms like my planning firm that operate in both Canada and the US that have provided better than CRM 2 disclosures for years, not because it was required but because it was the best thing to do for the consumer regardless of which side of the border they were investing on.

It is important not to ignore the drag on your investment portfolio that is caused by higher fees on mutual funds and other investments in Canada. For example, if you are able to choose a good index fund that reduces your annual expenses by 2 percent on a $100,000 portfolio, assuming a 6 percent annual return, your money will double to $200,000 in roughly 12 years or about six years earlier on the lower-cost portfolio than the one with the extra 2 percent drag in fees. With compounding, this gives you about a 50 percent greater return on your investments. Over one's working career this higher compounding rate could mean the difference between being able to retire comfortably and start your cross-border lifestyle at age 60 or being forced to wait until age 70 or even later. In the lower interest and/or return environment we have been in for the last decade, the drag of higher fees on mutual funds and other similar investments has been magnified.

There is also the relatively new form of investments called exchange traded funds (ETFs) that are portfolios of stocks or bonds that primarily follow either customized indexes or popular indexes such as the Toronto Stock Exchange Index or the Dow Jones Industrial Index. They are similar to mutual funds; however, ETFs trade like individual stocks and have several cost and tax advantages over mutual funds. ETFs, because they trade like stocks, can be bought at any stock exchange in either Canada or the US. This is not possible with mutual funds, as Canadian mutual funds can only be purchased in Canada and US registered mutual funds can only be purchased in the US. A large number of US ETFs have management expense fees as low as 0.05 percent per year, while most Canadian ETFs have fees ranging around 0.6 percent with a few as low as 0.1 percent. Still, this is less than you would spend on mutual funds, particularly if Canadians purchase US ETFs. These lower costs, liquidity options, and tax advantages may spur you on to add some US-domiciled ETF funds to your investment portfolio. In a flat or down market, paying the higher Canadian management fees can absorb most or even all of your total return available from that particular market.

If you are considering investing in mutual funds in the US as a non-resident, you'll find that without a US address and Social Security Number (SSN) or Individual Taxpayer Identification Number (ITIN), you'll have difficulty at most brokerage firms. For this and other regulatory reasons, we recommend non-residents enjoying the Vacationer or Snowbird lifestyles buy ETFs through a Canadian or online brokerage firm.

Returns from mutual funds or ETFs aren't guaranteed and will fluctuate according to market conditions. Many growth funds averaged a gain of 10 to 15 percent on an annual basis during the 1990s and beyond. The 2008–2009 market crash obliterated a good portion of the gains accumulated over the previous decade. It should be noted that the 1990s was a very unusual period in history for investors, with both stock and bond returns well above long-term averages. In the current very low interest-rate environment and with lower corporate profits on stocks, investors of all types should reduce their expectations going forward and adjust their financial plans accordingly. Funds will generally have negative returns one year for every two positive years, so should be considered long-term investments not to be dropped at the slightest downturn. These returns are a result of economic conditions and the type of fund managed.

Interest and dividend distribution from US mutual funds and ETFs earned by non-resident investors that are held outside of retirement or pension type investments like RRSPs (US investments held inside of Canadian RRSPs can generally have any non-resident withholding tax reduced to zero by filing the form W8-BEN with the investment provider), are subject to a 15 percent US withholding tax that can be taken as a full tax credit on your Canadian tax return. From an IRS perspective, capital gains and capital gains distibutions are tax-free in the US for Canadian non-residents, but all capital gains must still be reported to CRA. Mutual fund and ETF investments in the US — whether or not purchased in Canada — may also be subject to non-resident estate tax on amounts exceeding $5.45 million USD, including all other US property as outlined in Chapter 5. The Canada/US Tax Treaty has added US stocks, including mutual funds and exchange traded funds, to the list of investments that Canadians can make that are exempt from non-resident estate tax. This applies only to Canadians whose world estates are less than $1.2 million USD. I will take a closer look at investments that are exempt from both US income and estate taxes in a later section of this chapter.

MONEY MARKET FUNDS

Money market funds are offered by both banks and mutual fund companies. When purchased through a US bank, these accounts are merely daily-interest savings/checking accounts. They are currently paying no more than 0.5 percent interest and are insured by the FDIC if purchased through a bank.

Money market mutual funds in the current very low rate environment yield even less than bank money market accounts, but hold various types of short-term government and corporate securities directly. There is no FDIC insurance on money market mutual funds, but if you select a portfolio of strictly US government securities, the underlying bonds have a similar government guarantee without the FDIC's $250,000 limit.

Money market mutual funds are fully liquid and there are no sales charges to get into or out of a fund. Many also provide free check-writing services. For non-residents, it is much easier to open a money market account at a US bank than elsewhere.

LIMITED PARTNERSHIPS

US limited partnerships (LPs) are similar to Canadian LPs. They offer an opportunity to participate directly, with limited liability, in various businesses and investments, while providing professional management.

A non-resident investing in American LPs will be required to file a US non-resident tax return since they are considered to be doing business in the US, whether or not taxes are due. Taxes paid in the US will give Canadian taxpayers a corresponding credit on their Canadian returns providing there was Canadian taxable income from the partnership.

Rates of return and safety factors for the LP investor will vary as much as the types of LPs available. Great caution is advised when choosing an LP, and professional advice from a qualified investment advisor or Certified Financial Planner is highly recommended.

LPs are considered long-term investments and generally require you to commit your investment until the LP matures, normally five to seven years or beyond. They are more suited to resident investors, but a large number of them will accept non-residents. The fair market value of an LP may be subject to non-resident estate tax on those individuals who have worldwide estates of more than $5.45 million as provided by the Canada/US Tax Treaty as explained in Chapter 5.

REAL ESTATE

Real estate investments in Canada and the United States depend on the same three principles: location, location, location! Investors must do their homework in order to be successful. This location question transcends the Canada/US dollar exchange rates as well. Just because exchange rates are currently not as good as they were a few years ago for Canadians it does not mean that the location of their real estate investment should ignore US real estate investment opportunities; each property purchase should be weighed considering all the factors. Real estate prices in most Sunbelt areas are still a relative bargain compared to many Canadian cities even after currency exchange is considered. No real estate, regardless of location or how it is purchased comes with any guarantees of positive returns and if leverage/borrowing is used could you could lose part or even all of your investment.

Canadians choosing to invest in the United States will find much more paperwork than they may be accustomed to because of the many consumer protection regulations that Canada has not yet adopted. They may also encounter some unfamiliar terminology. For instance, rather than using an attorney to complete the paperwork, most US investors are required to use the services of a title insurance or escrow company. They complete the necessary paperwork and provide trust services for the equitable exchange of funds between buyer and seller. They also provide the mandatory title insurance required to ensure there is clear title to the property. The buyer typically pays for this insurance, which can range from $500 to $1,000 or more on an average residence.

Marriage involves less paperwork than divorce, and real estate is easier to purchase than to sell from the paperwork side as well. When a Vacationer or Snowbird/non-resident sells property in the US, he or she is required to file a non-resident US income tax return, Form 1040NR, reconciling capital gains or losses in the year of sale. Review Chapter 4 for more detailed discussion on the paperwork for Canadians who are not Settlers renting or disposing of US real estate. Without proper clearance certificates from the IRS, the non-resident may be subject to federal and state withholding taxes. These US filing requirements are in addition to the normal Canadian filing requirements for any Canadian resident selling any property whether it is located in Canada or the US.

If you are placing a mortgage on your property, find an institution familiar with the unique requirements of US non-residents and resident aliens. RBC, BMO, and TD banks all have large presences in the US. Even if there are no branches near you, you can usually do most of the work on the telephone and online to obtain mortgage financing. It is important to shop around but the Canadian banks will at least help you transfer credit ratings from Canada and help you through all the new terminology and procedures of placing a mortgage on a US property. You will likely be confronted with additional mortgage costs known as "points or closing fees." These are the institution's way of covering the upfront costs of handling the mortgage, and may reduce or discount your mortgage interest rate.

US Real Estate Investment Trusts (REITs) through the mutual fund format are also a very good way for Canadians to invest in US real estate. They can provide investors with a diversified solid portfolio of residential, commercial, or industrial properties which are professionally managed and over time generally provide 4 percent to 8 percent cash flow to the investors annually. The REIT will complete all of the US paperwork for you and issue you appropriate tax slips with appropriate withholding depending on how the fund is structured.

The equity value of your US real estate, together with your other worldwide assets, may be subject to estate taxes over the $5.45 million for an individual or $10.9 million for a married couple exemptions allowed under the Canada/US Tax Treaty.

EXEMPT INVESTMENTS

Throughout this book I have referred to exempt investments, meaning US investments that are exempt from both income and estate tax for Vacationers/Snowbirds/non-residents. If you are a US citizen, green card holder, or a Settler/resident of the US these exempt investments either don't apply to you at all or very much differently; see Chapters 9 and 10. You should already be familiar with the fact that exposure to US taxes can be a direct function of the type of investment you make in the United States. The following list of exempt investments will help you identify investments that could eliminate unnecessary tax burdens for non-residents, so that you can develop a safe, income-producing portfolio of US investments. If your US assets or investments are not included on the list below, they most certainly are included in what the IRS considers the taxable estate for a non-resident of the US. Exempt investments include:

- Banking deposits, including CDs, savings accounts, checking accounts, and money market funds (in general, any kind of deposit at these institutions). A completed IRS Form W-8BEN (see Figure 4.6) must be filed with the savings institution.
- US Treasury bonds, notes, bills, and agency issues.
- US corporate bonds. A completed Form W-8BEN must be filed with the company issuing the bond or with the brokerage account where you purchased and hold the bond.
- American Depository Receipts (ADRs).
- Specially structured mutual funds that are designed by the investment company to specifically hold investments that are exempt from US estate taxes for nonresidents.
- Some investment companies or brokerage houses offer money market funds where the securities in the portfolio consist of only government and corporate bonds that have been noted above as exempt securities. A completed Form W-8BEN must be filed with the brokerage firm.
- Life insurance death benefits, regardless of the amount.
- Canadians whose world estates are less than $1.2 million USD ($2.4 million for married couples with joint property), will be allowed under the current Canada/US Tax Treaty to add US stocks,

including mutual funds shares and ETFs, to this list of exempt investments for estate-tax purposes only. Please review Chapter 5 to understand what can be included in a person's worldwide estate from the IRS perspective. The US stocks or US mutual funds will still be subject to the treaty withholding on dividends of 15 percent, unless they are purchased through your Canadian broker inside your RRSP.

UNDERSTANDING INVESTMENT RISK

Investors think of risk in two erroneous ways. The first, is that investment risk reflects only potential downward movement in the value of an investment. In reality, risk is a measure of market volatility or variations. No one, normally, would consider something continually going up in a volatile manner to be risk. Therefore, risk reflects both the probability of upward and downward price fluctuations.

The second assumption is that market risk is the only kind of risk that exists in today's investment marketplace. Market risk is the degree an investment's price behavior correlates with the general market for that investment. A good example of this is company stocks, whose value will generally reflect movements in the stock market as a whole.

This section outlines at least seven types of investment risk with basic instructions of how to mitigate each one with a special emphasis on those types of risk that can most affect Vacationers, Snowbirds, or Settlers living the cross-border lifestyle, regardless of their country of residence:

- Specific risk reflects risks inherent to one investment in particular. A purchaser of Ford stock would be concerned about problems pertaining to Ford, such as the amount of company debt, potential labor problems, effective management, and so on. This type of risk might be eliminated or at least greatly reduced by properly diversifying a portfolio.
- Market risk is best exemplified by the stock or real estate markets. Market values of individual stocks or parcels of real estate tend to follow movement in the stock market or regional real estate markets. Market risk can pose a substantial short-term risk to investment principal. If your investment horizon is longer than three years, market risk in the stock market decreases rapidly and tends to decrease the longer the time period of your investment horizon. It is important to understand that to mitigate this risk you must not only select your individual time horizon that you can leave your money invested before you need to start consuming

the funds, but if you don't deal with specific risk through proper diversification the length of time you invest may be irrelevant. As in the previous example if you used only one stock like Ford, and Ford was in a long-term deteriorating market for automobiles it may never recover its value regardless of how long you hold it and it may actually go out of business.

- Inflation risk is the most insidious and harmful risk to long term investors because its effects are not immediately obvious. Inflation reflects a loss of purchasing power, and primarily affects fixed investments such as bonds, term deposits, GICs, CDs, and fixed annuities. If an investor had $10,000 in Canada Savings Bonds that yielded 5 percent per year in income, and inflation averaged 3 percent that year, what would happen to the value of the bonds? The bonds would still be worth $10,000 on the investor's annual statements, but would the investor still be able to purchase $10,000 worth of goods and services? No, because of the 3 percent annual inflation, the investor's $10,000 would be worth 3 percent less, or $9,700 and this silent devaluation would continue year after year! If you add income tax of close to 50 percent to the equation at these inflation rates and returns, you are experiencing an annual loss in your investments of approximately 1 percent. Income from the bonds is also worth 35 percent less, compounded for each year of inflation! If the investor held these bonds for ten years, and inflation averaged 3 percent per year, he would get a check from the Canadian government for $10,000, but the bonds would purchase only about $7,500 worth of goods and services. This type of risk may be reduced by adding inflation hedges to a portfolio or using inflation indexed government bonds such as TIPS (Treasury Inflation Protected Securities). Inflation hedges are generally defined as investments that, over long periods of time, have a tendency to rise at least at the average inflation level (examples would be blue-chip stocks, real estate, gold, minerals, and basic food commodities such as rice and wheat).
- Interest rate risk reflects how movements in interest rates affect the value of investments. Anyone whose income depends primarily on interest rates has seen their income plummet during years of low available interest rates. Term deposits that came due for renewal during those years also renewed at very low rates. Interest rate volatility over the last 20 years has made bonds and term deposits much riskier to hold, particularly in a portfolio that has little or no diversification. With the recession of 2008 and 2009

many investors were spooked into holding cash and fixed income investments which means not only did they lose money to inflation and taxes each year, they missed one of the best stock markets in history. Currently interest rates are so low it is difficult to get positive fixed income yields. Many European banks (and Canadian banks are considering the same), are actually charging investors for holding cash on their behalf. Paying banks to hold your money is not a good way to get ahead in any investment strategy. This risk can be reduced by shortening and laddering the maturities of these fixed investments using several different maturity dates to avoid the risk of being locked in low rates for too long and so you have certificates coming due on an annual basis. This will make your average rate of return more stable over a long term.

- Currency risk is similar to inflation risk in the way that it affects investments. This type of risk is especially important to Canadians and was discussed in Chapter 3. Changes in the value of currencies can affect purchasing power the same way inflation does. For instance, if the Canadian dollar were to depreciate 5 percent in a year in relation to the American dollar, Canadians could purchase 5 percent less in American goods. This type of risk may be eliminated by diversifying a portfolio in the global sense so that all world currencies, either directly or indirectly, are included in the portfolio strategy. This is particularly important for Canadians wishing to live the amazing cross-border lifestyle, as they should place a strong emphasis on US-dollar investments to generate US-dollar income throughout their investment strategy.
- Economic risk affects investments much as market risk does. Stocks and real estate tend to do well when the economy is brisk. Gold and utilities are examples of "counter cyclical" investments, which perform well when the economy is down. Economic risk is best mitigated through a proper diversified portfolio including commodities such as gold, which has always been the traditional investment that provides insurance against any potential form of severe economic collapse and should be included, at least in a small percentage, in all investment portfolio strategies.
- Government risk affects both Canadian and American residents. This type of risk results from both governments' frequent changes to the tax laws — often with negative effects for the investor. A major recent example was the Canadian government's elimination of the tax benefits on income trusts in Canada with their Halloween surprise in 2006. Canadian investors who had a large part

or even all of their portfolio in these income trusts saw the value of the portfolio drop in excess of 30 percent literally overnight. A similar event occurred in the US in the mid-'80s when the US government eliminated special tax benefits to real estate investors. As a result, the entire industry was changed dramatically in a matter of months and thousands of investors lost millions of dollars. This type of risk is best reduced by diversification and helping to elect investor-friendly governments.

By knowing all of the risks inherent in investing and prudently diversifying investments, the informed investor can enjoy a high, tax-favored income at low levels of risk. The effects of inflation and wide currency swings can be minimized. The 2008–2009 credit crisis with the ensuing stock market crash, unfortunately, has helped most investors understand risk much more completely than they ever have (and probably have ever wanted to) in the past. This market was such that few risk reduction strategies other than investing in short-term high-quality government securities and gold worked at all, at least temporarily. The perfect storm created by the market conditions produced what would be the investment equivalent of a 200-year flood and will likely change investor attitude toward risk for a generation or more to come. In retrospect this great recession was one of the best investment opportunities in a generation or even in a lifetime; market returns helped approximately double the portfolios of investors who stayed the course throughout with an intelligently diversified investment strategy from 2009 to 2015.

THE REWARDS OF GLOBAL INVESTING

In 1990, Merton Miller, William Sharpe, and Harry Markowitz won the Nobel Prize in economics for their pioneering work in quantifying returns and risk from a portfolio perspective. Their research turned up some rather surprising results. It turns out your grandmother was right after all; don't put all your eggs in one basket. The market may not compensate you for the additional risk with higher returns. There is also no such thing as a free lunch. Decrease your overall risk and you may also decrease returns over the long run.

Most surprising were the results attained by combining two assets that behave differently. Take a stock that performs well during economic downturns and take a cyclical stock (a stock that tends to vary in value according to certain economic cycles). Both are expected to return 11 percent over the long run. If you buy equal portions of both stocks, the long-run return will be 11 percent. But year-to-year volatility will decrease, because one stock will do well when the other does poorly. In fact, adding an asset that may be considered risky by itself may actually reduce the total risk of the overall portfolio by adding value when everything else has gone south — because it operates somewhat independently and often in an opposite manner to the overall portfolio!

What does this have to do with international investing? International stock and bond markets do not move in lockstep with the US and Canadian stock markets. In fact, when compared with other major world economic areas such as Europe and Asia, the US has the top-performing market less than 50 percent of the time. Consequently, if one ignores these other economic areas for a diversified strategy they are either missing out on great additional returns and/or taking a much higher risk by concentrating on just one area of the world. By combining foreign stocks and bonds with US and Canadian investments, we may lower risk and enhance returns over the long run. Invest in foreign securities and you attain diversification through exposure to different economies. Over the last 30 years, many markets have grown faster than the US or Canadian stock markets. This means added profits for investors. Opportunities are also emerging with the modern development of Eastern European countries and Russia, and of course India and China.

Currency risks are also hedged were mitigated with a globally diversified portfolio. Canadian investors in US and other foreign securities would have benefited greatly from currency gains when the Canadian dollar dropped from $1.00 USD to $0.68 USD in less than three years from early 2013 to early 2016. However, Canadians who invested strictly in US investments between 2003 and 2007, when the Canadian dollar went from $0.63 USD back up to $1.10 USD, would have seen their returns suffer greatly. In a global economy, diversifying globally to avoid currency risk is very important.

More aggressive investors may find excellent opportunities in emerging markets. Some of these markets have boomed for many years but performed as bad or even worse than North American markets during 2008–2009. These emerging markets, by most measures, oversold and are not doing well in the current general slow world economy, remain a very good growth opportunity once world conditions stabilize again. While we don't recommend that a portfolio contain only emerging market stocks, an exposure of 10 percent or so may aid returns and lower portfolio risk.

How do you select and purchase shares of stocks or bonds in these markets? By using a mutual fund or exchange-traded fund, indexed with baskets of securities, in the exact markets you choose. Stock selection is left to sponsors who focus on the country in question and select the stocks for the index. This expertise can be crucial since financial disclosure and accounting standards are rarely as investor-oriented as they are in North America. Funds buy large blocks of stocks or bonds and transaction costs are reduced. Shares of funds can be bought and sold quickly and inexpensively and offer instant diversification.

CHOOSING AN INTERNATIONAL INVESTMENT MANAGER

I have talked about many forms of risk, but I purposely ignored what I believe is the major risk keeping investors from getting good, solid, long-term returns from their portfolios. That risk is investing according to one's emotions. Investing according to what you feel is very dangerous to your investment health. Most investors, after listening, watching, or reading the deluge of available financial and economic information feel they need to make almost daily adjustments to investments because the world sky seems to be falling or there's some new hot stock that is having a real run and they need to jump on the bandwagon. The general public investor most often fails to realize that all this hype one way or another is just investment pornography driven by the media to make money by getting more investors to do more things, more often in the areas that make them, as advertisers or service providers, the most money. Simply put, their best interest is quite different than yours of having a good solid return on your portfolio. Therefore if you allow emotions created with all of this investment pornography to make your decisions you inevitably will succumb to long-term poorer performance while driving yourself crazy trying to sort through contradictions and different points of view.

A recent study by one of the world's leading investment companies, Vanguard, found that hiring a professional manager increased the returns that investors earn on their portfolios by 2 to 3 percent over the long haul. The Vanguard study determined one of the main reasons for this increased return was that investment managers protected the investors from making their portfolio strategies and adjustments according to emotions instead of determinable facts.

The key to successful investing is formulating a long-term, internationally diversified portfolio policy based on your own objectives and preferences. The first words out of a potential investment manager's mouth should be questions related to your personal investment objectives. These objectives should contain concise information regarding the returns you expect, and the level of risk or volatility you are willing to assume. Be leery of investment advisors who simply take your money with no questions asked and throw it in a big investment pool, without any customization to your individual needs. It is very important that they understand you and your needs before even a nickel is invested.

It is also important to consider present and future income needs from the portfolio, investment time horizon (the length of time you have invest the funds), liquidity requirements (how quickly can you sell your investments to produce cash for unexpected personal needs or expenses), income and estate tax information, and your current estate plan. You should be active in these early stages when the portfolio policy is being formulated, and again when your individual situation changes. Charles D. Ellis's book *Investment Policy*, second edition, published in 1993 by Business One Irwin, is considered a classic in this area.

Unfortunately most financial advisors may be little more than salespeople enjoying upfront commissions based solely on volume. There is little incentive for an advisor to monitor a client's account after a commission is received. In the US, less than one-third of advisors operate on a fee-only basis instead of commission. In Canada over 90 percent of financial advisors operate solely or largely on a commission basis. It is primarily this pressure to sell more at higher prices that allows financial scandals to go unchecked for such long periods, because so many investment salespeople and company executives are making so much money on all transactions or stock options created when the general public is convinced there are huge gains to be made without risk. I believe the financial crisis created in 2008 was caused by the major banks and brokerage firms repackaging high-risk mortgages and selling them as high yielding, secure financial products. Had there been full disclosure and these products not been pushed by a large army of commissioned salespeople, this entire crisis could have been avoided. Moreover, advisors working on a commission basis earn more by selling or shifting existing investments whether or not there is good reason to do so. This latter procedure, if done excessively, is called churning and is illegal. The key to successful investment performance is active, professional portfolio management. The most important consideration is the client's goals and best interest, closely matched to the manager's investment philosophy.

Why is formulation of a long-term portfolio policy emphasized here? Because some studies from the *Financial Analysts Journal* (Gary Brinson, L. Randolph Hood, and Gilbert L. Beebower, "Determinants of Portfolio Performance," July-August 1986, and Gary P. Brinson, Brian D. Singer, and Gilbert L. Beebower, "Revisiting Determinants of Portfolio Performance: An Update," May-June 1991) show that more than 90 percent of investment variability generated by large pension plans results from following a long-term investment policy. Less than 10 percent of portfolio variability was attributed to "stock picking" or market timing (switching funds between investments or asset classes in response to perceived changes in the economy). The successful investment advisor will pay close attention to those decisions that may generate 90 percent of their portfolios' returns or variability.

There seems to be an inherently unfair bias in the way the investment marketplace treats "retail" or individual investors, versus "wholesale" or institutional investors. What are these differences, and how can investors overcome them? How can you ensure equal treatment?

Let's examine some of the differences. The retail marketplace is largely transaction-based. Stockbrokers, commissioned financial planners, and insurance salespeople are compensated according to the number and size of transactions they effect. The more they sell you, the more money they make. The focus is not always on managing an investor's funds for the long term, but on switching from investment to investment.

Even banks collect commissions indirectly. Term deposits or bank CDs return an interest rate plus a guarantee of principal for a specified period of time. The banks invest the funds in government and corporate debt securities, mortgages and leases, and other investments. The return is often significantly higher than what is paid out to bank depositors.

The institutional marketplace, which includes pension funds, insurance companies, exchange traded funds and mutual funds, is performance-based. Portfolios are often managed by one or more managers, whose compensation is based on how big the portfolio gets. They are paid for performance rather than buying or selling investments. Here, the incentive is to reduce commission costs, since commissions reduce the size of the portfolios they manage.

Individual investors are constantly bombarded by the media and salespeople with information about the latest investment guru, the hottest stocks, or the best market pundit. Lots of excitement is promised but very little of substance happens. Investors often buy on the premise that the broker, salesperson, or financial planner can pick "hot stocks" or other investments and can time favorable moments to switch between stocks, bonds, or cash, depending on market conditions. If market timing and security selection contribute less than 10 percent of a typical portfolio's return, why do the media and retail investment marketplace focus so much time and energy promoting these advisors who claim to have exceptional abilities in these areas? Because strategies that lean heavily on security selection and market timing generate many more transactions (read: commissions) than establishing and sticking to a long-term investment policy.

Although many institutional investors use stock picking and some form of market timing, more have become asset allocators. This involves diversifying investments between cash equivalents, stocks, bonds, and other asset classes. Asset allocators don't try to forecast the markets, the economy, or interest rates. They believe these markets and indicators are unpredictable over the long run and diversify their holdings and use a buy-and-hold strategy to minimize transaction costs and income taxes.

How can you level the playing field? Find an investment advisor who focuses on formulating a long-term investment policy based on your needs and preferences, which is 90 percent of the ball game. In choosing an investment manager, you should consider the following:

- Choose a manager compensated on the basis of performance or a flat fee, not commissions.
- All things being equal, choose the manager with lower management fees.
- Make sure the manager cannot make "big bets" with your portfolio. Choose a fund or firm whose management philosophy requires the manager to be diversified to some degree.
- Choose a manager who will manage on a tax-efficient basis.
- Choose a manager who uses no-load mutual funds, exchange traded funds, and/or a discount brokerage arrangement to transact securities trades, thus minimizing your investment costs.

Border Guide readers may participate in a cross-border Q&A through the new Cross-Border Forum. You can easily post questions about the contents of this book. To post comment, go to keatsconnelly.com and click on the *Cross-Border Forum* tab at the top of the first page.

CROSS-BORDER Q&A

DOES US LAW FORBID NON-RESIDENT BROKERAGE ACCOUNTS?

I have searched in vain for a way out of my dilemma; the Florida broker I had dealt with for about a year was forced to close my account. Apparently, regulations prohibit a non-US resident brokerage account, with or without a W-8BEN, no matter which address I use. Please explain how I can resolve this.

— Edward S., North York, Ontario

Your dilemma may be solved by contacting either Vanguard Investments or Charles Schwab Global. Vanguard is one of the largest mutual fund and exchange traded funds investment companies in the US. Charles

Schwab is the largest discount brokerage firm in the United States. Both of these companies are excellent to deal with and have mechanisms for non-residents of the US to open full brokerage accounts. Vanguard can be found on the Internet at vanguard-international.vanguard.com and Schwab at schwab-global.com. There is a little more paperwork involved to set up these accounts, but they give you full access to trade in your account as you require. You may have luck with other brokerage firms or investment managers that are licensed in both Canada and the US for these non-resident alien (NRA) accounts as well.

I believe your stockbroker was confusing his company's policy and procedures with those of the regulatory bodies, as there are no laws that I am aware of that prohibit non-resident accounts as long as they are done properly.

HOLDING SECURITIES IN STREET FORM AND US TREASURY NOTES

If I hold US Securities in street form in my Canadian account, are they still subject to the $60,000 USD limit for estate tax? Technically, the answer is probably yes, but are there reporting procedures between the two countries? Finally, I have read about US Treasury notes. Are these available to Canadians? If so, where and how?

— Ronald Z., Corunna, Ontario

Holding securities in street form, as you already guessed, does not exempt them from non-resident estate tax. Any US securities, unless they are specifically exempt, add to the taxable estate of non-residents. Tax exempt securities that would likely be purchased through a brokerage firm include Certificates of Deposit from US banks, US government Treasury bills, Treasury notes, and Treasury bonds. US securities are taxable for non-resident estate tax purposes, whether the securities are held in Canada, the United States, or elsewhere in the world. Canadians whose world estates are less than $1.2 million USD can, under the current Canada/US Tax Treaty, hold US stocks and similar securities as exempt from the non-resident estate tax. In addition, the Treaty also provides Canadians access to the US estate tax exemption of $5.45 million USD.

There are now formal agreements between Canada and the US for reporting investments by residents of the opposite country. In addition, the Canada/US Tax Treaty allows for the exchange of tax information in either country at any time. The IRS and CRA have been using this treaty clause quite frequently to catch taxpayers not reporting income.

The answer to your final question about purchasing US Treasury notes is that you can hold as many as you desire, and if you use an online broker such as Charles Schwab Global (schwab-global.com), you can purchase them online at a very reasonable cost.

My wife has dual US/Canadian citizenship and we are looking at buying a property in Florida to use for at least 6 months of the year if not permanently. What options would she have for a mortgage, would she qualify as an American with lower down payments or would she be treated as a foreigner and have to use a larger down payment of 20 to 30 percent?

— KW, Hamilton, ON

With your wife as a dual citizen, she can do anything in the US that any other US citizen can do including purchasing property and getting a mortgage. However, there are several US lending institutions that will loan money to Canadians who are not US citizens to purchase US property as well. Down payments required are usually a minimum of 20 percent, however if you shop around you can usually find a mortgage company that will allow less. RBC, BMO, and TD all have good mortgage loaning policies for Canadians purchasing property in the US.

KEEPING A CANADIAN BROKERAGE ACCOUNT AS A US RESIDENT

I am a retired Canadian and a recent green card resident of Florida. My income (except for US Social Security) is all Canadian and I have an investment portfolio with a Toronto brokerage firm. This account consists of bonds and mortgage-backed securities. Trading in this account is infrequent and usually only to replace investments that have matured. My broker has recently advised me that SEC regulations prohibit him from making Canadian trades for a US resident! Is this a unique situation? There must be a great many Canadians in the US who own Canadian securities. This creates a very serious situation for me and I would appreciate your comments and your advice as to what steps I might take. Are there Toronto firms that could do trades for me if necessary?

— Darwin M., Sarasota, Florida

Your broker is correct; in order for him to legally deal with a US resident both he and his company must be licensed in your state of residence. Many Canadians in the United States have received similar notices from their brokers. Negotiations between Canadian and US securities regulators did partially solve this problem, at least with respect to RRSPs. From a simplification standpoint, life would be easier for you financially if you just moved your assets south. US brokerage firms can do everything

Canadian brokerage firms can do, including holding Canadian securities, and they can normally do it at lower costs, particularly if you deal with Charles Schwab or Fidelity Investments, both of which offer great discounted brokerage services.

This can be solved easily by setting up a US brokerage account and transferring the cash and securities into it through a broker-to-broker transfer. US brokerage firms can and do hold just about any listed Canadian bonds and stocks that would normally be traded on any of the Canadian exchanges. Those they can't accept, such as Canadian mutual funds, should be converted to cash before the transfer. Generally you will be able to do everything you are currently doing in your Canadian account at far less cost. Seek out the assistance of a professional, experienced cross-border financial planner for this transferring project as there are income and estate implications that need to be addressed to maintain your best financial health, not just the investment licensing and returns.

CAN CANADIAN BROKERS ACT FOR US RESIDENTS?

I am retired with no employment income. I do trade commodity futures through a US-based broker, using a computerized system. The net results are reported to Canada Revenue Agency. I intend to carry on this activity during the winter months from my temporary US address and would like to know if the results might be considered income earned in the US and therefore liable to be reported to the IRS. A complicating factor is that the income might never be actually received in the US since a trade could be initiated in one country but come to fruition in another.

— Gordon C., St. Catharines, Ontario

If you are able to ensure that your trading is simply a capital transaction and is subject to tax as capital gains (or losses), then you have no worries about being taxed in the US if you don't spend more than 182 days a year there and you file the Closer Connection Form 8840 with the IRS annually by June 15. If you follow these two requirements, the Canada/US Tax Treaty clearly states that your capital gains are taxable only in Canada, even though you may be in the United States for part of the year.

If this trading is regular enough that it might be considered your only job, there is a possibility that any income could be classified as business income. If you are considered to be doing business in the United States, this business income would be taxable in the US and included as part of your world income in Canada. If you have no immigration status or authorization to work in the US, you are an illegal alien.

I suggest you check to see if your US broker is licensed to do business in Ontario by the Ontario Securities Commission. If not, they could be trading for you against US Securities and Exchange Commission regulations, and you could have little or no consumer protection for inappropriate advice or someone's running off with your funds.

TRANSFERRING ACCOUNTS AND FINDING A US-BASED BROKER

My family and I became US residents in 2013 on an L-1 visa. For stocks and securities trading we dealt with TD Waterhouse investor services while in Canada, but they insist that they can no longer trade on our behalf. They blame US SEC rules, but I have seen conflicting information about this. TD Waterhouse in Canada does offer a US division that will carry my accounts in Canadian dollars, but I am not certain that I should go through the necessary exercise or that the downside has been made clear. Are there any alternatives for someone in my position? Is there any significant risk or loss of flexibility in transferring my accounts?

— Murray K., Farmington Hills, Michigan

Your brokerage firm is correct. They cannot legally trade accounts for US residents, unless both the broker and the firm are licensed in your state. Also, there are generally some state securities requirements that could make it illegal for them to deal with you. Canada and the US have negotiated a securities agreement that may alleviate this problem, at least for RRSPs. Trading in RRSP investments in Canada while you are a US resident can now be done in most of the US states, providing you and your Canadian brokerage firm meet specified criteria.

Your alternatives depend on your goals regarding the kind of investor you are, whether the accounts are RRSPs, and whether you plan to be a permanent US resident. Generally, it would simplify your financial life immensely if your accounts were in the US. It would be much easier for you to manage and administer, particularly for income tax reporting. You should also be able to reduce your brokerage costs, as competition in the US tends to keep transaction costs very low. My colleagues and I like to recommend Charles Schwab, Fidelity Investments, or TD Ameritrade as the best all-around discount brokers in the United States. You can provide them with a list of your securities and they should be able to tell you which ones can be held in the US. They can also initiate the transfer of your account. Generally, most listed Canadian stocks and bonds can be held in your US account. Canadian mutual funds would have to be liquidated and turned into cash to transfer to the United States.

Coming to America 8

Moving to the United States

Many Canadians would never dream of moving to the US, while others spend thousands of dollars attempting to adopt the Settler cross-border lifestyle and obtain legal status as US residents. There are other Canadians who live in the US illegally year-round, or who stay longer than rules allow for a Vacationer or Snowbird. With the relative ease of crossing the border, and the ability to remain in the US for extended periods of time, why should someone consider becoming a Settler or legal resident?

For some people, US residency means a new business opportunity. With the newly elected governments raising taxes to the highest levels in decades to balance budgets and/or "redistribute wealth," others have had enough of paying more than half of their earnings in high taxes. Others just prefer the warmer climate down south. This chapter is designed to assist those people who may want to move from the Vacationer or Snowbird cross-border lifestyle to the Settler category while never having to worry about counting the number of days they spend in the US. Chapters 9, 10, 15, and 16 will help you determine whether US residency and the Settler lifestyle would be a good move for you financially, after taking into consideration the key cross-border issues of income tax, estate tax, and medical. For those seriously contemplating a move, all the issues in this and the next three chapters need to be addressed simultaneously for maximum benefit of your chosen, most amazing cross-border lifestyle.

Immigration can be a complex and lengthy procedure under current law and should not be attempted without the services of a good US immigration attorney. Use this chapter as the initial guide to the numerous opportunities Canadians have to develop a Settler/US residency lifestyle.

HOW TO BECOME A LEGAL RESIDENT OF THE US

There are normally two legal ways to immigrate to the United States. The first is through a business or a professional relationship. The second is through the sponsorship of a close family member. This is about as simple an explanation as it gets about who is entitled to immigrate to the United States. After that, the whole process becomes complex and often appears contradictory. Figure 8.1 provides a chart of the basic business categories under which you may acquire either a permanent or something-less-than-permanent resident status.

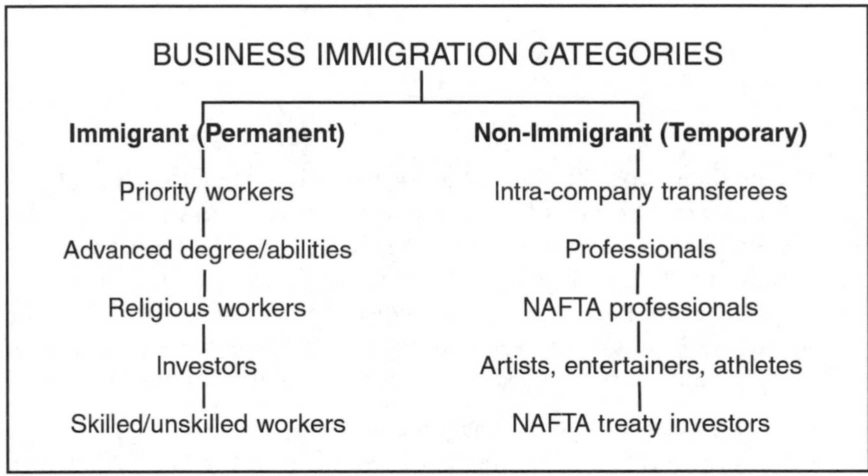

FIGURE 8.1

You can see from Figure 8.1 that there are numerous opportunities for US immigration for persons with business contacts. Business and professional immigration categories will be explained in greater detail in the next section. Where does this leave the retired person who wants to immigrate and retire to a cross-border lifestyle in the US Sunbelt? That's where some advance planning can pay big dividends. Those who have recently retired or are about to retire should consider keeping any business or professional relationships long enough to assist you in getting permanent immigration status. Those who are retired, investing in a small US business with a full-time manager or just a USCIS specially authorized investment can be a suitable means of obtaining a visa or legal permanent resident/green card that allows you to adopt a full Settler lifestyle to legally live in the US year-round with the Swinging Door that allows you full access back to Canada whenever you want for whatever reason.

Those with no applicable business or professional means may wish to look for any possible close family connections that can give them legal status in the US. Figure 8.2 addresses the key family relationships that can prove useful for immigration purposes. For most purposes, family relationships that are defined by USCIS as close include parents, children, or siblings of the applicant.

IMMIGRATION CATEGORIES

This section lists some of the basic qualifications for each of the business and family immigration categories outlined in Figures 8.1 and 8.2.

Immigrant or Lawful Permanent Resident (LPR) status is also known as a green card. This is similar to Permanent Resident status in Canada. The green card is no longer even green. Every so often it is given a new look to impede fraudulent reproduction. Current versions include an expiration date, holograms, and one or more biometric IDs. It is now like a driver's licence and must be renewed before the expiration date. Unlike a driver's licence you don't lose your status because your card expires. The main purpose of the expiration date is to force people to update their pictures, addresses, and to install the latest anti-forgery upgrades.

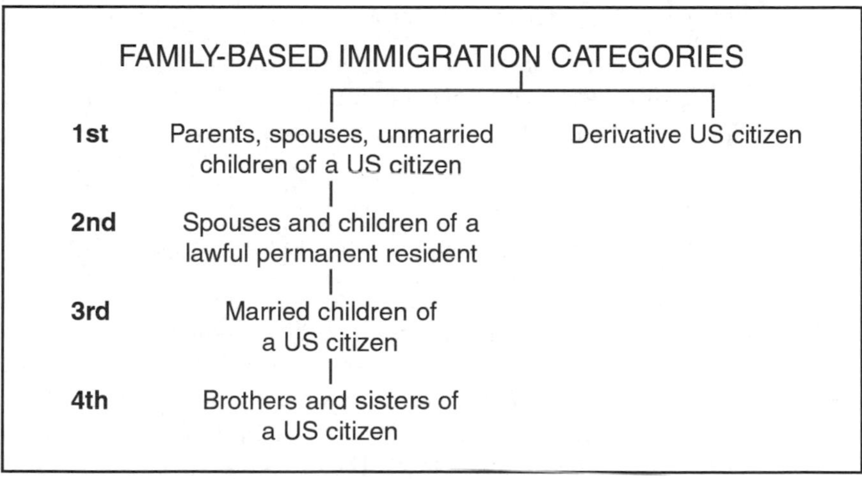

FIGURE 8.2

GREEN CARD OR EMPLOYMENT-BASED IMMIGRANT CATEGORIES: FIRST PREFERENCE EB-1

Priority Workers. There are three priority worker classes, known to the US Citizenship and Immigration Service (USCIS) as EB1-A, 1-B and 1-C categories:

1-A: Extraordinary-ability immigrants in the sciences, arts, education, business, or athletics. The regulations define extraordinary ability as a level of expertise indicating that the individual is one of a small percentage who have risen to the very top of a particular field. No employer sponsorship or labor certification is required. A Wayne Gretzky, the CEO of a large company, or a Nobel Prize winner would be examples for this category.

1-B: Outstanding professors and researchers. Applicants in this category must be coming to the United States to conduct research full time for a university or private firm. They must display documented achievements in their fields. The university or the private research company applies to the USCIS for this visa.

1-C: Executives and managers. An executive or manager who has been employed by the US employer's Canadian affiliate, parent, subsidiary, or branch office for at least one of the three years preceding the application qualifies for this category. This is a good opportunity to obtain a green card for those businesspeople who have a business in both countries. This category is very similar to the L-1 intra-company transferee visa in the non-immigrant petitions noted later in this chapter.

There are no waiting lists for these three priority green card categories. Processing times vary with government workloads. Processing time should be less than six months from date of application.

SECOND PREFERENCE, EB-2

Professionals Holding Advanced Degrees (2-A) or Exceptional Ability Immigrants (2-B):

2-A: Advanced Degree. This category includes people with PhDs and master's degrees. Five or more years of progressive work may be accepted in lieu of the advanced degree, providing a Bachelor's degree has been acquired. Unless they qualify for the national interest waiver discussed below, applicants for this category must have an employer petition on their behalf for a position that requires this advanced education and obtain a labor certification from the US Department of Labor. To obtain labor certification, the employer must demonstrate that there are no US workers who are qualified and available to fill the position.

2-B: Exceptional Ability Immigrants. USCIS provides for admission of a person with exceptional ability in the field of art, science, or business. If you can convince USCIS that it is of US national interest (because of a potential for significant positive contribution to the US economy) to waive the employment and labor certification requirement, this petition can be submitted directly without an employer sponsor. Like many aspects of immigration rules, the term "exceptional ability" has not been clearly defined. It is a lower standard than "extraordinary ability" in three first preference categories noted above but still requires a degree of expertise significantly above the ordinary. 2-B applicants must have an employer petition for them and must obtain a labor certification, unless they are granted the national interest waiver for those requirements.

Historically, there have been no waiting lists for these categories. Processing times vary with government workloads. Processing time should be less than one year.

THIRD PREFERENCE, EB-3

Skilled and Unskilled Workers. This catch-all category is for immigrants with offers of employment. This category is further subdivided into the following:

3-A: Professionals with Bachelor's degrees and labor certifications.

3-B: Skilled workers performing a job requiring at least two years of higher education, training, or experience.

3-C: "Other workers." This subcategory is for positions that require less than two years of higher education, training, or experience.

This third preference category is notoriously subject to delays and backlogs. Expect the process to take one year or longer.

FOURTH PREFERENCE, EB-4

Religious Workers. Must have been a member of and worked for a denomination for at least two years and seek entry as a minister (need a baccalaureate degree), a professional working in a religious capacity, or another religious organization worker.

Processing times vary with government workloads. Processing should take a little more than one year.

FIFTH PREFERENCE, EB-5

Immigrant investors: This is sometimes referred to as the "gold card." It is similar to the program Canada has used for years to attract foreign business entrepreneurs. Because of the large investment and job creation requirements and other restrictions, the EB-5 green card category has been greatly underutilized since its inception in the early 1990s. However, in 2002 the USCIS introduced a second option, the Regional Center program, which is ideal for the retiree or inactive investor who wishes to immigrate to the US. Both of the EB-5 programs provide for a Conditional Lawful Permanent Residence — in other words, a conditional green card — for two years until all the requirements listed below are met (after which full green card or LPR status is granted).

- Regular Program: Establish a new or expand an existing commercial enterprise in rural or special high-unemployment areas with an investment of $500,000, or with an investment of $1 million in another area that will benefit the US economy and create at least ten full-time jobs for US authorized workers. Direct involvement of the investor in the day-to-day operations or at least active management of the business is expected, including living near the location of the business investment.
- Regional Center Program: The investment requirement for these EB-5 programs is generally the lower $500,000 amount because the investments are deliberately created in the targeted areas of high unemployment or areas of desired economic expansion. The ten-employee requirement of the Regular program is replaced with a less restrictive "indirect employment creation," which allows the investor to qualify for an EB-5 green card without directly hiring ten people to work in the company being invested in. Consequently, the investor can qualify by presenting evidence that ten jobs will be created throughout the Regional Center economy, a much easier hurdle to face. The EB-5 management requirement is minimal in that the investor can be a limited partner and still qualify for the green card, making this program much more acceptable for those who are not interested in day-to-day management or actively running a business. The investor is not required to live where the investment is made; he or she can, for example, live in Florida and invest in Washington state. There are generally several Regional Center Programs for the investor to choose from in many states and with a great deal of choice in the specific business opportunities available. Investors should be cautious who they choose for their sponsors, they are not all the same and vary greatly in business experience and reliability, and there has been considerable fraud committed by several sponsors which has made the USCIS tighten up the regulation of Regional Centers. The only major concern an investor has is to choose the right investment; the program managers will do the rest, and in approximately

14 months on average the investor will have his or her conditional two-year green card. (This processing time varies greatly according to the investment project chosen and the workload of the USCIS processing staff and has been as short as 4 months and as long as 18 months recently.) At the end of the two years, the green card becomes permanent with full rights of permanent residency, and an opportunity for US citizenship becomes available. The investment can be sold at any time after the permanent green card has been obtained; in fact, many of these investments self-liquidate five to seven years after inception. Choosing the right investment cannot be overemphasized, as the program should give investors a fair return on their investment, and the green card should be considered a secondary benefit. Under mandate by Congress, Regional Center EB-5 petitions are given priority by USCIS which, among other benefits, often results in a quicker approval process.

The procedure for obtaining an EB-5 investor green card is relatively straightforward. The investor must produce five years of tax returns and other financial records to substantiate the legal source of investment funds. The source of the funds can also be in the form of a loan or gift from a friend or relative. The investor must also present evidence that traces the capital from the investor directly to the enterprise being invested in (including bank transfers and other documentation).

If the investor is already in the US legally as a visitor or other visa holder, he or she then applies for a green card through USCIS. Customarily no interview is required. Approval usually takes 6 to 18 months. If the investor still lives in Canada, an application for the green card is generally made at a US consulate; however, for consular processing purposes, an interview is necessary (which for Canadians means a trip to Montreal). Approval of the green card in this case takes on average about 10 or 11 months, approximately the same as through USCIS.

For all of the above categories, an accompanying spouse (the acceptable Canadian definition of a spouse does not necessarily qualify for US immigration unless there is an actual legal marriage including same sex marriages) and minor children under the age of 21 can be included with the application to receive the same green card status as the applicant.

EMPLOYMENT-BASED NON-IMMIGRANT CATEGORIES

For all the non-immigrant visas noted below, a spouse and dependent children are allowed to accompany the visa holder for the same amount of time in the US and will be issued their own special visas. However, the spouse of an L- or E- visa holder may obtain employment authorization. The spouses and children of all other visa applicants are not allowed to work legally in the US unless they can get their own non-immigrant working visas based on their own qualifications. This is a particularly important consideration for young families in which one of the spouses receives a US job offer in one of these categories. If little planning is done to develop a long-term strategy, the family will be at a disadvantage. The children and the spouse will be prevented from working at any time during their stay in the US. The entire family may be forced to move back to Canada at the expiration visa of the primary applicant. It is important that an employee negotiating a job offer gets a firm commitment from the employer to sponsor the entire family for green cards as soon as it is practical once they are in the US as non-immigrant visa holders.

1. Intra-Company Transferees. This category is classified as the L-1 non-immigrant status and can last, with renewals, up to seven years. There are two parts to this visa L-1A, Manager/Executive where managing is an essential function and L-1B which requires specialized knowledge of sponsoring companies' products, services, and/or processes. This visa requires an ongoing relationship between a Canadian company and a US parent subsidiary, branch office, or affiliate. The visa applicant, as noted above, must be an executive, manager, or a person with specialized knowledge or training needed for the US company, and must have worked for the Canadian affiliate for at least one year out of the three years preceding the transfer to the US. Although this visa is for seven years maximum, time spent outside of the US is not included in the actual qualifying time for the visa. Consequently, for example, if over the seven-year period with your L-1 you have spent two years total cumulative time in Canada or traveling outside of the US, you could get your L-1 extended for the additional two years.
2. Professionals and Other Temporary Workers. This category is divided into four subcategories and these visas can last, with renewals, up to six years. The four categories are as follows:

   H-1B: Professionals in special occupations requiring a college degree or equivalent work experience.

   H-2A: Temporary agricultural workers that are in short supply.

   H-2B: Temporary non-agricultural workers in short supply.

   H-3: Trainees. The H-1B category can be granted for an initial three-year period, extendable to a six-year maximum. The

H-2A, H-2B, and H-3 categories can be granted for up to one year initially, and are extendable to three years for H-2A and H-1B or two years for the H-3. There is a cap on the number of these visas granted each year, and there is currently a waiting list. The H-1B has become so popular that all applications received with in a two-day filing window each year enter a lottery for the limited number of available visas, even if the other requirements are met. The annual quota is established on the first day of October.

3. Artists, Entertainers, and Athletes. There are two non-immigrant categories available for these emigrants from Canada. These are known as the P and O statuses and both are limited to the period of (a) particular event(s). The O visa is for extraordinary artists, entertainers, businesspeople, and athletes and can last for three years initially, then is renewable yearly thereafter or for the time period of the event(s), whichever is less. The P non-immigrant status can last for up to five years, extendable to a ten-year maximum. There is a cap on the number of these visas as well.
4. North American Free Trade Agreement (NAFTA) Treaty Traders and Investors. The Canadian Free Trade Agreement with the US became effective January 1, 1989, and was superseded by NAFTA, which came into effect January 1, 1994. The Immigration section of NAFTA provides for the temporary entry of business visitors, eliminates barriers to trade, facilitates across-the-border investment, provides for joint administration and dispute resolution, and emphasizes trade and the movement of people.

This means that Canadian citizens can now obtain the E-1 Trader visa or the E-2 Investor visa under NAFTA. These are usually renewable indefinitely, as long as the qualifying investment remains ongoing. These visas are considered the next best thing to permanent residency. Requirements for an E-2 visa are the following:

- The applicant must be a Canadian citizen.
- A substantial investment in a bona fide US enterprise must be made. A substantial investment is not clearly defined but the State Department has issued a sliding scale guideline. If the value of the enterprise is less than $500,000, the applicant must provide 75 percent of the investment. The amount of the investment must be an amount normally considered appropriate to establish a viable enterprise of the nature contemplated. Most viable applications

investing at least $100,000 or more with other capital readily available are accepted and with the latest tightening of rules on these visas these numbers are becoming hard to justify for most businesses and USCIS are looking for larger capital commitments from the applicants. A good business plan is essential, particularly if the applicant has limited capital to put into the new enterprise.

- The investor must be in a position to "develop and direct" the entity in which he has invested. Generally, that means the investor must have at least 50 percent ownership or control interest. Although not mandatory, the E-2 applicant will be more easily granted a visa if they have a history or experience in the type of business in which they are investing.

Certain "essential employees" of the investor may also be eligible for E-2 status. They must be employed in a supervisory or executive capacity or have special skills needed by the employer. Often a business-partner spouse could obtain his or her own E-2 visa under this option.

There is no requirement for a minimum number of employees to be hired, but the number of employees needed to operate the business in addition to the E-2 investor must be sufficient to make the enterprise successful. The investment must do more than support the investor and his or her family, so the more employees, the better the chances the visa will be granted.

The company employing the visa applicant must be at least 51 percent Canadian owned and controlled.

Processing times for these categories vary depending on government workloads, the complexity of an application, and whether the government requires additional data or documentation to make a determination. Canadians must go for an interview for these visas at the US consulate in Toronto before final approval. Processing is typically two to four months, though a decision can be rendered in two weeks or less if premium processing is selected for an additional fee, and the application is thoroughly prepared and well documented at the time of initial filing.

Although the E-1 does not seem to be as popular as the E-2 the requirements are very similar. However, the E-1 is a trader visa that requires your firm to have a large volume of international trade of goods, services and technology and more than 50 percent of the trade must be between the United States and Canada.

NAFTA PROFESSIONALS

This category is a unique one and is called the TN status. It permits people to come in as non-immigrants on the basis of their being a "professional" as listed on a schedule to NAFTA, and they have a simple written offer from a US employer to use the particular professional skills they possess. The Trade NAFTA (TN) visa is generally valid for three years and may be renewed for an unlimited duration as long as the visa holder maintains his non-immigrant intent (recently the USCIS has started to turn down TN visa holders who are renewing three or more times in certain professions and circumstances). Non-immigrant intent is not clearly defined but the TN visa holder must show that they have, at least at some point in the near future, the intent to return to Canada. A good example of clear intent to return to Canada would be maintaining a residence there, but this is by no means mandatory. You need a separate TN visa for each employer that you may be doing work for in the US since the TN visa is specific to only one company at a time.

The list of professionals includes accountants, engineers, scientists, research assistants, medical and allied professionals, scientific technicians, disaster-relief insurance claims adjusters, architects, lawyers, economists, computer systems analysts, management consultants, and others. It includes professors but omits teachers at the high school level. The professionals require at least a Bachelor's degree. Work experience will be allowed to replace education requirements for management consultants only. TN processing is done by US immigration officers at ports of entry. Processing time should be less than an hour.

FAMILY-BASED IMMIGRANT CATEGORIES

Family-based immigration is predicated on the fact that a close family member who is already a US citizen or green card holder can sponsor other family members for permanent residence in the US. There is also the possibility that a person looking to immigrate to the US may already be a derivative citizen through family history. This is covered in detail in the next section. There are five main categories for family-sponsored immigration. The immediate relative category is separate from other family-based immigration because it is not numerically restricted. This category is for spouses, unmarried minor children, and parents of US citizens. New spouses obtaining green cards by marrying US citizens will receive two-year temporary green cards and must go through an interview process after the two years before permanent cards are issued. The purpose of this process is to thwart marriages of convenience whose purpose is to obtain legal immigration status fraudulently. Those who saw the movie *Green Card* will better understand what this process entails with its detailed questioning of the spouses to ensure they are truly married.

In all but one of the other four categories, the family member sponsoring the green card or LPR of another family member must be a US citizen (see Applying for US Citizenship later in this chapter). These categories are subject to quotas and waiting lists of a few months to several years. They work on a priority or preference system:

- First preference: Parents, spouses, and minor unmarried sons and daughters of US citizens. At the present time there is a processing time of about 6 to 12 months in this category if filing is done at the US consulate in Canada (currently the only consulate in Canada being used for all final green card processing is in Montreal). If the filing is done from the US side of the border through an adjustment of status because the applicant is legally in the US as a visitor or with some other non-immigrant visa status, expect a processing time of less than 12 months depending on the USCIS processing center used. Usually those processing their applications in the US can request work permits and advance parole and be granted these in about 12 to 16 weeks from the date of application. Advance parole is just a special permission document which allows applicants to stay legally (they may also work if granted a work permit) in the US and also allows them to leave and re-enter the US while they are waiting for permanent green cards. For adult (over the age of 21) unmarried children of US citizens, the total wait/processing time is currently about eight years.
- Second preference: Two sub-categories:
  - — Spouses and minor children of lawful permanent residents or green card holders. There is currently a wait of about one and a half years in this category.
  - — Adult unmarried sons and daughters of lawful permanent residents or green card holders. There is a waiting period of more than six and a half years in this category.
- Third preference: Married children of US citizens. There is a waiting period in this category of more than ten years.
- Fourth preference: Siblings of US citizens. There is a waiting period in this category of nearly 12.5 years. Even though the waiting list may be quite long, it is worthwhile getting on this list as a change in legislation could either reduce the waiting period and/or

increase quotas, and people already on the list could move much more quickly. There have been recent proposals before Congress to eliminate the fourth preference altogether but so far this category has survived. Because the second, third, and fourth preference green card waiting lists are so long, prospective applicants should also apply for one of the non-immigrant visas mentioned earlier in this chapter (if they qualify) while they are waiting for their green card application to be approved. Care must be taken as to which visa is obtained, since some visas (like, for example, the TN visa) do not allow dual intent. Dual intent means that you are in the US on a temporary visa that requires you to return to your home country at the end of a specified time, and you are simultaneously applying for permanent status. The USCIS considers dual intent an irreconcilable conflict with certain visas, and therefore will reject applications for these visas if there is dual intent. Many other visas, such as the L-1 and E-2 visas, do allow dual intent.

DERIVATIVE CITIZENSHIP: ARE YOU A US CITIZEN?

With Canada and the US so closely related in geography and history, there has been substantial migration of residents across the 49th parallel. As a result, many Canadians, although they might never have lived in the US, might be US citizens solely on the basis of their ancestry. This is known as derivative citizenship.

Derivative citizenship was first established in law by Congress in the late 1700s. Since then, Congress has amended the rules as to who is eligible for derivative citizenship status at least a dozen times. Consequently, the rules to determine derivative citizenship can be quite complex.

Figure 8.3 illustrates a possible flow chart regarding how to determine whether you are a US citizen. The “Yes” notations indicate possible derivative citizenship if all other qualifications are met as outlined in the figure.

The flow chart gives you some idea about who may qualify as a derivative citizen, but with the 12 or more congressional amendments to the citizenship rules, it becomes a very complicated issue. For example, it is possible for one member of a family to acquire US citizenship on the day of his or her birth, while a sibling born later may be out of luck. After May 24, 1934, US residency of the US citizen ancestor became a vital ingredient in establishing a person’s American citizenship entitlement. In addition, during certain periods of time, Congress required the potential derivative citizen’s parent(s) to meet some residency requirements. Figure 8.3 is further explained in the following summary:

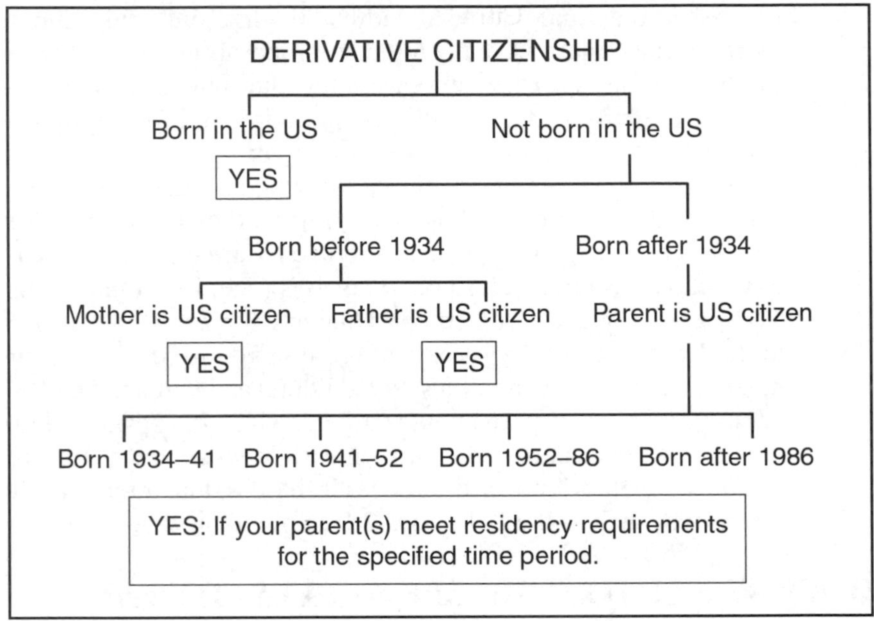

FIGURE 8.3

- Born in the US: If you were born in the United States, it is likely that you have retained your US citizenship, unless you have actively renounced it. Before 1990, US-born people taking up citizenship, or even just voting, in another country were considered to have renounced their US citizenship. Since then, the State Department has published new guidelines to determine retention of US citizenship: they now presume a person intends to retain US citizenship, even if that person obtains naturalization in or declares allegiance to another country. This new policy is retroactive. This means that it applies to people who might think they have lost their US citizenship, including those who have been told by the US State Department that they have lost their citizenship. A recent client was told 30 years ago by the State Department that he had lost his citizenship. He wrote to the State Department after visiting the US Consulate in Vancouver and they revoked their past Loss of Citizenship declaration. The client had his citizenship back in less than eight weeks.
- Both Parents Are US Citizens: If both your parents were US citizens at the time of your birth, you will generally have a claim to US citizenship if one or both of your parents ever "resided" in the US. This applies even if you have never lived in the US yourself.

- One Parent Is a US Citizen: If only one of your parents was a US citizen, you may be a US citizen if you and your parent have resided in the United States for the requisite time periods as summarized below:
- Born on or before May 24, 1934: If you were born before this date and your father was a US citizen, you are eligible for US citizenship. The law was changed effective October 6, 1994, to give mothers the same rights as fathers in conferring citizenship on their children.
- Born May 25, 1934, to January 13, 1941: Canadians born in this period are subject to two conditions. First, the US-citizen parent must have had a prior US residency. Second, the would-be derivative citizen must retain his citizenship through a two-year continuous presence (although not necessarily an uninterrupted stay) in the US. The terms "residency" and "presence" have no clear definition, but are interpreted through facts and circumstances and previous case law. We had a client born to a US-citizen parent during this period, who as a child spent most of her summers at an uncle's residence on the New England coast of the US. By adding up all her summer visits, she qualified for her two years' presence in the US.
- Born January 14, 1941, to December 24, 1952: Similar to those Canadians in the preceding category, the prospective derivative-citizen and the US parent are subject to residency requirements. Here, the US parent must have ten years' US residency, at least five of which were after age 16. The two-year continuous presence requirement for the potential derivative-citizen was also in force.
- Born December 25, 1952, to November 13, 1986: If you were born in this period, your US parent must have been physically present in the United States for ten years, at least five of which were after age 14. After October 10, 1978, the retention through residency requirement for the potential derivative-citizen was abolished.
- Born After November 13, 1986: The US parent must have five years of previous physical presence in the United States, at least two of which were after age 14. No residency is required of the prospective derivative-citizen.
- As of October 1994: A new law allows a person who was a citizen at birth, but who lost that citizenship by failing to meet the physical presence requirements, to reapply to regain US citizenship.

Once you've established that you're eligible for derivative citizenship, the biggest and most rewarding challenge comes from documenting the facts of the US parent's relationship and residency. Prospective derivative-citizens often need to become ancestral detectives, searching through old family and government records to shed new light on their pasts. Family Bibles, voter registrations, census records, sworn statements of family members: all have been used successfully to establish entitlement for US citizenship status.

APPLYING FOR US CITIZENSHIP

United States citizenship is acquired through three methods:

- Birth
- Derivation
- Naturalization

Obtaining citizenship derivation was explained in the previous section on derivative citizenship. In general, any person born in the US is considered a US citizen even though his or her parents may have been just passing through the US at the time of birth. You may apply for or confirm your citizenship status either by completing a Form N-600 with the USCIS or by simply submitting an application for a passport to the US State Department. Most people will find the passport route the quickest and most hassle-free method. The State Department is not nearly as bogged down as the USCIS, so if your passport application is rejected you will know about it much earlier and will be able to begin the appeals process that much sooner if you feel you have a legitimate claim.

Acquiring US citizenship by naturalization is available to those who have a five-year continuous legal permanent residence in the United States. In other words, you must have had a green card and have been physically present in the United States without any interruptions of longer than six months over a period of five years. There are a few exceptions. Those married to US citizens have only a three-year continuous residency requirement. For naturalization, one needs to demonstrate physical presence for the required amount of time, good moral character, and a minimum knowledge of English, US history, and government.

Naturalization is a relatively simple process that begins with submitting application Form N-400 to the USCIS, along with a specified fee (currently about $700 including a fingerprint fee), two color photographs, and proof of some of the information requested in the application. Visit the US Citizenship and Immigration Service's website to get copies of the forms and to determine the latest fees (uscis.gov). The most difficult question on Form N-400 requests the details of every trip you have taken outside the United States since you received your green card. An oral examination is required after filing the N-400 to prove some basic knowledge of US history and government (on the USCIS website they offer 100 questions from which the interviewer will normally take one or two verbally to test your knowledge) and English proficiency and verify eligibility for US citizenship. After a successful examination, a US District Court judge or an immigration officer will confer citizenship on you at a swearing-in ceremony. This entire citizenship process, depending on your county of residence, may take 5 to 12 months to complete.

However American citizenship is acquired, it can provide the ease of US access that many Canadians seek. Those who are dual citizens of Canada and the US cannot be denied entry to either country or be restricted to a certain number of days they can spend in out of either country. We remind Canadians who are considering US citizenship (or any US immigration to become Settlers, for that matter) to use the services of a competent cross-border financial planning practitioner to address the tax consequences of such a move before they attempt to obtain or reinstate US citizenship. Those who fail to heed this advice could face some adverse tax consequences once they obtain citizenship unless they can qualify for the Streamlined Voluntary Disclosure or other tax exemptions/procedures mentioned in Chapter 4.

DUAL CITIZENSHIP: IS IT POSSIBLE?

There are few issues — besides which way the Canadian dollar is going — that are more hotly debated by Canadians in the US than whether one is or can become a dual citizen of the US and Canada. To begin with, there is such a thing as dual citizenship, even though you may have a difficult time finding an immigration official in either Canada or the US who will admit that it exists or tell you anything about it. There is no formal procedure to apply for dual citizenship. You acquire it by applying for US citizenship and not relinquishing your Canadian citizenship (or vice versa).

Dual citizenship exists for Canadian citizens under two premises. First, there is the case of a Canadian green card holder and lawful permanent resident of the US, who is becoming a naturalized citizen. Since February 15, 1977, when Prime Minister Pierre Trudeau made his famous statement "once a Canadian, always a Canadian," Canada has not revoked its citizenship upon the US naturalization of its citizens. Changes to the Canadian *Citizenship Act* in April 2009 allow for Canadians who lost their Canadian citizenship before 1977, by taking up US citizenship or some other citizenship, to reclaim their Canadian citizenship. Canadians in these situations hold citizenship status in both countries.

Second, there are Canadian-born persons who meet the criteria for US derivative citizenship status as outlined earlier in this chapter; they can hold both a Canadian and a US passport at the same time. They are dual citizens as well.

Dual citizenship does not come from any formal application for dual citizenship but by default. Currently you can hold dual citizenship if you are a Canadian citizen who qualifies for US citizenship by simply applying for US citizenship and not formally renouncing your Canadian citizenship. Your new Canadian passport will indicate your dual citizenship. The US basically ignores the notion that someone applying for American citizenship may want to remain the citizen of another country at the same time, and does nothing to formally recognize or deny this dual-status situation. The reluctance of the US Citizenship and Immigration Service (USCIS) to accept dual citizenship may stem from a fear of divided loyalties and citizenship by convenience.

Canadian/US dual citizens are envied for having the best of both worlds because they are in no way restricted from living, working, or vacationing in either country for any reason, for their entire lives. In addition, these dual citizens can pass this status on to their children by assisting them to obtain green cards in the categories noted earlier in this chapter. Also, children born directly to dual citizens can also become dual citizens providing they take action to do so prior to the age of 28.

Since I am currently a dual citizen and both my daughters, Sarah and Rebekah, were born in the US, I applied for their Canadian citizenship in 2007. Now they are both dual citizens. The changes to the Canadian *Citizenship Act* will not allow my daughters or other children in similar situations to eventually pass Canadian citizenship, and therefore dual citizenship, on to their children unless the children are born in Canada.

THE GREEN CARD LOTTERY

From time to time, the US Congress allows for an immigrant visa lottery. This is a free lottery, which offers a large number of visas on a random determinant basis with no employment or family-based qualifications required. Congress decides from which countries it will take entries, based on which countries they feel have not received a fair shake in the immigrant categories through the normal visa process and for other political reasons.

Congress holds what is now called Green Card Through the Diversity Immigrant Visa Program lottery of 50,000 applicants each, generally once a year. Canadians were eligible for these bulk lotteries but have been excluded from subsequent lotteries since 1993. However, if you are a citizen of some other country but are living in Canada, you may be eligible for the lottery under the non-Canadian citizenship lottery quota. Typically, the entry process is made public several months before the draws are made in the fall and each person is allowed only one application. Spouses, if also eligible, may each file separate entries.

The entries are very simple to complete, and contrary to advertisements from immigration services you do not need to pay, nor do you gain any advantage from having someone prepare and submit your application.

Those who are interested in future lotteries should contact USCIS periodically. Check the USCIS website for the lottery dates and to find out which countries are eligible for submission, at www.uscis.gov. The most recent lottery accepted only electronic applications.

LEGAL RETIREMENT IN THE US

Even though statistics show large numbers of Canadians spend much of their retirements in the US Sunbelt, there is no such thing as a retiree's visa. A separate visa category for retirees did exist once, but it was closed down in the mid-1970s due to some changes in US immigration rules. In 2014, the US Senate actually voted on and approved an immigration bill that included to what might be called two retirement visas, one special visa for Canadians that would allow them to spend up to eight months legally at a stretch in the US and the other a more general visa for retirees to live year-round in the US but not be allowed to work. Because it was part of a much larger immigration bill, the Canadian retirement visa was one of the least controversial aspects of the bill. However, because of the other large controversial aspects of the bill, the US House of Representatives wanted to split the bill into sections before they voted on it but that never happened as the bill died on the order paper with the 2014 US midterm election and has yet to be revived. However, all immigration policy is a political football and it is difficult to predict how soon, if at all, any form of retirement visa will again be available. This surprises many Canadians who do not intend to become any burden whatsoever on the US economy, but who just want to retire as Settlers in the US and spend the hard-earned dollars accumulated over their working years there.

Canadians who retire in the United States not only find a bit of sunshine for themselves, but they also help brighten the lives and economies in the communities where they make their homes. If you agree that the United States needs a retiree immigration visa status, share your thoughts with Uncle Sam. Write to your favorite Congressperson or any of the political representatives in any state where you winter or travel.

Although immigration is now a hot issue, you can help diffuse some of the controversy by sharing some of your positive contributions. Remind Congress that Canadians create hundreds of thousands of jobs and support the US economy with real estate purchases, travel costs, retail sales, taxes, and just by being nice folks! Each time an immigrant is bashed by some opportunistic politician, the chances of the retiree visa diminish. Make your voice count now! Even though you may not be able to vote, the people who work at the businesses you support certainly do.

Since there is no retirement visa yet, how, then, can you legally retire and become a Settler in the United States? In this chapter we have covered many immigration options, all of which apply to anyone, officially retired or not. In spite of this, most Canadian retirees or businesspeople probably travel to the United States as temporary visitors under the Vacationer or Snowbird lifestyle. Because of the relationship between Canada and the United States, entering each other's countries as a visitor is free of any formalities, at least for the time being, even though there are certain requirements that must be followed.

There are really two types of non-immigrant status for these people: visitors for business and visitors for pleasure (which were both briefly discussed in Chapter 1). Visitors for business are B-1 visitors. Visitors for pleasure are B-2 visitors. The USCIS normally allows Canadians six months when they enter on this temporary visitor status. The B-1 and B-2 visas for Canadians require no formal application or documentation. All that's required to be allowed into the United States on this status is a simple statement with respect to the time and purpose of your visit. Although B-1 and B-2 visas allow you to remain in the United States for only six months, there is no prohibition against leaving the country and re-entering to start a new six-month stay, even if it's only a day trip to Mexico in between. However, if you are entering the United States with the sole intention of remaining there as a resident, you may be considered as entering under false pretenses as you are abusing the intent of visitor status visas. If this is the case, you will be considered an illegal alien and could be barred from entering the US for any reason for periods extending up to five years for the first offense. The new US restrictions requiring visitors to check in and out of the US with full biometric identification regardless of their mode of travel currently mean that the amount of time a visitor spends in the US will be tracked very closely.

In Chapters 1 and 2, we discussed the differences between being a legal resident of the United States for tax purposes and being one for immigration purposes. Consequently, leaving the United States after six months as a visitor and then re-entering may work on a limited basis for immigration purposes, but it will also subject you to a whole new set of tax rules as you become a US taxpayer on your world income. Refer back to Chapter 4 for more on the tax implications of remaining in the United States for more than six months per year.

Always travel with your Border Kit mentioned in Chapter 1 and avoid the Red Flags also mentioned in Chapter 1, regardless of your status under any of these immigration rules, just to make your virtual Swinging Door work for you and your lifestyle as effectively as possible.

CANADIAN RESIDENTS HOLDING GREEN CARDS

It is estimated that thousands of Canadians who currently reside in Canada also hold US green cards — legal permanent resident (LPR) status. Often, these people are not sure what they should do with their green cards: if they should leave them in the drawer, move to the United States, throw them away, or get in touch with the USCIS for direction. Anyone holding a green card under these circumstances needs to carefully consider his or her options before deciding whether to use it or lose it.

In strict technical USCIS immigration terms, when green card holders take up permanent residency outside the United States, they have abandoned their LPR green card status. If they are still in possession of the green card they could use it to take up full-time residency in the United States, as long as they appear in all respects to be US residents. Some Canadians have had their cards seized when entering the United States because they gave immigration officials reason to believe that they were no longer permanent residents of the United States.

Keeping your green card active entitles you to all of its privileges, such as being able to live and work year-round in the United States. On the other hand, a green card comes with corresponding responsibilities, such as filing tax returns and maintaining a presence in the US. The tax consequences of holding a green card are discussed in Chapter 4 and the tax advantages are given in Chapters 9, 11, and 16. Since it is very difficult for most people to obtain green cards, Canadian residents who have them should carefully consider all their options before making a decision. Those who have had their green cards longer than eight years may be subject to the expatriation rules, effective June 17, 2008, which are detailed in Chapter 4. There is no middle ground here, as the USCIS allows no lengthy stays outside the US without having to meet admission criteria for re-entry. The only way to keep your green card is to use it, but from an income tax standpoint you are a US taxpayer as long as you possess and have not physically relinquished your green card to USCIS. This situation is one of those circumstances discussed earlier in which you may have no legal immigration status in the US but you are considered a US taxpayer by the IRS. The following guidelines should help those who wish to maintain their green card LPR:

- Use your green card every time you enter the United States.
- Maintain clear evidence of residence. For example, file US Income Tax Returns, use a US driver's licence and vehicle registration, keep US bank and investment accounts, all with a US address that belongs to you and that you return to very frequently.
- Keep your Alien Resident Card (green card) information current. You can update by filing Form I-90 if your name changes or you are past the expiration date of your card (please note that just because your card expiration date has passed you still have your legal US permanent resident status, the expiration date just means your card needs to be updated) and Form AR-11 for change of address.
- Ensure trips to Canada or abroad don't exceed one year from your last US entry date. If you anticipate an absence from the United States for longer than one year, obtain a Re-entry Permit (USCIS Form I-131) before leaving. Re-entry Permits are generally valid for a maximum of two years but can be renewed several times.

If you are certain there will be no advantages to keeping your green card, mail it along with Form I-407 by return receipt it to any US Consulate/Embassy office or surrender it next time you cross the border. As noted in the US Tax Legislation Concerning Expatriation from the US section in Chapter 4, long-term green card holders may be subject to some specific US tax rules when they give up their green cards. Extreme caution and professional advice are recommended before you give up a green card or US citizenship.

MARRIAGE TO A US CITIZEN

Every year, probably thousands of Canadians marry American citizens. Many of these are second marriages, where the respective spouses have been widowed by their previous partners. Many others are couples who met at US colleges or workplaces.

These marriages will trigger several important decisions that, if ignored, could lead to some major tax problems or missed opportunities. Some of the questions facing these cross-border couples are the following:

- Where do they, as a couple, actually reside?
- Where and how do they file tax returns for maximum advantage?
- How do they revise their estate plan to fit a cross-border situation, including avoiding double estate-taxation and taking advantage of all available deductions, while also remaining fair to children from former marriages?
- How do they maximize government benefits such as CPP/QPP, OAS, Social Security, and US or Canadian Medicare?
- How do they merge the two separate families in the two countries to suit their own personal goals, financial or otherwise to live the cross-border lifestyle they choose?
- What immigration issues do they need to cover and what do they say to immigration officials when entering the country to which their spouse is not a citizen or legal resident (and vice versa)?

All of these issues are covered indirectly through discussions in other chapters. This section will attempt to address them all in this particular context. Cross-border marriages may be a common occurrence, but there is little guidance available for cross-border couples, who will particularly need assistance with a cross-border financial planning analysis. Unfortunately, because of this lack of easily attainable help, we have been finding an increased level of stress and frustration at the hassles these couples (who are normally widows or widowers from long, previous successful marriages) are getting from increased scrutiny at the borders (in both directions), from overzealous immigration control people. All these couples want is to be able to enjoy their cross-border lifestyle and travel back and forth between their respective countries to spend time with their families and enjoy their final years. Recently we had a couple in this situation who traveled a lot together before they were married, and who were tired of the hassles they got at the border (as to what their intentions were, with respect to why they were traveling together and whether they were going to get married). Therefore, they thought they would fix the problem and put an end to the border interrogations by getting married. However, the first time they crossed into the US as a married couple, the Canadian husband was banned from entering the US for a year. He was told that he would only be allowed into the US if he spent the time and money to get a special K3 visa and apply for a green card.

Talk about a stressful and frustrating time for this couple! In fact, he was so angry at the US Customs and Border Protection that he didn't ever want to go to the US again. Had this couple known what they needed to do, and when and where they needed to get married to avoid these immigration problems, there would have been no border-crossing hassles at all along with putting a lot of money back in their pockets through tax reduction. This kind of situation seems to be happening time and time again when Canadians marry Americans (or vice versa).

The first area of concern for cross-border couples is which country to call home. For a retired married couple, this becomes largely a matter of choice; for those who are still working, where their skills will be most effectively employed and jobs available will be the important factors. A Canadian citizen spouse can sponsor a US citizen spouse for permanent resident status in Canada, or a US citizen spouse can sponsor a Canadian citizen spouse for a green card in the United States. (It should be noted here that it can be much easier to cross the border together if you can explain to the border officials that you both are legal residents in the same country. Otherwise, many red flags come up with immigration officials, and it can be very stressful trying to explain your situation every time you cross.) The third option is for each spouse to remain a resident of his or her original country and a non-resident of the spouse's country. This third option presents some unique tax and border-crossing difficulties, as noted above, and is recommended only in unusual circumstances, and even then only on a short-term basis.

Many couples in this situation make their decisions based on the economic realities of where they can get the best results from their combined financial resources. The major issues to consider here are income and estate taxes, medical coverage, and the cost of living.

The cost of living, especially when you include income tax and the Goods and Services Tax (GST), is generally accepted to be lower in the US, particularly with the recent strengthening of Canadian-dollar exchange rates. Depending on a couple's lifestyle, large savings can be achieved by spending the majority of their time in the US.

Income taxes are covered in detail in both Chapters 4 and 9. Estate tax issues are discussed in Chapters 5, 11, and 16. Chapters 5 and 15 cover Medicare, medical insurance, and the entitlements to government-sponsored programs, such as US Social Security, the Canada Pension Plan/Quebec Pension Plan, and Old Age Security. A complete review of these chapters, preferably before the marriage takes place, will go a long way toward making your marriage a more fruitful and happy one.

Even after reviewing all the issues in the previous chapters and making the appropriate calculations, it should be abundantly clear that there is no easy answer as to where a Canadian-American couple should reside. It really depends on personal preference, along with a combination of all the other factors applied to your personal situation. A complete cross-border financial planning analysis can help you determine the financial implications of either move. Hiring a cross-border financial planning professional is recommended for couples in this situation as their guidance should result in a good return on the investment of time and money. Ideally, both spouses should attempt to become dual citizens to maximize flexibility for themselves and their families, for the rest of their lives.

WHAT TO DO IF YOU ARE REFUSED ENTRY TO THE US

A traveler's greatest fear when crossing an international border is being hassled by some overly officious immigration officer. Many of you have heard stories about friends or relatives being detained or turned away for no apparent reason. Perhaps their vacation plans were ruined because an immigration officer misinterpreted an innocent remark. You may have even had this happen to you. Are you really defenseless against the onslaught of a border guard who is just having a bad day? Absolutely not! Here are some things you can do to ease your exits and entries to and from the US, and eliminate some of the stresses involved with dealing with immigration. Refer back to Chapter 1 for all the items you need to set up your virtual Swinging Door on the border or your chosen lifestyle as a Vacationer, Snowbird, or Settler. Following all of these recommendations will help ensure smooth travels back and forth as many times as you want. However, if you are refused entry to the US and can't see any quick resolution, ask for a deferred ruling at the USCIS office nearest to where you will be staying in the US. You may be allowed to enter the US until a hearing is set up, and you will get to present your case in a more favorable environment. You may also ask for parole, which will also allow you to enter the US and give you enough time to straighten out the particular concern in question. You will also have the time to engage an immigration attorney. These deferred hearings are extremely difficult to arrange due to new powers granted to border officials in 1997, that allow them to act more like an on-the-spot judge and jury. Deferred hearings and parole require additional paperwork and effort on the part of the immigration official. So if you don't know to ask for them, officials are very unlikely to offer you these options.

Border Guide readers are encouraged to participate in a cross-border Q&A through the new Cross-Border Forum. After registering, you can post questions about the contents of this book. Questions will be moderated and/or answered by a cross-border financial planning professional in a timely fashion. You can also post comments or create discussions with other readers to share experiences and swap cross-border financial planning tips. To post a question or comment, go to keatsconnelly.com and click on the Cross-Border Forum tab at the top of the first page

CROSS-BORDER Q&A

PROFESSIONAL CANADIAN WANTS TO WORK IN THE US

I am a Canadian Certified General Accountant with a Bachelor of Commerce undergraduate degree. I am currently employed in the public education K-12 sector as a Chief Financial Officer in a large school district in British Columbia, Canada. I am very interested in relocating to California with my spouse and child to work in my professional capacity. To date, I have made application to several opportunities that I have found on the Internet in the K-12 and college sectors. How should I respond to employers with respect to eligibility to work in the States (i.e., what is involved and how long will it take for me to be eligible to work in California)?

— Phil T., Maple Ridge, British Columbia

You should tell your prospective employers that you have the qualifications to get an H1B visa for full-time employment, which can be obtained on an accelerated basis in about three weeks (provided that you pay a $1,000 fee and have the application filled out by the potential employer, and provided that there is a quota opening available for this visa). Then, once you start your job, they can sponsor you for a green card (as the H1B is only good for six years, maximum). You should also have a good immigration attorney. Let me know if you need a referral. If there are no H1B visas available you should also be able to qualify for a TN visa.

PLAN AHEAD FOR CROSS-BORDER MARRIAGE

My fiancée and I are engaged to be married. We are both 65 plus and retired. This is a new and different venture for us because I am a citizen of the United States and she is a Canadian. We have so many unanswered questions we hope you can help us with:

1. *Would it be beneficial for each of us to apply for American and Canadian citizenship? I understand that I would have to sponsor her application to the USCIS for permanent resident alien status. Is the acceptance of this application a green card? And if you keep this green card for three years, does this entitle you to US citizenship?*

What is the procedure? To apply for the green card, is it acceptable to live six months in Canada and six months in the United States?

2. *How do I apply for Canadian citizenship?*
3. *Would it be advisable to apply for dual citizenship?*
4. *When we are married, will we continue to submit our income tax forms to our individual countries? Or because we will be married, does that mean we will both have to submit to both countries? My income is approximately $50,000; hers is about $41,000.*
5. *I own two condos in Florida; she owns one. If we rent two of these, the rent about covers the cost of ownership. Would it be advisable to sell two of these condos and invest the money received? I presently have investments worth $75,000 in the United States. She has about $95,000 invested in mutual funds in Canada. She owns a condo in Ontario and currently we plan to spend six months there and six months in Florida. However, there may come a time when we prefer to spend eight months in Florida and four months in Canada; hence the need for dual citizenship.*
6. *Is a living trust a good thing? My will has been prepared in Florida and hers in Ontario. Are these acceptable in each other's residence, or must they be prepared in both places?*
7. *Upon death, which countries laws will our estates be treated by?*

— J.T., Sanibel, Florida

Your questions are very good and very relevant for anyone in your situation. Most of the questions require lengthy, detailed analysis and answers to put you in a position to take the correct action. I will give you the key issues you need to resolve to obtain the answers to your questions. There are several steps you need to go through before or immediately after you are married to determine the best course to take. The first step is to determine which country you are going to call your tax home. This should be the country where you get married and start the immigration process for the immigrating spouse. Once you are married, you should remain in that country until the immigrating spouse has legal documentation not only to legally remain there, but to leave and re-enter the country. This will determine what tax filings, estate-planning documents, immigration requirements, medical coverage, and other forms of insurance you will require. If you attempt to be residents of both countries, or if one spouse is to be a resident of Canada and the other a resident of the US, you will have an endless state of confusion about which tax, estate, and immigration requirements apply and which don't. You want to be in a position to have to file the least number of returns and pay the least amount of taxes, but residency and/or US citizenship all affect what returns you file.

A cross-border financial planning analysis is definitely in order to determine which country you should call your tax home. This plan will determine the amount of income tax you would pay according to which country and which scenario you are looking at, and will net out any potential increases or decreases in other costs such as medical coverage and estate taxes. From the information you have provided I would expect you would pay the least amount of tax in the US and get increased Social Security pensions there; consequently you should sponsor your new spouse for US green card. She will qualify for US Medicare and a US Social Security pension, based on your Social Security benefits obtained, after one year and also for US citizenship after being married to you for at least three years by spending at least six months each year in the US for each of those three years. The plan should confirm this as to which country is best for you from a financial standpoint. Then it becomes easier to determine whether to become a dual citizen, what tax returns you should file, what changes have to be made to your wills or trusts, what changes have to be made to your investments, and what medicare and other government benefits you can obtain. Also as part of the planning the cross-border planner can better can answer your question is whether you should sell your rental properties or keep them for cash flow.

I realize I have not answered your questions directly, but the issues go much deeper than you have anticipated and are not easily addressed until some cross-border financial planning analysis is completed.

DERIVATIVE CITIZEN WANTS TO SPONSOR SONS

I am 53 and an only child. My father passed away ten years ago. He was born in Vancouver and moved to LA with his mother in about 1930. He was married twice to American citizens and was also in the US Navy. His last divorce was in about 1942, and both his divorces were done in the US. His Navy records indicate naturalization in 1942 (he used to be British). I have no documentation to show he was a US citizen other than Navy papers, marriage and divorce papers, birth certificate, etc. He stayed in the US for over 12 years and I have records of all previous addresses. He married my mother in 1948 and lived in BC for the rest of his life. He never voted in Canada because he claimed he was a US citizen. He also collected US Social Security in 1990 and a portion of that was left to my mother when he died (my mother died in 2008). In 2004 I became her US trustee to look after her Social Security, and she and I were both given Social Security cards.

I have two sons who want me to become a dual citizen so that eventually they can also have the option of working in the US. I have been working on this for two years for proof of my father being a US citizen. Even though I have lots of paperwork on his personal history, I don't have documents to show that he was legally a US citizen. I contacted the US Navy six months ago for a search and have not yet heard from them. What do you suggest?

— Gail L., Vancouver, British Columbia

You should be gathering documentation for the purpose of applying for a US passport rather than a Certificate of US Citizenship. You are probably a US citizen already by birth, through your father. However, with all of the concerns regarding security these days, it is possible that the passport office will ask you to go back and apply for a Certificate of Citizenship first; this may happen if the quality of your documentation is poor. In spite of this, applying for a passport is your quickest and easiest route to determine if you are considered a US citizen. Passport application is normally processed in only four to eight weeks so you'll know very quickly an answer to your dual citizenship status.

The US Navy may or may not have a copy of your father's naturalization certificate. US Citizenship and Immigration Services is the agency most likely to have a copy. It may take six months or longer to get copies of records from either the Navy or USCIS.

Once you have proof (such as a US passport or US Certificate of Citizenship) that you are a US citizen and that you are living in the US or have the intention of living in the US, you can sponsor your sons for green cards. Once they've lived in the US for five years, they can apply for US citizenship and therefore become dual citizens of Canada and the US.

US CITIZENSHIP IS A MATERNAL MATTER

I am interested in finding out about becoming an American resident. I retired eight years ago from a career in the Canadian Armed Forces and the federal government. My wife and I own a condominium in Canada where we live during the summer months. We also own a home in Florida near Tampa where we spend up to six months per year.

I am particularly interested in knowing more about derivative citizenship. I was born in Ontario in 1931. My father was Canadian but my mother is American, born in Chicago, Illinois. I understand there is some US legislation that would allow me to claim US citizenship. I believe it is known as the Equity in Citizenship Act. I have not been able to track any progress in this legislation. Perhaps you could inform me of its current and future status.

On the pessimistic assumption that there is no future for this legislation, I wonder what other avenues are available to me. Is there any possibility that a claim in court for American citizenship based on the inequities of the present legislation would prove successful?

— D.W., Mount Hope, Ontario

I have great news for people in your position. The Immigration Technical Corrections Bill was passed October 6, 1994. This means that those born before 1934 to US citizen mothers have derived US citizenship from their mothers. Before this Technical Corrections Bill, citizenship could be derived only through a US citizen father.

Your best bet is to apply for a US passport to affirm your US citizenship status. A strong note of caution: Complete a comprehensive cross-border financial planning analysis first to ensure you are aware of the tax implications of being a US citizen.

KNOW US RULES FOR RESIDENCY CHANGE

My husband and I are thinking about residing in Florida on a permanent basis about five years from now. We will be 75 and 76 respectively at that time and feel that the 1,300-mile trip from northern Ontario will become too difficult. We need to know the following:

1. *Health insurance: How will it affect us?*
2. *What do we need to do to achieve resident status but keep our Canadian citizenship?*

We both have government pensions and pensions set up by ourselves. There would be no income from the United States except small amounts of interest income from bank accounts.

— A.C., Clearwater, Florida

1. Health insurance in the US is relatively easy to obtain under the Affordable Care Act once you have legal residency in the US. You can also buy into US Medicare if you have been a legal permanent resident for five years, are a US citizen, or have worked in that country for a minimum of ten years. There is also limited coverage from insurance carriers outside the United States for those over 65; a good international insurance broker may be useful for your health insurance coverage in the United States. Don't forget about

long-term nursing care insurance, since US Medicare and other health insurance policies don't cover extended care for long-term disabilities or incapacities. This coverage can be obtained at any age (up to around 85) from numerous US insurance companies.

2. To achieve residency you need either a family or a business to sponsor you for a visa or a green card (Legal Permanent Resident status). This may be difficult under current law as there are few options available for retired persons unless you have $500,000 to invest in a Regional Center Program to get an investor green card under the EB-5 category.

 Once you have legal immigration status in the US, income tax would not likely be a problem for you since rates in Florida are much lower than they are in any Canadian province. You would have to file a return on your world income in the United States and you would cease to file any returns in Canada if you became a US resident. CRA would withhold a non-resident withholding tax of 15 percent on all your non-CPP/QPP or OAS pensions and 0 percent on interest earned in Canada, and you would receive credit for this tax when you filed your returns in the United States. CRA will not withhold any tax on CPP/QPP and OAS payments for non-residents. You need to calculate the difference between your reduction in tax, food, clothing, and housing costs, and the cost of your health insurance to see if you'll come out ahead. For more information on these topics I suggest you obtain advice from a cross-border financial planning professional.

RECLAIMING CANADIAN CITIZENSHIP IS A COMPLICATED, LENGTHY PROCESS

I became a US citizen in 1974, three years before the new Canadian citizenship law in 1977. I would like to reclaim my Canadian citizenship without jeopardizing my US citizenship. Is that feasible without resorting to an application to a citizenship court? Are you aware of any challenges to claim dual citizenship on any basis for a case similar to mine?

— Brian M., Kanata, Ontario

There is good news for people in your situation. Amendments to the Canadian *Citizenship Act*, effective April 17, 2009, allow people in your circumstances to reclaim their lost Canadian citizenship. The easiest way for you to confirm your renewed Canadian citizenship status is to apply for a Canadian passport.

GREEN CARD GONE? START OVER AGAIN

My spouse and I are in good health and financially independent. We are aware that since the mid-1980s there has been no separate visa category for us due to changes in the US immigration rules. You state in your book that those who have had a five-year continuous legal permanent residence in the United States and have not had any interruptions over six months, are eligible for US citizenship by naturalization.

Both of us had green cards from the 1960s until we surrendered them to US immigration in 1979 for family reasons. I would appreciate your comments on the following questions:

1. *Since we had a green card and were physically present in the United States without any interruptions over six months for five years, are we eligible for naturalization via application form N-400?*
2. *Regarding taxation, is the criteria residency or citizenship?*
3. *Where does dual citizenship fit into this situation?*

— Hollis and Anne G., Gravenhurst, Ontario

Sorry; when you turned in your green cards in 1979, you gave up the qualifications you had to become naturalized US citizens. You could have become naturalized US citizens at that time in 1979, but since you are no longer legal permanent residents of the US, you cannot use the USCIS Form N-400. In effect, you have to start over and get another green card for legal permanent residence, and then have them for five years before you apply again. If you had any children while you lived in the United States who are US citizens, they can sponsor you for the new green cards.

BORN IN THE US, DUAL CITIZENSHIP NOT LOST

My husband and I had three children, all born in the United States and US citizens until they became Canadian citizens in 1992. We had always assumed that by doing this, they lost their US citizenship. Is this true?

— Ethel M., Indian Harbor Beach, Florida

When your children became Canadian citizens in 1992, they did not lose their US citizenships. Under US immigration rules introduced in 1992, they would not be considered to have given up their citizenship unless they had the intention to do so. They can likely reinstate it by applying to the US State Department for a passport or by contacting the US Immigration and Naturalization Service for an N-600 form.

OBTAINING A GREEN CARD

We are retired and financially independent Canadians and we want to retire in Arizona. What are our chances of immigrating to the United States? What is a green card and how do we get one? Does it help that I have a brother who is a green card holder and living in Florida?

— Axel R., Phoenix, Arizona

There are two basic ways of immigrating to the US. One is to achieve permanent resident status through a job, and the other is through a relative. In your case, since your brother already has a green card, immigration through a relative seems like the better possibility. However, a lawful permanent resident (or green card holder) cannot petition for siblings. He or she must become a US citizen to do so. Citizenship normally requires five years of permanent residence, unless the permanent residence was acquired through a US-citizen spouse, in which case he or she need only wait three years before filing an application for US citizenship.

Once sworn in as a US citizen, your brother may immediately file a visa petition for you in the category of fourth preference. However, at the current time, the "quota wait" for fourth preference for Canada is approximately 13 years. If this seems out of the question, you could try the business routes to immigration. If you have $500,000 to invest, you may also be able to obtain a green card in a matter of months through a Regional Center EB-5 investor green card program.

DERIVATIVE CITIZENSHIP

My parents were both US citizens, but I was born in Canada and have lived there all my life. I am now 69. Could I obtain US citizenship easily if I wanted to? Similarly, my wife, who is 66, also had US citizens as parents. Would it be any easier for her to get US citizenship?

— Donald E., Scottsdale, Arizona

One or both of you may already be US citizens. You must prove your derivative citizenship by filing Form N-600 (Application for Certificate of Citizenship), along with supporting documentation, with the US Citizenship and Immigration Service (USCIS) or by applying for a US passport from the State Department.

Based on your ages, citizenship could only have been transmitted through either or both of your respective parents. You must discover whether your parents ever knowingly abandoned their US citizenships before your birth, by taking an oath of allegiance to the government of Canada and forswearing allegiances to all other nations.

In the event that documentary evidence is lacking for one of your derivative citizenship claims it would only be necessary for one of you to prove US citizenship. The other could immigrate as the immediate relative of the US citizen, a category for which there is no quota or wait.

HIRING AN IMMIGRATION ATTORNEY

When should I use an attorney to help me immigrate to the United States? What would it cost relative to my status? How long does it take?

— Alice C., Tucson, Arizona

There is no law that says immigration documents may not be filed by an individual. However, there may be alternatives available to you that you may find out about only through a consultation with an attorney. Certainly, if you have a problem with the Immigration Service, you would be well advised to get professional assistance immediately. Most immigration attorneys work on an hourly basis, but expect to pay over $5,000 for even a basic visa; complicated situations can be substantially more.

IMMIGRATION STRATEGIES AND THE NEED FOR FINANCIAL PLANNING

My husband and I wish to immigrate to the United States. My husband is a civil technologist currently employed by a road construction firm. I run my own advertising and promotions firm, registered as an Ontario corporation.

1. *How can we immigrate with a minimum of fuss and expense? (I have heard rumors about bringing in $100,000 and hiring one employee.) What are the costs involved? Also, my husband's sister has lived and worked in Michigan for the last 15 years. If she becomes an American citizen, could she sponsor us and could we both get jobs and work? How long would it take for her to get US citizenship and sponsor us?*
2. *Would it be to our advantage to get jobs in order to immigrate or is it a disadvantage to me, especially since I have an existing corporation?*
3. *If we are no longer Canadian residents, I assume there are tax advantages, but does this lack of residency affect our current investments, such as our family home (must we sell?), our RRSPs held in a Canadian brokerage house, our life insurance held by Canadian firms, etc.?*

— Laura P., Toronto, Ontario

1. From what you have told me, the best alternative for you to immigrate to the US would be through your business. By forming a similar business in the United States, you have created the means

for you to qualify for a visa under Treaty Investor Route (E-2) or a regular intra-company transfer (L-1), or even the new green card category (E-1C) for established businesses (similar to the L-1).

The E-2 is likely the quickest and easiest to achieve. Many immigration attorneys recommend you invest $100,000 or more in the US business to qualify for this type of visa. Immigration attorneys working for our clients in non-capital intensive service industries similar to your business have received E-2 visas for investments of less than $100,000. Even though there is no requirement to hire US workers, the more employment you can create and the more capital you have, the better off you will be.

The best long-term route is the green card route through a transfer from your established Canadian company to the US-affiliated company you would set up. The green card confers permanent residency status, whereas all the other visas may be subject to continuing requirements and/or have expiration dates.

Your husband's sister can become a naturalized US citizen if she has had her green card for five years or longer. It is currently taking 7 to 12 months from the date of application to complete this process. Once she is a citizen she can sponsor your husband for permanent resident status (or a green card). However, there can be a waiting list in this category of as much as 13 years. It wouldn't hurt to get on this waiting list, as sometimes quotas change and the waiting list disappears or at least shortens.

The maze of rules and regulations can be overwhelming. I recommend that you use a good immigration attorney in the area where you are likely to relocate. Be prepared to spend $5,000 to $7,500 on legal fees to get the job done both of you. If you are well organized and can do a lot of the necessary work yourself, the legal fees could be lower, but they will increase if you do not have a concrete plan of action that you can outline to the attorney.

2. You will not be able to procure legal employment in the US unless you have a visa or some special skills or education that allow you to get a work visa (for example, if you have a PhD or other post-secondary degree(s) or equivalent experience). If so, your immigration attorney will direct you to these special categories.
3. As far as financial matters are concerned, there are some good planning opportunities and some pitfalls. These are difficult to condense. I recommend you complete a comprehensive financial

plan, with the assistance of a professional planner who is knowledgeable in both Canadian and US tax, investment, estate, and insurance requirements.

IS US CITIZENSHIP REQUIRED FOR ESTATE TAX EXEMPTIONS?

My husband and I are both Canadian citizens by birth who became permanent US residents and green card holders in 1997. We live permanently in Florida. Our question is whether we should become US citizens to take advantage of the $5.45 million exemption from estate tax, since you mentioned that only US citizens can take full advantage of this exemption.

— M.S., North Miami, Florida

It is Canada's choice whether you keep your Canadian citizenship. Only the country conferring citizenship can require a person to relinquish prior citizenship. For the time being, Canada allows individuals to retain Canadian citizenship after becoming US citizens.

Since you are a green card holder domiciled in the US, you already qualify for the $5.45 million estate tax exemption and so does your husband. You do not have to become citizens to qualify for these exemptions.

As a US citizen you gain the ability to defer estate tax on estates over $5.45 million to the second spouse's death by using the unlimited marital deduction. You may use a qualified domestic trust to take advantage of the unlimited marital deduction as an alternative to becoming a citizen.

If you or your husband's estate(s) are worth more than $5.45 million each, you need to consider your options with the help of a professional estate planner. If you still have assets in Canada you'll need a cross-border financial planning professional.

STAYING ON BOTH SIDES OF THE BORDER

My husband and I have lived and worked in Canada since 1995. I retired in 2015 but my husband is still working and would like to continue until he is eligible for Canadian Pension. We are both 57 years old.

2015 came sooner than we expected, and are not ready to move to the US yet. We plan on moving permanently when my husband retires in 2019.

We bought a retirement home in Florida. I have been living in Florida for six months and in Canada for six months since we received our green cards in May 2015, thinking I was within the bounds of immigration laws of both countries. We file both US and Canadian income taxes and opted out of the Homestead tax deduction offered for first-time home buyers in

Florida. On my recent trip to the United States, I was questioned at length by US immigration officials in Toronto. I was told I should give up either my green card or my OHIP card. My questions are the following:

1. *Can US Immigration confiscate either my green card or OHIP card? Is there a law that entitles them to do this?*
2. *Does six months in the United States constitute legal permanent resident status? Does it have to be six consecutive months and only in one particular state?*
3. *If I were to give up my green card, would US Immigration issue me one easily later on when my husband retires? Would it take very long?*
4. *I am covered by my husband's company health plan. If I move earlier and live permanently in Florida, will I still get free medical health coverage without my OHIP card?*
5. *We own properties in Canada and all our investments are there. In light of the continuing decline of the Canadian dollar, the increasing high cost of health care in the United States, and the new non-resident tax deduction in effect on CPP and OAS, would we be better off to forget about residing permanently in the United States and instead spend six months in Canada and only go for six months in the winter to Florida as Canadian tourists?*

— Elaine F., Toronto, Ontario

1. US Immigration has the authority to take your green card if they can determine you are not living permanently in the US, a requirement in order to keep your green card. They cannot take your OHIP card; only OHIP can do that and they may do just that once they discover an OHIP member has a green card.
2. You should not reside outside the United States longer than six months at any stretch and maintain full US residency ties at all times to maintain your green card.
3. Whether you can get another green card depends on how you got it. If you got it in the lottery, you would have to wait for another lottery and hope you are lucky. If a family member sponsored you, you would have to reapply, a process that is taking anywhere from six months to five years, depending on preference status.
4. You should check with your husband's company benefits department; they will be able to answer this easily. Most plans require you to be a member of OHIP to get full health insurance coverage.

OHIP requires you to live at least five months a year in Ontario. I recommend you shop for US coverage as soon as possible, there are many reasonably priced health insurance options in Florida, since OHIP may ask you to give up your OHIP benefits because you have a green card. If you live in Florida for at least six months a year, US immigration should also not be a problem, and you should be able to maintain your green card. In addition, you should do other things a US green card holder would normally do like to get a US driver's license, bank accounts, credit cards and give up the Canadian equivalents of these residential ties. You likely save taxes if you only file your taxes in the US as well, you will need to do an exit return from Canada by putting an exit date on your next T1 filing with the CRA.

5. These kinds of questions require you to have a knowledgeable cross-border financial planning practitioner do a detailed cross-border financial planning analysis. Your planner can compare all the tax, immigration, and insurance issues and provide you with the information you need to make an educated choice. Only you can decide which country will be best for you.

Please note that your husband does not have to work until age 60 to receive CPP. He only needs to wait until age 60 (the earliest age at which he can apply) to start receiving CPP payments.

REASONS FOR BEING REFUSED ENTRY AT THE BORDER

An immigration officer refused us entry into the United States last November because we rented our house in Canada for six months while we were away. Why? When I mentioned I was born in North Dakota, he said if I hadn't renounced my US citizenship, I could hold dual citizenship. Can I do this?

— E.W., Arizona City, Arizona

It sounds like the immigration official at the border was being a bit overzealous, but if he was concerned that you were living in the United States permanently he had every right to refuse you entry as a visitor. However, he was correct that you probably are a dual Canada/US citizen.

Remember that whenever you enter the US you are presumed to be entering permanently unless you can prove otherwise. You must supply this proof, if asked. Carry a border-crossing kit that includes property tax notices, recent utility bills, proof of Canadian medicare, vehicle and driver's registration, pay stubs, and bank and investment account records to prove that you are going to remain residents of Canada.

It is relatively easy for you to confirm whether you are still a US citizen by applying for your US passport at the nearest passport office. Since you were born in the US and don't appear to have done anything intentionally to renounce your US citizenship, you most certainly still are a US citizen and you could easily sponsor your husband for a US green card so you both could become US residents. After three years with a green card your husband can also become a dual citizen so that you can spend any time you want in the US or Canada for the rest of your lives. However, with US citizenship may come tax obligations, along with some excellent potential tax reductions if you desire, that you will need to address before you proceed any further. I suggest you contact a knowledgeable cross-border financial planning practitioner to analyze your specific situation.

BANNED FROM THE UNITED STATES

My husband and I are Canadian citizens with a winter home in the United States. We overstayed the six-month limit, and when my husband returned to Canada he was told by US officials that he could not come back into the United States for five years or face fines and jail time. I am still in the States (and past my deadline as well). Do you have any advice?

— M.C., Fort Myers, Florida

There is not much you can do, except get legal with US Immigration as soon as possible by leaving the US. When you return as a visitor, make sure you have clear proof with you that you have not become a resident of the US. You should carry a border kit that contains such items as a copy of your current Canadian tax return, latest utilities paid in Canada, and home title or lease agreement if you rent, as well as your provincial medicare card, Canadian driver's licence, and return-trip airfare purchased in Canada or if traveling by car, have a Canadian provincial plate on the car. This Border Kit should always be kept current and should be available every time you enter the US. You should never stay in the US longer than six months at a time without returning to Canada unless you have proper immigration status.

Your husband will have difficulty overcoming the five-year ban. He needs to hire a good US immigration attorney who will go through the very limited procedures to get this ban overturned, which will likely only be possible if your husband has a good reason for his overstay.

The Grass Is Always Greener

Canadian versus US Taxation Policies

One of the major considerations for people thinking of adopting a Settler cross-border lifestyle temporarily or more permanently with the United States is how much income tax they may be able to save. For the first time some Canadians are facing a combined federal and provincial marginal income tax rate of close to 60 percent and most, including Alberta which was once Canada's tax haven, are around 50 percent rates. Canadians are frustrated by the seemingly endless spiral of federal and provincial income taxes because they are on top of all the other taxes such as PST, GST, HST, gasoline, beer/wine/liquor, and property taxes which are also creeping up. Most Canadians accept higher taxes as the price of Canada's social welfare system, but recently the higher taxes seem to have come with commensurate decreases in government services. Some Canadians have voted with their feet by becoming taxpayers in the US and reaping a major tax cut. Tax differentials between Canadian and US taxpayers is the greatest in favor of the US since the first edition of *The Border Guide* was published in 1992. It is estimated that most Canadians would receive significant tax reductions through adopting a Settler lifestyle with the US even after they purchased an unlimited US medical insurance program under the Affordable Care Act mentioned in Chapter 6.

For those Canadians who wish to adopt the Settler lifestyle this chapter will address tax-saving opportunities and will provide good guidance of how the tax savings can enhance their cross-border lifestyles by increasing their after-tax spendable income, whether measured in Canadian or US funds. In addition to substantial increased after-tax income available for the Settler's lifestyles, they will also be able to take advantage of the much lower cost of living in the US. This cost of living reduction is usually 20 to 40 percent for most necessary living expenses or purchases. Chapters 14 and 15 will discuss the opportunities in investments, medical coverage, insurance, and US Social Security benefits.

In Chapter 4, I outlined some of the basic tax rates and tax deduction comparisons between the United States and Canada. These comparisons can now be incorporated into a cross-border financial planning analysis from the perspective of someone who is actually transitioning to or contemplating a transition to the United States to enjoy the Settler lifestyle. I will use real-life examples showing how some Canadians have effectively used cross-border financial planning professionals to maximize the benefits while minimizing the pitfalls of moving south. Because of constant changes to taxes in both countries, it is important to understand that the tax comparisons in this chapter are a moving target; therefore, it is vital that you get the latest information and incorporate any changes made after the printing of this edition of *The Border Guide*.

First, our discussion looks at a line-by-line analysis of each type of taxable income and deduction, and then I tie it all together using full, comprehensive case studies of Canadians who have gone through professional cross-border financial planning services. Please note all the dollars indicated in this chapter, and other chapters for that matter, are entered in Canadian dollars unless otherwise indicated.

KEEP MORE OF YOUR CPP/QPP AND OAS

A popular misconception among Canadians is that they lose Canada Pension Plan or Quebec Pension Plan (CPP/QPP), and/or Old Age Security (OAS) benefits after exiting Canada. In fact, the opposite is true and they will actually receive more of their benefits on an after-tax basis. The Canada/US Tax Treaty amendment, as effective January 1, 1996, provides some very interesting tax advantages for those Canadians who are collecting or are eligible for CPP/QPP and Old Age Security.

Because of provisions contained in the treaty, both your CPP/QPP and OAS are no longer taxable at all by Canada Revenue Agency (CRA) for US residents and are totally free from non-resident withholding tax. When you file tax returns in the US as a resident, CPP/QPP and OAS are reported and taxed in a manner similar to US Social Security. Married couples with incomes of less than $32,000 USD (including the CPP/QPP and OAS) or single persons with less than $25,000 USD of income do not pay any US tax on this income. Consequently, CPP/QPP and OAS are completely free from both Canadian and US taxes for people in this income bracket. For those at higher income levels, 85 percent of the total CPP/QPP and OAS is added to income and taxed at the standard US tax rates; the other 15 percent is tax free. The maximum federal US tax rate on this income as US residents is 34 percent, even if your income exceeds the highest tax bracket.

Since January 1996, Canadian residents in the US have no longer been subject to the OAS 100 percent clawback tax rules as they would be as residents of Canada. This means Canadians moving to the United States as Settlers who have been subject to the OAS clawback on income of more than $73,756, would be entirely exempt from the clawback regardless of the size of their income once they become US residents. For a high-income married couple, getting out from under the OAS clawback can mean an immediate tax saving on their OAS alone of up to $13,000, depending into which US tax brackets they fall. Even those Canadians who have sufficient income to put them in the highest US bracket that have surplus foreign tax credits from other sources, such as RRSP withdrawals, may use these foreign tax credits to zero out any US taxes due so they pay 0 percent net tax on their OAS (that normally would have been at 100 percent net tax had they remained Canadian residents). This is one of the most ironic situations in cross-border planning: You have to leave Canada to get a benefit that it takes 40 years of living in Canada to qualify for. I often tell people to take this minor windfall of $13,000, and take a nice cruise once a year, then send a thank-you note to CRA.

Let's look at a real example of what this one item can mean. George and Susan transitioned from Ottawa to become Settlers in Florida, with $13,000 of CPP and $6,800 of OAS benefits each; both are receiving the maximum of these benefits. This couple is retired and near the highest Canadian tax bracket (Ontario, 53.5 percent) and both are subject to the OAS clawback; the applicable US tax bracket in Florida is 25 percent. (See Figure 9.7 later in this chapter for details of their incomes. All dollar amounts in Figures 9.1 through 9.8 are in Canadian funds, and I have used the tax rates from Figure 4.6.)

As you can see from Figure 9.1, with the treaty and exemption from OAS clawback rules for non-residents, George would see a drop in his average tax rate from 70 percent to a maximum of 22 percent. This is on his combined CPP and OAS income. The resulting tax saving of $9,947 is significant, especially when you consider that George's wife is in a similar situation. In addition, if George and Susan have foreign tax credits available the entire $4,208 US tax due to the IRS can be reduced to zero. Their combined savings would double to $19,894 or, with foreign tax credits, to $28,310 per year. So before George and Susan even consider any potential tax reductions on investment and other pension income, they are in line for a raise of $1,660 to $2,360 a month! Figure 9.7 shows George and Susan's complete sources of income. It is important to note here that although George and Susan are in approximately the top 5 percent of all income earners in North America, they are only in the middle

CANADIAN AND US TAX RATES ON CPP AND OAS INCOME, 2009

Income	
CPP	$13,000
OAS	$6,800

	Canadian Resident	US Resident
Taxable income	$19,500	$16,830
Tax due	$13,735	$4,208
Effective tax rate	70%	22%
Total savings		$9,947

FIGURE 9.1

US income tax brackets, generally American residents need to be in the top 1 percent of income earners (over about $500,000 US) to be in the highest brackets under the US federal tax system.

INTEREST INCOME-TAX FREE, IF YOU WISH

In the United States, municipal bonds are a form of local government bond that pay interest without attracting income tax at either federal or state levels. These are the bonds cities use to fund infrastructure such as public buildings, roads, airports, and hospitals.

As a result, someone earning a great deal of interest can zero out the tax liability on any amount of interest they earn by holding these municipal bonds. Some of these types of bonds may be subject to US alternative minimum tax. When you consider that interest in Canada is taxed at rates of up to 58 percent in some provinces, a zero tax rate looks pretty attractive. From the investment planning aspect (see Chapter 14), it's not wise to place most of your investment portfolio into municipal bonds, or any other asset class for that matter. Municipal bonds are currently paying rates of interest higher than those of any Canadian bank deposits — around 4 percent compared to about 2 percent on Canadian term deposits or GICs. If you're in a top Canadian income tax bracket, you will keep less than half of the 2 percent you earn on a GIC. A 4 percent rate on a tax-free bond would yield 400 percent more after taxes if you were a US resident. That is an incredible increase in income on an investment that provides a fixed income with a relatively low level of risk. In fact, at maximum Canadian tax rates, you would have to earn more than 8 percent or better on a GIC to net the same amount on an after-tax basis that a 4 percent tax-free municipal bond does. When was the last time anyone saw 8 percent paid on a GIC; persons already retired may never even see this higher rate again in their lifetime?

In various federal budgets over the past couple of decades, Canada's parliament has gradually eliminated the ability to defer income taxes on Canada Savings Bonds, annuities, and long-term term deposits or GICs. This means that all interest earned on any investment must be paid on a current accrued annual basis, and cannot be deferred to a later date when the interest is actually received. For anyone saving for retirement, the ability to defer income tax to a future date, particularly when he or she may be in a lower tax bracket, can dramatically increase total return. For example, if you had $100,000 earning 10 percent interest over 15 years, and were in a 50 percent tax bracket, you would net only $107,900 if you paid the tax on a current or accrual basis under present Canadian tax rules. You would net $158,850 of earnings after tax if you could defer paying all the tax until the 15th year, which is still possible for US residents. This amounts to more than a 47 percent increase in income from a basic investment. That's why RRSPs — with their ability to defer taxes on current income — work so well over the long haul for those Canadians that are in a lower tax bracket when they withdraw RRSP proceeds or

CANADA		**UNITED STATES**	
	Interest Income		
42,500		$14,167	Tax Free
		$14,167	Tax Deferred
		$14,167	Taxable
		$42,500	Total
	Tax Due		
$22,738		$3,542	
	Amount left after tax		
		$38,958	
$19,762			
	Tax saved		
		$19,196	

FIGURE 9.2

are forced to convert it to an RRIF. In addition to receiving a deduction for your RRSP contribution, the interest and other income accumulate tax-deferred. In the United States, the ability to defer tax on interest is not limited to RRSP-like investments. Taxpayers can deposit unlimited sums into investment vehicles, called deferred or variable annuities, which allow for tax-free compounding and deferral of interest, dividends, and capital gains for any number of years. Tax is paid on the income only when it is taken out of the annuity at a time of your choice and the withdrawals can be spread over any number of years. Even so, it's still not prudent to place all your investments into tax-free or tax-deferred investments from an investment or estate-planning standpoint.

Let's call on George and Susan again to look at the interest-income portion of their tax picture, and then compare this with their tax savings potential if they move to the United States. In the example used in Figure 9.2, we assume they have $850,000 of joint investments in interest-bearing vehicles such as bonds and GICs, earning an average rate of interest of 5 percent, for a total of $42,500. After moving to the United States, they split their portfolio into one-third tax-free municipal bonds earning 5 percent or $14,167, one-third tax-deferred annuities earning 5 percent or $14,167, and leave the remaining one-third in investments similar to those in their Canadian portfolio earning 5 percent or $14,166. Amounts in Figure 9.2 (and through Figure 9.8) are shown in Canadian funds. Please note, these interest rates whether in Canada or the US vary greatly and the rates used in this example are strictly hypothetical to illustrate how interest can be taxed differently in the US than in Canada.

In Figure 9.2, George and Susan's interest income, after taxes are paid, is more than 97 percent higher. It should be noted that one-third of the investment portfolio is in a tax-deferred annuity and will be subject to tax when withdrawn in the future. But tax deferred can be tax saved if deferred long enough. In the 25 percent tax bracket that George and Susan fall into in the United States, you only have to defer the tax for approximately eight years before you can save the entire amount.

There is a common misconception that moving to the US means accepting lower interest rates on savings. In fact, US interest rates are now higher in most cases, particularly on the tax free municipal bonds depending on where the Bank of Canada is setting its rates.

PENSIONS: PARTIALLY TAX FREE

There are major differences between the US and Canada in the way pensions are taxed. The CRA taxes all pensions by including 100 percent as taxable income, minus an equivalent exemption of $2,000 each year. All Canadian pensions now qualify for income splitting which can allow some tax reduction if you have a lower income spouse. Income splitting has never been necessary in the US since most couples file their returns jointly anyways so they in effect get an automatic income split. The IRS allows pensioners to receive the portion of the pension resulting from the taxpayer-non-deductible-contribution tax-free. If an individual made 50 percent of the annual contributions to her company pension, roughly half of her pension at retirement would be tax-free. The actual amount received tax-free depends on current interest rates and the life expectancy of the employee at the time she starts receiving the pension. The IRS, for example, considers a pension annuity created from an RRSP (which would be fully taxable in Canada) as just a regular annuity. Only the annual interest earned is considered taxable. Thus for those considering a Settler cross-border lifestyle a significant portion of the monthly payments from your RRSP-created pension would be tax free.

Finally, for those Canadians who have worked in the US during their career and qualify for US Social Security, the IRS provides more tax-favored treatment, depending on total current income from all sources; anywhere from 100 percent of US Social Security to a minimum of 15 percent can be received tax-free.

Let's look at George again. He receives $65,000 a year from a company pension that he contributed to over his 30-year employment. Under new rules the IRS will consider 100 percent of his pension as included taxation in the United States. Susan did not have a company pension but purchased a 20-year RRSP term annuity. She receives $50,000 a year from this, and her return of principal from the annuity would be approximately $25,000 per year. In her case, approximately 50 percent of her annuity would be excluded from US taxes. Figure 9.3 shows the net effect on taxes on George and Susan's pensions by moving to the United States. George and Susan would effectively cut their tax on the pension portion of their income by 73 percent. Obviously, this would represent a major raise for them, allowing them to keep $92,500 of their pension after tax, instead of only keeping $53,475 as Canadian residents. These tax savings combined with those in the previous section from CPP and OAS, give George and Susan nearly $60,000 a year (or $5,000 a month) additional income from their combined pensions — just by adopting the Settler lifestyle in the US. If you look at this another way, George and Susan would have to earn or find from somewhere else an additional $130,000 of income per year in Canada as Canadian residents to have the same after-tax result as if they moved to the US, just in terms of the total of all forms of pension income alone.

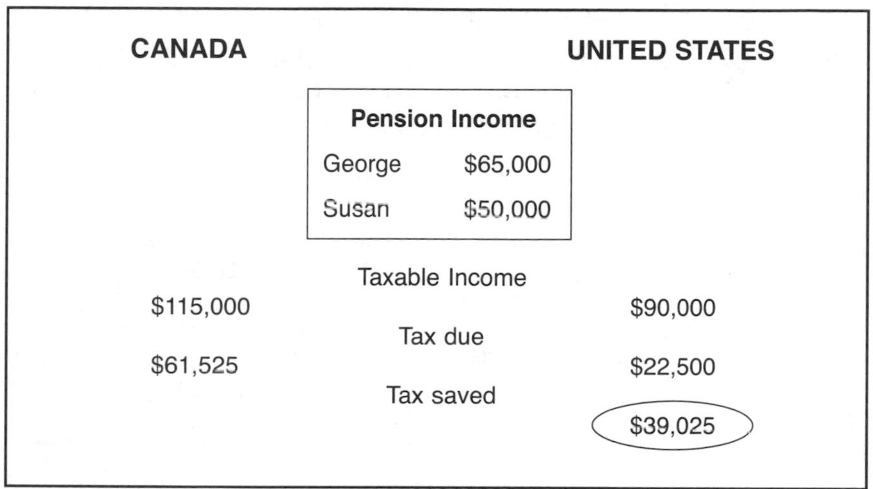

FIGURE 9.3

EMPLOYMENT INCOME

Earned income in the US is taxed similarly to how it is taxed in Canada, it is added to taxable income. Earned income is taxed at your highest marginal tax rates in both countries. This makes tax comparisons between Canada and the US very simple.

Although Susan is retired, she still does some management consulting for her former employer. She receives a fee of $30,000 a year. Figure 9.4 compares the taxation on this income between the two countries.

Susan is entitled to a whopping 53 percent tax reduction if she becomes a US resident. This amounts to an effective 40 percent after-tax pay raise without even having to talk to her boss. The tax savings result from the fact that the maximum tax rate is 53.5 percent in Ontario and 25 percent (39.6 percent maximum in top brackets) in Florida on the same amount of income. (See Figure 9.8 for another province (MB) and state (AZ) comparison for a different hypothetical couple with different income sources.)

Susan can place her maximum $5,400 into an RRSP and deduct this amount from her $30,000 employment income in Canada. In the US, however, she is able to place up to $21,500 — more than twice the RRSP deductible amount — into one of several deductible individual retirement account options available to her (for example, a simple IRA or single-member 401(k) plan).

I have deliberately not included Canada Pension Plan contributions or US Social Security contributions that may be required to be

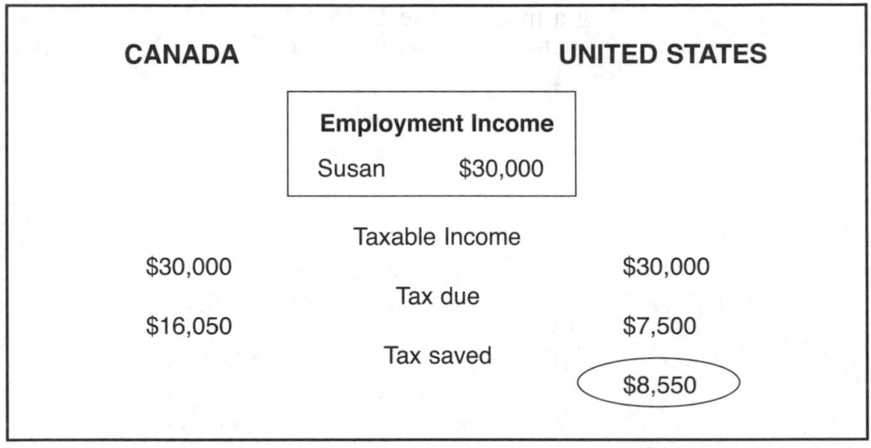

FIGURE 9.4

paid on Susan's earned income. Social Security contributions are higher than CPP contributions by about 50 percent, but the benefits of Social Security, particularly for George and Susan, could be anywhere from 100 percent to 200 percent more beneficial per dollar of contribution. Since this is a very complex issue to try to explain thoroughly, I have just chosen to exclude it from these calculations, but in actuality it is a major planning opportunity for Canadians to be able to double dip into US Social Security and Medicare (see Chapter 15 for a complete discussion on US Social Security and Medicare).

CAPITAL GAINS

Capital gains receive some favorable income tax treatment in both Canada and the US. Since October 2000, Canadians have been allowed to exclude 50 percent of any capital gains from their taxable income. Consequently, Canadian capital gains are taxed at a maximum of over 25 percent in most provinces (27 percent in Ontario, 24 percent in Alberta). In the US, the maximum federal tax rate on long-term capital gains (those held longer than one year) is 20 percent in the highest income brackets and 0 percent in the lowest brackets (it should also be noted that for those married couples with taxable incomes in excess of $250,000 USD, a 3.8 percent surtaxes may apply on capital gains and other taxable investment income under the Affordable Care Act). Since there is generally considerable risk in the types of investments that produce capital gains, most prudent people do not have a large percentage of their assets tied up in this area of investment. Consequently, the tax savings on capital gains are generally not enough to create any significant advantages either way when contemplating a move to the US to become a Settler, unless you have a small or closely-held business that is highly appreciated which would create a large capital gain on the sale (see Chapter 16).

Those who buy and sell real estate for investment purposes or as their occupation, will appreciate that in the US they have the ability to roll the tax on a gain from the sale of one property to another purchase of equal or higher value, which is an excellent tax-saving device. By rolling their gains from the sale of the real estate into a new property the US resident/ Settler can take the one quarter to one half of the sale proceeds that may have gone to the government in taxes and invest it in new property to earn new rental income and gains; one could do this for their entire lifetime without paying any tax on real estate gains.

There is also no deemed disposition tax at death on appreciated assets in the US, as there is in Canada. In fact, the beneficiary gets a free step-up in cost basis to fair market value of the property upon the death of the owner. The step-up in cost basis means it is as if the beneficiaries purchased the property on the date of death of the owner at its fair market value. A surviving spouse or other beneficiary who inherits highly appreciated property can sell it free from capital gains tax. Some US estate tax may be charged for non-spousal beneficiaries on estates of more than $5.45 million USD, the US individual exemption from estate taxes.

George and Susan would like to sell some growth mutual funds and real estate. For the current year, they have received capital gains distributions and other trading profits from their mutual funds of $8,000. They also sold a piece of property they had for ten years, which netted them a gain. Figure 9.5 displays the results.

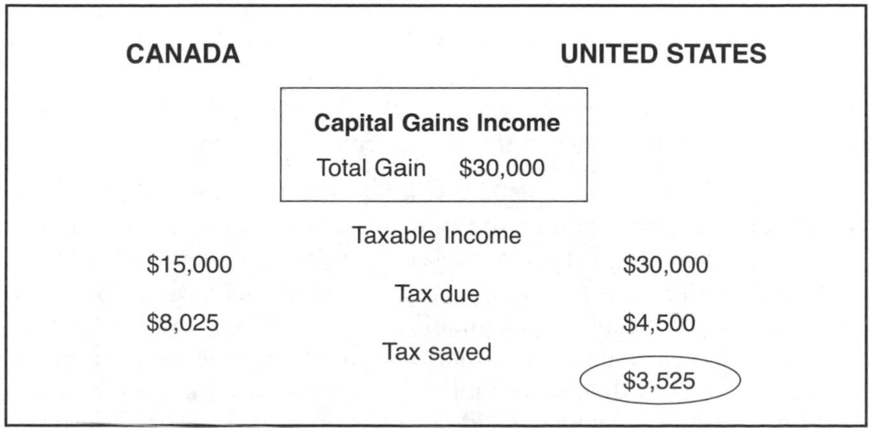

CANADA		UNITED STATES
	Capital Gains Income Total Gain $30,000	
	Taxable Income	
$15,000		$30,000
	Tax due	
$8,025		$4,500
	Tax saved	
		$3,525

FIGURE 9.5

The tax reduction on capital gains is over 43 percent in the US, even though only 50 percent of the gain is taxable in Canada. In the US, George and Susan may realize greater tax savings on their capital gains by setting up the mutual funds as a variable annuity. These funds provide for the unlimited deferral of capital gains, interest, and dividend income until the deferred income is actually withdrawn. Alternatively, in the US, they could invest the property proceeds into a new property and not pay any capital gains tax until they sell the property.

DIVIDENDS

Dividends are taxed very differently in Canada than they are in the US where qualified dividends are taxed the same way as capital gains: at a maximum rate of 20 percent, or 0 percent in the lower brackets. US qualified dividends are dividends from all private or public US and Canadian companies (or dividends from other treaty countries with the US).

Canadian eligible dividends would be the type of dividends earned by owning some of the larger Canadian publicly-traded corporations, whereas non-eligible dividends would normally be dividends paid from private Canadian corporations on income that had received the small-business tax rates inside the corporation. Foreign dividends, including US dividends in Canada, are taxed at the same marginal rates as interest income, which is 53.5 percent maximum in Ontario. This makes the maximum tax rate 39.3 percent on eligible Canadian dividends and 45.3 percent on non-eligible dividends in Ontario, compared to 15 percent in Florida for someone in George and Susan's tax bracket.

George and Susan have $10,000 of eligible dividend income. Figure 9.6 compares the net result of their dividend earnings in each country. George and Susan get a 38 percent tax reduction on dividend income by becoming Settlers to the US. As noted in the section Capital Gains in this chapter, they can use mutual funds in the form of variable annuities to defer income on dividends in the United States, and pay no current tax.

In both the US and Canada dividends are taxed twice, once at the corporate level and again at the individual shareholder's level. If you own a small, private dividend-paying corporation, both levels of tax must be considered to do a fair comparison. For someone with a Canadian-controlled small business that qualifies for the small-business tax rate on active business income, the total tax paid on dividends at both the corporate and individual shareholder levels in the lower income brackets could be less on the Canadian side of the border on corporate incomes less than $500,000 (depending on the province and other factors). In the

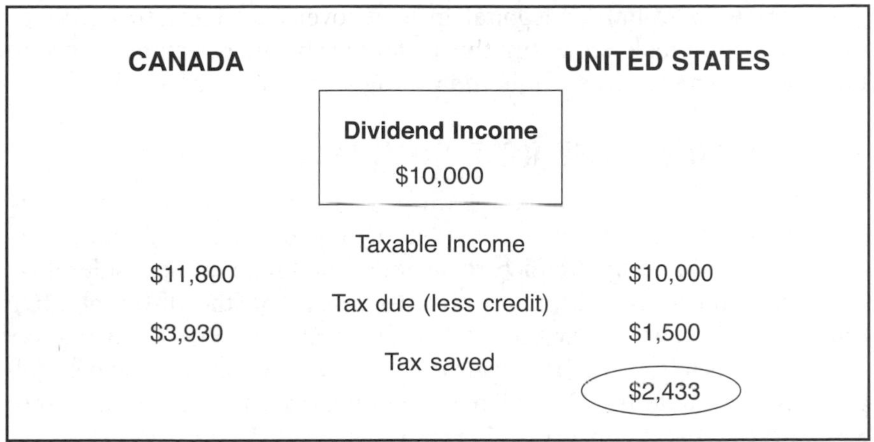

FIGURE 9.6

United States, it is generally better to pay salaries and bonuses to owner shareholders or to use flow-through company structures that pay no tax at the corporate level, than it is to pay corporate taxes and dividends. Salaries or dividends from the flow-through companies can be taxed only once, at a maximum federal individual rate of 39.6 percent for total amounts with taxable US income levels of more than $675,000 CAD.

ALIMONY

Alimony is taxed very similarly in both the US and Canada; it is fully taxable to the recipient and fully deductible by the payer. Consequently, someone receiving alimony who is also moving to the US will normally keep more of his or her alimony by paying less tax.

However, there is one important cross-border planning tip you should know if you are currently undergoing a divorce and your spouse is a US citizen or a green card holder (or can get a US visa of any type) who wishes to move back to the US. By including in the separation agreement certain legal language regarding spousal support, as specified by the IRS, the Canadian alimony-payer can continue to deduct the payment on his or her Canadian tax return, while the US resident spouse is not taxed on the payments for US purposes. The IRS specifications to make this work are complex but are pursuant to Internal Revenue Code Section 71(b)(1)(B) and Regulation 1.71-IT. Essentially, the alimony payer needs to make a declaration in the agreement that he or she will not deduct any alimony payments for US tax purposes, but since the payer in this case is a Canadian resident and not required to file a US return, it makes no difference.

Appropriate cross-border legal help is necessary to make this strategy work, but it can make an enormous difference to the recipient spouse to have the income tax-free, while the paying spouse is unaffected.

TOTAL INCOME: THE REAL COMPARISON

The examples used in Figures 9.1 through 9.6 are useful for comparing taxes on major income sources on a line-by-line basis. They do not, however, provide the complete picture, as it does not take into consideration personal deductions, the progressive tax rates, and the different filing options available in the two countries. The best way to do a realistic tax comparison is to take the total world income with deductions and simultaneously calculate the Canadian and US tax (as if the individuals were residents of either country), and then net out the final tax figures.

Since we are already somewhat familiar with George and Susan, we will do their total tax comparison in Figure 9.7 first. George and Susan are both retired, so we will also look at Bill and Mary, who are medical doctors that are still working; they have dependent children in college (Figure 9.8). These tax comparisons are based on the estimated 2016 tax rates as available at the time this book was published in the United States and Canada, so they may contain small differences from similar returns that could be filed based on actual rates.

George and Susan are both over 65 and own a summer cottage near Ottawa and a single-family dwelling in Naples, Florida. They pay property taxes, have no mortgages, and made no donations for this year; therefore, they take the standard deductions for their age rather than itemizing these expenses. Susan contributes the maximum amounts to her RRSP and IRA in Canada and the US respectively. They have no sources of income other than those detailed in Figures 9.1 to 9.7.

George and Susan have cut their tax bill by 65 percent by moving to the US and have increased their after-tax income by nearly $4,250 per month. If we were to assume that their joint life expectancy is 20 years and that they could invest these annual tax savings to earn an after-tax return of 5 percent, they would accumulate a total of approximately $1,700,000 in additional net worth over their lifetimes — or just enjoy the extra income with more travel, golf, or other retirement activities.

The tax reduction enjoyed by George and Susan is quite typical of those who retire in the Sunbelt. Larger savings can be achieved with more comprehensive cross-border planning. People whose income comes primarily from RRSPs or RRIFs and other investments can realize even greater savings than George and Susan did if they do proper planning.

MOVING TO THE US TO CHANGE EMPLOYMENT

Now let's take a look at Bill and Mary, who are in their early 40s and have two children in college. Bill is an anesthesiologist who earns $300,000 CAD net annually from his practice. Mary is also a doctor who works in a medical clinic as a general practitioner, with a salary of $150,000 CAD. They have some joint term deposits that earn about $10,000 per year in interest, making their total income $460,000. They have a large mortgage on their home in Winnipeg with payments of $4,500 per month, interest only, and both make the maximum contribution to their RRSPs each year. Their property taxes are $6,000, vehicle licence is $1,000, and their two children still live at home. Both have job offers in Arizona, at the same income level in order to simplify this comparison (a good anesthesiologist in Arizona would earn in excess of $850,000 and a general practitioner in excess of $250,000), adjusted for current exchange rates (for this example, $1 CAD equals $0.72 USD), and want to compare after-tax income between Manitoba and Arizona. Figure 9.8 shows the results of that comparison.

Even though their circumstances are quite different from George and Susan's, Bill and Mary achieve an even greater level of tax reduction — about 65 percent. They would realize an after-tax raise in monthly income of nearly $8,400, or $100,577 per year.

This tax saving is partly due to lower US federal and Arizona tax rates, but also because they deduct their large mortgage interest payments, property tax, and state income tax. They make their maximum contribution to their Individual 401(k) pension plan and a Health Savings Account (HSA), rather than an RRSP. Bill and Mary would also have to pay Social Security taxes in the United States. Although Social Security benefits are larger than those from CPP, so are their contributions. To keep the tax comparisons simple, we have not included any CPP, EI, or Social Security payments in the net taxes due. Also not taken into consideration for either couple, would be the savings in the US due to no Goods and Services Tax (GST). The GST/HST savings could amount to several more thousands of dollars a year, depending on their spending habits as US residents. Sales taxes for Arizona are about the same as the Manitoba provincial sales tax, while property taxes are much lower (and are tax deductible) for an equivalent house in Arizona.

Our two couples, George and Susan, and Bill and Mary, both have high incomes. Those in lower income brackets will generally experience proportionate tax cuts ranging from a one-third to two-thirds reduction in overall tax on the same amount of income, in both countries by adopting

INCOME

	George	Susan	Combined
CPP	$13,000	$13,000	$26,100
OAS	5,800	5,800	13,600
Pension	65,000	50,000	115,000
Interest	22,250	22,250	42,500
Dividends	5,000	5,000	10,000
Employment	0	30,000	30,000
Capital gains	15,000	15,000	30,000
Total income	**$120,450**	**$135,480**	**$255,900**

CANADA		UNITED STATES	
Adjustment to Total Income			
Dividends	+$3,800	Tax-free interest	–$14,167
Capital gains	–$15,000	Tax-deferred interest	–$14,167
OAS repayment	–$13,600	Simple IRA	–$21,500
RRSP	–$5,400	Susan's pension	–$25,000
		Pers. exemption	–$11,000
		Standard deductions	–$17,500
		OAS and CPP	–$5,940
Taxable income			
	$255,900		$186,300
Federal tax credits			
	$7,200		
Net tax due			
	$78,800		$27,740
Tax savings			
			$51,060

FIGURE 9.7

BILL AND MARY
(Adjustments to total income of $460,000)

CANADA		**UNITED STATES**	
RRSP contribution	–$50,000	Pers. exemption	–$22,200
		AZ state tax	–$12,500
		Property taxes	–$6,000
		HSA/SEP contrib.	–$149,000
		Mortgage interest	–$54,000

CANADA		UNITED STATES
$300,000	Taxable income	$215,300
$3,400	Federal tax credits	
$155,377	Net tax due	$54,805
	Tax savings	$100,570

FIGURE 9.8

the Settler/US resident lifestyle. As outlined in Chapter 6, Canadians of all ages and pre-existing medical conditions can get easily affordable healthcare in the US. However, if you wish to adopt the Settler cross-border lifestyle and want your tax savings to at least cover your medical insurance premiums over the cost of travel insurance your current Canadian taxes for an individual should be around $10,000. At this level of Canadian taxes/taxable income it is very likely you will have zero US taxes to pay so consequently the $10,000 you pay in Canadian tax that would normally be set off to Ottawa and never seen again may be reallocated to medical insurance in the US, so that you can enjoy your Settler cross-border lifestyle with no net increase in expenses. Ironically, how nice is it to have the CRA, through tax reductions by adopting a Settler lifestyle, effectively pay for your US healthcare.

CANADIAN NON-RESIDENT WITHHOLDING TAX

Canadians who choose to adopt the Settler cross-border lifestyle but still receive Canadian income have to look at the Canada/US Tax Treaty for the rules governing taxation of the income sourced in Canada. The Treaty, as described in Chapter 4, was created to prevent citizens and residents from being taxed twice on the same income, while at the same time allowing both countries some limited power of taxation according to the income source and type.

In Figures 9.1 to 9.7, George and Susan provide us with a typical example of a situation where the Treaty comes into play. They have a number of income sources that cannot be changed, including their CPP, OAS, and pensions. This means that Canada Revenue Agency, under the Tax Treaty, may be able to levy some tax on some of this income as that of non-residents, since it is sourced in Canada. The IRS will have taxation rights on the income. The Treaty ensures that George and Susan will not be double-taxed on any of this income, by specifying how the income will be taxed and allowing for tax credits in one country for taxes paid to the other. The table in Figure 9.9 lists the withholding tax rates of Canadian-sourced income that a Canadian is likely to encounter on major forms of income when moving to the US. Under the Treaty Canada has no right to tax CPP/QPP or OAS, including the 100 percent OAS clawback tax, once the Settler is considered a resident of the US under treaty rules.

The non-resident tax rates indicated in Figure 9.9 are withheld at the source, such as they are at the bank that pays the dividends or the company that pays the pension. It is the responsibility of the payer to withhold the correct treaty rate from the non-resident's income and forward that amount to CRA. It is the responsibility of the non-resident to notify any applicable payer that the recipient is, or is becoming, a resident of the United States for income tax purposes. If the improper amount has been withheld, CRA will send a bill to the non-resident and demand payment. If CRA cannot locate the non-resident and the payer was at fault for withholding too little, the payer can be held liable for any taxes due.

If the correct withholding has been done, the non-resident is not required to file a tax return with CRA and the non-resident tax slip issued by the payer, usually an NR4 slip, is considered the complete tax filing necessary. However, there are special filing options for those non-residents with rental income or pension income, if the withholding rate is higher than the actual tax would have been had that person been a resident of Canada. For example, if a non-resident has rental property that earns no net profit, he or she could elect to file a non-resident return under Section 216 of the Canadian *Income Tax Act*, netting out income and expenses and paying no tax rather than a 25 percent withholding on the gross rental receipts. Similarly, under Section 217 of the *Income Tax Act*, someone receiving a Canadian pension whose tax rate would have been less than the 15 percent withholding tax (had he or she been

CANADIAN NON-RESIDENT WITHHOLDING RATES, 2016	
Interest	0%
Gov't bonds	0%
Dividends	5% or 15%
CPP/QPP and OAS	0%
Pensions/annuities/periodic RRIF	15%
Lump-sum RRSPs	25%
Rental income	25%
Management fees	15%
Capital gains	Variable %
Royalties	0–15%
Income trusts	15%

FIGURE 9.9

a Canadian resident with that pension income only), can file a special return and claim a refund. In addition, he or she could apply to CRA for a reduced withholding rate on future payments on Form NR5.

On capital gains income from the sale of Canadian real estate, non-residents must either face withholding rates of up to 25 percent of the full value of the property being sold or file for a clearance certificate (Form T2062) from CRA prior to the sale of the capital property. When CRA issues the clearance certificate, it will determine what portion of the gain is taxable and will authorize the buyer to withhold at a rate that ensures total tax payment. The seller must file a Canadian non-resident return as a final reconciliation of the transaction for the year in which the sale occurred.

Payments from RRSPs and RRIFs are considered pension payments subject to the 15 percent withholding rate as long as they are periodic. Periodic means the RRSP must be in the form of an annuity with payments to the pensioner until at least age 90 or ten years, whichever is less. Periodic payments from a RRIF must not exceed 10 percent of the value or twice the annual minimum payment as calculated using your age, the value of your account, and CRA tables to qualify for the 15 percent withholding rate, rather than the lump sum rate of 25 percent. (More on this in Chapter 10.)

FOREIGN TAX CREDITS

The US has an extremely generous foreign tax credit regime. I have mentioned foreign tax credits on numerous occasions already in previous chapters and will continue to mention them throughout the rest of the book. They are so very important when cross-border planning, and when their use is optimized they can make a difference in reducing US taxes by tens or hundreds of thousands of dollars on an annual basis. Foreign tax credits are a dollar-for-dollar reduction in taxes paid and are far superior to deductions, since deductions only reduce your taxes by a percentage of your income equal to your top tax bracket. For example, if you had a $1,000 foreign tax credit, your taxes could be reduced by $1,000, but if you had a $1,000 deduction and were in a 25 percent bracket, the deduction would only reduce your taxes by $250.

Taxes paid to Canada, or most any other foreign government for that matter, end up on your US tax return in the form of these foreign tax credits when you are a US resident. These credits remain in an account at the IRS under your name, not unlike having a non-interest bearing checking account, and the IRS gives you the current year plus ten additional years (and one year carry back) to spend/use these credits or lose them. It is very much simpler and extremely less painful to tell the IRS to take your taxes payable from your foreign tax credit account, than it is to cut a check from your regular bank account to pay the exact same tax.

In addition to the time limits to use up your foreign tax credits, the IRS has a couple of requirements that you must fulfill before you can draw on your foreign tax credit account: The income must be foreign from a US perspective and it must be of a similar type of income. The IRS has two main separate accounts for these credits. One for passive income that would normally be generated from investments, like interest, dividends, capital gains, rental income, etc., and another for general limitation income that would normally be earned income from employment or active business income. Some types of income are technically able to go into either the passive or the general limitation account baskets. It requires much foresight and experienced planning to make sure the credits are placed in the correct basket, and that the foreign income you earn will be in the same basket, so you can draw on the correct account when you need to reduce your taxes. Often, poor planning generates foreign income of one type, while the foreign tax credits are in the other account and then expire unused. The final factor the IRS uses to dictate how many foreign tax credits you may use to reduce your tax in any particular tax year is a ratio of your foreign income compared with your total world income. For example, if you had income of $200,000 in any given year, and half of it was foreign, you could only use foreign tax credits to reduce up to 50 percent of your tax payable for that particular year. An experienced cross-border planner also knows how to generate foreign income instead of US-sourced income in order to optimize the use of any remaining foreign tax credits each year. This is not a simple task for the novice to attempt. I estimate that millions of dollars of unnecessary income taxes are paid when Canadians become US Settlers, because their advisors and tax preparers don't understand how to take advantage of these foreign tax credits, and thus they are giving money to the government that they are not legally required to give.

To illustrate more clearly how this system of withholding taxes and credits works, let's go back to George and Susan again and see what actually happened when they left Canada for the US. We assume that they converted all of their interest-bearing bank deposits in Canada to the US into special bonds generating foreign income, just as their cross-border financial planner recommended. CRA agreed that a 25 percent withholding tax on their capital gains on their Canadian real property of $30,000 was suitable and equal to the actual total tax due. (You can refer back to Figure 9.7 if you wish to review George and Susan's income sources and taxes due, as Figure 9.10 only summarizes these numbers.)

Figure 9.10 indicates that because their non-resident withholding by the CRA totaled $29,250 which is more than the taxes actually due to the US IRS, George and Susan would owe no tax to the US. Since the Canadian non-resident withholding tax was allowed as a foreign tax credit on their US returns and pretty well 100 percent of their income would be considered foreign by the IRS, they can effectively zero out their US income taxes with the foreign tax credits. The excess unused credits left after George and Susan zeroed out their US tax can be carried forward for up to ten years, to be used in a year when the withholding tax would be insufficient to provide a full credit against the US tax due on foreign income). George and Susan's case has been simplified somewhat in Figure 9.10 to show the overall effect of the withholding and credit system under the Canada/US Tax Treaty.

Border Guide readers are encouraged to participate in a cross-border Q&A through the new Cross-Border Forum, which is a platform where, after registering, you can easily post questions about the contents of this book. You can also post comments or create discussions with other readers to share experiences and swap cross-border financial planning tips. To post a question or comment, go to keatsconnelly.com and click on the Cross-Border Forum tab at the top of the first page.

CROSS-BORDER Q&A

CRA WANTS TAXES FROM US RESIDENT PAID AFTER EXIT FROM CANADA

My wife and I left Canada in January 2011 to work in the US; I have an H1B Visa with a green card pending. However, in 2012, my wife returned to Canada to continue her PhD. I visit her and she visits me in the US. Here are some facts:

- *I spend all but a few weeks of my time in the US every year.*
- *My only source of employment income is from my US employer who sponsored me for my H1B visa.*
- *I have owned a permanent residence in Washington state since I left Canada.*
- *I have filed and paid US taxes as required by the IRS every year.*
- *I have maintained a checking account in Canada.*
- *Every year since 2014 my wife files a Canadian return at Canadian tax time.*

In any event I have recently received a letter from Canada Revenue Agency stating that I owe taxes from 2012-2015 (because of my significant ties — my wife, and bank account, I have been determined to be a Factual Resident by CRA). I have informed them that I am a resident of the US for tax purposes. What should I do in these circumstances?

— Anonymous

The only thing I agree with about what CRA is telling you is that you likely are a Factual Resident of Canada under Canadian rules. However, as a Factual Resident you are entitled to benefits of the Canada/US tax treaty, which, based on the facts you outlined, clearly indicates you are a Treaty resident of the US. The Treaty overrides Canadian domestic Factual Resident rules, providing you file a Canadian tax return and declare your treaty benefits. Consequently, you should go back and file Canadian tax returns for the years in question as a Factual Resident and include all of your US income on this return. Then exempt it all on line 256 of the T1 return under Article IV of the Canada/US Tax Treaty.

Even though having your wife in Canada is a significant tie, the Treaty treats you as a separate taxpayer and if you review the tiebreaker rules of Article IV in the Treaty, you will find that your key ties under the Treaty definitions are with the US. Under CRA rules, Section 250 (5) of the Canadian Act, it states if you are a Treaty resident of the US, you are automatically a non-resident of Canada for income tax purposes. You should also make it perfectly clear to CRA that it is your intention to stay in the US (i.e., show them your green card application) and that it is the intention of your wife to join you there on a long-term basis once she finishes her PhD. If, after you file these returns and have claimed the treaty exemptions, your collections officer at CRA still insists on collecting tax from you, you can file a notice of objection within 90 days and appeal the decisions. You would have a very good chance of success through the appeals process based on the facts you have presented. An alternative strategy for your wife is that, under the Treaty, students are considered a resident for tax purposes in the country where they came from to become a student in Canada, which in her case is the US. This would mean she would only file tax returns on her income in the US.

PILOTS FLYING FOR AIR CANADA HAVE SPECIAL CANADIAN INCOME TAX RULES

I am a dual citizen currently residing in Washington state. I am an airline pilot based out of Vancouver and began working for Air Canada at the start of 2012. Prior to this, I was employed by a US carrier flying domestically in the US. I suspect I will need to file both Canadian and US tax returns starting in 2012. What special filing rules apply to me and how to allocate my income correctly between Canada and the US?

— ***Anonymous***

You didn't state whether you are flying domestically for Air Canada or internationally or both. Consequently, I will give you examples of each combination. Flying domestically in Canada is more complicated than if you are flying internationally to and from Canada. Domestic flights you make are prorated equally between the provinces where you take off/land, whereas, with international flights only a small percentage of the flight is taxed in Canada. Here are some examples:

- If you fly nonstop from Vancouver to Toronto, half the flight is credited to Ontario and half to BC.
- If you fly from Calgary to Edmonton all of the flight is credited to and taxed in Alberta.
- If you then fly from Calgary to Toronto, half of that flight leg goes to Alberta and half to Ontario.
- Vancouver to Chicago gives about 8 percent to BC and the US gets the rest.

- Calgary to Chicago — Alberta gets about 8 percent and the rest goes to the US.

The airlines can normally provide you with the tables of what percentage of your time and wages would be allocated to each country when flying internationally. You will need to provide your entire flight schedule with each respective return. Filing returns in this situation can be quite complex and we do recommend that you seek professional advice from somebody experienced in filing US and Canadian tax returns together.

CONVERTING E-2 VISA STATUS AND HOLDING CANADIAN RRSPS

In August of 2012, after obtaining an E-2 visa, I moved to the United States and purchased a business and a home. I am a Canadian citizen, residing in the United States with my wife and children, and would like to establish permanent immigrant status. I own a rental property in Florida through a numbered Ontario corporation. My income is derived from the business in the United States and from dividends received from less-than-arm's-length Canadian corporations. As of 2014, I have elected to be taxed in the United States. I still hold an RRSP in Canada and own a private Canadian corporation.

I realize these are rather complex issues, but I would like to hear from you.

1. *In whose name should any US assets be held?*
2. *What should I do with my Canadian assets?*
3. *What should I do with my Canadian RRSP?*
4. *What should I do with my US rental property?*
5. *What can be done to convert my E-2 non-immigrant status to immigrant status? My sister is a US resident and holds a green card.*

— Jimi H., Wilmington, North Carolina

Your questions cover some very complicated issues. Consequently, the answers will also be complex, depending on your ultimate objectives and other extenuating circumstances.

1. The titling of your US assets generally would follow the same procedures you would use in Canada. Business assets would likely best be owned by the business itself, depending on whether you are operating under a sole proprietorship or are incorporated. Personal assets would be in your and/or your spouse's name. You should also look into using a family living trust with provisions for a qualified domestic trust to own all your assets. This trust would help organize your estate to help avoid probate in Florida, North

Carolina, and Ontario, and make better use of the US estate tax exemptions.

2. Unless your Canadian assets are of such a nature that there are no comparable assets available in the United States that can produce a similar return on your investment, your life will be greatly simplified if you liquidate all your Canadian assets. Maintaining a Canadian corporation when your intentions are to reside permanently in the United States can create double income and estate tax, possibly subject you to a higher rate of income tax and force you into special Internal Revenue Service reporting on your Canadian personal holding companies. This extra accounting and potential taxes will generally outweigh any benefit of maintaining the Canadian Corporation unless it is a major thriving business that can afford the extra expenses and reorganization to be more tax efficient with the US.
3. RRSPs and what to do with them when you move to the United States will be explained in the next cross-border question below.
4. Your US rental property in the Ontario company should be moved out of the Ontario company into either your own name or possibly a US corporation similar in purpose to the Ontario onc. On the US side of the border, there is no tax advantage to holding small rental properties in holding companies. In fact, you would likely be at a tax disadvantage by using a US holding company unless you use US flow-through type corporations that pass the tax obligations on to the shareholders yet still give you liability protection of a Corporation, not to mention all the extra costs involved with corporations. There are both Canadian and US tax implications in taking this rental property out of the Ontario Corporation, which are too complex to be discussed here. I recommend you seek professional help with this and any other changes you are contemplating, as mistakes can be costly.
5. If your sister has been married to a US citizen and has resided in the United States for more than 3 years, she can become a US citizen and sponsor your green card immigrant status. The waiting time for this type of sibling sponsorship of the green card can be as long as 13 years from application, so you would need to keep renewing your E-2 visa until that time. You have some other options to obtaining immigrant status through your company, which may require a somewhat difficult labor certification. I would advise a consultation with a good immigration attorney.

MAKING RRSP CONTRIBUTIONS FOR THE YEAR YOU LEAVE CANADA

My husband and I are taking up new positions in Florida and will be leaving Canada on what appears to be a permanent basis. Do you have any recommendations as to what to do with our RRSPs? Is it to our advantage to make RRSP contributions in the year we leave? What will happen once we leave Canada if we keep our RRSPs in Canada? Can they be transferred to a retirement plan in the US, or should we cash them in before we leave?

— Lucetta S., Safety Harbor, Florida

First, let's deal with the question of what to do with your RRSPs before you leave Canada. Assuming you both have employment income in the same year you are leaving, cashing in your RRSPs would add greatly to your total income for the year, and likely be taxed at your maximum marginal tax rates of 53.5 percent in Ontario. Unless you want to lose half of all your accumulated RRSP savings to CRA, you should explore other alternatives to cashing them in before you leave Canada.

There are some alternatives that may allow you to withdraw the full balance of your RRSPs at no or very low Canadian taxes.

If your RRSPs consist of mutual funds, stocks, or other appreciated assets, we recommend you realize these gains before you become US residents. You would realize the gains by either liquidating all the investments and transferring the proceeds directly into a new RRSP savings account or short-term deposits. If you have mutual funds, this transaction can be accomplished generally at no cost by merely switching from one fund to another, within the same family of mutual funds. This exercise to realize your gains does not affect your Canadian tax one bit, because your investments remain sheltered within your RRSP. However, for American tax purposes, should you liquidate them while you are United States residents, you will pay more US tax unless you complete this gain realization process. The United States can tax capital gains on your investments, so by realizing these gains before you take up residency you are establishing a higher cost basis, and hence lower US capital gains when the investments are eventually sold.

Before you leave Canada, I recommend you make your maximum contribution, including any unused carry forward contributions from previous years not used, to your RRSPs for the current year. With Canada's new RRSP rules, which base this year's contributions on last year's income, you can take advantage of some great tax savings. For example, if you and your husband each earned up to $35,000 from your Canadian employment in the current year before you left the country, and could make the maximum RRSP contributions of $26,000 each, based on last year's earnings, you could eliminate any tax on your income in Canada during your year of exit. Your RRSP contributions and your personal credits should qualify you for a full refund of any tax withheld. At these levels of income, we would estimate a refund of more than $10,000 each in the short year of your exit.

After taking up residency in the United States, withdrawals from your RRSPs, if planned correctly, can be a great source of tax savings. Without proper planning, they can create unnecessary US taxes, and could be taxed by both the United States and Canada.

There are no provisions between Canada and the United States for a direct transfer of your RRSP to the US equivalent, an Individual Retirement Account (IRA). However, you can cash out your RRSPs and pay as little as zero taxes on a net basis, once you leave Canada, and use the net proceeds to contribute your maximum to your IRAs or other tax-deductible qualified plans in the United States.

The background of how Canadian RRSPs are looked at by the US Internal Revenue Service will help explain the problem and how to plan around it. The IRS considers your RRSP an ordinary investment, without the deferral of tax that CRA provides. As a US resident, if you were to leave your RRSPs in Canada, the IRS would tax you on all interest, dividends, and capital gains on your account, even though you may not have actually received them. Income on which you are taxed but that you do not receive is called phantom income. The Canada/US Tax Treaty allows you to make an election annually on your US return to defer the payment of US federal tax (individual states generally do not and are not required to follow tax treaties but since Florida has no state income tax at the individual level state taxes will be of no concern) on the RRSP phantom income, until it is actually withdrawn. Withdrawals of your principal contributions to the RRSP are not taxed by the IRS at any time.

You should know that CRA will tax all lump-sum RRSP withdrawals by non-residents at a flat 25 percent withholding rate, and periodic withdrawals at a 15 percent rate.

The question of what to do now should be somewhat easier to explain, now that you have some background. Since CRA has made it next to impossible for younger RRSP holders to have their withdrawals classified as periodic payments, a series of lump-sum withdrawals at the 25 percent withholding rate is probably the best alternative. The reason why you might want to do a series of lump-sum withdrawals rather than just one big withdrawal is to spread the withholding tax over more than one year so you have the better possibility of either deducting the withholding tax or using it as a foreign tax credit.

Other than the withholding tax, you have no further Canadian obligations with respect to your RRSPs. However, you are going to have to reconcile the income earned on this RRSP with the IRS, by adding it to your US taxable income every year you have a balance in your RRSPs. You will receive foreign tax credits for the tax withheld by Canada on your US return. There are a number of alternatives to consider when reporting the income on your US return, but without knowing your US tax information it is difficult to speculate as to which alternative would be best. You will likely need some professional help in this area.

RECOVERING WITHHOLDING TAX ON CANADIAN INCOME

My two brothers and I own a family farm in Saskatchewan, rented out since 2002. One brother lives in Ottawa, the other in San Diego. We all depend on the income from the wheat sales.

My previous year's US taxes gave me no tax relief on my Canadian income and I got no relief from my Canadian taxes. Did the Canada/US Tax Treaty change that much recently? I am a widow living on Social Security plus a small income, so I feel I should have gotten some refund.

— Freda M., Tampa, Florida

While you are in a unique situation, it should not be difficult to resolve. You may file a short-form Canadian tax return to get back some of the withholding tax from CRA. On this return, you should include only the portion of income from the Saskatchewan farm allocated to you, deduct any expenses you have related to this income, and then collect any refund due, any taxes that you pay in Canada on your Canadian sourced income will be considered a foreign tax credit to you in the US and will reduce your US taxes dollar-for-dollar on this income at least at the federal level. The state of California does not recognize and therefore will not give you a tax credit for taxes paid to any Canadian province. The deadline for filing such Canadian returns is July 1 following the year end, so you may be out of luck for the previous year, but will likely benefit for the current filing year, your US and Canadian tax preparers should know what to do with these filings including deducting proper expenses and utilizing foreign tax credits to reduce or eliminate your US federal taxes, including re-filing previous US returns to get refunds. If they do not I suggest you get more knowledgeable tax preparers experienced in filing both US and Canadian tax returns on cross-border/international issues. If you cannot find someone, contact us, we have a wholly-owned subsidiary that can assist you.

US RESIDENT WITH CANADIAN INCOME TRUSTS

I am now a US resident and am doing my US taxes for the first time. I have several Canadian energy trusts that I have been buying and selling, and I have received investment income from them. How do I report these investments on my US tax return?

— Dana L., Phoenix, Arizona

Canadian income or energy trusts present some unique concerns for US tax reporting requirements. Some of them are registered as a corporation in the US and therefore taxed as such, and others are trusts that are taxed in the same manner as US Real Estate Investment Trusts (REITs), with the full flow-through of the tax liability to the individual owners of the trust whether the income is interest, dividends, or capital gains. As a consequence, the investors would normally receive a 1099 income slip from the corporate registered income trusts and a K-1 from the others. However, most of the Canadian income trusts don't issue a US K-1 because they are Canadian. You may have to do a bit of detective work to translate the Canadian interest, dividends, capital gains, ordinary income, and return of capital amounts from each of your income trusts based on the Canadian tax information provided from the income trusts themselves into an equivalent US K-1 that you can report on your US tax return. This may be difficult; I suggest visiting the websites for each of the trusts you own and looking for the information you need. Canadian income trusts should be withholding 15 percent non-resident withholding tax on all distributions they send to a US resident, including distributions which are returns of your capital.

10 A Cross-Border Lottery: Don't Forget to Turn in Your Ticket

Canadians on the whole are very good savers and most have squirreled away a significant sum of money in Registered Plans such as RRSPs, Locked In Retirement Accounts (LIRAs), Individual Pension Plans (IPPs), Retirement Compensation Arrangements (RCAs) and many other employer-sponsored tax-deferred arrangements. However, most Canadians don't realize that the Canada Revenue Agency is happier than them with these large retirement accounts, as in most provinces now they may take more than half of those funds when they are withdrawn. For those in the highest tax brackets combining both federal and provincial income taxes, the government's share of your hard-earned RRSP or other registered type plans savings could be close to 60 percent.

Although Canadians have had legal lotteries of many different forms for many decades, because of the low odds of winning, most have never won any tax-free lottery winnings to fund their lifestyles. You do not even have to buy a lottery ticket to get the equivalent of an extremely large lottery of tax-free cash, literally guaranteed by current tax rules if you are a high income earner, if you choose to adopt the Settler cross-border lifestyle and become a US taxpayer, under the Canada/US Tax Treaty. This chapter will provide readers with the insight of how to claim their equivalent tax-free lottery winnings from their retirement accounts.

WITHDRAW YOUR RRSP TAX-FREE ON A NET AFTER-TAX BASIS

This section deals with some of the financial planning tools that can help you get your equivalent cross-border lottery by taking as much as legally possible of CRA's portion of your retirement accounts, that they are entitled to if you are resident of Canada and are not able to take, under current Treaty rules, if you are considered a tax resident of the US (as a Settler normally would be). By taking advantage of the Treaty non-resident withholding tax rates on RRSPs and utilizing foreign tax credits as discussed in the previous chapter, you can withdraw large sums from your RRSP and effectively pay a greatly reduced tax, or, with the right circumstances and planning, pay no net taxes at all as a US resident taxpayer. Please note that you cannot simply move to the US, contact CRA, and tell them *The Border Guide* said you could withdraw the money in your RRSP tax-free. CRA will always gets some withholding tax in the form of either the 15 percent on periodic payments or the 25 percent on lump sum payments. You can only get close to withdrawing your RRSP tax-free on a net basis if you recover every dollar of withholding tax taken by CRA, through foreign tax credits allowed by the IRS on certain types of future income. Not everyone will be able to do this. I would suggest that without the assistance of an experienced cross-border financial planning professional, the chances of getting your RRSP out of Canada at a zero net tax are extremely slim. It is exceedingly difficult even for an experienced professional to be able to accomplish this challenging feat. However, most everyone will have access to their equivalent tax-free lottery by moving their RRSPs out of Canada at a substantially lower tax rate than if they remained a Canadian resident, even if they try to do it themselves. In many cases, these cross-border financial planning techniques can provide a major source of funding and incentive for adopting the Settler cross-border lifestyle, as the tax savings, especially on the larger accounts, can be tens or hundreds of thousands of dollars!

Even though this section continually refers to RRSPs (Registered Retirement Savings Plans), consider them a proxy for other Canadian registered investments, such as Registered Retirement Income Funds (RRIFs), Individual Pension Plans (IPPs), Deferred Profit Sharing Plans (DPSPs), Life Income Funds (LIFs), Locked-in Retirement Accounts (LIRAs), Locked-in Retirement Income Funds (LRIFs), and Retirement Compensation Arrangements (RCAs). All generate similar foreign tax credits and similar equivalent lottery winning opportunities for US residents.

SETTLERS: DON'T LEAVE HOME WITHOUT YOUR RRSP

The issue of what to do with RRSPs when Canadians become US taxpayers by adopting the Settler lifestyle or become residents in the United States is more often than not overlooked, especially for those who fail to complete a cross-border financial planning analysis. When taking up residency in the United States, Canadians can find their RRSPs a great source of tax savings, in effect their personal tax-free lottery, if they plan for them correctly. Without proper planning, RRSPs can create unnecessary US taxes and can potentially be taxed by both countries. Most people ignore planning for their RRSPs, think there is nothing they need to do, or have even been advised to leave their RRSPs in Canada by unknowledgeable or self-serving advisors.

How Canadian RRSPs are viewed by the IRS will help explain some of the problems surrounding them and illustrate how you can take advantage of the differences in the rules. The IRS considers your RRSP an ordinary investment by looking right through the RRSP trusteeship and CRA's deferment of income tax rules. The IRS deems an RRSP to be a simple grantor trust, under US rules, in which the grantor or contributor pays tax on all the income as it is earned or realized. This is a key element of the mechanism to give RRSP savers access to the equivalent lottery from these kinds of plans as explained below.

When you are a resident of the US for income tax purposes under the Treaty, the IRS will consider an RRSP the same way it would treat the underlying investments of the RRSP had it not been a registered investment. For example, if you as a US resident earned bank interest during the year in your RRSP, the IRS would want you to report and pay tax on that interest as if you had earned it in a regular bank account. The IRS will consider the contributions you made to the RRSP before you became a US resident (as well as the accumulated interest, realized gains, or dividends in it) as tax-paid principal under the grantor trust rules. (Note that this IRS tax-paid treatment for interest and dividends does not apply to unrealized capital gains at your entrance date into the US, nor does it apply to US citizens or green card holders who have been residents in Canada.) Once you are a US resident, citizen, or green card holder, the IRS will tax the interest earned and paid during the year inside the RRSP unless they elect under IRS tax rules to defer it. Similarly, dividends and capital gains on your RRSP account are subject to US tax as they are paid or realized each and every year, without the deferral of tax provided for by CRA, to gain unless they elect to do so with the IRS under US return filing. At first glance this seems like a major problem, but knowing how the IRS taxes RRSPs and similar plans gives cross-border financial planning practitioners a great tool to help Canadians get their RRSPs out of Canada at low or even no net taxes.

If you were to become a Settler and leave your RRSPs/RRIFs in Canada (or if you are a US citizen or green card holder with RRSPs/RRIFs), regardless of where you live, the IRS will tax you as a US resident on all interest, dividends, and capital gains earned on your account, even though you may not have actually received these funds. Income that you do not actually receive but are taxed on is called "phantom income." Many Canadians with RRSPs have been in the United States for years and never realized that they have a United States tax liability on this phantom income. The Canada/US Tax Treaty protocol that came into effect in 1996 allows you to make an election annually on your US return to defer the payment of US tax on the RRSP phantom income until such time as it is actually withdrawn. In order for the deferment of tax on the income to be effective, a form requesting this deferment must be attached to your US tax return every year for each RRSP or RRIF owned. For tax years after 2004, the IRS has created Form 8891, which must be completed for each RRSP/RRIF for each year to take advantage of the tax deferment. Deferment is considered the default election and the election is irrevocable once made for the current year and subsequent years. Although Form 8891 is relatively straightforward, I find that in at least 90 percent of all US tax preparers complete the form incorrectly. This is primarily due to the fact that RRSP/RRIF trustees or custodians do not report income in a manner the tax preparer can determine the amount of deferred income correctly on each RRSP each year and it would take an extremely large amount of time for the tax preparer to go through monthly statements manually and make currency conversions for each and every dollar of interest, dividends, and capital gains earned throughout each tax year for each RRSP or RRIF. However, unless the form is completed correctly by the tax preparer it leaves the taxpayer opened to substantially higher taxes and penalties from the IRS and the little benefit the deferment offers could be wiped out entirely.

Ironically, those to take what appears to be the easier logical choice and defer the income on their RRSPs/RRIFs once the Settler/taxpayer becomes a US tax resident, for most US taxpayers, the deferment option on Form 8891 may the worst choice from an overall income tax reduction strategy as discussed in the next section of this chapter.

The election to defer income on registered plans under the Treaty and IRS rules only applies to RRSPs, LIFs, LIRAs and RRIFs, it does not apply to other retirement type plans like Individual Pension Plans, Retirement Compensation Accounts, and Deferred Compensation Plans.

Also note that if you live in a state that has state income tax, state income tax may also be due on the phantom income every year, regardless of whether you have filed the election with your federal tax return (as states are not party to the treaty or its elections). In fact, California, in 2003, put RRSP holders on notice that it did not allow any deferral of Canadian RRSP and similar plan income, and furthermore would come after them if they didn't report the income annually and pay full California state income tax on it. Many Canadians were caught off guard by these state rules and paid dearly for it. Withdrawals of your principal contributions to the RRSP are not taxed by the IRS or by states at any time.

TEN KEY REASONS TO REMOVE YOUR RRSP FROM CANADA

What, then, is the best thing to do with your RRSPs or RRIFs after leaving Canada and adopting the Settler or US resident lifestyle? There are no provisions between Canada and the United States for a direct transfer of your RRSP to the US equivalent, an Individual Retirement Account (IRA). Consequently, you have only three options: withdraw the RRSPs; report the realized income each year and pay the tax on the phantom income; or make the annual elections under the treaty to defer federal tax on the income. If you are intending to become a Settler and reside permanently or at least for many years in the United States and you wish to partake in your maximum equivalent tax-free lottery from your registered plans, I recommend the first solution, complete or staged withdrawal, for these ten key reasons:

1. If you leave your RRSP in Canada, not only are you subject to the tax rules of both Canada and the US simultaneously, but you are subject to any future Canadian tax legislation that could restrict future withdrawals more than current laws do now. For example, in June 2015, the CRA made reductions in the minimum RRIF withdrawal percentages at age 71. Although these reductions in the minimum withdrawals could help a few Canadian residents temporarily, it reduces the amount that a resident of US may take at the 15 percent Treaty withholding rate rather than the 25 percent lump-sum withdrawal rate. In 2004, the IRS brought in substantial new rules affecting foreign pensions, which can spill over into RRSP and other registered plans. In short, the writing is on the wall; take action while there are still major opportunities to get your equipment cross-border lottery winnings from these plans.

   In addition to these tax complications, expect CRA to continue tightening their restrictions or increasing the withholding rates on RRSPs, as they are constantly looking for more revenue. Just like the old sayings "make hay while the sun shines" and "get out while the getting is good," you can cash in your RRSPs now and pay as little as zero net tax, as noted above, once you leave Canada. Why wait for future legislation in either Canada or the US to come along that will restrict your options or increase your tax due?

2. People with estates of more than $5.45 million USD or who live in a state which has its own estate tax may face double taxation. The double tax arises because Canada will withhold 25 percent from your RRSP at your death, and this amount may not be allowed as a credit against state estate tax due. Estate tax credits are allowed at the federal level on taxes paid on RRSPs/RRIFs at death providing timing of the estate tax returns and the taxes paid are done in such a manner to maximize these credits, otherwise additional taxes or unnecessary taxes may be paid on these Canadian registered plans (see point 5 below for details of how this double tax can apply on income with respect to the decedent). If you reside in one of those states that has its own estate tax regimes as mentioned in Chapter 5, you most certainly will face double taxation since the Treaty does not apply at the state level. In addition, many Canadian provinces now require residents to file separate provincial tax returns and they, like individual US states, may not allow credits for foreign taxes paid. Why pay any tax, even on one level, when you can get rid of the tax entirely by getting your RRSP out of Canada? Similarly, regardless of the size of your taxable US estate, having significant assets in a foreign country locked into the special rules that apply to RRSPs makes it very difficult to use standard estate-tax reduction planning techniques available to most US residents. With the added complexity of having RRSPs in Canada for US residents in my more than 35 years in the US, I have yet to see even the most competent of US estate attorneys properly design estate documents to deal adequately with RRSPs back in Canada so your chances of getting a properly drafted estate plan by the US estate attorney when you have RRSPs or other qualified plans in Canada is slim to none unless you can find an experienced cross-border attorney.
3. Another reason to cash in your RRSPs after becoming a US resident is to avoid currency speculation. (In Chapter 3, I covered the hazards of unknowingly becoming a currency speculator.) Keeping an RRSP in Canadian dollars when you are likely to need US dollars for retirement is exposing yourself to unnecessary currency risk, as you are not properly matching your retirement income with the expenses of retirement. This difference could reduce retirement income in US dollars to such an extent that you find yourself forced to work longer than planned or part-time in retirement. Why take this risk? If the exchange rate on the Canadian dollar improves, you have still protected yourself. Since most Canadians in the US will continue to have CPP and OAS or

other sources of Canadian income, they will still benefit from the improved exchange rate. Even though you can invest up to 100 percent of your RRSP in Canada in US funds, it adds a level of complexity and cost to your entire RRSP strategy that you receive no marginal benefit from, since it can be done better and at lower cost on the US side of the border.

4. As noted earlier in this section, the individual US states are not party to federal treaties such as the Canada/US Tax Treaty, although many states do voluntarily provide their residents the income tax benefits of a treaty. In states with a state income tax that do not voluntarily follow the Treaty, an additional level of tax may apply each year even though you may have elected to defer the IRS tax under the treaty. For example, if you are a Canadian with RRSPs who takes up residence in the state of California and have elected to take the deferral of the RRSP income at the federal level, you will pay up to 13 percent state tax annually on the RRSP phantom income. This tax would not be recoverable in the United States under California state tax rules, so it would in effect be a very costly double tax.
5. At the death of a US resident who has deferred tax on RRSPs under the treaty, the US rules of Income in Respect to the Decedent (IRD) apply. Most Canadians are aware that when they die owning an RRSP or an RRIF they are taxed on the plan balance as if they cashed the entire plan on the day before they died. Consequently they are taxed at the highest Canadian rates on the entire amount of the plan. In the US, the IRD rules transfer the tax liability on the amount of deferred income to the beneficiary, and he or she pays the tax each year on the income received for that year (the income from these plans can be amortized over the remainder of the life of the beneficiary), at his or her personal rate. The beneficiary is allowed a tax deduction for the tax paid on the IRD if the decedent had paid US estate tax. Since CRA taxes the decedent and the IRS taxes the beneficiary, there is an automatic double tax because tax credits can't be transferred between taxpayers. IRD results in double tax generally whenever it occurs, particularly where there are non-resident beneficiaries. Under IRD rules, at the death of a US resident who had elected to defer tax on RRSP income, the maximum tax rate goes from zero (if the RRSP had been removed from Canada) to 60 percent or more, including state taxes. This is not a tax to be ignored.

6. Getting your RRSP out of Canada early in your US residency can be to your advantage. In a practical investment sense, competition favors an investor in the US through lower commissions on securities, transactions, and lower management fees on mutual funds and exchange traded funds (ETFs). Mutual fund management fees and expense ratios are generally 2 to 3 percent in Canada, while in the US they average 1 to 1.5 percent — generally half the cost for a similar mutual fund. In addition, the larger selection of US mutual funds and ETFs allows you to choose no-load index funds with expense ratios as low as 0.05 percent. Compared to leaving your mutual funds in Canada, this cost savings over a number of years can be substantial. Over approximately ten years, particularly in this low interest rate environment, this extra cost on your RRSP investments can by itself be greater than the 25 percent non-resident tax you would pay to get your RRSPs out of Canada now (so these costs can, in effect, be a hidden tax).
7. The US SEC requires that your Canadian broker and the Canadian brokerage firm holding your RRSP funds be licensed in your state of residence. The securities they sell you must be US-registered before they can legally transact security trades for you as a resident in the US. As a result, you may be stuck with all the stocks, bonds, and mutual funds you own in your RRSP, without being able to change investments to react to changing market conditions after you leave Canada. On June 23, 2000, the SEC and various provincial securities divisions in Canada came to an agreement on a partial solution to this problem of trading inside RRSPs for US residents. The US SEC offered an exemption to Canadian brokers trading on behalf of US resident RRSP/RRIF holders with certain restrictions. Some of the restrictions eliminate many people from taking advantage of this exemption. Some US states did not follow the SEC's lead and will not give Canadian brokers any legal trading rights for their residents. Consequently, after years of waiting for this US SEC exemption, few people with RRSPs in Canada will be able to take advantage of it. Why bother with this hassle with the Canadian brokers when you can deal with US brokers at a much reduced cost once you have withdrawn the funds from Canada?
8. Those RRSP investors who invest in appreciating assets such as stocks or growth-type mutual funds will almost certainly face a double tax on their capital gains. This double tax comes from the manner in which the Canada/US Tax Treaty sources the capital

gains. The Treaty says that gains on securities are sourced to the country of the taxpayer's residence. Consequently, US residents with Canadian RRSPs will have all their gains classified as US-sourced. Foreign tax credits generated on the withholding upon cashing the RRSP cannot be used to offset the US tax owing on the gains since tax credits are only allowed against foreign income. Since capital gains are no longer considered foreign because of these treaty sourcing rules, a double tax results. The minimum tax on capital gains from an RRSP for a US resident, not including any state taxes, is 40 percent (the 25 percent withholding plus the 15 percent US tax on capital gains) rather than just the 25 percent withholding tax on principal, interest and dividends.

This double tax on capital gains is the reason it is strongly recommended that, before entering the United States, all RRSP holders sell their appreciated stocks, ETFs, bonds, and mutual funds to get a stepped-up cost basis for US purposes. A stepped-up cost basis is the term for when someone sells a security and buys it back at the same price in order to move the cost for tax purposes from the original purchase price to the current price. This step-up in basis will eliminate the double tax on any gains accumulated before you become subject to US taxes under the treaty sourcing rules, but will not help you with the tax on the capital gains after you become a US resident even if you make the treaty election to defer the tax each year.

For those US residents that elect to for the US federal taxes on their RRSPs in Canada by filing IRS Form 8891 are giving up the lower tax rates the IRS allows on dividends and capital gains. Once you take the election all of the deferred income will be taxed as ordinary income at your highest original rates in the US rather than the reduced rates for the capital gains and dividends. This lost US benefit, over long period of time be extremely costly to those leaving their RRSPs and other qualified plans in Canada.

9. There is something to be said for simplicity in one's financial life. Leaving your RRSP in Canada when you are a US resident complicates your tax and investment management life substantially. You constantly need to find US tax and investment advisors who understand RRSP reporting procedures, a difficult job at the best of times, for most of them are struggling just to keep current on the usual IRS rules and regulations. You will be lucky just to find a US advisor who knows where Canada is let alone deal with it in complicated tax matters. The cost of qualified advisors and all the

reporting they must do on your behalf, particularly if you get the wrong advice, can often outweigh the benefits of any tax deferral you might obtain by leaving the RRSP in Canada and electing the treaty deferral. Even if you have only one RRSP, as a US resident you face up to four relatively complex forms and elections that your tax preparer must include with each year's filings at the federal level. The following IRS forms are or may be required when you have an RRSP in Canada: Form 8891, Form 8938, Form 8833, Form 3520, Form 3520A, Form FinCen 114, Form 1116, Form 1116AMT. Most of these forms are required each and every year on each RRSP; others are only required when you make a withdrawal or an election. Even if you can find someone who knows how to complete these forms, it is expensive to get them filed and your tax return could be an inch thick. Even worse, if you fail to file the correct forms in a timely manner, the penalties could be prohibitive and cost you the entire value of your RRSP and more. For example, if you fail to file Form FinCen 114, the penalty is a fine up to 50 percent of the value of each account or five years in jail. If you have more than one RRSP, many of these forms must be prepared separately for each RRSP, and if you have a state tax return to file, additional forms and taxes could be required to be prepared at the state level each year, a gain with the additional complexity and costs. Most knowledgeable tax preparers will normally charge more than twice the amount for a Canadian in the US if they have RRSPs left in Canada, and as noted above if they make the wrong elections or file the wrong forms or file them incorrectly they can cost you additional interest and penalties.

10. In a Tax Court of Canada case, *McFadyen v. The Queen*, the judge cited as evidence of a residential tie with Canada the fact that Mr. McFadyen, a non-resident of Canada, had maintained an RRSP in Canada, and subsequently assessed him with Canadian taxes on his world income for three years. If you want to ensure CRA doesn't attempt to tax you as a Canadian resident, do not leave RRSPs in Canada; they might become a target following this Tax Court of Canada ruling.

In spite of all these reasons to get your RRSP out of Canada once you become a US resident, there is a tendency for most Canadian advisors to continue to recommend that Canadians moving to the United States leave their RRSPs in Canada. The key reasons for this advice are believed to be a lack of understanding of the above noted complications, unnecessary costs and double-tax problems, and how far-reaching the adverse consequences of holding RRSPs can be for US residents. In addition, because of the way most Canadian advisors are compensated on RRSPs, it is in their own self-interest to keep the RRSPs in Canada where they can continue to collect commissions and other fees.

CASHING IN YOUR LOTTERY TICKET EQUIVALENT RRSP

After discussing all of the reasons why you should never leave your RRSP or equivalent registered plans in Canada once you become a US resident I will give you a better idea of how to cash in on your own personal equivalent lottery by getting your RRSP out of Canada as quickly as possible. The first part of the lottery is very simple, you are cutting your maximum tax rate on your RRSP and registered plans from the resident Canadian rates of well over 50 percent for high taxable income individuals to a maximum of 25 percent. Consequently, 25 percent of a $1 million RRSP is equivalent to winning a tax-free lottery of $250,000 or if you have planning assistance, withdraw the 15 percent Canadian withholding level, and your lottery equivalent is $350,000. Not bad winnings and you didn't even have to buy a lottery ticket. As noted earlier, this lottery winning equivalent is virtually guaranteed under current Canadian, US, and Treaty rules when the rules are followed correctly so the odds of winning are 100 percent rather than on a regular lottery where your odds can be one in several million. A second part of this equivalent lottery comes from the withholding tax that actually goes to Canada once you remove the RRSP and bring it to the US. This with withholding tax as noted in the section can be partially or totally recovered through proper cross-border financial planning by an experienced professional. This planning is not guaranteed to recover all of the taxes paid to Canada but with the proper long-term strategy a Canadian Settler can usually cover most if not all the taxes paid to Canada through US foreign tax credits. If they are able to recover all of the Canadian withholding through US foreign tax credits their equivalent lottery winning on the million-dollar RRSP noted above goes from $250,000 to over $500,000.

Making withdrawals from your RRSP that maximize benefits and minimize taxes is not simple and should not be done without the supervision of a qualified cross-border financial planning practitioner. This is one area of cross-border planning where a simple error can be costly and irreversible. Using a knowledgeable professional can pay big dividends.

The timing of the withdrawals is critical. You need to match Canadian withholding taxes with US taxability of foreign income. This correct matching of taxes paid to Canada and available foreign tax credits in the US can mean the difference between paying 25 percent (40 percent on capital gains as noted above) or 0 percent tax on a net basis on your RRSP balance. When calculating the usable foreign tax credits on a US tax return, all sources of foreign income must be considered.

I have been inundated with a large number of requests from readers asking me to include more specific examples on withdrawing RRSPs at the lowest possible rate. As noted above the first part of your equivalent RRSP lottery is pretty simple, just become a Settler/US resident and cash in the RRSP; the second part is to recover tax credits paid to Canada which is the complex planning point that I am discussing in this section.

Many would like to attempt withdrawing their RRSPs tax-free on a net basis on their own and I would strongly advise using a knowledgeable professional. I am reluctant to provide these examples because this is one area that is far too complex and dependent on too many factors for me to even attempt to present it in any condensed written form. Any RRSP or other qualified plan withdrawal planning for non-residents of Canada is affected by this partial list of factors:

- Your age, health, and marital status and your spouse's age and health
- Your and your spouse's life goals and objectives
- Whether you have children and where they live
- Type, amounts, and sources of your current and future income and that of your spouse.
- Amounts of past, current, and future non-resident tax paid or to be paid to CRA by you and your spouse
- Your and your spouse's net worth
- Location and tax basis of non-RRSP assets
- Size of your and your spouse's RRSPs
- The types of investments in your RRSPs
- Whether any of your RRSPs are "locked in" by provincial legislation
- Whether you are still a Canadian resident for tax purposes
- How long you've been a resident in the US and what is your immigration status
- Whether you have previous US tax returns in which you reported RRSP income incorrectly

- Your need for current or future cash flow
- Your state of residence in the United States
- The province in which the RRSPs are located
- The type of registered account, that is, RRSP, LIRA, RCA, etc.

The many factors affecting RRSP withdrawal planning can be mind-boggling, particularly when you consider the number of combinations and permutations so many factors create. Trying to deal with all these factors is like reading how to remove someone's appendix and then setting out to do it: you may be lucky but the odds are against you. Consider interest rates on RRSPs, foreign income, amounts withdrawn, and available US tax credits in order to withdraw your RRSP from Canada in the shortest time at the lowest possible tax rate. If you aren't careful or fail to use competent professional advice on your RRSP withdrawals, as a non-resident of Canada you can miss the maximum opportunities with your equivalent lottery winnings to reduce taxes significantly. Worse yet, taxes and penalties can wipe out a great deal of your equivalent lottery winnings.

For smaller RRSPs, namely those of less than $100,000 in value, staged withdrawals can be controlled to match the foreign tax credits available. Section 217 of the *Income Tax Act* allows people who withdraw between $10,000 and $25,000 from their RRSPs and who have little or no other taxable income to file a return and obtain either a full or partial refund of the withholding tax. CRA amended its Section 217 filing requirements in 1996, including other world taxable income in a formula that provides tax relief only on a proportionate basis of Canadian-sourced income that qualifies for the Section 217 treatment in relation to total world income. Consequently, this option is no longer viable for those with substantial US or world income. Section 217 filings work well for the RRSP belonging to a non-working spouse with no investment income.

Other than the correct non-resident withholding tax on withdrawal as a US resident, you have no further Canadian obligations with respect to your RRSPs, and no need to file a return when making withdrawals, unless you qualify for a refund under Section 217 or incorrect withholding was done at source, as is all too often the case. If you are a Canadian non-resident, make certain that on all lump-sum RRSP withdrawals the payer takes exactly 25 percent non-resident withholding tax. If the payer takes more than 25 percent, you have a great hassle trying to get a refund of the overcharge from CRA by filing an NR-7 form, and if the payer takes anything less than 25 percent on the RRSP, you will need to file and pay the shortfall, often with interest and penalties.

BREAKING THE LOCK ON LOCKED-IN RRSPS

Canadians who have worked for employers within Canada find, much to their disappointment, that a good portion of their pension benefit is "locked in" when they leave the company before retirement age. This lock-in is a result of employment pension plan regulation at the provincial level. All provinces and territories have such legislation, designed to prevent employees from spending their accrued pension benefits before retirement age. If a company's operations are regulated by the government, regardless of which province the company is located, its pension plans are in turn regulated or locked in under federal regulation that parallels these provincial lock-in rules. In effect, the provinces and the federal government feel the employees aren't responsible enough to roll their pension benefits into an RRSP and leave it there only for their eventual retirement, so they force the employees to roll the vested company contributions of their pensions into a Locked-In Retirement Account (LIRA) or a Life Income Fund (LIF).

Funds cannot be withdrawn from a LIRA, except in special emergency situations as defined by the applicable provincial legislation, and under federal legislation withdrawals under any circumstances were prohibited until the federal 2008 budget. At the normal retirement age set by the original company plan in which the employee was a member, the LIRA owners, if they wish to make withdrawals, can convert their LIRAs to Life Income Funds (LIFs) or Locked-In Retirement Income Funds (LRIFs). These both operate like Registered Retirement Income Funds (RRIFs) except that the start date at which withdrawals can be made for most provinces is age 55 and there is a maximum withdrawal rate each year, as well as the usual RRIF minimum. One additional option for LIRA holders is to use the LIRA funds to purchase a life annuity.

Until the year 2000, provincially regulated LIRA holders who became non-residents of Canada had no options other than the two mentioned above. This subjected US-resident LIRA holders to numerous reporting requirements annually to the IRS and state tax authorities, potential double income and/or estate taxes, estate-planning issues, and investment planning issues, not to mention currency risks. Review the previous section of this chapter for more details of the concerns of US resident RRSP/LIRA holders. In other words, being locked in with your RRSPs (in the form of a LIRA, LIF, or LRIF) as a US resident is somewhat punitive!

All Canadian provinces now allow non-residents under certain conditions to break the lock on their Canadian LIRAs, effective on various dates from July, 1999 to June, 2015 depending on the province. As of these dates, LIRA owners who have been non-residents for two or more years can break the locks on their LIRAs if they can get written confirmation from CRA that they are non-residents. If the LIRA owner is married, a spousal waiver of any benefits from the LIRA is also required. CRA written confirmation can be obtained by filing Form NR73, Determination of Residency Status. An answer should be received approximately eight weeks after submitting the NR73 to CRA.

Employees of federally regulated industries, such as airlines, railroads, and communication companies, regardless of their provinces of residence, can also qualify to break the lock-in on their LIRAs obtained from these companies as Settlers/non-residents of Canada. To qualify they must currently be and have been non-residents of Canada for at least two years. By providing proof of non-residency to the LIRA trustee, he or she can break the lock-in and forward the funds to you, less the 25 percent non-resident withholding tax. The province of PEI is following the federal regulations in all respects for all lock-in plans in the province until it creates provincial legislation of its own. Yukon, Northwest Territories, and Nunavut also follow the federal legislation on locked-in plans.

Dealing with RRSPs and LIRAs as a non-resident of Canada can be a tricky business. We recommend, at all times, that you seek the advice of an experienced and qualified cross-border financial planning expert.

REGISTERED EDUCATION SAVINGS PLANS (RESPs)

People residing in the United States and owning RESPs for their children, grandchildren, or other relatives will be taxed on the annual realized income earned in their accounts in the same manner as explained for RRSPs/RRIFs/LIRAs in the previous two sections. However, there are no corresponding Canada/US Tax Treaty elections to defer the income buildup inside of these plans to avoid the annual tax, and IRS Form 3520 needs to be completed and filed each year on an RESP (the fines for failure to file Form 3520 can amount to penalties of up to 5 percent of the assets in the plan and 35 percent of the income from the plan for each year the form has not been filed correctly). The Canadian tax deferrals and other benefits remain the same for US resident holders of RESPs. However, there is one key problem with account withdrawals unique to non-resident RESP owners: They cannot withdraw any earnings from the account, even if they want to pay the taxes on it, unless it is used strictly for qualified education assistance payments. This presents a real problem for RESP holders who no longer have any eligible relatives left to be able to use the RESP income built up or they are nearing the end of the 35-year lifespan of the RESP. It is believed this is an oversight on CRA's part because this RESP income can be stranded in Canada indefinitely with nobody being able to benefit. Consequently, RESP owners who are moving to the US need to consider withdrawing the RESP income before becoming non-residents from Canada and pay the appropriate tax and penalties to rescue funds that they and their relatives may never be able to use before the income is stranded. An alternative we have used successfully, is to transfer the ownership of the RESP, prior to leaving Canada, to a grandparent, uncle, or aunt who still lives in Canada as long as you can trust them to use the plan benefits for your child for his or her education eventually. Because they are still residents of Canada and you have no incidents of ownership in the RESP plan as a US resident, there is no additional IRS form or special reporting to do on your US return and yet your child can still benefit from the plan when he or she goes to college. Non-residents may withdraw principal from RESPs without difficulty or penalty. However, if you did establish the RESP for a Canadian relative such as a grandchild while you were a resident of Canada, it will be much easier if you simply give the RESP to the parent of the grandchild or directly to the grandchild before you exit Canada. Non-residents of Canada can contribute to their Canadian relative's RESP but they should not establish the plan or own a plan of behalf of a relative.

Border Guide readers are encouraged to participate in a cross-border Q&A through the new Cross-Border Forum. After registering, you can easily post questions about the contents of this book which will be moderated and/or answered by a cross-border financial planning professional in a timely fashion. You can also post comments or create discussions with other readers to share experiences and swap cross-border financial planning tips. To post a question or comment, go to keatsconnelly.com and click on the Cross-Border Forum tab at the top of the first page.

CROSS-BORDER Q&A

MARRIAGE TO CANADIAN WITH AN RRSP

I am an American citizen, and my fiancé is coming to the US from Canada to get married. I found I completely agreed with your ten reasons why one should liquidate RRSPs before leaving Canada. However, if we sell all of my fiancé's RRSPs, should we convert to an RRIF? My fiancé invested at the tail end of the boom and is suffering losses. What is the best way of minimizing taxes on his withdrawals? Do we have to do a staged withdrawal, and what are the matching foreign tax credits you refer to in your book? Of course, we would like to have a 0 percent tax liability.

Your book did not mention what to do with life insurance. Should we liquidate before we leave? Will the Canadian government view this as a tie?

Finally, my fiancé owns a house with his parents: joint ownership with right of survival. Should he have his name removed from the title? His parents still live in the house. Will the Canadian government view this as a tie?

— Marry Y., San Jose, California

Your questions are quite common for your situation, and there are many questions that you have not yet asked but will likely also need answered. However, I will need more information before I can provide advice, so I suggest you review the section Withdraw Your RRSP Tax-Free on a Net After-Tax Basis in this chapter, giving special attention to the factors listed there. Without knowing these factors and completing an analysis, my answers could be off considerably.

You are right in wanting to get answers to your questions before you are married and your future husband becomes a US resident. One bit of positive tax news is that your fiancé should be able to write off the losses in his RRSP portfolio in the US.

A US resident may maintain life insurance from Canada without income tax or other major problems; but there may be some estate tax issues, as covered in Chapter 4. The death benefits will be in Canadian dollars, so you will need to continually monitor the exchange rate to make sure your husband has enough insurance.

It is difficult to say what your fiancé should do with the ownership of his parents' home without more information, but it should not be of concern with respect to residential ties to Canada because of the Canada/US Tax Treaty tiebreaker rules.

DEFERRING TAX ON RRSP UNDER TREATY

I am a dual citizen, my wife is Canadian with a green card, and my children are dual citizens. We have been residing in Washington state for five years now. I am a physician. We figured most things out on our own when we moved to the US, and fortunately it looks like we did pretty well. My wife and I have about $85,000 in RRSPs in Canada. We have nothing else there, except a checking account to pay insurance premiums (which is only funded by me with after-tax US dollars and used for no other reason). I have been filing elections to defer tax in the US on the RRSPs as per the treaty. We do not know if we will ever return to Canada, but would never close that door. You are the first person I have ever heard to recommend taking the RRSPs out of Canada. What is the most tax-efficient way to approach the process, *since I am over 30 years away from being able to take distributions and I have a high income in the US? I never did anything to step up the cost basis before leaving the country, but have since consolidated our RRSPs all in one place. (As you know, Washington state was an early adopter of legislation that allowed us to manage our RRSPs from the US). We use Phillips, Hagar and North, an excellent company with regards to management fees and returns, even when compared with US fund managers. Since it is a small amount of money, would it be better just to leave it, not knowing where we will live in the future? Might that be akin to hedging currency risk for future retirement? This is really my only outstanding issue. Whether to do it, and if so, how? Is there more information on this particular scenario, or do I require professional help to make a judgment?*

My second question relates to being a high-income earner in the US and moving back to Canada. I believe there would be onerous tax implications for me, since I would trigger Alternative Minimum Tax (AMT) on the US return, and would have to pay 10 percent of the AMT regardless of the tax treaty and credits (at least this is my understanding). This, in addition to an already high Canadian tax rate. It sounds like I would have issues with my Roth IRAs as well. As an aside, your book has depressed me a bit, because I realize that it may be incredibly prohibitive to ever go back.

— Andrew J., Snohomish, Washington

My question to you is why complicate your investment strategy and your income tax filing by leaving a small RRSP in Canada at all? It is costing you more than you think and every year the file you need to keep for the IRS keeps getting thicker and thicker. After 20 or more years this will become quite unwieldy. Having an RRSP while you are a US resident invariably adds several hundreds of dollars to your accounting and tax preparation bills each year unnecessarily; you are better to pocket this expense or use it for something else.

Yes, PH&N are a very good company, but if you go to Vanguard or Fidelity in the US, you can get excellent funds for about one-tenth the cost. Over the life of your investment, the approximately 1 percent more per year that you are paying to PH&N can amount to a 10 percent tax equivalent each year because of this additional money management cost (when you are averaging even a 10 percent total return, which is a stretch currently). This extra cost of investment and trying to keep up with the US tax complications every year removes any benefits you might get from tax deferral by attempting to keep your RRSP in Canada.

Waiting to withdraw the funds until after you are back in Canada guarantees you will pay higher taxes than the 25 percent you would currently pay in the US — not much of a reward for deferring. Don't forget you can use the 25 percent non-resident withholding tax not needed to pay all the deferred taxes now on your US return to reduce US taxes for up to ten years through foreign tax credits. This makes a current withdrawal even more beneficial, whereas the longer you defer, the larger your tax bill will be. Eventually the 25 percent non-resident withholding tax will not even cover the US tax on withdrawal, and you will need to pay out of pocket. In addition, what happens if Canada Revenue Agency decides to increase the non-resident withholding tax to more than 25 percent as they easily could?

Don't be discouraged about going back to Canada to retire. If you do some advance planning, as I mention in Chapter 12, you can minimize taxes. Some new IRS rules that took effect in October 2004 make AMT using foreign tax credits no longer an issue.

SHOULD YOU COLLAPSE YOUR CANADIAN RRSP?

I read an article entitled "Don't Collapse Your RRSP if You Move to the US." It stated that I would lose money if I moved my RRSP and it would be to my advantage to leave my RRSP in Canada as a US resident. I have been a US resident green card holder for two years, and my wife and I have $350,000 in RRSP mutual funds in Canada. We are unlikely to return to Canada in the foreseeable future. As you can see, due to the size of our RRSP, this is an important issue and the advice in the article appears to conflict with the advice you and others have given us in the past, which is to cash in my RRSPs. Is this something new or is there some other reason for the advice given in this article? My wife's US income is about $20,000 and mine is about $90,000. Would a Section 217 filing apply to us and could we get a refund of the non-resident withholding from CRA?

— Kurt K., Seattle, Washington

There are some good reasons why the strategy mentioned in the article will not work for the majority of Canadians moving to the US with RRSPs. I feel the author of the article did not do proper research and/or works for a company that benefits from charging fees for managing your RRSP in Canada; they would lose if you move those funds to the US and therefore they only outline benefits of keeping your RRSP in Canada rather than the pitfalls.

Stepping up the basis in your RRSP, as recommended in the article, by buying the assets from your own RRSP would be considered a non-event by the IRS. This would be similar to changing brokerage firms by transferring your RRSP from one firm to another. To qualify for a step-up in basis in your RRSP before you enter the US, the securities must be sold to a third party (your spouse doesn't count, either). You can switch mutual funds to other funds in the same family to get a step-up in your cost basis before you take up a US residency without transaction cost. As you are already in the US this would not apply to you.

In addition, a Section 217 filing won't help obtain refunds of the non-resident withholding tax for those with incomes of more than $20,000. This is generally practical only for those with world incomes around $15,000 including the RRSP withdrawals, not the $30,000 mentioned in the article. For those with incomes of more than $20,000, it becomes more practical to use foreign tax credits in the United States rather than to look for a refund from CRA. The article overlooked several other key issues that I believe would lead most people to conclude that they should take their RRSPs out of Canada soon after departing for the United States:

1. Leaving your RRSP in Canada exposes you to significant government risk. In other words, you are at the mercy of CRA or the IRS's ability to change the rules on these investments and greatly increase your tax. The withholding tax on RRSP lump-sum withdrawals used to be 15 percent; now it is 25 percent and we expect it to keep rising even higher. Make hay while the sun is shining! The current 25 percent withholding on lump sum RRSP withdrawals may be the lowest you'll ever get and still about 50 percent reduction of the tax you would pay by withdrawing the RRSP as a Canadian resident now or in the future.
2. Getting your RRSP out of Canada greatly simplifies your financial life. You will be subject only to US tax rules and you won't need the specialized tax and investment advice that comes with maintaining an RRSP as a US resident. This specialized advice is not only expensive, but hard to find since most US or Canadian advisors don't have any experience with RRSPs for US residents and don't have the time required and/or the desire to get up to speed on these unique issues, because they would come across them so rarely unless their business was specializing in cross-border financial planning.
3. The article failed to address the complications of state income tax rules, which vary somewhat from state to state. American states are not bound by any federal tax treaties, so the election to defer US taxes on income in the RRSP at the federal level would have no effect at the state level in many states. This would result in an unnecessary and added level of tax.

4. Once your RRSPs are withdrawn, you can put the net proceeds in the United States into a very broad range of tax-free or tax-deferred investments without all the restrictions of an RRSP.
5. On average, mutual funds in Canada charge about double what they do in the United States. Management expense ratios average 2 to 3 percent in Canada, while in the United States you have a large selection of no-load mutual funds with expense ratios as low as 0.05 percent. Based on the size of your RRSPs, the savings in expenses alone could be close to $10,000 a year.

There are at least five other reasons why you should not leave your RRSPs in Canada once you are a US resident, but the ones I've listed should be sufficient to convince you what to do with yours.

CROSS-BORDER RRIFS CAN BE A TRICKY BUSINESS

I am considering cashing in $350,000 in Canadian RRIFs and investing the proceeds in the US. Our bank in Canada advises me that a Canadian withholding tax of 25 percent applies to all payments above the minimum, which has 15 percent withheld. The RRIF withdrawals will also be taxed in the US, but subject to tax credits. From what I have been able to deduce, it would be advantageous for me to move at least some of the RRIFs from GIC investments to mutual funds to be able to utilize these tax credits fully. Our Canadian bank is prepared to make this switch of assets. We are inclined to bite the bullet and pay the 25 percent Canadian tax. Is there a way to avoid the 25 percent Canadian tax and instead pay 15 percent?

— G.N., Fort Myers, Florida

You can withdraw twice your annual minimums or 10 percent of the value, whichever is greater, at the beginning of the year from your RRIFs at the 15 percent non-resident withholding tax rate. Up to twice the minimum RRIF or the 10 percent withdrawals is considered periodic under the Canada/US Tax Treaty. Lump-sum withdrawals over the two-times-annual minimum are taxed at the 25 percent non-resident rate. The only part of your RRIF that is taxable by the United States is your earnings — interest, dividends, and capital gains in your plan each year. The rest is considered tax-free withdrawal of principal. You'll need some help from a fee-only financial planner to help you plan these withdrawals. Doing it on your own can mean you miss out on tax credits and could make costly mistakes, as there is more to consider than meets the eye when making these RRIF withdrawals as a US resident.

11 Don't Let the Tax Door Hit You in the Behind on the Way out

DEALING WITH DEPARTURE TAX

WHAT IS A DEPARTURE TAX?

It would be nice to be able to say that the Canadian departure tax (also known as the exit tax) is much ado about nothing, but most Canadians give it a great deal of thought when considering adopting the settler cross-border lifestyle or moving to the US Sunbelt. This chapter aims to show that the departure tax does get more attention than it deserves. We can start by defining what departure tax is. Departure tax is the tax that Canada Revenue Agency levies on taxpayers' capital assets when they become non-residents of Canada. CRA requires a taxpayer who is exiting Canada to go through a deemed disposition or a deemed sale of certain assets on the date of departure. For tax purposes, under CRA rules, a deemed sell is always taxed as an actual sale of assets. As noted in earlier chapters, Canada taxes residents on their world income only while they are actually living within its borders. Consequently, all one has to do to no longer be subject to Canadian tax rules is depart from Canada. Canada's answer to this simplistic method of avoiding Canadian tax is to collect all the taxes due on any capital gains that have not yet been taxed prior to the taxpayer's departure, hence the departure tax. The best way to understand the departure tax is to understand what is not subject to the tax, since there are many myths and misunderstandings as to what is included in this tax. The following is a list of assets that are NOT subject to any departure tax when emigrating from Canada:

1. Canadian real estate or resource properties
2. Canadian business capital property (including inventory), if the business is carried on through a permanent establishment in Canada
3. Pensions and all registered plans (including RRSPs, RRIFs, LIRAs, RCAs, and DPSPs)

4. Employee stock options subject to tax in Canada
5. Interest in life insurance policies or annuities in Canada
6. Rights to certain benefits under employee profit-sharing plans, employee benefit plans, employee trusts, retirement allowances, and salary deferral arrangements
7. Interests in certain trusts in which the trustee and the trust assets will remain in Canada

Now that we've looked at what is not subject to tax, it is a little bit easier to understand what is subject to the departure tax:

1. All stocks (including closely held Canadian-controlled private corporations), bonds, mutual funds, exchange traded funds, limited or general partnership interests, and other similar securities that are not inside registered plans noted in (3) above
2. US real estate and other foreign real estate
3. Certain rights or interests in foreign trusts
4. Personal property that has appreciated in value such as artwork or antiques

If you compare the two lists above as to what is and what isn't subject to departure tax, you can easily surmise a large number, in fact most Canadians would not be subject to any departure tax at all. Those Canadians who may be subject to departure tax have several options to mitigate, defer, or eliminate this tax altogether, as noted in the next section.

TAX ON EXITING CANADA

When Canadian residents move to the United States, CRA requires that they file exit or final tax returns for the year of their departure. This exit return is a regular T1 form filed by the usual April 30 deadline following the year of departure, with the exit date clearly indicated on the first page of the T1 and all the appropriate schedules, forms, and disclosures completed as required. For most persons adopting the Settler cross-border lifestyle, this will be the final CRA return. The important forms to be filed with an exit T1 are Form T1161 (List of Properties by an Emigrant of Canada) and Form T1243 (Deemed Disposition Property by an Emigrant of Canada), which lists and calculates the net capital gains on those owned items subject to the exit tax. Each property deemed to be disposed of is deemed to have been re-acquired by the individual at the time of emigration at a cost equal to the proceeds of the disposition of the property. Any capital gains tax due may be paid with the return or deferred using the procedures noted in the next paragraph.

To elect to defer this exit tax you must complete and file Form T1244 with your exit tax return. You are required to post suitable security with CRA equal to the tax due. The tax due need not be paid until the assets subject to the deemed disposition tax are actually sold. It is important to realize that since CRA charges no interest on the tax due, by electing to defer, you are in exactly the same situation as if you stayed in Canada holding the same securities or properties. Given this, why are so many emigrants overly concerned about leaving Canada and paying an exit tax? All too often, concern with the exit tax is a result of not knowing the basic rules or of relying on advisors who aren't able to or don't want to explain the rules to the taxpayer. Many times during my cross-border planning career, I have heard individuals say to me, "My accountant, who has been my advisor for too many years to mention, told me I can't leave Canada because I would have way too much departure tax to pay." If you hear this phrase or something similar, I believe you need to seek out a new advisor who looks out for your best interests. The old advisor may be wrongfully preventing you from having that swinging door on the Canada-US border that allows you the cross-border lifestyle you wish.

Using the election to defer taxes is just a worst-case scenario; there are many cross-border options to legitimately minimize or eliminate any exit/departure tax that may be due. These options include, but are not limited to, the following:

- Most investment portfolios have some securities in a gain position and some in a loss position. On your exit, you may offset the losses against gains and therefore be subject to tax only if there is net gain on the portfolio. It should be noted that CRA does not allow the same kind of gain-loss offset when dealing with personal use property. For example, you may have a large deemed loss on an item of personal property on exit such as a car and a large gain on a wine collection but on your exit return you could not offset the loss on your car against the gain on your wine collection. Consequently, you would be forced to either drink all the wine before you left Canada or alternately pay capital gains tax on the appreciation on the wine collection over what you paid for it. CRA also distinguishes between personal use property and what it defines as listed personal property. Personal use property tends to be ordinary personal items like cars and sofas etc. Listed personal property is something more extraordinary like works of art, jewellery, stamps or coins; everything else not on this list is considered personal use property. Listed personal property gains or losses can offset one another on the exit return.

- Use the Canada/US Tax Treaty to eliminate the tax entirely on a net basis by turning the so-called exit tax into foreign tax credits that can be used to reduce US income taxes on a dollar-for-dollar basis once you've taken up residency in the United States.
- Use the small-business capital gains exemption for qualified active businesses (for husband and wife this could mean up to $1.7 million of tax-free capital gains).
- Utilize capital losses carried forward that may be available from previous investment losses or failed investments.
- If your spouse is not emigrating from Canada with you, transfer assets to him or her on a tax-free basis and you would have no exit tax when you departed Canada.
- If you have assets that are not deemed to be disposed of when you cross the border and have a net loss built into them — such as a terrible real estate investment — you may elect to go through a deemed disposition of this property on your exit and use the loss to offset other capital gains that are subject to the exit tax. Care must be taken when dealing with the depreciable property such as buildings as there can be recapture of previous depreciation.

There is also a reporting requirement for those exiting Canada with total property holdings exceeding $25,000. They are required to report all of their property on CRA Form T1161 with their exit returns for the year of departure.

If you did not sell or do not wish to sell your Canadian principal residence before departing Canada, you need to be aware of some special rules under the Canada/US Tax Treaty that can help you reduce future capital gains tax on the sale of your Canadian home while you are a US resident. In Chapter 3, when we compared the basic differences in taxation between the United States and Canada, we saw that Canada does not tax capital gains on the sale of a principal residence while the United States will tax those gains in excess of $250,000 ($500,000 per married couple). The Canada/US Tax Treaty helps you avoid this problem by making it appear, for tax purposes, that you purchased the Canadian home at its fair market value the day you entered the United States, provided you file the appropriate Treaty election with your US tax return for that tax year. As a result, you are only required to pay tax on gains on this property from the date that you became a resident. Note that this step-up in basis for your principal residence applies only to non-US citizens or non-green card holders. Other capital property (thanks to changes to the Canada/US Tax Treaty in September 2000) that is subject to the deemed disposition on exit from Canada may also get a new cost basis for US tax purposes equal to the fair market value of the property on the exit date. To receive the special tax treatment, the individual must file a treaty election Form 8833 with the US tax return for the year of departure from Canada. It is highly recommended that Canadians who keep their principal residences when moving to the United States get a fair market appraisal just before leaving Canada and keep it for future tax reference when making the treaty election.

Upon your exit from Canada, you must either elect a deemed disposition of your principal residence on your exit tax return, or convert it to rental property. This will step up your Canadian cost basis on the ultimate sale of the property to further reduce possible capital gains taxes in Canada, as you would have received the tax-free principal residence exemption had the residence been sold before your departure.

Canadians emigrating from Canada to become settlers/residents in the US should get professional advice from a cross-border financial planning expert as far in advance of their exit date as possible, unless they have very small and simple accumulated assets. This process tends to be very complex, and mistakes can be very costly.

CANADIAN DEPARTURE CHECKLIST

If you're exiting Canada for the US or another treaty country, the treaty will generally provide clear rules as to what income can be taxed, at what rate, and by which country. Your exit from Canada should be as clean as possible to avoid CRA attacks on your residency or non-residency status. There are several key actions you should follow when exiting Canada, and if you follow these rules you will likely have little problem with CRA attempting to tax your world income in Canada. In the 1998 federal budget, CRA introduced a new rule that stated that if a Canadian was deemed a resident of another country under a treaty with Canada, he or she would automatically become a non-resident of Canada for all domestic purposes. This new rule makes it much less likely that CRA will ever challenge the fact that you have not exited Canada and try to tax you at Canadian tax rates after you have moved to the US. However, some items are not covered by treaty provisions. In order to avoid paying full Canadian tax rates, we've developed a checklist. These tips can assist you in establishing Canadian non-resident status after your departure, thereby avoiding future controversy with CRA. The items are listed in no particular order, but the first five are considered important and you do not have to implement every one of them, providing you follow at least one of the four Key Treaty tiebreaker rules as discussed in Chapter 4. Remember that there is no single thing you do but rather the combination of facts and circumstances that determines residency.

1. Sell your Canadian principal residence or rent it out on a long-term lease (six months or longer) on or about your date of departure, preferably before your exit date. Having unrestricted access to year-round accommodation in Canada, regardless of whether you own it, is considered having a principal residence in Canada. A cottage or other seasonal residence generally would not be considered a principal Canadian residence. If you buy or rent in the United States, the Canada/US Tax Treaty will cancel out CRA's claim for Canadian residence even if you still own a place in Canada. This principal residence determination is the first rule of the Canada/US Tax Treaty tiebreaker rules (detailed in Chapter 4).

2. Make sure you spend as much time out of Canada after your exit date as possible, particularly in the first two years. Under no circumstance spend more than six months a year in Canada after your departure. Keep your visits to Canada relatively short in duration (four to six weeks) and as infrequent as possible.

3. If you have a business in Canada or Canadian employment income, develop proof that you are not required to be in Canada on a continuous basis to operate the business. Other employment or business income should be earned in the same manner that a US person who has never resided in Canada would earn it. Try to do all your work from the US side of the border. You are allowed to earn up to $10,000 in Canada without being subject to Canadian tax under the Canada/US Tax Treaty. If you exceed this amount, you must file Canadian tax returns and pay Canadian taxes at the full rates on your income earned in Canada, even though you may be a non-resident. Please review the Canada/US Tax Treaty tiebreaker rules outlined in Chapter 4; if there is any doubt or concern with any of these first three items, the Treaty is always the final determinant.

4. Close all your Canadian bank and brokerage accounts, including RRSPs (review all the issues concerning RRSPs detailed in

Chapter 10), and move them to the United States. Maintaining a checking and/or savings account at a Canadian bank generally is okay, providing it is clearly set up as a non-resident account.

5. Notify any Canadian payers of Canadian-sourced income such as banks, brokers, pension payers, and government agencies in writing that you have left Canada and are to be considered a non-resident for all purposes as of your exit date. Give them your US address to forward all future payments and statements.
6. Cancel your Canadian medical coverage before your exit date or within the provincially allowed grace period after your departure. Make sure you have US health insurance in place before you leave Canada.
7. You must be a legal resident in the United States before you can exit Canada for tax purposes. Ensure that proper US immigration documentation is in place before you depart from Canada.
8. Cancel all church, club, or equivalent memberships in Canada or at minimum convert the regular memberships to non-resident memberships. All churches and most clubs will allow you to visit or use their facilities as a non-resident.
9. Cancel all your Canadian credit cards, your driver's licence, and your vehicle registration. Establish all of these in the United States (see the next section of this chapter when attempting to establish credit for the first time in the US).
10. Accept no mail deliveries at any address in Canada. Have all mail forwarded to the United States. Do not have personal mail sent to a Canadian relative or business address in Canada.
11. Change wills and other legal documents to reflect US residence.

In general, always think and act as a visitor to Canada in all respects. It is sometimes good to just think of yourself as entering Canada as a visitor for the first time and acting accordingly.

TRANSFERRING YOUR CREDIT RATING TO THE UNITED STATES

Many Canadians moving to the US are shocked to discover their hard-earned good credit rating in Canada cannot get them even a simple Visa card in the US. We have had clients with a high net worth be turned down for a thousand dollar credit limit Visa card. This problem can usually be overcome by knowing what to tell a credit card company, or whoever you are borrowing from, what they need to do to verify your credit history. The people doing the credit check will normally need your Social Security Number (if you do not have an SSN you will need to get one before you embark on this process, otherwise your chances of success will be slim as every US citizen and legal resident of the US must have an SSN) into the three major US credit bureaus and see what comes back. Since you are a new resident, likely with a new Social Security Number, usually nothing will come up. No credit will be advanced, since lenders usually consider someone with no credit history a poor risk. The trick, if they are smart businesspeople and prepared to listen, is to give them your Canadian Social Insurance Number so they can call the Canadian bureaus. Explain that credit bureaus in Canada operate on a very similar basis as they do in the US. Even provide them with a copy of your Canadian credit report and the numbers (provided below) for the credit bureaus in Canada for them to verify. Don't assume that they even know where Canada is, let alone how Canadian credit bureaus work. At least two of the three major US credit bureaus are the same in Canada as in the US, although the Canadian divisions are separate and normally do not communicate with their US counterparts unless you force the issue. I would guess that 98 percent of the banks or credit card companies to which you may be applying for credit in the US would not know this basic fact but when enlightened by you would feel comfortable calling Canada to get your history. If they call a Canadian reporting agency with your SIN, they can access your complete credit history.

It is important to obtain a hard copy of your Canadian credit rating from one of the Canadian credit services. Equifax (1-800-465-7166, www.equifax.ca) and TransUnion (1-800-663-9980, www.tuc.ca) are the credit bureaus in both Canada and the US so they are the easiest to work with in these circumstances. Without direction from you, clerks at most lending institutions will simply reject you because their rule books don't tell them what to do in this situation. Be persistent with this process and insist on speaking to higher levels of management in the organization you are wishing to receive credit from. Eventually you should find someone experienced enough to understand the situation and who will act accordingly. American Express is the only credit card company I am aware of that will transfer your Canadian account to the US, including all member benefits, without cost or hassle just by calling their customer service line.

Three major Canadian banks, RBC, TD, and BMO, have substantial number of branches or federal charters in the US. Because of the demand from their Canadian clientele, these banks have developed systems to port Canadian credit ratings from Canada to the US so that they can follow US regulations when providing credit to Canadians who have adopted the Settler/resident lifestyle with the US. Consequently, if you want or need a mortgage or a US credit card, these three Canadian banks are good place to start and establish your credit rating to the same level you had earned in Canada.

All US residents need to be familiar with their FICO (the Fair Isaac and Company) score. The FICO score was created several decades ago as a measure of one's credit worthiness. Your FICO score can range from 300 to 900, the higher the score the better your credit rating. With a 600 or less FICO score, you would be considered a poor credit risk. There are five major factors used to determine your FICO score: your payment history (35 percent), the length of your credit history (15 percent), amounts owed currently (30 percent), amount of new credit recently applied for (10 percent), and the type of credit used — such as loans with collateral (e.g., mortgages) or just open lines of credit with no collateral (10 percent). Consequently, new residents to the US, using these factors, will likely have a very low FICO score unless they can get credit history transferred successfully to the US. This low score can stick with you for a long period of time. Each of the three US credit bureaus, Equifax, TransUnion, and Experian are required by law to give you a free copy of your credit report and FICO score once a year and it is recommended that you take advantage of this service every year to monitor your credit for fraud or someone using your credit illegally.

US ESTATE PLANNING

Necessity is often the mother of invention. Since there is a greater need for comprehensive estate planning in the US, a number of very good and proven techniques have been developed. There are many tools in the estate planning toolbox available in the US, that can be used to create flexible and less costly estate plans to implement and maintain. These techniques help make management of your estate easier while you are alive and then provide for a smooth transition to your heirs. Many of these techniques will work equally well for Canadians who become residents of the US and can be used to cover assets remaining in Canada.

When you are moving or contemplating a settler lifestyle to the US, cross-border estate planning needs to be a top priority, as there are many complex issues that could lead to unnecessary estate settlement costs and death taxes if not addressed before you take up residence in that country.

Normally the first matter of business in cross-border estate planning is a comparison of what your estate costs and taxes are in Canada and the

US, to see if there is an advantage in either country. It is not very often in this book that I can state a general rule that applies in almost every case, but I can say that couples with estates of less than $11 million USD (or nearly $15 million CAD) have an unquestionable death tax advantage as residents of the US. Since there are spousal trusts and other roll-over options for surviving spouses in Canada and qualified domestic-marital deduction trusts in the US to permit the transfer of assets tax-free between spouses, I will concentrate on estate tax and settlement costs at the death of the second spouse, to measure the full impact of these costs and make a proper Canadian-US comparison. Figure 11.1 gives an example of this situation, using a reasonably well-off couple with an estate of $2,230,000 CAD from the province of Ontario.

The Canadian death taxes in Figure 11.1 are calculated by taking the amount subject to the deemed disposition tax at death of the surviving spouse and adding the Ontario probate fee.

The total deemed disposition tax is $498,800 CAD; US non-resident estate tax is zero under the new Canada/US Tax Treaty and the probate fee for an estate of this size in Ontario would be $33,450 CAD. Thus, a total death tax of $532,250 CAD would be payable by this couple's estate if they were Canadian residents at the time of their deaths. If this couple, or at the very least the surviving spouse, does not undertake some preventive planning, their heirs will pay what amounts to a total of $532,250 CAD in Canadian inheritance or estate tax after the second spouse's death. These taxes will be due within six months of that person's death or by April 30 of the following year, whichever is sooner.

When comparing US and Canadian taxes, many Canadian accountants, financial planners, and attorneys are quick to pontificate that Canada does not have an estate tax. Just because CRA doesn't call the tax at death an "estate tax," as Figure 11.1 illustrates, it doesn't mean that most Canadians won't face a much higher estate tax in Canada than US residents who own similar estates. The IRS doesn't try to disguise its estate tax, and because of the high exemptions allowed, less than 1 percent of all US residents are subject to an estate tax.

If this couple took up residence in the US and had a similar asset mix at the time of death, they would have absolutely no US estate taxes due, since the size of their estate would be only about $2 million USD, less than their combined total of $11 million USD in US estate tax exemptions. This couple could deal with their RRSPs as outlined earlier to get them out of Canada at no or very low income taxes on a net basis. In addition, the beneficiaries of the estate from the US residents would re-

Assets		Amount Subject to Canadian Death Tax
RRSP/RRIF	$800,000	$800,000
Cdn. Residence	400,000	0
Mutual Funds	300,000	
	(Original cost at $150,000)	75,000
US Residence	400,000	
	(Original cost at 100,000)	150,000
Land	150,000	
	(Original cost at $50,000)	50,000
Term deposit	100,000	0
Personal	80,000	0
Total	**$2,230,000**	**$1,075,000**
Canadian resident death taxes	$535,000	
US resident death taxes	$0	

FIGURE 11.1

ceive a free step-up in basis on any appreciated assets left in the estate so they could be sold without capital gains taxes. In Chapter 5, I listed some of the double-tax consequences of having assets in both Canada and the United States, and earlier in this chapter I listed things to look out for when leaving Canada. The complexity of these issues underscores the necessity of consulting with a cross-border financial planning professional to ensure you maximize the opportunities and minimize the pitfalls.

For estates of more than $11 million USD per couple, or $5.45 million USD for individuals, other estate-planning techniques can be used to deal economically with almost any estate tax (see Figure 5.2 for the estate tax rates). US residents with estates exceeding their personal estate tax exemptions, and who are concerned about depletion of their estates as discussed in Chapter 4, will use one or more trusts set aside and funded with income tax savings to pay any potential estate taxes, even when they run into millions of dollars.

The January 1, 1996 protocol to the Canada/US Tax Treaty added a very useful provision that allows the executor of a Canadian citizen descendant to opt out of the US unlimited marital deduction on the first spouse's death and receive an extra exemption equivalent to the $5.45 million USD current amount. This means that those couples who have estates of between $11 million USD and $22 million USD, divided equally between the spouses, can escape US estate taxes altogether using this single Treaty provision at the first spouse's death. In addition, there are many other effective estate tax planning techniques for larger estates, which go beyond the general scope of this cross-border guide.

In the section Living Trusts in Chapter 5, we outlined a number of benefits in using a living trust in an estate plan. These trusts are used in the US for estates of any size, to assist in minimizing probate costs and delays. Combined with wills with pour-over provisions that are designed to place assets either left on purpose or accidentally outside the trusts into them at death, powers of attorney and living wills, these trusts round out a cross-border estate plan. (Powers of attorney are also explained in Chapter 5.) A living will is a separate document that deals with the possibility of your becoming incapacitated, to the extent of your being connected to life support systems with no hope of recovery. It tells your family and medical professionals your wishes under such circumstances.

Border Guide readers are encouraged to participate in the new *Cross-Border Forum.* To post a question or comment, go to keatsconnelly.com and click on the *Cross-Border Forum* tab.

CROSS-BORDER Q&A

CANADIAN EXIT PROCEDURES

Is there a beneficial purpose in submitting Canadian Form NR73, Determination of Residency Status (Leaving Canada)? Specifically we are both retired and own a condo in the US. We have been renting a small home in rural Saskatchewan. We would like to establish residency in the US, and we would like to keep our small rental home as a seasonal residence. Should we show on form NR73 that we are leaving personal possessions in Canada; keeping a Canadian bank account; keeping a brokerage account; and keeping our Canadian passports?

Apart from the above we will cancel our Saskatchewan driver's and vehicle licences and close all memberships, our post office box, government medicare, and telephone. We have paid the instalment on our taxes due, transferred our auto club membership to Washington State, notified all payers of change of residency, and sent in a change of address for periodical subscriptions and all others we can think of, including charitable organizations to which we contribute. Mail is being forwarded to our US address.

With this situation, and those boxes checked on form NR73 mentioned above — assuming it were to be submitted — what might be the response from CRA, after the 12-week current waiting period?

— Darlene G., Yorkton, Saskatchewan

You are not required to file an NR73. We generally recommend you do not file one unless you are specifically requested to by CRA. If you follow the exit checklist in this chapter, you can generally assume that you have safely exited Canada for tax purposes. Nothing that you listed regarding what you are leaving in Canada would likely cause CRA to classify you as a resident of Saskatchewan. However, you should move your brokerage account to the US and keep only minimal amounts in your bank accounts. There are securities regulations that make trading in your Canadian brokerage account illegal from your broker's standpoint, unless the firm and broker are also licensed in Washington State.

TRANSFERRING CANADIAN CREDIT HISTORY TO THE US

My husband holds an L-1A visa, and I have an L-2 visa that is valid until April 2013. I took your advice and called American Express to transfer my credit from Canada to America. They told me that they have made some structural changes in that I would have to be the one to call the Canadian office, cancel my card, then call back to the American office and apply for a card again. The information they would need from me would be my employment information and bank information. Obviously, I told them that I do not work, and they refused me a card. Unfortunately, since my husband is not an American Express cardholder, he was refused as well.

I also tried calling Equifax in the States and explained my situation. They told me to call the Canadian branch and get my credit information from Canada. Shouldn't the States have a copy of my credit information? That's the whole point of my not getting any credit here: America doesn't have any credit file on me! They told me that when and if I apply for any type of credit card or anything else I need, I would have to present a copy of my Canadian credit information. I find that ridiculous! Is this the way it works? I am in the process of mailing my personal information to the Canadian Equifax office to get my credit file.

I was also wondering if I need to cancel my Canadian life insurance policy now that I am an American resident.

— Soula P., Vancouver, British Columbia

Some people have managed to get Equifax to make the call to Canada and get the credit history transferred; others have had to do what you are doing. I don't know why there is such inconsistency in the Equifax procedures, but both ways do work. In addition, try TransUnion, the other credit reporting agency both in Canada and the US.

Also check with RBC, TD, and BMO branches in the US, as they have been very helpful in assisting Canadians to transfer their credit ratings to the US. There is no need to cancel your Canadian life insurance policy, but if you are still able to get new insurance, it will be more convenient to replace your Canadian policy with an American one. Don't cancel your existing policy until the new policy is in place.

KEEPING A CANADIAN COTTAGE AS A US RESIDENT

On your Canadian Departure Checklist, you mention selling of your principal residence, and you also mention that a "cottage or seasonal residence generally would not be considered a principal Canadian residence." In the next sentence you mention that "if you buy or rent in the United States, the treaty will cancel out CRA's claim for Canadian residence even if you still own a place in Canada."

When looking at CRA Form NR73, Determination of Canadian Residency, I understand that a cottage is indeed considered a "secondary tie" to Canada and thus would not be a principal residence (which would be considered a primary tie). However, if one had enough ties remaining to be considered a resident of Canada (and owned only a cottage and not a home), and if it came down to the residency tiebreaker, and since the first tiebreaker in the treaty is a permanent home, would CRA at that point consider the cottage to be a permanent home in order to send the decision to the next tiebreaker (which is the center of vital interests)? I began thinking about this while reading your book and thought I would ask about it.

— Krista B., Ottawa, Ontario

Keeping a cottage as a secondary tie to Canada has never, to my knowledge, been a problem for any of the clients or *Border Guide* readers with whom I have worked. There are two reasons for this. First, if CRA were to try to tax you as a resident, you could argue that primary residence trumps secondary residence, and therefore you would pass the first Treaty test. However, should that fail, the next treaty test is for vital interests, over which you have nearly full control, and you could make these weigh in favor of US residency, thereby passing that test. You should ensure that you can pass at least one test clearly and should have a good backup plan to be able to pass one other, just in case you are declared a resident when you don't want or plan to be.

There's No Place Like Home 12

Returning Residents

There are estimated to be more than two million Canadians living in the US. Many of them took jobs or were transferred for employment purposes, leaving their families and their roots behind. Many have completed their US employment or are baby boomers who are deciding what kind of cross-border lifestyle they would like to live now that they are no longer tied to jobs. Many will decide to stay where they are because they have developed new social and family networks; many others will head south to the US Sunbelt; and some will head north to Canada and their roots. In the past few years my colleagues and I have helped complete cross-border planning for several of these people returning to Canada and we have had many requests to add information to *The Border Guide* that would be of assistance to them and others in the same situation.

This chapter discusses issues and suggests solutions for Canadians returning to Canada to live permanently, or deciding whether to be a Vacationer, Snowbird, or Settler as discussed in Chapter 1. US citizens being transferred to Canada for employment, or wishing to retire in Canada, face similar issues to long-term US-resident Canadians returning to Canada; however, there are enough differences between these groups that Chapter 13 deals specifically with cross-border financial planning issues for US citizens moving to Canada.

As with most cross-border planning, the longer you plan in advance the better the return you will get on your time, effort, and expenses. Planning must be completed before you cross the border to take advantage of some of the pre-entry techniques to reduce or eliminate taxes, and to gain opportunities that aren't available once you are in Canada. Good cross-border planning dictates that no doors should be closed nor bridges burned, and an optional plan to move back to Canada should have been included in your plan to move to the US in the first place.

IMMIGRATION TO CANADA

Canadians who have retained their Canadian citizenship, or are dual citizens, will have no problem when entering Canada. Those who have been out of Canada for a long time and are concerned that by taking up US citizenship they have lost their Canadian citizenship need not worry if they took up US citizenship after 1977 when Prime Minister Pierre Trudeau introduced his "once a Canadian, always a Canadian" policy. After that date Canadians were allowed to retain citizenship when taking up that of another country (unless they made a formal renunciation of their Canadian citizenship). New rules brought into effect in the Canadian *Citizenship Act* in April 17, 2009 has retroactively reinstated Canadian citizenship for those who may have lost it prior to 1977 by taking up citizenship in the US. However, these new rules only allow children born to Canadian parents living in the US to inherit Canadian citizenship, not grandchildren. Canadian citizenship can only be passed on to the first generation born in the US to a Canadian citizen. If you have never been a Canadian citizen, you will need to obtain permanent resident status under one of several Canadian programs, or be granted a visa under the North American Free Trade Agreement (NAFTA) before you will be allowed to move to Canada legally. Canadian immigration options for US citizens moving to Canada will be discussed in detail in Chapter 13.

GIVING UP YOUR US CITIZENSHIP OR GREEN CARD

If you are a US green card holder and are making a move to leave the US for a period exceeding six months, you will be deemed to have abandoned your green card status as a legal permanent resident of the US. However, in a practical sense, if you don't voluntarily surrender your green card at the border, or to a US Citizenship and Immigration (USCIS) office, you should be able to retain the use of the card if you follow some basic guidelines. If you have been a green card holder for more than five years and wish to keep your options open about moving back to the US at some point, it is recommended that you become a US citizen before you move back to Canada. I wish I had a dollar for each of the countless Canadians who have given up their green cards when they moved back to Canada from the US, and then regretted doing so, or wished they had taken up US citizenship when they had the chance, so that they could to go back to the US for personal or financial reasons. In Chapter 1, we discussed how the Platinum Level Frequent Traveler status is afforded to a dual citizen, where he or she can live, work, or travel in either country for any amount of time without restriction. Those with a US green card, as noted below, have a few considerations to deal with and therefore have only

Gold status. With planning, Platinum or Gold status allows the option of paying the lowest tax rates between Canada and the US.

There are potentially large tax compliance issues if you retain your green card. The IRS taxes green card holders as it taxes US citizens wherever they live. As part of your cross-border plan, it is best to review all the implications of retaining or giving up your green card and take the appropriate action. Because part of cross-border planning is to keep the door open to live and pay taxes in either country, we suggest legally retaining your green card or becoming a US citizen, unless absolutely certain that you will never return to resident status in the US. Normally you can retain your green card legally if you maintain a presence in the US such as a home, investments, a driver's licence, etc., and if you return to the US at least once every six months and continue to comply with the IRS by filing annual tax returns. Filing US tax returns doesn't necessarily mean you end up paying more taxes since the tax rates in the US are generally lower on nearly all income items. If you definitely will never return and are giving up or abandoning your green card, you are treated by the IRS like an expatriating US citizen for tax purposes if you have had the green card for more than 8 of the past 15 years. This is detailed in Chapter 4 in the section US Tax Legislation Concerning Expatriation from the US.

It is not easy getting US citizenship or a green card. Giving them up should not be taken lightly. It should not be done without advice and analysis by a qualified US tax expert or cross-border financial planner.

INVESTMENT GAINS AND INCOME

In Chapter 4, we compared the major forms of investment income on a line-by-line basis. Canadian residents pay substantially higher taxes on every major form of investment income, so those who rely on investment income need to prepare themselves for a large reduction in after-tax income after moving back to Canada. Because of the continuous fluctuations in the value of the Canadian dollar relative to the US dollar, Canadian residents of the US who move back to Canada without both kinds of currency protection planning (as discussed in Chapter 3) may see their nest eggs affected substantially by currency fluctuations.

Canada Revenue Agency (CRA) allows you a tax-free step-up in the cost basis on entering the country (see Chapter 11 for the departure tax rules). This means, for Canadian tax purposes, that you are deemed to have sold all your capital assets on the day prior to your entering the country and to have reacquired them at their fair market value on that day. Consequently, only the gains that accrue after you become a Canadian resident taxpayer are taxable by CRA. This deemed step-up in cost basis upon re-entering Canada has no effect for US tax purposes. If you are still a US citizen or green card holder and would like to become a Canadian resident, the sourcing rules for capital gains need to be understood. These rules determine in which country the gains will be taxable, under the Canada/US Tax Treaty capital gains sourcing rules (as previously noted in Chapter 10). All your gains, with the exception of US real property, will be classed as Canadian gains once residency in Canada is established. The sale of appreciated stocks and bonds or other capital property after you become a Canadian resident will, in certain cases, trigger a US tax with no offsetting Canadian foreign tax credits. In the previous chapter, I defined "double tax" and why you need to plan to avoid it. The bottom line is that you pay tax on the same income two or more times. If this sounds like double-talk, that's because, unfortunately, that's exactly what it is. Regardless of when it happens, paying an unnecessary extra level of tax is painful and usually can be avoided with proper planning with a cross-border financial planning professional.

Those to whom the expatriating rules noted above and in Chapter 4 do not apply, and who have given up their green cards or US citizenship, may escape both Canadian and US tax on any gains accrued on assets before entering Canada. If you fit into this situation, having a tax-free holiday on all your capital gains can be an enormous benefit. Those Canadian residents who remain US citizens or who are green card holders generally will find it best to consider triggering the US capital gains or electing under the new Fifth Protocol of the Canada/US Tax Treaty to get a new stepped-up in cost basis without selling the appreciated assets before entering Canada to avoid any future double-tax problems on their appreciated assets. It is very important to obtain fair market value appraisals on all assets on the date you leave the United States and enter Canada, as you will definitely need those cost basis numbers for future tax filings.

Income earned or accrued on investments prior to entering Canada (including dividends and interest) will be taxed only in the US. After entering Canada the investment income will be taxed by CRA only for those who are no longer US citizens or green card holders. US citizens and green card holders will need to report this income annually in both countries on an ongoing basis, paying the highest rate of tax imposed by either country. Because Canada allows foreign tax credits only on US investment income to the extent of the Canada/US Tax Treaty withholding rates, US citizens or green card holders are advised to move their income-producing investments to Canada or employ other investment strategies to avoid paying a double tax. The IRS will allow full foreign tax credits for investment income earned in Canada, so no double tax should be levied on IRS returns filed after Canadian residency is established.

Canada does not have tax-free or tax-deferred investments other than RRSP-type registered plans or Tax-Free Savings Accounts (TFSAs). This means a US citizen or green card holder holding tax-free US municipal bonds or tax-deferred annuities of any type and who is resident in Canada will pay Canadian tax annually on all the interest and dividends earned on these investments, whether he leaves the income to accrue in the US or not. This kind of investment situation is an example of the double-tax situation that should not be ignored. People with these types of investments should seriously consider liquidating them before becoming Canadian residents, paying the tax on the deferred income inside the annuities at the lower US rates, and investing the proceeds in Canada, where the income will be taxed on a current basis by CRA and will create foreign tax credits for future US tax filings.

Since as a Canadian resident you will have to pay full taxes on any municipal bonds you own, you may require professional investment planning help. By cashing the bonds in and reinvesting them, you may be able to obtain higher yields on the taxable bonds. In effect you'll have more interest income to help pay for the taxes due as a Canadian resident.

US RETIREMENT PLANS

Qualified retirement plans and Individual Retirement Accounts (IRAs) in the US are the equivalent of the Canadian RRSP-type registered plans in Canada. They can consist of any combination of Individual Retirement Accounts (IRAs), Roth IRAs, 401(k) plans, Roth 401(k) plans, 457 plans, 403(b) plans, Simplified Employee Pensions (SEPs), and Savings Incentive Match Plans for Employees (SIMPLEs). Like Canadian RRSPs, contributions to these US plans are deductible, and all of these plans allow interest, dividends, and capital gains to accrue on a tax-deferred basis until they must be withdrawn starting at age 70½ (age 71 for RRSPs). The key exception to this rule is the Roth 401(k)s and Roth IRAs, which are after-tax contributions, and in which all investment income is tax free in the US regardless of when it is withdrawn (past age 59½); there is also no forced withdrawal. Once US residents holding any of these US retirement plans become Canadian residents, they may continue to defer the taxation on the buildup of income until withdrawal in a manner similar to that for RRSPs, with the exception of the Roth IRA and Roth 401(k).

The Fifth Protocol to the Canada/US Tax Treaty, effective January 1, 2009, has provided a major tax benefit to those moving to Canada who have accumulated a large Roth IRA or 401(k) while in the US. Under this new protocol, Roth IRAs are considered pensions. Canada must therefore provide the same tax-free benefits to plan holders as the IRS. Consequently, before moving to Canada US residents with any IRAs, 401(k) plans, or similar qualified plans, should seriously consider rolling them all over to a Roth IRA before taking up Canadian residency. This recommendation will generally still stand even if you need to pay US taxes to do the rollover to the Roth IRA. Roth 401(k) plans were not specifically addressed in the new protocol, but these plans can be rolled over without tax or penalty very easily to a Roth IRA. Roth IRAs provide an incredible benefit for Canadians moving back to Canada or Americans moving to Canada for the first time, as there is no other investment where one can have such large sums of money and pay no tax to either Canada or the US on any income earned or principal withdrawn for the rest of their lives. The IRS is unknowingly helping people in this situation; starting in the year 2010, it removed the income restrictions above which no contribution to the Roth could be made, which was $100,000; these new rules now allow more individuals to roll regular IRAs or other qualified plans into Roth IRAs in any amount, at any income level.

It is very kind of CRA to allow returning Canadians or US citizens to continue to defer tax in almost all of their US retirement plans (except the Roth IRA plans, which are tax-free as noted above). However, the catch is that CRA will tax 100 percent of any withdrawals from these non-Roth IRA retirement plans for Canadian residents at full Canadian rates even if withdrawals are made in the first year of Canadian residency. As a result, those moving to Canada with these regular IRAs and qualified plans will pay, on average, twice as much tax as they would have as US residents on any withdrawals, particularly if the withdrawals bump them up into the maximum Canadian tax brackets and make them subject to OAS clawbacks (review Chapter 4 and, in particular, Figure 4.6 for a comparison of US and Canadian tax rates).

As described in Chapter 11 and illustrated in Figure 11.1 for Canadian registered plans, the full value of US qualified plans and IRAs for Canadian residents are similarly taxed at Canadian maximum rates on the date of death (unless you have a spouse to roll the plan over to). This is in sharp contrast to the option US residents have on their retirement plans, besides the spousal rollover, which is to have their estates pay out the qualified plan or IRA to their children or grandchildren over their respective lifetimes. This very useful option allows the family to get another twenty to eighty years of deferral (or tax-free payments in case of Roth IRAs) out of their qualified plans and IRA plans. This extra deferral period can provide thousands or even millions more after-tax dollars to the family of the original US retirement plan holder that will be lost to Canadian residents regardless of citizenship status.

Anyone entering Canada with the US retirement plans noted above may be advised to forego future tax-free deferrals on the income buildup inside the plans. It makes very little sense to defer income in retirement accounts when the tax on withdrawal is going to be higher than tax savings realized when the original contributions were made. If you are retired or have the necessary flexibility, it may be best to withdraw all the non-Roth IRAs and qualified retirement plans at US tax rates gradually before you take up residence in Canada (if you are never likely to return to the US) and roll the proceeds to a Roth IRA as explained earlier in this section. If you are retired and your chief source of income is from investments, you could convert most of your investment income to tax-free or low-taxed income. Then start rolling over your qualified plan or regular IRAs as rapidly as possible, spread over enough years to keep your average tax rates in the US as low as possible. In the US, even if you have a large qualified retirement plan and are over age 59½, you could still withdraw up to $467,000 USD a year and not get into the highest US tax bracket for married, jointly filing taxpayers. Once you have rolled over all of your qualified plans or IRAs to the Roth IRA at the lower US rates, you can enter Canada with tax-paid funds. You could earn a substantial amount of tax-free investment income for life. The tax savings on this course of action are enormous. On larger qualified plans you can easily save enough tax to buy yourself a house free and clear, with money that would have gone to CRA in the future. To complete a withdrawal and subsequent rollover to the Roth IRA you will need the help of a qualified cross-border financial planning expert, as there are too many factors, combinations, and permutations that need to be considered to complete it efficiently, and mistakes or missed opportunities can be very costly.

US STOCK OPTIONS, BONUSES, AND DEFERRED COMPENSATION

Those who have any US-acquired stock options, yet-to-be-paid employment income or bonuses, or are members of deferred compensation plans, need to be alerted to some potentially adverse tax consequences when taking up Canadian residency. Canada Revenue Agency will tax any of this income at full Canadian rates if it is paid to a Canadian resident, even though it was all earned before he or she entered Canada. Even if you took up Canadian residency last week and got that long-awaited, hard-earned bonus from your US employer this week, not only will you pay Canadian tax rates on the bonus and lose close to half of it, but it will also still be taxable in the US. However, CRA will allow a foreign tax credit for the tax paid to the US (but this will usually cover only a portion of the Canadian tax due). This can come as quite a shock to a first-time or returning Canadian resident being whacked with this "welcome to Canada tax." The best way to avoid this problem is to not take up Canadian residence until you have exercised all of your US stock options, received any residual wages or bonuses, and cleared out your deferred compensation plan. This is one area of pre-entry planning where a simple solution applied in a timely manner can save you a great deal of tax.

The latest Canada/US Tax Treaty protocol, effective January 1, 2009, means that there is finally another planning option for those with stock options. The treaty now states that stock options that were earned in one country and exercised in the other will have the tax apportioned between the two countries according to the number of days spent working in each country from the time the stock options were granted and exercised.

US SOCIAL SECURITY

Providing you have qualified under US rules, you and your spouse will continue to be eligible for US Social Security and Medicare benefits if you become Canadian residents. Only 85 percent of any Social Security pension benefits paid to you as Canadian residents will be taxable at your full Canadian tax rates. For most people this will mean an increase in taxes paid on Social Security income over their lifetimes. The maximum tax rate on Social Security in the US (for those with taxable incomes of more than $467,000 USD) is 34 percent at the federal level, whereas in Canada as a Canadian resident, your maximum tax rate would be about 44 percent (for those with incomes of more than $125,000 CAD, depending on your province of residence, and assuming the Social Security payments would not increase or make you subject to the OAS clawback).

CANADIAN OAS AND CPP/QPP

Qualification for the Canada Pension Plan (CPP) and Quebec Pension Plan (QPP) is based on Canadian employment earnings at any time since the CPP/QPP plan was introduced in the early 1960s. So if you worked in Canada during this period up to age 65, you will be eligible for some CPP/QPP pension. If you are retiring and moving to Canada and are still under 65, it would be worth your while to find or create some Canadian employment income each year so that you will receive a CPP/QPP pension at 65. Qualifying for Canadian Old Age Security is based only on the number of years lived in Canada between ages 18 and 65. To receive a full benefit you need to have 40 years in Canada. The full benefit is about $6,800 per year for life, indexed partially for inflation. Partial benefits are paid based on the fraction of the 40 years you have spent in Canada. If you lived 20 years in Canada between 18 and 65, you would receive half the maximum annual OAS benefit. If your total number of years in Canada is less than 20, in order to get a benefit, you will need to apply under the Canada/US Social Security agreement to get credit for your time in the US. OAS may be clawed back by CRA through a tax rate of up to 100 percent on the amount of OAS received (for Canadian residents beginning at about the $73,500 CAD income level).

CANADIAN FOREIGN REPORTING

Canada Revenue Agency has recently introduced an entire series of reporting requirements designed to try to catch those thousands of Canadians who have parked money offshore and are not reporting the income on their Canadian returns. These rules dictate that Canadian residents who have investments, bank accounts, foreign trusts, or corporations (or are beneficiaries thereof), or investment real estate located outside Canada worth a total value of $100,000 or more must list these accounts on a special CRA form T1135, and report earnings on the appropriate Canadian T1 return schedules. Failure to complete this reporting will invoke penalties for each year of non-compliance, effectively confiscating the foreign assets after only a few years of trying to hide any of these funds from CRA. Consequently, anyone moving from the United States to Canada will likely face these reporting requirements for every year that they maintain US qualified plans, IRAs, investment accounts, bank accounts, or US investment property totalling a worth more than $100,000.

Because the penalties are so severe, care must be taken not to miss any foreign items that CRA requires you to report. Since CRA and the IRS regularly share information and help each other enforce penalties under the Canada/US Tax Treaty, it would be very foolish indeed to think CRA wouldn't find out about any US assets or income that was not reported according to these new rules.

UNITED STATES TO CANADA — YOUR ESTATE PLAN

Anyone moving temporarily or permanently across the Canada-US border in either direction must replace, or at the very least modify, their estate-planning documents. A well-drafted US estate plan can become ineffective after a move to Canada. A US living trust for which you and/or your spouse are trustees will become a foreign trust for IRS purposes and be subject to many complex tax rules. From a CRA standpoint, the trust would be considered a Canadian-resident trust and required to file its own annual tax return in addition to following many other CRA rules discussed later in this section. A correctly drafted and valid US will would be valid in most Canadian provinces. Trying to submit what amounts to a foreign will to a Canadian probate court is not very practical. It would be time-consuming and costly convincing a Canadian judge that the US will was valid. It would be beneficial to have your US will redrafted by a Canadian lawyer in your province of residence, adding any modifications required by that particular province. If you are going to have assets remaining in the United States, it would be best to use a cross-border lawyer trained and experienced in both Canadian and US estate laws to make sure the will can be easily used and probated in all the jurisdictions in which you have assets. As an alternative, if you cannot find a cross-border lawyer you can have the Canadian lawyer contact a US counterpart in the state(s) in which you have assets to review the Canadian will.

Although this is more time-consuming and costly, it could pay off greatly in the ease with which your estate is settled. US citizens and green card holders must include provisions in their wills to deal with potential US estate taxes and related exemptions or options. Some lawyers may try to convince you to have two or more wills, one for each jurisdiction that you have assets in. Although there are some merits to this advice, I do not generally recommend it. It is difficult enough to keep track of one will for most people never mind two or more wills. Having more than one will increases the number of opportunities for mistakes or challenges from beneficiaries as to which will should be the governing one.

Powers of attorney (POAs) for both general matters and medical matters are very important, but often neglected, documents in any Canadian or US estate plan. The POAs need to be enduring (Canadian terminology) or durable (US terminology), which means they will still be valid even in the event of the writers' incapacity. Some POAs can be drafted with "springing powers," stating that they have no effect until incapacity occurs. Our recommendations here are very similar to those regarding wills: Use a competent lawyer or lawyers in your province of residence and state(s) where your assets are located to ensure your POAs are effective when and where needed. Since you are still alive when your POAs are to be used, and they can easily be drafted using even the forms provided by the institutions where you have accounts, such as banks, it is generally okay to have a POA for each jurisdiction or even at each financial institution in which you have assets. US medical POAs, for most states, include living wills, which have provisions to determine when and who would "pull the plug" if you were in a vegetative state with no hope for recovery. Some Canadian provinces have not yet recognized living wills or even enduring medical POAs, so these documents may be of no legal use there. We still recommend the use of living wills and enduring POAs even if your province of residence does not formally recognize them yet, as they help family members make better decisions for you, and more and more judges are recognizing their validity.

Living trusts of various forms are very common in the United States and therefore are widely accepted by banks, investment firms, and other financial institutions. The same cannot be said for Canada, although their use is beginning to catch on, very slowly. For those over age 65, CRA now allows the use of alter ego trusts, which are very similar in design, use and administration to US living trusts. Upon a move to Canada, the trust also takes up Canadian residence if you are its trustee under CRA rules. In addition, CRA imposes certain rules on trusts that US residents do not have to deal with. For example, in Canada, trusts must file their own tax returns to report income (this is not required for most US trusts since the tax liability flows directly to the trust's grantors, beneficiaries, or creators), and there is a 21-year rule that requires that all assets in the trust be deemed disposed of and any capital gains taxes paid (the IRS has no similar rule at all in the United States). Although these CRA rules dealing with trusts may increase the cost of administering living trusts in Canada, it doesn't mean that you necessarily scrap your US trusts once you cross the border. Living trusts will still be valid in Canada and can be very useful to avoid Canadian probate fees, to ease the administration of your estate, and to look after you and/or your spouse if you are incapacitated. These trusts can help those who remain US citizens or green card holders take advantage of US estate tax and generation-skipping taxes. Some US trusts may require slight modifications once their grantors or creators effectively become Canadian residents, to deal with some of CRA's rules or provincial idiosyncrasies. Simply put, moving from the US to Canada complicates your estate plan, in my estimation, by a factor of at least three. Again, professional legal help from a cross-border lawyer is recommended.

MEDICAL COVERAGE

One item that is easy to deal with in moving to Canada is the ease in applying for and receiving Canadian medicare, regardless of your medical condition. Most provinces only require you to be a resident for 90 days or less before full medical coverage takes effect, providing you apply for it through the applicable provincial agency. Alberta and New Brunswick allow returning residents immediate access to medical coverage, with no waiting period. Some provinces charge a nominal quarterly fee for the coverage, depending on your age, while others include the costs in the general taxation system to make it appear free. One thing returning or new Canadian residents will appreciate with the Canadian medicare system is the lack of paperwork for patients. However, they may miss the wide range of choices, full access to specialists, and modern medical facilities without waiting lines available in the United States.

Some people moving to Canada may have their cake and eat it too with respect to Canadian and US medical coverage, by having full access to all medical facilities and doctors in Canada and the United States. If you are over 65 and have qualified for US Medicare, you can retain this coverage even as a resident of Canada. Consequently, you can have access to the Canadian medical system through your provincial medicare and to the US medical system through US Medicare. For example, if you lived in Vancouver and needed a hip replacement but there was a long waiting list for the surgery there, you could cross the border to Blaine, Washington, a few miles away, have the surgery, and be fully recovered before your wait for surgery in Vancouver was even over. Also, many returning Canadians still winter or travel in the United States, so having US Medicare gives them very economical travel insurance that is not restricted by age or medical condition and is not limited to emergency care only. This certainly is having the best of both worlds, medically speaking.

For both Canadian and US Medicare, supplements are recommended to fill any gaps of coverage and to give you better access to private hospital beds.

Both US Medicare and, to a lesser extent, Canadian medicare are inadequate when providing long-term nursing care benefits. We recommend that both US and Canadian residents have adequate long-term care insurance to protect their assets from having to be consumed by any lengthy stay in a nursing home or similar facility. Some United States long-term insurance carriers will pay benefits for nursing home stays in either Canada or the United States without any additional premium cost. I highly recommend one of these carriers for your long-term care insurance, as my experience indicates that maximum flexibility in choosing a nursing home in either country is most beneficial. You should have a daily benefit in your policy at least equal to the average daily costs in the long-term facilities in the geographical areas where you are likely to be.

DEDUCTIONS LOST

Chapter 4 compared deductions allowed by the IRS directly to CRA rules, so I will only summarize and review these differences. The key deduction most people would miss moving from the United States to Canada would be the mortgage interest deduction on up to two principal residences, and property taxes on all properties. The other major deduction lost would be that for the state income taxes allowed by the IRS; CRA doesn't allow any equivalent deduction for provincial taxes paid. Minor deductions allowed by the IRS but not CRA would be for tax-preparation fees, certain legal fees, financial planning fees, and motor vehicle licence fees. Although it's not really a deduction, most US taxpayers would also miss the tax-free treatment of interest from municipal bonds and the ability to defer interest, dividends, and capital gains income through variable annuities for as much and as long as they want. Also, as noted earlier in this chapter in the section Investment Gains and Income, one can expect that the income taxes on most forms of investment income will increase about 50 percent on regular investment income to over 100 percent greater on tax-free bond interest or deferred dividends and capital gains over the required taxes paid on the same amount of income in the US.

COST OF LIVING ADJUSTMENTS

Having assisted employees and Canadian long-term residents with moves to Canada over many years, I know it is difficult to determine what the increase in cost of living may be. It varies between areas and depends in individuals' buying habits and current Canada-US exchange rates. However, most people can expect an approximately 30 percent increase in costs for basics such as food, clothing, transportation, and principal residence purchases. Part of this increase is due to Canada's GST/HST.

US DEPARTING ALIEN INCOME TAX RETURN

All resident aliens — that is, US green card holders, visa holders or visitors deemed resident of the United States under the Substantial Presence Test as noted in Chapter 4 — leaving the country more or less permanently, are required to get a Certificate of Compliance (also known as a sailing permit) from the IRS. The sailing permit is obtained by filing IRS Form 1040-C at your local IRS office at least two weeks before your departure date. Form 1040-C is essentially an interim tax return for the year of your departure to ensure the IRS can collect the tax due on interim income earned for the departure year before your departure date. If the IRS is satisfied they have collected enough tax from you through withholding or with the 1040-C return, they will issue you the sailing permit to allow you to leave the country. You are still required to file your regular IRS Form 1040, Dual Status return, by June 15 following the year of departure to make a final reconciliation of the taxes due in the year of departure as the 1040-C is not considered a final return.

The surprising thing about filing Form 1040-C is there are no apparent penalties for not filing it and there is no one to review your sailing permit as you leave the United States. As most people who travel internationally know, when you cross the border from the United States to Canada, the first people you report to are Canada Border Service Agency employees, who are not the least bit interested in whether you have a sailing permit from the IRS or not, and would likely laugh at you if you showed it to them. Note that there definitely are penalties levied by the IRS if the final 1040 is not filed and any tax is not paid in the required time. If you are a US citizen or a green card holder, and are not giving it up, there is no such thing as a final Form 1040 or a need to complete Form 1040-C (as you are required by the IRS to file a full Form 1040 annually on your world income).

CANADIAN PRE-ENTRY REVIEW

In order to summarize this chapter and to assist those contemplating a move back to Canada (or a first time move to Canada) from the United States, I have listed the key issues to be considered:

- Higher overall taxes on most sources of income. Review Chapter 4 and Chapter 9 for a detailed analysis of the tax differences between Canada and the United States.
- Loss of the tax-free status of interest on municipal bonds and/or Roth 401(k) plans.
- Maintain the tax-free status on Roth IRAs.
- No tax-deferred income tax on any form of deferred annuities, long-term deposits, or compounding interest bonds.
- Allowance to continue to defer tax on income buildup on US-qualified retirement plans and IRAs; however, the entire plan's value will still be subject to much higher Canadian tax rates when withdrawn.
- OAS clawback of up to 100 percent of Old Age Security benefits (this is only applicable to Canadian residents who have spent enough time in Canada to qualify for the OAS pension).
- Access to both Canadian and US Medicare (for those who have a sufficient number of earning quarters to qualify for it prior to leaving the US) from the Canadian side of the border.
- Modifications to wills, living trusts, powers of attorney (POAs), and other estate-planning documents required upon moving to Canada.

- The cost of the actual move, the new estate-planning documents, and a cross-border financial plan. There is also generally a substantial increase in general cost of living.
- The consequences of giving up US citizenship or a green card, and conversely, the cost of keeping US citizenship or a green card as a Canadian resident may be significant. You must thoroughly investigate prior to taking these kinds of actions.

After reviewing all of these factors you may feel that the positive attributes outweigh the negative ones, and decide that a move to Canada is in the cards. However, if the negative factors, such as the increased tax burden, are unacceptable, you should stay put in the US. If the family and social pressures of moving back to Canada are conflicting with your desire to avoid higher Canadian taxes, perhaps a "have your cake and eat it too" solution is the answer and you can adopt a Settler cross-border lifestyle. You can follow the Canada/US Tax Treaty rules to maintain US residency for tax purposes, yet own a second home in Canada, get on Canadian medicare, and live there for up to six months a year (or more in certain circumstances). Regardless of which goal and objectives you are trying to attain, a complete cross-border plan needs to be initiated and implemented in a timely manner to ensure the pitfalls of the cross-border move are minimized and all the opportunities for tax savings are exploited. A cross-border financial plan will ensure that your personal and family goals are suitably achieved.

Although Chapter 13 is written specifically for US citizens moving to Canada for the first time, it also contains relevant information for Canadians returning to Canada after a period of US residency.

Border Guide readers may participate in a cross-border Q&A through the new *Cross-Border Forum.* Upon registering, you can post comments or create discussions with other *Border Guide* readers to share experiences and swap cross-border financial planning tips. To post a question or comment, go to keatsconnelly.com and click on the *Cross-Border Forum* tab.

CROSS-BORDER Q&A

MOVING BACK TO CANADA

Relocation between Canada and the United States is not just a one-way street to the South. A lot of Canadians return to Canada after years of living and working in Florida as US residents. These people would love to hear something about their tax-planning opportunities as well, such as deferred

US annuities. Florida tax planners are in general not really knowledgeable about Canadian tax law and changes in the past.

— Enocho B., Naples, Florida

Great question. Since we live in such an ever-changing society, good cross-border planning will generally keep all doors open so that people moving out of Canada may move back without adverse tax or other consequences.

Tax-planning opportunities and concerns arising when moving from the United States back to Canada are numerous and are not necessarily the reverse of the planning procedure of the original move to the United States.

Unrealized gains on stocks, bonds, and investment real estate are best realized before leaving the United States for Canada. The maximum capital gains rate in most provinces is close to 25 percent, whereas the US maximum is now 20 percent. If you don't realize the gains prior to your entrance into Canada, you will have a Canadian cost basis equal to the value of the properties or securities on the date of your return to Canada. If you have become a US citizen or have had a US green card for longer than eight years, it is very important to go through this exercise and examine the new treaty elections, available in the Fifth Protocol to the Canada/US Tax Treaty as of January 1, 2009, to avoid potential double tax.

If you have a large capital gain built up in the personal residence you own in the United States, you should take advantage of the $500,000 tax exemption by selling the residence before you leave the country, or you could lose it. Canada will not recognize this US exemption, nor will the United States recognize the Canadian capital gains exemption for the principal residence.

If you have acquired IRAs, 401(k) plans or other qualified plans in the United States, which are equivalent to Canadian RRSPs, you may get some great tax breaks when you head back to Canada, providing you roll them over to Roth IRAs before exiting the United States. You must pay regular US tax on the amount rolled over from the regular plans to the Roth IRA. However, the tax you pay to the US before the rollover will generally be less, particularly if you plan well in advance, than what you'd pay if you kept those tax-deferred plans as a Canadian resident. Without the Roth IRA rollover, Canada will tax you at full rates on the principal, interest, and dividends on withdrawals from these accounts once you become a resident. Consequently, if you still own regular IRAs or other US-qualified plans when you return to Canada, you will pay the higher Canadian tax rates on all your withdrawals. If all your US retirement plans have been rolled into a Roth IRA, you will earn interest, dividends, and capital gains free from tax by CRA and the IRS for the rest of your life. There is no other method available in Canada to accumulate such a large amount of investment income tax-free for life.

If you own deferred annuities of any type when you move back to Canada, they will lose their ability to shelter income buildup from current Canadian taxation. Canada requires you to report all interest, dividends, and realized capital gains on deferred annuities on a current basis and will not allow you to accrue this income to defer the payment of tax. Annuities are best cashed in and invested in term deposits or similar Canadian investments, or converted to annuity payout options.

If you are collecting US Social Security, under the Canada/US Tax Treaty you will be allowed to exclude 15 percent of it from Canadian taxation. If you are a US green card holder when you take up permanent residence back in Canada, you will be required to surrender it without maintaining significant ties to the US. If you don't surrender your green card to the USCIS, you are going against US Immigration regulations and the IRS will continue to tax you as a resident. If you have become a US citizen or a dual Canadian/US citizen, much of what I outline here as planning opportunities will apply differently to you, unless you directly and formally surrender your US citizenship. If you are a dual citizen and are a resident of Canada, you will need to file full returns in both Canada and the US on your world income, and take allowable credits back and forth to avoid being double-taxed on that income.

When you re-enter Canada, be prepared for a tax shock. There is no tax-free or tax-deferred income available in Canada unless you do the Roth IRA rollover noted above. Also available are the new Tax-Free Savings Accounts (TFSAs), although the contribution amounts are very limited. Features of TFSAs include fewer deductions and significantly higher marginal tax rates and the amount of income required to reach the highest rates is much lower. If your primary sources of income are interest and pensions, you can expect your income tax bill to nearly double. You will benefit from Canada's medical care system and more generous social welfare systems. So what you give up in taxes, you may well recover in social security, particularly if you are in the lower income brackets.

In any case, when you are moving cross-border in either direction, you need a detailed plan with the assistance of a cross-border financial planning professional who is fully knowledgeable about both sides of the border to direct you through the maze of opportunities and pitfalls.

GREEN CARD MUST BE GIVEN UP

I am a Canadian citizen and have been a US resident for the last five years. I plan to return to Canada. I am 75 years old. My assets will be two US bank accounts, US Treasury bills worth about $300,000, a mobile home in Alabama, Canada Pension, and Old Age Pension. My plan is as follows:

1. *Enter Canada formally on January 1.*
2. *Apply for OHIP medicare in Ontario.*
3. *Keep my US bank accounts and US Treasury securities.*
5. *Apply for W-8BEN designation of my assets to be US tax exempt.*
6. *Give up my green card to qualify.*
7. *Keep my mobile home in Alabama for now.*

Is my plan satisfactory? Any pitfalls? When do I give up my green card?

— J.B., Elberta, Alabama

There appears to be no reason why you can't go through with your plan to return to Canada. OHIP will require a 90-day waiting period before you will be covered. CRA will be happy to see you back as they will collect tax on your OAS, CPP, and the interest on your US Treasury bills. There is no requirement for you to file a W-8BEN form for your US Treasuries, as they are not subject to non-resident withholding tax, but you will need to file it for your bank accounts. Remember that exemption from US taxes does not mean exemption for Canadian purposes. You must report all your US income to CRA. You will have to give up your green card, but make certain you will never need it again before you give it up as they are difficult to obtain these days. Good luck!

RETURNING CANADIAN RESIDENT LOSES HOMESTEAD EXEMPTION

I am a Canadian citizen and live in Florida six months of the year. I have a green card. I have a residence in Ontario where I live for the other six months. I would like to return to Canada as a full-time resident. Should I sell my house here as I would no longer get the Homestead and widow's allowance exemptions? What should I do with the green card?

— D.S., Boynton Beach, Florida

The procedure to become a Canadian resident, since you are already a Canadian citizen, is simply to move back to Canada and re-establish your residential ties, such as applying for OHIP, a driver's licence, and filing a Canadian tax return. You will need to effectively give up your green card by mailing it to US Citizenship and Immigration Services (USCIS) or surrendering it at the border. Make sure you are prepared for possibly higher Canadian income taxes before you give up US residence.

If keeping your Florida Homestead Exemption is the only reason you are keeping your property, you should sell it as you will lose your exemption if you are no longer a resident of Florida. However, it certainly is not necessary to sell this residence if you still want to visit Florida during the winters and need a place to stay.

MOVING BACK TO CANADA — THE SEQUEL

In 2002 we were transferred to the US by a subsidiary of a large Canadian company. My husband worked there until retiring in 2012. We applied for and received our resident alien status in June 2002. In 2012 we returned and resumed Canadian residency in order to take advantage of OHIP. We did not apply for or receive Medicare. We own a home in the US where we spend six months every year. My husband has a small company pension, Social Security, stock, investments, and IRAs. Our total US assets amount to approximately $400,000 and we file a 1040NR and a Form 8840. Our assets in Canada exceed this amount and include our home, property, company stock, investments, RRSPs, GICs, company pension, OAS, and CPP. We regret our decision to return to Canada and we wish to reinstate our US resident alien status. We still have our green cards and, since purchasing The Border Guide, *are now aware of the implications. Would you advise us or inform us as to where we can obtain information on the following:*

1. *How we do reactivate our NR status?*
2. *Can Medicare be secured prior to reestablishing residency?*
3. *Do we need an estate planner and legal counsel?*
4. *Should we begin using our green cards upon entry to the United States and reinstate residency?*

— Sid and Nancy V., Holiday, Florida

Since you have been living six months out of every year in the US and still have your green cards, you are probably permanent legal residents there and have likely not abandoned your green card status. However, you have been filing the wrong returns with the IRS for residents and should go back and re-file all the returns that were completed incorrectly. You need to file Form 1040, not 1040NR returns and not file Form 8840 at all. This should get you in compliance with both IRS and USCIS and may also get you some tax benefits to top it off.

1. As noted above, you may have retained your US status.
2. Medicare can be applied for from January 1 through March 31 every year and will become effective July 1 of the year in which you apply, so you may have to cover the gap from January to July with alternative coverage.
3. You definitely do need professional help, but not just for estate planning as you have several other financial, tax, investment, and insurance issues to address. A good cross-border financial plan can save you a lot of money and aggravation in these areas.
4. I have to answer this one with a conditional yes after you have covered all the other issues discussed above.

TAX TREATY CAN REDUCE WITHHOLDING ON 401(K) PLANS

I am a retired Canadian citizen who, while living in the US, participated in a 401(k) plan. I now wish to commence monthly plan withdrawals. The plan managers advise they are required to withhold tax at the rate of 30 percent. Your guide discusses the Canada/US Tax Treaty and leaves me with the feeling the 30 percent withholding tax is too high. If I am correct, can you refer me to the current IRS bulletin so that I can share it with them? P.S. Including this withdrawal, my wife and I would have a total gross US income of about $4,000, which includes some common stock dividend payments.

— P.F.L., Caledonia, Ontario

The plan manager is technically correct with its withholding rate of 30 percent according to IRS domestic rules. However, you should qualify for a treaty reduction under the Canada/US Tax Treaty to 15 percent, providing your withdrawals are periodic by IRS definition. To apply for the treaty-reduced withholding, you will need to file IRS Form W-8BEN.

For residents of Canada, all IRA, 401(k), 403(b) and other US plan withdrawals are 100 percent taxable by CRA at your marginal Canadian rates. Any US non-resident withholding tax you pay will become a credit for you on filing your annual Canadian T1 return, provided the withholding was done at the correct Canada/US Tax Treaty rates. If you are in the 50 percent Canadian tax bracket and have 15 percent non-resident withholding by the IRS on 401(k) withdrawals, you will pay an additional tax to CRA equivalent to 35 percent of your US plan distributions.

MOVING BACK TO CANADA AND OCCUPYING RENTAL PROPERTY

My husband and I have been residents of the US as green card holders for over six years. I will be moving back to BC next year, but he needs to remain in the US for about two years more, so he technically will remain a resident of the US longer than me. We have a house that we still own equally in Canada that we have rented out since we left Canada in 2002. How long do we have to occupy the house before we will be eligible for the tax-free capital gains exemption on our principal residence in Canada? When I move back, is there anything I need to do to change the status of my house?

— Martha H., Houston, Texas

As soon as you move into the house, you will trigger a capital gains tax for the increase in value from the day you left Canada to the day you returned. This gain has to be reported on line 127 of your first Canadian tax return, and taxes must be paid accordingly. You may also make an election to defer the tax until you sell the residence. Since your husband will remain a resident of the US, he will have to file a Canadian non-resident tax return and also pay Canadian taxes on this "deemed disposition of your rental property" as a non-resident. However, you will have the luxury to wait until April 30 of the year following your move back to Canada to pay the taxes or defer your half of the taxes due under Section 43 (3) of the *Income Tax Act.* As a non-resident of Canada, he must file CRA Forms T2062 and T2062A immediately upon occupancy of the residence. Non-resident withholding taxes will be paid at that time on your husband's half of any gains. There is no form to file for the 43(3) election, you just request it by filing a letter with your first Canadian return.

Once you have moved back into your BC house, any increase in value will be tax free, as it will be your personal residence. You can never get rid of the tax liability on increase in value while you were in the US.

There are some US issues you need be aware of with respect to your US principal residence exemptions, particularly if you still own a residence in Texas that your husband will live in while you move back to Canada. In this circumstance, you will need to continue to file your US returns "married filing jointly" or you could lose your half of the $500,000 USD principal residence exemption that the US has for married couples. Also, if your husband has had his green card for more than eight years before he moves back to Canada, he will have the US expatriation rules apply to him that can cause adverse tax consequences. Seek professional advice for him from a cross-border financial planning expert when he returns to BC on a permanent basis.

Moving to Canada, Eh 13

US Citizens or Residents Moving to or Investing in Canada

It is estimated by the US embassy in Ottawa that there are more than a million Americans living in Canada on a regular basis. Canada welcomes thousands of new immigrants and visitors from the US every year. Just as Canadian visitors fall in love with certain areas of the US and purchase property there, for similar reasons Americans visiting Canada often want to either purchase Canadian property for recreational use or as an investment.

Chapters 3 through 7 dealt with Canadians visiting and investing in the US as Vacationers or Snowbirds, and Chapters 8 to 11 have addressed Canadians adopting a Settler cross-border lifestyle in the US. Although many of the issues discussed in these chapters are not relevant to Americans immigrating to or investing in Canada, Americans face many similar cross-border issues when they move north. I therefore recommend that American readers review these chapters, paying particular attention to the concerns of US citizens and green card holders living in Canada, and the differences in both income and estate taxation between Canada and the United States. Chapter 12 and this chapter discuss the residency status of new or returning immigrants to Canada and certain Canadian tax regulations that apply to Americans who invest in Canada. To get the full picture, both of these chapters should be read by Americans moving to Canada for the first time.

We will begin by addressing American visitors wishing to invest in real estate or other securities in Canada. Later in the chapter, we will discuss issues of particular interest to Americans immigrating to Canada.

AMERICANS PURCHASING PROPERTY AND INVESTING IN CANADA

Thousands of Americans currently own or are in the process of buying Canadian real estate. The Vancouver real estate board estimates that one-third to one-half of all new condos in downtown Vancouver are owned by Americans. Similarly, there are many areas around the Canadian side of the Great Lakes where the majority of the property owners are American. Here are the key concerns Americans buying and holding real estate in Canada need to be aware of:

- When you purchase Canadian real estate for your own personal use, you may pay a Goods and Services Tax (GST), currently equal to 5 percent of the purchase price. In other provinces — currently, New Brunswick, Newfoundland, Nova Scotia, Ontario, and Quebec — you may instead pay the Harmonized Sales Tax (HST), which ranges between 12 and 14 percent of the purchase price depending on the province. Whether GST or HST applies depends on the type and ultimate use made of the property and may depend on provincial regulations.
- When you sell your Canadian property you are subject to Canadian capital gains tax, which will normally be withheld by the buyer's attorney until you get a clearance certificate by completing Form T2062 (Non-Resident of Canada for a Certificate of Compliance Related to Disposition of Taxable Canadian Property) in advance of the sale. Forms T2062 and T2062A must be filed by the vendor in advance of the sale or within 10 days of the date of the sale (the T2062A only has to be filed if the client has taken depreciation on the property and the tax on the recapture is calculated). Failure to file will incur a penalty of $25/day to a maximum of $2,500 (if the property is jointly owned by husband and wife, the maximum penalty is $5,000). Even if the withholding tax is nil, you would still be subject to the penalty for late filing. With the T2062 you indicate the sale price, the adjusted cost base (ACB) of the property, and the capital gain. The tax withholding is 25 percent of the estimated gain. On the T2062 you cannot include your costs of disposition (i.e., legal costs, real estate commissions, etc.). You have to submit all the documentation to verify the sale price, which usually consists of the Purchase and Sale Agreement, and documentation for the ACB, which is usually your lawyer's Statement of Adjustments when you purchased the property. You must still file a Canadian non-resident tax return by April 30 following the year of the sale — it's on this return you get to deduct expenses of the property sale. In most provinces and territories, Canadian capital gains tax is higher than US capital gains tax. However, the Canada/US Tax Treaty will provide you with a tax credit on your US tax return for the same year for any taxes paid in Canada, so at least you are not double-taxed. On the

US return Form 1040, you must adjust both your cost of the property and the sale price for currency fluctuations. Your US gains/loss will normally be different on the US and Canadian returns.

- Most Canadian provinces and territories have a probate fee (review Chapter 5 for details about these fees), so if you die owning Canadian property, you will be subject to provincial government probate fees as well as the cost of probate in Canada. The cost of probate may be substantial, as you will likely need both a Canadian and a US attorney. If you have a US will, it must be submitted to a Canadian court to prove its validity under Canadian rules. If you do not have a will, your Canadian property will be subject to provincial intestate rules, which may be substantially different from intestate rules in the state where you are resident.
- If you die owning Canadian property, you are subject to the Canadian equivalent of an estate tax. Known as a deemed disposition tax on death, this is a Canadian capital gains tax on the increased value between when a property was bought and its value at your death. You may also be subject to US estate taxes. If so, you will need to know how to use the Canada/US Tax Treaty to prevent double-taxation on death if you need to pay both the Canadian and US estate taxes. If you have a worldwide estate that is less than the US estate tax exemption of $5.45 million, the Canadian deemed disposition tax at death becomes the equivalent of a double tax because for US purposes when someone dies, US beneficiaries get a free step-up in cost basis of the property they inherit. Thus, no tax would be due under US rules on the property, but Canada does not provide a similar benefit. This potential extra tax needs to be planned for in the US citizen's estate plan.
- Some provinces have a land transfer tax of 1 to 2 percent that must be paid every time a property changes ownership.
- The title on your property is very important. Each form of ownership has specific tax and estate implications. Americans who have US living trusts may be advised to purchase their Canadian property in the name of the trust. This could help them avoid Canadian probate fees, estate settlement costs, and deemed disposition taxes at death. There is a limitation on trusts with Canadian property that requires the property either be transferred out to the beneficiaries of the trust or is deemed to be sold and any capital gains tax paid after 21 years. This is unique to Canadian property and has no US equivalent, so if

the tax is paid on this deemed disposition it may create a double tax with the IRS similar to the double tax described above, because there will be no offsetting credits unless the property is sold. The Fifth Protocol of the Canada/US Tax Treaty has a provision to allow the US person or trusts when subject to deemed disposition rules in Canada to elect to also go through a deemed disposition for US tax purposes, so that tax paid to Canada will be timed in the same year in which it can be taken as a foreign tax credit on a US tax return. This means America are paying tax early and/or a tax that would not be necessary on a US property.

- If you already own a Canadian property and wish to transfer it to your US living trust, Canada Revenue Agency considers the transfer a "taxable event" (it is treated as if the property were sold on the date of transfer). Capital gains taxes are due in the year of transfer to the trust. If the property is in a province that has a land transfer tax, this tax may also be due at the same time.
- If you are going to rent out your Canadian property, you are subject to full Canadian income tax on the rental income. You have the option, under the Canada/US Tax Treaty, to pay a flat 25 percent of the gross rental income directly to CRA as the rent is received. Under Section 216 of the Canadian *Income Tax Act*, you may elect to file Canadian non-resident tax returns annually and pay regular Canadian tax on the net rental income. Under Section 216, in addition to the annual tax return, you must file CRA Form NR6 each year before you begin receiving rental income to establish the non-resident withholding rate CRA calculates for your agent to collect on the monthly rental checks. Your agent, whom you need to identify on the NR6, must be a Canadian resident. If you open up a Canadian bank account to assist in collecting rent and paying expenses, do not neglect to file the IRS required reporting forms annually for foreign bank accounts, Form 114, as the penalties can be quite severe for failure to file.

Even though I have attempted to simplify ownership issues, you have probably gathered that these issues can be extremely complicated for Americans owning property in Canada. I recommend that any American wishing to purchase property in Canada get advice from a cross-border financial planning professional before making the purchase.

Other popular Canadian investments made by Americans who are not residents of Canada include stocks, exchange traded funds (ETFs), and private equity investments in closely held Canadian businesses.

Canadian stocks and bonds are available to most Americans through US brokerage firms. Many Canadian stocks are actually listed on both Canadian and US stock exchanges, which makes trading easier for Americans wishing to buy or sell such stocks. Interlisted Canadian stocks can be tracked in either Canadian or US funds, but the Canadian stocks that are only available through Canadian stock exchanges are generally available in Canadian dollars only, which means that Americans purchasing the stocks must bear the currency risk in addition to the normal investment risk when buying stocks. However, as non-residents, Americans will normally not be able to open brokerage accounts in Canada because of securities regulations. Under the Canada/US Tax Treaty, American residents are exempt from any capital gains tax on trading of Canadian stocks; such gains are only taxable in the US. If any of the Canadian stocks pay dividends, the treaty will allow CRA to withhold 15 percent non-resident withholding tax and to provide a full foreign tax credit for the US resident's tax return.

Canadian exchange traded funds (ETFs) are very similar to American exchange traded funds. They resemble indexed mutual funds but trade like individual stocks. Canadian ETFs can be purchased on major Canadian stock exchanges and through most US brokerage firms.

Many successful US businesspeople have significant holdings in Canada. They continue to invest in Canada as opportunities arise through personal and business contacts. Such investments can create significant US tax burdens if the businessperson does not correctly structure his or her ownership in private Canadian businesses. Many private Canadian companies are considered Controlled Foreign Corporations (CFCs) or Passive Foreign Investment Companies (PFIC) under IRS rules. For US residents, US citizens or green card holders, owning CFCs or PFICs can result in considerably higher taxes, double-taxation, and loss of foreign tax credits on the Canadian income in the corporation. To avoid these negative tax consequences of owning closely held Canadian businesses, US business investors must seek to structure their corporate deals in the form of joint ventures, partnerships or limited liability partnerships that flow all income directly to them, without any corporate tax. In addition, US investors can use a relatively new corporate form called Unlimited Liability Companies, which exist in the provinces of British Columbia, Nova Scotia, and Alberta but are recognized in all other provinces. Unlimited Liability Companies are taxed by CRA as regular Canadian corporations but for US tax purposes there is a flow-through of corporate income directly to the US shareholder, in the same manner as with Limited Liability Corporations and S-Corporations in the US. The Canada/

US Tax Treaty protocol in 2008 recognizes US LLCs owned by US residents as flow-through entities for Canadian purposes when these LLCs are conducting business in Canada, rather than the CRA taxing them as regular corporations. S-Corporations operating in Canada require special approval by the CRA to avoid double taxes or less of foreign tax credits. This permits US residents to invest in Canada through LLCs or S-Corporations and still get Treaty benefits, since the income flows through to the individual US residents who own these entities.

IMMIGRATING TO CANADA

Canada, like the United States, has many business and family categories by which people can apply for immigration. The key categories used by Citizenship and Immigration Canada (CIC) are outlined below:

1. **Skilled Workers**

   Skilled workers with good education, work experience, and knowledge of English or French may immigrate to Canada based on the number of points they receive from a scoring formula based on six factors. Total score from the primary six factors must exceed 75 out of 100 before one may be considered for immigration to Canada in this category. The six factors are Education (maximum of 25 points); English and French Language Ability (maximum 24 points); Work Experience (maximum 21 points); Age (maximum 10 points); Arranged Employment (maximum 10 points); and Adaptability (maximum 10 points). For example, if you had a PhD with work experience of at least four years, spoke English and French, you were under the age of 30, had a job offer in Canada, and a well-educated spouse who also spoke English and French, your score would be close to 100 and immigration to Canada would likely be straightforward. However, if your education, language ability, and/or work experience were weak, your chances of reaching the minimum score to immigrate in this category would be very poor. In an attempt to speed up the process for immigration for skilled workers, Canada introduced a new active recruitment model known as the Expression of Interest (EOI) system. Under EOI, skilled workers can, by answering basic questions for CIC on their work history, education, and skill sets, get preapproval and an expedited processing of their admission to Canada, providing they meet the requirements with appropriate scores from six factors noted here.

2. **Business Immigrants**

Canada has implemented a new program for business entrepreneurs to get a visa and permanent residence in Canada. This program is called the Start-up Visa Program, which has four basic requirements for a business entrepreneur. The first requirement is a letter of support from a designated angel investor group, venture capital fund, or business incubator. The entrepreneur must secure a minimum of $200,000 CAD if the investment comes from a designated Canadian venture capital fund or $75,000 CAD if the investment comes from a designated Canadian angel investor group. There is no minimum investment requirement from a business incubator; however it must be accepted into an incubator program.

The second requirement is that the business entrepreneur must hold at least 10 percent of the voting rights in the business individually or jointly with up to five other start-up visa applicants that hold more than 50 percent of the voting rights in the business. The third requirement is basic language skills in either English and/or French, and finally that the person has an adequate amount of money to settle and provide for the cost of living prior to earning an income from the business.

In addition to the Start-up Visa Program, Citizenship and Immigration Canada has an Investor Venture Capital Pilot program for all provinces with the exception of Quebec. The requirements for this program are quite substantial; you must have a personal net worth of at least $10 million CAD, and be willing to invest at least $2 million CAD in the Immigrant Investor Venture Capital Fund. You must also have minimum language skills in English and/or French and a postsecondary degree. Since the requirements for this visa are quite substantial, the CIC has had very little interest in this program and I would expect that it may be abandoned soon.

3. **Provincial Nomination**

Most Canadian provinces and territories have programs that encourage immigrants to settle in their jurisdictions. These Provincial Nominee Programs (PNPs) are primarily employment-driven, allowing the provinces to select immigrants to assist in developing specific areas of provincial economies. For example, a province may want to hire a foreign doctor to cover a particular rural area in the province and will nominate that physician to the CIC for immigration. If the selected physician fulfills the provincial requirement to remain and serve in that rural setting for the specified number of years, usually about three years, that physician can become a permanent resident of Canada and may move or live anywhere in the country. This person also becomes eligible for Canadian citizenship after living in Canada for at least 1,460 days.

4. **Family Class Immigration**

   Canadian citizens and permanent residents living in Canada who are 18 years or older may sponsor close relatives or family members who want to become permanent residents of Canada. Sponsors must promise to support the relative or family member and their accompanying family members for a period of three to ten years, depending on their age and relationship to the sponsor, to help them get established in Canada.

5. **Quebec Immigration**

   Quebec is responsible for selecting immigrants who wish to settle in Quebec. In fact, Quebec has a special status with Citizenship and Immigration Canada that allows it to set its own immigration criteria, almost like a separate country. Quebec skilled workers are not assessed on the six selection factors of the Federal Skilled Workers Program. Quebec sets its own criteria for skilled workers, which are normally less restrictive than the federal factors, and they focus the language skills on French only, with very little emphasis on the ability to speak English.

6. **North American Free Trade Agreement** (NAFTA)

   Under NAFTA, US businesspeople get quicker and easier temporary entry into Canada than other applicants. NAFTA applies to four specific categories of businesspeople: business visitors, professionals, intra-company transferees, and traders or investors. Each of these categories has its own requirements to gain temporary access to Canada to conduct business. In general, unless the individuals qualify for permanent resident status under one or the other categories noted above, they will have to return to the US when their temporary visas expire.

Once you become a permanent resident of Canada, you may apply for Canadian citizenship (after living in Canada for at least 1,460 days). If you are a US citizen, the United States does not require that you give up your US citizenship to become a Canadian citizen. Therefore, in effect, when you become a Canadian citizen, you are considered a dual citizen of Canada and the United States.

WHEN DO YOU PAY TAXES IN CANADA?

As noted earlier in this chapter, US visitors are taxed in Canada only when they have income that is sourced in Canada. They pay Canadian income tax to the Canada Revenue Agency directly or through a non-resident tax withholding system under the Canada/US Tax Treaty. Visitors who have sojourned in Canada for periods that total 183 days or more in a year are deemed to have been residents of Canada throughout that taxation year. This deemed residency rule could potentially subject visitors to Canadian income tax on their world income. It is important that visitors who spend 183 days or more in a year in Canada protect themselves from being taxed on their worldwide income by filing Form T1 with CRA for the tax year in question. On this tax return they may claim Canada/US Tax Treaty protection from full taxation on their world income because the treaty considers them residents of the US under the residency tiebreaker rules. (Review Chapter 4 for the treaty tiebreaker rules to ensure that under these rules you would be considered a non-resident of Canada.)

Generally speaking, the CRA considers any immigrant who becomes a permanent resident of Canada taxable on their world income on the day they obtain their status and apply for Canadian medical coverage. Permanent residents must then file their first Canadian tax return, a Form T1, by April 30 of the following year, using the date they became permanent residents as the start date on the return. If you are both a permanent resident of Canada and a US citizen, you must file tax returns in both countries, and use the many facets of the Canada/US Tax Treaty to ensure that you are not taxed twice on the same income. US citizens must file annual US tax returns regardless of where they live in the world.

In almost all circumstances, once you become taxable by CRA as a resident of Canada you will pay higher to significantly higher income taxes than you would in the United States, depending on the amounts and sources of your taxable income. (Review Chapters 4 and 9 for more information on specific differences between Canadian and US taxation systems and to learn about ways to take advantage of tax-saving opportunities.)

Some important tax considerations for first-time residents of Canada are outlined in the three sections that follow.

COST BUMP ON PROPERTY UPON IMMIGRATING TO CANADA

Once an individual enters Canada to become a resident for tax purposes, under Canada Revenue Agency rules he or she is deemed to have sold each property owned immediately before entering Canada — for proceeds equal to the property's fair market value — and purchased it back at that same value on the same day. This deemed disposition is called the "cost bump" or "step-up in cost basis" because, for Canadian tax purposes, it's as if the property was sold and then repurchased on the day before the person entered Canada. CRA taxes only those gains that accrue after the individual becomes a resident of Canada.

However, this cost bump does not apply to property that is already taxable Canadian property. For example, if you already own a residence in Canada that you purchased sometime before entering Canada as a resident for tax purposes, that property will retain its original cost for Canadian tax purposes. If you sell the property in the future, you'll pay capital gains tax based on the difference between the purchase price and the price for which you sell it. If you make this property your principal residence, any capital gains that accrue while you are a Canadian resident will be tax-free.

US citizens immigrating to Canada have some important issues to consider regarding their capital property when they enter Canada as residents. If they fail to work through these options, they could be double-taxed when they sell properties and investments owned at the time they entered Canada. This potential for double-taxation is best illustrated by a simple example. Assume you, as a US citizen, immigrated and became a Canadian resident owning a stock that you paid $1,000 for, and that had a fair market value of $10,000 on the date that you entered Canada. For US tax purposes the purchase price would be $1,000; for Canadian tax purposes the cost basis would be $10,000, the value of the stock when you entered Canada. If, after you had been a resident of Canada for a year, you decided to sell the stock, which had reached a value of $20,000, you would have a Canadian capital gain of $10,000 (the $20,000 fair market value less the Canadian cost basis of $10,000 equals a $10,000 gain), on which you would be taxed in Canada, paying about $2,500 in income tax. You would have a US taxable gain of $19,000 (the $20,000 fair market value less the original cost of $1,000 equals a gain of $19,000), on which you would pay about $2,850 tax in the United States. Under the Canada/US Tax Treaty, once you become a resident of Canada, capital gains are considered "sourced": originated in your country of residence. Because of this sourcing rule, the profit on the sale of this stock is considered a Canadian taxable gain and therefore no foreign tax credits for the taxes paid to the US would be allowed (because from a Canadian tax perspective the gain is not foreign). This means you end up paying capital gains taxes in both countries, totalling $5,350. If you had done some tax planning before entering Canada, you could have avoided paying tax on the same income in both countries.

This situation is referred to as double-taxation. The tax may not be exactly double; in fact, often it is more than double. Double-taxation really hurts when it hits unexpectedly, especially when it amounts to many thousands of dollars. In the example given above, you could have eliminated double-taxation if you had sold the stock before you entered Canada as a resident and bought it back on the same day. In this circumstance you would pay the US tax on the capital gains, but thereafter your US and Canadian cost bases would be the same, and you would not pay double tax. It should also be noted here that the effect of the double tax may be reduced for US citizens by taking a credit for the Canadian taxes paid on the gain on their US return.

If the property the US citizen is selling is US real estate and if the state in which the property is located imposes its own income tax, this state tax can also create some double tax possibilities as Canada will not give credit under the treaty for state tax paid. The opposite is also true as several Canadian provinces (the ones that now require a separate provincial tax return rather than having the federal government calculate and collect their taxes) also do not allow foreign tax credits dictated under the Canada/US Tax Treaty.

Individuals who are immigrating to Canada and who own considerable investment portfolios and properties located outside Canada are well advised to consult a cross-border planning specialist before entering Canada as residents.

IMPORTANT TAX CONCERNS FOR AMERICANS MOVING TO CANADA

Chapter 12 discusses many important tax considerations for Canadians returning to Canada after a long period of residence in the US. Since many people in this situation are also US citizens or long-term green card holders, most of these important tax considerations also apply to Americans moving to Canada for the first time. Rather than repeat tax issues discussed in Chapter 10, I recommend that Americans immigrating to Canada review that chapter. However, I will also summarize these considerations in this chapter and point out any peculiarities that may apply to Americans immigrating to Canada for the first time.

- US citizens heading to Canada with IRAs, 401(k) plans, or other qualified plans are, on average, going to double the amount of income taxes they will need to pay when they eventually withdraw income from these plans. In Chapter 12, I provided several solutions to mitigate this doubling of the tax obligations on deferred income plans primarily by rolling them over to a Roth IRA.

- Income tax on an investment portfolio can increase dramatically when a US taxpayer becomes a Canadian taxpayer. Tax-free and tax-deferred income from investments becomes fully taxable annually in Canada. Capital gains in Canada are taxed at slightly higher rates than in the US, but it is important to watch out for potential double-tax situations noted earlier in this chapter.
- Any US resident immigrating to Canada with bonuses, severance payments, vacation pay, or deferred compensation earned in the US but not yet collected should delay immigration and collect this income while still a US taxpayer. If a person moves to Canada with any of this or similar kinds of employment income, he or she will pay Canadian tax rates on this income, which in almost all cases will be significantly higher than the taxes paid by US taxpayers.
- US stock options accrued while you are a resident of the US are best exercised before entering Canada and becoming a Canadian taxpayer. CRA will tax the stock options even though they were from US employment in the apportionment allocated under the treaty rules.
- Americans immigrating to Canada will continue to qualify for US Social Security and Medicare at age 66 (or to continue to receive benefits if they are already receiving them) while they are in Canada, providing that they qualified under US rules before they left the United States. Under the Canada/US Tax Treaty, when you collect US Social Security benefits in Canada, 15 percent of the benefit will be tax-free and the balance is taxed at Canadian rates. Chapter 15 discusses receiving both Canadian and US Social Security benefits at the same time, whether living in Canada or the US. Americans moving to Canada should review that chapter if they wish to maximize these benefits.
- Americans working in Canada will, under normal circumstances, pay into the Canada Pension Plan (CPP) or Quebec Pension Plan (QPP) and be eligible for a pension when they reach age 65. Canadian Old Age Security (OAS) is not based on work history; benefits are accrued to anyone who has lived in Canada between the ages of 18 and 65 (starting in 2023, the age of eligibility for OAS will gradually increase to 67). Full OAS benefits are paid at age 65 to those with annual incomes less than $73,350 and who

have lived in Canada for 40 years between the above-noted ages. If you live in Canada less than the full 40 years you are entitled to a fraction of the OAS benefit based on the years resident over 40, for example, if you had lived in Canada for only 20 years before the age of 65, you could receive up to half the current maximum benefit of $6,800 per year, indexed for inflation.

- American citizens working in Canada and participating in Canadian deferred income plans such as Registered Retirement Savings Plans (RRSPs) or employer-sponsored pension plans can't assume they will receive a US deduction or be exempt from paying tax on the income earned in these plans (although their fellow Canadians won't pay until the money is withdrawn from RRSPs). Since American citizens must file US tax returns each year, the IRS will not recognize tax-deferred status of Canadian registered retirement plans. In Chapter 10 there is a discussion of how the IRS views and taxes Canadian RRSPs and similar plans. Review this and the unique tax filing requirements for US citizens in Canada later in this chapter. Special reporting forms need to be completed and attached to your IRS Form 1040 and your Canadian T1 tax form each year. For the first time, in 2009, the Fifth Protocol to the Canada/US Tax Treaty allowed American citizens and green card holders working in Canada to deduct contributions to Canadian employer-based retirement plans, to the same limits they would be able to deduct for similar plans through a US employer. These deductions for contributions to Canadian RRSPs or similar plans are only allowed for the first five years of residency in Canada. The distributions from these plans, regardless of where the US citizen or green card holder is resident at the time of distribution, will also be fully taxable by the IRS on the same basis as US qualified plans.
- If you continue to own US life insurance policies that accumulate cash values after you have moved to Canada, you need to be aware that CRA will only allow the tax-free accumulation of income in a Canadian-exempt insurance policy. CRA will require a Canadian resident to annually report the growth of a US insurance policy under the foreign investment entity rules, using the mark-to-market approach. You will pay income tax on any income earned inside the US insurance policy. If you are still insurable at reasonable rates you may consider replacing your US life insurance policies with Canadian insurance policies as needed once you are Canadian resident. It is best to use term insurance only. There is

no investment portion built into the policy so there is no difference in how these policies are taxed in either country.

- Americans wishing to give up their US citizenship when immigrating to Canada should review Chapter 4, which details the tax implications of completing an expatriation.

CONVERTING YOUR US ESTATE PLAN TO A CANADIAN ESTATE PLAN

Generally speaking, if an American immigrates to Canada, with a valid will from their US state of residence, their will would be recognized as a valid will in Canada. However, ancillary estate documents such as living wills and powers of attorney, which are extremely important documents when you are incapacitated either permanently or temporarily, may not be usable in Canada. Consequently, it is highly recommended that you draft a new set of estate-planning documents as soon as possible after entering Canada. These documents should be drawn up by a Canadian attorney intimately familiar with the needs of US citizens living in Canada.

Any American who immigrates to Canada leaving property, investments, retirement plans, and/or family members in the US will complicate their estate plan considerably. For example, if you own properties in the US and are living in Canada, your will or testament will need to go through probate in each jurisdiction in which any of the property is located. That means your executor will most likely have to hire an attorney to assist with the probate process and filing the required federal and state/provincial estate tax returns in each jurisdiction. The executor will then have to try to coordinate all the attorneys to close out the estate. Anyone who has been an executor of a friend or relative's estate understands the settling of an estate can be a very lengthy, complex process even when only one provincial or state jurisdiction is involved. Adding additional jurisdictions — especially between two countries — makes the executor's job more difficult and increases the cost of estate settlement.

Intelligent use of cross-border trusts and titling of assets can mitigate the complications and the costs of estate settlement, but these options sometimes create additional complications of their own. The use of the standard US "living trust" can help to avoid probate in multiple jurisdictions; however, once the settler and/or trustee becomes a resident of Canada, a new set of complicated tax rules applies to the trust. Unlike the IRS, which allows a complete flow-through of income to the creator, beneficiary, or settler of the trust without any tax at the trust level, CRA treats living trusts as separate taxpayers from the settler. This means that

Form T3 must be completed annually in Canada for the trust, and care must be taken to distribute the trust income correctly to the beneficiaries so they are not double-taxed. In addition, CRA requires a deemed disposition of all the assets in the trust every 21 years, requiring capital gains tax to be paid on any appreciation on the assets in the trust at that time. Americans moving to Canada with existing US living trusts must at the very least amend their trusts to adjust for these Canadian tax rules. Trust settlers may want to consider distributing all the assets of a trust to themselves and closing down the trust before entering Canada after carefully weighing the advantages and disadvantages of maintaining the US living trusts as Canadian residents.

A major consideration in your estate plan is where your executor is located. If you choose one of your children as executor of your estate and he or she is not located in the same province or even the same country as you are, he or she could run into obstacles that can delay the settlement of the estate and increase the cost of the settlement. Most provinces or states require outside non-resident executors to post large bonds to ensure all taxes are paid by the estate before the executor distributes any assets. In short, your estate will be settled much more quickly if the executor is located in the same jurisdiction in which you are resident at death.

If your beneficiaries are in both Canada and the US or other countries abroad, special provisions should be considered to account for the differences in tax rules, and to ensure beneficiaries are treated fairly. US IRAs and qualified plans may also create double tax situations for the estate plan of a US citizen or green card holder living in Canada; review Chapter 10 for a discussion of this estate planning concern. Several differences need to be accounted for in an estate plan with beneficiaries in multiple countries. Some differences in taxation offer Americans living in Canada great planning opportunities to reduce or eliminate estate taxes and settlement costs; other differences will have costly consequences.

Americans immigrating to Canada and leaving IRAs, 401(k) plans or other US-qualified plans in the US should review all their beneficiary designations at the brokerage firm or bank where the plans are held. They must ensure that at death these plans can be rolled over to a spouse or transferred directly to a child or other beneficiary without having to go through probate in either country. Another complication created by leaving these plans and other portfolio investments in the US is a simple administrative issue that can develop into a major problem for Canadian residents. Most US brokerage firms and other investment companies will refuse to deal with non-residents of the US, even if you are a US citizen. Consequently, your US portfolios either inside of IRAs and qualified plans or outside of these plans become frozen and no transactions other than complete liquidation can happen. Because banks and trust companies are regulated differently than the brokerage firms, you will likely have more success leaving your IRA accounts in one of these institutions than with a brokerage firm if you are moving to Canada.

For the purposes of understandability and legibility, I have greatly simplified the complexities of cross-border estate planning in this discussion. If some of the issues mentioned above seem difficult to understand, this only underlines the importance of consulting a good cross-border financial planning professional to assist you in dealing with all such issues.

UNIQUE TAX FILING REQUIREMENTS FOR US CITIZENS IN CANADA

As discussed earlier in this chapter and in several previous chapters, US citizens and green card holders living in Canada must continue to file annual US tax returns (Form 1040), whether or not they have any US-sourced income. A married US couple would normally file just one tax return annually, a "married filing joint" return. After moving to Canada, they would have to file three tax returns: the joint US return plus individual Canadian returns for each of the spouses, since CRA does not allow fully jointly filed returns. Of the estimated one million US citizens living in Canada, I suspect that considerably less than half meet this requirement of filing US tax returns to keep in compliance with the IRS. The main reason for non-compliance is simply a lack of knowledge.

Many US citizens living in Canada don't know that US tax returns must be filed, or if they do know, they don't understand the consequences of failure to file. Many of these people have a misconceived idea that they don't need to file if they have no US-sourced income, and they believe exemptions under the Canada/US Tax Treaty will protect them. They may have filed US tax returns in the past and, as is most often the case, zero taxes were due to the IRS. They concluded there was no need to continue filing in the US. This is an entirely false sense of security; many IRS and CRA forms must be filed simply for reporting purposes, with typically no tax due. However, the penalties for not filing these reporting forms in a timely fashion can be so onerous, the non-filer may as well give the tax authorities a blank cheque or an open door invitation to take every asset they own. The IRS, as of January 1, 2009, has become more aggressive in collecting penalties from American taxpayers, living in or investing in foreign jurisdictions, who have been reporting incompletely or not at all. In fact, a wealthy American received jail time in addition to heavy penalties for failure to report a Swiss investment account on his US return. A summary of the reporting forms the IRS requires on foreign accounts and the penalties for failure to file are provided later in this chapter. In Chapter 4, I indicated there is a Streamlined Voluntary Disclosure Program for US citizens or green card holders who may have missed filing proper US reporting forms, free from penalty if acted upon quickly.

Although the Canada/US Tax Treaty provides a great deal of protection to US citizens living in Canada (and vice versa), it can also be used to assist the IRS in collecting penalties if you fail to file the required reporting forms correctly and on time. In addition, if you fail to file a US return and then try to invoke treaty protection, you then may lose treaty protection altogether and face massive double-taxation because a great number of treaty elections cannot be filed retroactively. CRA also has some special reporting forms to report US or other foreign income and assets; if these forms are not filed, the penalties can be equally or even more onerous than IRS penalties. The importance of knowing what to file and when with both CRA and the IRS cannot be overemphasized. The following section outlines the unique forms that the US citizen or green card holder living in Canada needs to consider in addition to the normal forms and schedules when filing annually in both countries.

CANADA REVENUE AGENCY FORMS TO BE COMPLETED WITH THE MAIN TAX RETURN, FORM T1

- **Form T1135,** Foreign Income Verification Statement. On this form, you must list any foreign property when the total value of such foreign property exceeds $100,000 CAD. (If a US citizen left behind any property or investments in the US or another country, this information must be identified on this form.) For 2015 and later, foreign property with a cost of more than $600,000 but with a value throughout the year of less than $250,000 qualifies for a simplified reporting method. Failure to file this form can result in a penalty equal to or even greater than the value of the foreign property, particularly when reporting has been missed for several tax years.
- **Form T1141,** Information Return in Respect of Transfer or Loans to a Non-Resident Trust: This form needs to be completed if you or your controlled foreign affiliate has transferred owned property to a foreign trust or a non-resident corporation controlled by the trust. The penalties for failure to file this form are substantial. There is also an information reporting form, T1142, in respect to distributions from and indebted to a non-resident trust.

- **FinCEN Form 114,** Report of Foreign Bank and Financial Accounts (FBAR): This form is actually a Treasury Department form for the Financial Crimes Enforcement Network under the Bank Secrecy Act (BSA), not an IRS form; it is completed from information on Form 1040 and from bank or brokerage statements, but is filed electronically only with the Treasury Department by April 15 with a six month extension request available to October 15 every year when required. For each and every Canadian bank account, investment account, retirement savings account, or corporate account on which you are a signing authority in Canada or any other foreign country, and where the balance of that account exceeded $10,000 USD at any point in the calendar year, must be fully disclosed on this form. The highest balance reached in each account throughout the year must also be disclosed. The penalty for willfully failing to file an FBAR can be as high as the greater of $100,000 or 50 percent of the total balance of the foreign account per violation. Non-willful violations that the IRS determines are not due to reasonable cause are subject to a $10,000 penalty per violation. This is one form that you should not fail to file under any circumstances.
- **Form 5471,** Information Return of US Persons with Respect to Certain Foreign Corporations: This form is for US citizens owning more than 10 percent of the shares in a Canadian or other foreign company and is filed separately with the IRS international office in Philadelphia and a copy is attached to Form 1040 by the normal 1040 filing date, with extensions. The normal filing date for Form 1040 for US citizens living outside the US is June 15; they get an automatic extension from the regular April 15 deadline. However, US citizens in Canada can extend their US returns up to October 15 if required. Taxes may have to be paid based on your share of the accrued earnings and profits from inside a Canadian corporation as calculated by completing Form 5471. Completing this form is complicated and time-consuming, as it takes the Canadian tax data and translates it into the equivalent of a full US corporate tax return. Double-tax can result from the taxable flow-through of undistributed income from a Canadian company, because a corporation is a separate taxpayer from an individual therefore no foreign tax credits are available for the individual taxpayer to use on income allocation from the Corporation under these rules. Penalties for failure to file a Form 5471 on each and every Canadian corporation you own or control is $10,000, for

each annual accounting period, for each foreign corporation, plus penalties and interest for any taxes that were due.

- **Form 5472,** Information Return of a 25 percent Foreign-Owned US Corporation or a Foreign Corporation Engaged in a US Trade or Business: If you are living in Canada and still own 25 percent or more of a US closely-held corporation, it is required to file Form 5472 to disclose ownership by a foreign person or a US citizen living abroad. Penalties for US corporations with foreign ownership that fail to file Form 5472 are $10,000 for each occurrence.
- **Form 8938,** Statement of Specified Foreign Financial Assets: US taxpayers living outside of the US must report specified foreign financial assets in which they have an interest of total value of more than $200,000 USD on the last day of the tax year, or more than $300,000 USD at any time during the year (married taxpayers filing a joint tax return have threshold reporting of foreign assets valued more than $400,000 USD on the last day of the year or more than $600,000 USD at any time during the year). The foreign financial assets that are required to be reported on this form include virtually any form of financial accounts maintained by a foreign financial institution; stocks or securities issued by someone that is not a US person; any interest in a foreign entity; and any financial instrument or contract that has an insurer or counterparty that is not a US person. The penalty for failure to file Form 8938 by the due date is $10,000 not including any underpayment penalties for taxes not paid on any income produced the foreign financial assets. If you have reported the specified foreign financial assets in timely filed Forms 3520, 3520A, or 5471, you do not have to report them again on Form 8938.
- **Form 8891,** US Information Return for Beneficiaries of Certain Canadian Registered Retirement Savings Plans: This form is filed with Form 1040 by US citizens in Canada who wish to defer US tax on the income buildup inside any Canadian RRSP or similar registered plan that they have accumulated while in Canada. There is no penalty per se for not filing this form, but if you fail to elect to defer tax buildup on RRSPs and then you fail to report the income earned inside RRSPs on Schedule B or Schedule D, as applicable, on your Form 1040, you may have to pay penalties and interest on any tax due on this income. One Form 8891 must be filed for each RRSP owned.

- **Form 1116,** Foreign Tax Credit: Filing this form is important to eliminate double-taxation and is required when a US taxpayer is claiming credit under a treaty for taxes paid to a foreign country such as Canada. This form has several versions for different forms of foreign income and for alternative minimum tax calculations. It is fairly difficult to complete accurately. Form 1116 accounts for unused foreign tax credits and allows you to carry forward unused credits for up to ten years. Since a credit is a dollar-for-dollar reduction in tax, it is very important to continue to file these forms to track accumulated foreign tax credits. There is no penalty for failure to file this form, but if you don't file, you get no credit for taxes paid in Canada, which in itself could be very costly.
- **Form 2555,** Foreign Earned Income: This form is for US citizens earning employment income while living in Canada or other foreign jurisdictions. It allows the taxpayer to exclude up to $100,800 USD of income earned from employment in Canada each year. If you are filing as "married filing joint" and your spouse also has employment income, he or she will also qualify to exclude up to $100,800 USD of employment income each year. There is no penalty for failure to file this form, but you would lose an exemption.
- **Form 3520,** Annual Return to Report Transactions with Foreign Trusts and Receipt of Certain Foreign Gifts: These forms are required if, during the current tax year, a US citizen receives a distribution from or makes a contribution to what the IRS considers a foreign trust. Form 3520 is also used to report gifts of $100,000 USD or more from a non-resident individual or a foreign estate, or gifts of more than $15,601 USD from foreign corporations or foreign partnerships. Penalty for failure to file a required Form 3520 is the larger of 35 percent of the gross value of any property transferred to a foreign trust and/or of the distributions received from a foreign trust, or 5 percent of the gross value of the portion of the trust assets treated as owned by the US person.
- **Form 3520A,** Annual Information Return of Foreign Trusts with a U.S. Owner: A foreign trust with a US owner means filing Form 3520A in order for the US owner to satisfy the annual information reporting requirement. The owner of any portion of a foreign trust is responsible for ensuring that the foreign trust files this form, and furnishes the required annual statements to its US owners and beneficiaries. The US owner is subject to a penalty equal to the greater of $10,000 or 5 percent of the gross value of

the portion of the trust assets treated as owned by the US person at the close of the year.

- **Form 8833,** Treaty-Based Return Position Disclosure Under Section 6144 or 7701(b) of the Internal Revenue Code (also referred to as Treaty Election Form): Any US taxpayer who wishes to receive benefits from any tax treaty the IRS is party to must file this form with the IRS to provide full disclosure of all details of the treaty benefit desired. For example, under the Canada/US Tax Treaty, a US citizen living in Canada who is collecting Social Security income is not required to pay tax in the US on this income. The taxpayer would have to disclose this treaty benefit on Form 8833. There are no penalties for failure to file this form, but failure to do so may jeopardize substantial treaty benefits.

The above list of forms should not be considered all-inclusive but these are the most common forms that people either fail to file or file incorrectly. US citizens living in Canada should seek professional assistance for their tax preparation as there are far too many opportunities for mistakes when self-filing. There are many tax preparation firms in Canada that claim they can do US tax returns; however, only a few do a reliable job consistently; the majority of these are listed in Appendix E at the back of this book. As you can see from the large penalties or missed exemptions mentioned above, the cost of not filing or making mistakes when filing can be prohibitive. It is not unusual for a high-net-worth US citizen living in Canada to have Canadian and US tax returns several inches thick to keep in compliance with all these tax rules and forms.

OTHER POINTS TO CONSIDER

Here are a few other things you may need to consider or execute when immigrating to Canada:

- **Social Insurance Number (SIN):** This number is the equivalent of the US Social Security Number and must be used when filing Canadian tax returns, for payroll records, for opening bank accounts, and in general when dealing with the government and other bureaucracies. You need to apply for your SIN as soon as you get your immigration status approved. Citizenship and Immigration Canada will provide the forms to apply for a SIN.
- **Establishing a credit rating in Canada:** Since you are new to Canada and Canada has a separate credit reporting system, you can expect that banks and credit card companies will be reluctant to loan you money. Chapter 11 outlines what a Canadian needs to

do when moving to the US to establish a credit rating there. Since the issues are very similar for an American moving to Canada, please review this section and apply the suggested recommendations on the north side of the Canada/US border.

- **Applying for Canadian medicare:** Depending on which province or territory you are immigrating to, you may be eligible to apply for Canadian medical benefits as soon as you receive your permanent resident or visa status. Some provinces and territories have a waiting period of 30 to 90 days; others have none. Make sure you are covered with a supplementary plan until your full coverage takes effect. Three out of the ten Canadian provinces charge a small premium for their medical benefit plans. Please review Chapter 6 for information on how to contact the correct medicare office, and for ideas about how to cover your medical needs when traveling back to the US.

Border Guide readers are encouraged to participate in cross-border Q&A through the new *Cross-Border Forum.* After registering, you can easily post questions about the contents of this book. Questions will be moderated and/or answered by a cross-border financial planning professional in a timely fashion. To post a question or comment, go to keatsconnelly.com and click on the *Cross-Border Forum* tab.

CROSS-BORDER Q&A

US PERSONS RENTING OUT THEIR CANADIAN COTTAGE

I am an American citizen and my wife is a Canadian citizen (with green card status) and we reside permanently in the US. Five years ago, we purchased a cottage in Canada that we rent out every summer to various tenants. We have not filed any Canadian tax returns and have not included any income or costs related to the cottage on our US tax returns.

— Ray S., New York, NY

It is very important that you get into compliance with both CRA and the IRS by filing tax returns for the entire five-year period and that you continue to do so for all future years. If you do this on a voluntary basis you will find penalties and interest will be much more reasonable than if either tax department were to come after you based on information they have collected — for example, from a disgruntled tenant.

Since the property is located in Canada, CRA gets first crack at the tax. You must file a Section 216 T1 tax return in Canada, reporting all your rental income, taking allowed deductions, and then paying the applicable Canadian tax on any net profits. Since you have not filed a return, CRA is entitled to take 25 percent of the gross rent each year, even if you made no profit at all. By filing the returns you can deduct expenses and pay taxes only on the net rent. However, even if you made no profit, CRA may require that you pay interest on the withholding that was supposed to have been taken even though the withholding itself can be negated by filing a net income return. You would then take the same information, translate it into US funds and depreciation schedules, and place it on Schedule E of your US Form 1040. The taxes you paid to CRA can be taken as a credit on Form 1116, and applied against any taxes due on the rental income on your US return so that you are not double-taxed on this income. For future years, in Canada you will need to complete a CRA Form NR6 each year before you collect any rent for the year as this eliminates the need for withholding mentioned above.

CANADIAN RESIDENT DAUGHTER GIVING UP US CITIZENSHIP

My daughter, who is 40, became a dual US/Canadian citizen in 2000. Each year since, she has filed a US tax return declaring her salary and income investments (interest and dividend income, but not the amount and type of her investment portfolio). She has elected not to be taxed on her RRSP income (based on the Canada/US tax treaty). She is now considering revoking her US citizenship. What US tax implications should she expect as a result of this action? Do all the gains in her RRSP become taxable in the US? Are there other taxes she has to consider?

—Alan D., Cambridge, Ontario

Your daughter's thoughts of giving up her US citizenship deserve serious consideration before she makes that decision. So many people give up their US citizenship or US green card, then later in life wished they hadn't. Often my clients spend thousands of dollars and a great deal of time trying to get back into the US or to sponsor their children into the US. Depending on your daughter's net worth — i.e., if it is over $2 million USD or if her annual income tax is over $161,000 USD — there are considerable tax consequences from giving up US citizenship. There are new expatriation rules as of June 17, 2008 that need to be reviewed carefully and then followed for your daughter to eliminate any future problems with the IRS. In addition, the IRS/US State department are keeping a blacklist since 1996 which they say is to deny entry into the US to anyone who gave up US citizenship for tax reasons. To date they have never used this blacklist and it would be very difficult for them to enforce it; nonetheless it exists. Full tax on your daughter's RRSP and any other unrealized gains exceeding an exemption of $693,000 USD would be due upon her expatriation. Filing an annual US tax return is time-consuming, but I would recommend that your daughter seriously consider not giving up her US citizenship, so that she does not regret her decision later.

PRINCIPAL RESIDENCE EXEMPTION FOR US GOVERNMENT EMPLOYEE WORKING IN CANADA

I am one of many US government officials living and working in Canada. Like some of my colleagues, I bought my own house in Canada to live in. I understand my US government salary is exempt from Canadian tax under the Canada/US Tax Treaty, as I am considered a resident of the United States. I am a deemed non-resident of Canada under the Income Tax Act.

My question is: Is it possible for a deemed non-resident of Canada who is a US citizen to elect to file an income tax return in Canada as a resident, similar to a non-resident alien in the United States electing to file a US tax return as a resident alien? If so, would I be able to retain the exemption of my government salary under the tax treaty? Even though my worldwide income would be exposed to Canadian taxation, in my case, I do not think my non-salary income will be significant compared to the advantage of being able to utilize the principal residence exemption when I sell my home.

— Jack W., Ottawa, Ontario

You are exempt from taxation in Canada on your US government income under Article XIX of the Canada/US Tax Treaty.

You can apply for permanent resident status in Canada. If you become a permanent resident, you would file a normal Canadian T1 tax return, exclude your government pension under the treaty, and then be eligible for the full Canadian capital gains exemption on your residence as well as the US capital gains exemption on the principal residence (up to $500,000 for you and your wife on the US return you file).

14 Give My Regards to Wall Street

Investing as a US Settler or Resident

A sound investment strategy should be built around the basic concepts of asset allocation, risk allocation, risk control, and performance tracking. Due to the cyclical nature of our economy, attention to asset allocation is necessary. A country's economy changes from periods of prosperity and low interest rates, to times of recession and high rates. Proper asset allocation strategies allow portfolios to contain different types of investments that will perform well in various economic environments. Regardless of which way the economy is headed, you have a relatively steady return with good safety of principal.

The market crash of 2008 was precipitated by the credit crisis that started in the US and spread throughout the world. Even properly diversified portfolios suffered. The mainstream media exacerbated the crisis by doing whatever they could to strike fear into everyone's hearts in order to sell more newspapers. Although the economy has gradually improved, sound investment strategies still need to be followed to achieve long-term financial goals. Investors who were most affected by the 2008–2009 recession were those who panicked and abandoned their long-term strategies, believing the sky was falling and they would lose all their money. Investors who stuck to long-term plans were rewarded greatly and have seen one of the best periods of investment return in history.

The lessons of the market crisis from the most recent recession will help people focus on what really is important in their financial situation and help them learn how to control the things they can control so that the things that they can't control won't have the opportunity to knock them off track. The things people can control in setting and maintaining their financial goals are spending priorities, keeping investment costs down, minimizing income taxes, and developing an investment allocation suitable to their risk tolerance and cash flow needs. Everything else — which way the stock market is going, whether interest rates are going up or down, whether inflation or deflation is happening, which way world currencies are moving — all are out of our control. Looking at ways to reduce taxes can improve cash flow. A financial planning analysis which looks at a cross-border investment strategy could be one opportunity to reduce taxes and replace some of the income and assets lost.

In Chapter 7, I wrote a great deal about investment types, investment risk, and currency fluctuations, mainly from the perspective of the non-resident Canadian. Canadians who adopt the settler cross-border lifestyle take up tax residence in the US and need to consider all these factors, make some necessary adjustments, and position their investments in such a way that the proper balance between assets is achieved to realize their financial goals. Most Canadians moving to the US require specialized assistance in their portfolios, because they normally have a considerable amount of foreign tax credits that will expire unless their investments produce the income needed to use those credits efficiently. Proper investment design can turn each dollar of foreign tax credit into a dollar of tax reduction. Most people find this a difficult task, because not only are they treading new ground in the US, there are interlocking factors that need to be addressed simultaneously among the financial planning areas of taxation, estate, cash flow, and investments. Changes in one segment of your financial plan may require modification to several other areas. There are also cross-border considerations, since most Canadians moving to the US leave several investments in Canada. These investments need to be integrated into investment programs for the investors' maximum benefit.

INVESTMENT PRIORITIES

First determine what you want and need to achieve with your investment portfolio. Ask yourself what you want the money to do, how it will make your life better, and if there is enough for you to maintain your lifestyle. This may be restating the obvious, but my experience in financial planning has proven that many people neglect doing even a basic analysis of exactly what they want or need from their investment portfolios. Consequently, their current investments do not match their needs. Figure 14.1 is a quick exercise designed to help you determine your priorities.

The investment characteristics listed in Figure 14.1 are the main attributes you should consider when looking at investments. In the boxes on the right, rank these characteristics by assigning a numerical value from 1 to 9, 1 being the most important and 9 the least. Use the same number only once, so that when you are finished you will have a list of the nine main characteristics, in order of importance. This is a guide against

INVESTMENT PRIORITY CHECKLIST	
Inflation	❑
Tax advantages	❑
Safety	❑
Diversification	❑
Professional management	❑
Growth	❑
Liquidify	❑
Income now	❑
Income later	❑

FIGURE 14.1

which you can measure how well your investments meet your priorities. For example, if liquidity and inflation protection are important, and you have most of your money locked into term deposits, certificates of deposits, or GICs, your investments are mismatched to your needs, since those investments will provide neither inflation protection nor liquidity.

Professional money managers use some long-term historical asset allocation programs that compare your current portfolio with 20 or more years of historical data, to determine the overall level of risk or variability of your investments and their expected rates of return, assuming you leave the investments as they are. These programs can also recommend changes or optimize a portfolio, to achieve greater returns at reduced levels of risk. Of course, historical data cannot guarantee future results, but this sort of analysis is very useful in quantifying levels of risk, determining the relation between one investment and another, and looking at how changes to an individual portfolio can affect the risk and return parameters. More forward-looking advisors will use simulation tools to assist in the design of a portfolio customized to your needs and goals. Simulation tools can help your advisor develop a portfolio for you that will have the highest probability of meeting your goals over the span of your life or some other specified period. When setting up your US investment program, this type of analysis should be routine and can help provide you with greater security and increased return. However no system of portfolio design is going to have a guaranteed outcome. There are far too many variables to accurately predict the future.

The next step in developing your portfolio is determining your overall objectives. There are four key objectives or modes that can realistically be achieved by an investment portfolio.

1. OBJECTIVE — INCOME AND PRESERVATION OF PRINCIPAL

The Income and Preservation of Principal objective seeks a high level of current income with liquidity and relatively low annual principal fluctuation. It does not seek to maintain purchasing power against inflation.

Who Should Consider This Objective?

- Investors whose primary concern is current income.
- Investors who will tolerate only minor erosions of principal in any given year.
- Investors who are not concerned with the long-term effects of inflation on their purchasing power.

Typical Investors

- Retired individuals looking to enhance their income in order to live more comfortably.
- Conservative investors willing to accept a relatively small degree of principal fluctuation.
- Families who need to supplement their income.

Management Technique

Use mutual funds or exchange traded funds (ETFs) that invest in US or foreign government securities, investment-grade corporate debt securities, high quality mortgage securities, and/or investment-grade or insured municipal bonds. Equity exposure should be limited to 30 percent of the total portfolio.

2. OBJECTIVE — GROWTH AND INCOME

The Growth and Income objective seeks to provide income stream that averages an annual increase to make up for the loss of purchasing power due to rising inflation. It also strives to maintain portfolio purchasing power. This objective will entail some year-to-year volatility in portfolio values.

Who Should Consider This Objective?

- Investors with long investment horizons (five years or longer).

- Investors who want long-term growth along with stability of principal.
- Investors who want current income that could increase each year to offset inflation.
- Investors who can live with the possibility of some losses as well as gains in any given year, in other words, with a reasonable tolerance for variability in the marketplace.

Typical Investors

- Retired individuals concerned about the effects of inflation on their retirement income.
- Conservative working people looking to build a nest egg.

Management Technique

Use mutual funds or ETFs that invest in large-capitalization stocks and investment-grade debt securities. Investments in cash/short-term debt and fixed income funds will total 20 to 40 percent of the portfolio for each category. Maximum exposure to equity markets will generally be 60 percent.

3. OBJECTIVE — GROWTH

The Growth objective is to seek capital appreciation over the long run (three to ten years). Current income is not a consideration.

Who Should Consider This Objective?

- Investors with long-term investment horizons (five years or more).
- Investors who can live with the possibility of large losses as well as gains in any given year.
- Investors who have income from other sources and do not have to live on all the income generated from their investments.

Typical Investors

- Working people who are looking to aggressively build an asset base.
- Retired individuals who at present require little or no investment income to live on.
- Bank savers who realize that by keeping their investments solely in bank accounts they may be sacrificing opportunities for superior long-term investment returns.

Management Technique

Use mutual funds and ETFs that will not be limited by size or type of company. Investments in cash and fixed income funds will usually be minimal, but should make up at least 10 to 20 percent of the portfolio. Thus, maximum exposure to equity markets should be 80 to 90 percent.

4. OBJECTIVE — AGGRESSIVE GROWTH

The Aggressive Growth strategy offers potentially high long-term returns (five to ten years) at the cost of year-to-year volatility. This offers the highest potential for growth over the long run, but will probably be the most volatile with the greatest up-and-down rollercoaster ride of all the objectives in any given year.

Who Should Consider This Objective?

- Investors with long-term investment horizons (ten years or more).
- Investors who want a chance to maximize long-term growth.
- Investors who can tolerate potentially large year-to-year volatility in the value of their investments.

Typical Investors

- Aggressive retirees not needing investment income to live on.
- Aggressive middle-aged investors working to build a nest egg.
- Young investors not "now" oriented.

Management Technique

Use mutual funds and ETFs that will not be limited by size or type of company. Investments in cash and fixed income funds will usually be minimal. Equity exposure can range as high as 100 percent. It is anticipated that this objective will make use of small company funds in both developed countries and emerging markets to a greater degree than the Growth objective.

Once you have determined your objectives, you are probably 90 percent of the way toward developing your portfolio. The final 10 percent is important: the actual investment selection. A professional money manager can select and maintain the investments that match your objectives, making future modifications as your objectives change. The US provides a wide variety of investments to achieve any objective, many of which are tax-advantaged. These investments allow investors to achieve greater tax savings without sacrificing liquidity, diversification, or increased risk.

Social Security and Medicare 15

THE ART OF DOUBLE DIPPING

MAXIMIZING SOCIAL BENEFITS WHEN MOVING TO THE US

For many people, a major objective in developing a Settler cross-border lifestyle is to position themselves to qualify for both Canadian and US government social programs: Canada Pension Plan (CPP), Quebec Pension Plan (QPP), and Old Age Security (OAS) in Canada, and Social Security in the US. Qualifying for these benefits requires long-term planning. Canada Pension Plan benefits are earned by being employed in Canada for ten years or longer. Once you have exited Canada, the benefit goes with you. Similarly, if you are a US resident who qualifies for US Social Security, and you are returning or immigrating to Canada, these benefits will go with you. You can apply for CPP at age 60 or wait longer to qualify for increased benefits. The longer you wait, the more zero-income years you'll have if you are no longer working, which will reduce your average monthly earnings and offset potential increases by delaying payment of benefits. Widows, whether living in Canada or the US, can qualify for a reduced benefit based on their spouses' earnings records.

To qualify for full Old Age Security benefits, you need to have been a resident of Canada for 40 years past the age of 18. Anything less will result in a proportionate reduction in benefits. For example, if you had only 30 years in Canada after age 18, you would receive 75 percent of the approximate maximum $6,800 annual benefit.

For those receiving CPP/QPP and OAS there are great tax savings for you while receiving these benefits as a resident of the US. The same cannot be said for those collecting US Social Security in Canada because the tax rate on this income is most often higher.

Before I explain how to qualify for US Social Security, I want to make you aware of another, sometimes very beneficial, treaty between

Canada and the US: the Canada-US Social Security Agreement. This provides for a coordination of benefits so that citizens spending time in both countries are not disadvantaged by any loss of benefits.

As a result of this agreement, a Canadian moving to the US can qualify for a minimal US Social Security monthly benefit as early as age 62, by working as few as 18 months and earning as little as $500 per month and paying the 7 percent employee portion of the Social Security tax. The normal qualifying time without the benefit of the Canada-US Social Security Agreement is ten years of earnings. With US Social Security, the spouse of the qualifying person also automatically qualifies to receive approximately 50 percent of the amount of the qualifying person, even though he or she may never have contributed to the system. Although US Social Security can be applied for at age 62, maximum benefits are not paid until age 65 (if you were born after 1937, the age before maximum benefits are paid can be as late as age 67). A Canadian who marries a US resident who is receiving or who qualifies for Social Security from US employment can receive 50 percent of the spouse's monthly amount and US Medicare for life. To be able to apply for this spousal benefit the new spouse must wait until at least age 62 (age 65 if Medicare benefits are to be included) and the qualifying spouse is currently over the minimum retirement age of 65 to 67 and is receiving Social Security pension and Medicare benefits qualified for under their own employment.

Retired Canadians up to age 70 who become US residents should attempt to put in the minimum amount of qualifying time for Social Security and Medicare. This can be accomplished by earning about $6,000 USD a year (even if the entire $6,000 was earned on the first day of the year), working part time, doing some consulting work, or by holding a seat on a board of directors, even if it is your own company's board or that of a friend or family member. It doesn't matter whether or not the company is in Canada or the US. You need legitimate employment earnings equivalent to 18 months (or six quarters) of work to qualify for minimum pension benefits, and up to 120 months to qualify for free US Medicare Part A. Even a Canadian past age 70 (the optimal age, however, being 55) can continue to easily accumulate quarters of coverage to get a lifetime Social Security pension and US Medicare. The pension, unless you have substantial employment earnings well over the minimum, will not be significant but qualifying for US Medicare Part A is a major goal, since once one spouse qualifies, both spouses can get coverage at today's value of nearly $14,000 CAD tax free per year for life. Of all the investments you could make with a government guarantee, this will provide you the best return you will ever get from any retirement plan. As a long-time cross-border financial planning practitioner, all Canadians retiring in the US should obtain Medicare at or as soon after age 65 as possible, even if they are covered by a good employer medical plan. Unfortunately, as many retired employees have discovered, employer-sponsored medical plans can change or be eliminated after retirement.

If you worked in the US anytime after 1933 you likely will have accumulated useful quarters toward a monthly Social Security pension benefit and, with enough quarters, Medicare. This work time in the US could be something as simple as working part time while you were going through college in the US, a temporary transfer from Canadian employer to a US corporate affiliate or having a spouse that worked in the US prior your marriage and moving to Canada. You can easily find out if you have any quarters of coverage by logging on to the Social Security website, ssa.gov, and following the instructions to get a statement of your earnings.

The maximum US Social Security pension benefit for an individual who has contributed at maximum rates for 30 years or more is approximately $2,700 USD per month (this is equivalent to approximately $45,000 CAD per year or $67,500 CAD including the spousal benefit noted below; compare that with the maximum CPP/QPP benefit in Canada of approximately $13,000 a year). The benefit for a spouse without a US work history is an additional $1,350 USD per month (CPP/QPP have no living spousal benefit); a spouse with his or her own work history would qualify for a separate pension, and would receive the higher amount of that pension or the $1,350 USD spousal benefit. US Social Security benefits are entirely tax-free for a married couple with less than $34,000 total income; 50 percent of the benefits are tax-free if their total income is more than $34,000 but less than $46,000; at incomes above that, up to 85 percent of the benefits must be included in taxable income.

Canadians who have made contributions to a company pension plan may be able to claim a portion of their pensions as tax-free returns of principal while they are residents in the US. The exact amount of tax-free pension is determined according to the size of the pension annuity purchased, your age, and IRS regulations.

US MEDICAL COVERAGE

Canadians routinely hear about Americans being denied medical treatment because they have no money or insurance. Americans hear about the evils of Canada's socialist medical system, patients dying from inadequate care or while they are on long wait lists for surgery. In reality, things are seldom as grim as the media portrays them, and many of these horror stories have been exaggerated or taken out of context. The most important thing to remember about the US medical system is that it is not inherently more or less humane than the Canadian system, just different. The ideal medical coverage, in my many years of experience with family, friends, and clients is to have access to both the Canadian and US medical systems whenever you require them.

American hospitals and health-care providers usually operate on a profit-making basis, unlike their Canadian counterparts. They compete for patients. This results in improved access to the most sophisticated medical technology. A medium-sized American city often has more specialized diagnostic equipment (such as MRI or CT scanners) than is available in all of Canada. The downside of the equation is that patients under age 65 and not yet eligible for US Medicare must either pay out of their own pockets or buy health insurance to cover medical expenses. Those without either insurance or the funds to pay generally have access to free medical care through non-profit, government-provided county hospitals and doctors, which operate in much the same way that Canadian hospitals and doctors do, on a modified first-come first-served basis without any patient billing for services. County medical facilities provide the full range of medical services, but they are certainly not as convenient as those in the pay-for-service system. As with many Canadian hospitals, there are often waits for services and a limited choice of doctors.

For a new Canadian resident in the US, we recommend you purchase private health insurance. Canadians of any age with or without pre-existing conditions who become Settlers and residents in the US can get full US medical coverage immediately. Coverage can cost from about $450 to $750 per month, depending on your age and the deductible level you choose. To get a premium and plan choices you can go to healthcare.gov where there are federal and state exchange programs providing multiple coverage options and premiums for each option you chose. For most people these insurance premiums are tax deductible at the state level and to a lesser extent at the federal level, so the cost of the programs can be greatly reduced on an after-tax basis. In addition, the US has introduced a new savings program called Health Savings Accounts (HSAs). This program works much like a Registered Retirement Savings Plan. You can put up to $7,250 per year (plus an additional $1,000 if you are over 50) into the program, take a full tax deduction, then allow the contributions to accumulate in an investment account on a tax-free basis. Withdrawals from the HSA account are tax free if used for qualified medical expenses. Some Canadian retirees may find their pension plans will provide some US coverage. Retired federal government employees are eligible through

US MEDICARE ELIGIBILITY

Age 65 or older, and one or more of the following —

- five years or longer as a legal US resident or green card holder; or
- US citizen (including derivative citizens); or
- married to a US citizen or resident on Social Security who qualified through his or her own employment

FIGURE 15.1

their group plan, the Public Service Health Care Plan, for supplemental coverage that will pay all reasonable doctors' costs up to three times the Canadian rates. Also covered: prescription drug costs and a small amount toward daily hospital expenses in the US. This plan can work well when combined with US Medicare or a good hospital indemnity policy.

There are insurers who provide supplements to fill in gaps left by Medicare. These "medigap" policies currently cost $100 to $300 a month, depending on level and type of medigap chosen. Canadians who haven't contributed the minimum 40 quarters (120 months) to US Social Security through employment, or who are not married to a US resident or citizen who has made the necessary contributions, can expect to pay around $600 per month for US Medicare coverage Part A (hospital care: $450 per month) and Part B (doctors and outpatient care: $150 per month). Recent rules concerning Medicare Part B and the medical drug coverage Part D require those in higher income brackets to pay anywhere up to three times the regular Part B and Part D premiums in (those couples earning over $400,000 USD per year will pay the maximum premium).

For Canadians over 65 who do not meet the five-year-residency requirement for Medicare, there are several options. Chapter 6 referred to several international insurers who provide worldwide coverage at reasonable costs and for those who have pre-existing conditions the US Affordable Care Act can provide full coverage without exclusion premium adjustments for the pre-existing conditions.

US health insurance and Medicare do not cover extended care in nursing homes or similar facilities, and a separate policy is needed to cover these expenses. Many insurance companies offer this long-term care coverage, but great caution is advised. The minimum recommended coverage is $200 per day (this varies from state to state) for up to four years of benefits and with an inflation rider. People over age 75 could eliminate the inflation rider, as it tends to nearly double premiums. Premiums from a good A+ rated insurance company can range between $200 and $500 per month, depending on your age at the time the policy is taken out. This coverage can be applied for at any time, beginning at about age 40, and should be in place well before you reach age 60, whether you are a resident of Canada or the US at that time. Long-term care insurance is highly recommended (even in Canada for those not even contemplating a Settler cross-border lifestyle) as many public long-term care facilities are quite inadequate and overcrowded. There are many wonderful private pay facilities available.

Any medical coverage insurance premiums are deductible as an itemized medical expense on your US tax return. However, total monthly premiums can be higher than regular Snowbird travel insurance, especially for those who do not qualify for free US Medicare. This added cost must be weighed against the potential income tax and other savings of becoming a US Settler/resident. In George and Susan's example in Chapter 9, they are able to save over $2,000 a month in taxes just from their CPP tax reduction and OAS clawback; enough to pay for good medical insurance coverage in the United States.

APPLYING FOR US SOCIAL SECURITY

Imagine the dismay of a couple who have done ten years of planning so that they qualify for US Social Security and Medicare benefits, only to be told, upon filing the application, that they do not qualify. This scenario has happened to many readers of *The Border Guide*. In fact, in a couple of cases not only did the Social Security clerk tell applicants that they did not qualify, they also wiped out years of quarters of credits, which meant that these people had to start over in the qualifying process — not something one wants to do at age 70+.

So far, we're batting 1,000 in taking on the Social Security Administration with respect to these situations. The clerks were wrong in what they did, but did not (I think) err on purpose. Rather, they didn't understand how the Canada-US Social Security Agreement applied to these people. In this section I want to make you aware of some of these issues so that you can avoid the complications that can arise.

First, the Canada-US Social Security Agreement states that if you have less than 40 quarters of work but more than 6, you can use time spent in Canada to help qualify for benefits. To do so, you must file Form SSA-2490-BK (or form SSA-1294CN for persons filing in Canada), Application for Benefits Under a US International Social Security Agreement (some readers have had trouble getting this form from Social Security, but it can also be found at ssa.gov or forms.gov) at the same time you submit your normal Social Security application. Form SSA-2490-BK can help solve some problems and force clerks to send it through the appropriate channels to be processed. This can take some time, as US Social Security will contact the Canadian government.

The Canada-US Social Security Agreement also allows US citizens in Canada to use Canadian employment earnings to qualify for US Social Security benefits, provided that with the annual filing of their US tax returns they paid Social Security taxes on their Canadian income. (Even though the Canada-US Social Security Agreement allows this, internal Social Security rules do not deal with it.) These Canadian earnings helped some of our clients who were US citizens get many quarters of benefits earned while they were still in Canada, and we were even able to re-file up to three past years of returns and pay the Social Security taxes to get 12 additional quarters immediately.

AVOIDING THE WINDFALL ELIMINATION PROVISIONS

The final key benefit of the Canada-US Social Security Agreement is that it can help avoid the Windfall Elimination Provision (WEP), which can reduce a person's Social Security pension by up to 60 percent. The WEP applies to people who have earned pensions by working for an employer that did not withhold Social Security taxes (i.e., a government agency or an employer outside the US), but also worked for other employers that did withhold Social Security taxes long enough for them to qualify for Social Security benefits. The WEP was brought in to prevent such people from gaining an unfair advantage in the Social Security system. So what does the WEP have to do with people who have spent a good deal of their working careers in Canada and are applying for benefits? The Social Security clerks have a sad tendency to apply the WEP because they feel such applicants may gain a similar unfair advantage through not having contributed to Social Security for their entire working careers. However, hidden in the WEP rules is a statement that the WEP doesn't apply to benefits under a Social Security agreement with the US.

As you can see, most of these concerns arise because Social Security personnel do not apply the rules correctly. In their defense I must state that most Social Security personnel seldom encounter these rules. Yours may be the first and last case ever handled at that particular office that deals with Canadians applying for Social Security benefits. Thus, you have a strong advantage if you can help the SSA staff find and interpret the agreement rules. If the staff continue to misapply the rules, you can appeal their rulings in writing. The appeal goes to an administrative judge, who usually does a better job with international agreements. But do your homework and be very prepared.

Because of the increasing number of *Border Guide* readers who seem to be facing this WEP problem, I would like to point out a few of the more technical reasons why WEP does not normally apply to Canadians qualifying for US Social Security. These technical points, which are derived from the US Social Security Act and the Canada-US Social Security Agreement, are also available on the Social Security website: www.ssa.gov. These documents, although written in dense legalese, should be reviewed for supporting information for any petitions or appeals you might want to present before the Social Security Administration. By providing this information, I hope my readers can prevent the Social Security clerks and administrative judges from taking them down the wrong path and reducing their Social Security benefit entitlements. Here are the key points to read up on and present to Social Security Administration personnel:

- The Canada-US Social Security Agreement Part 1, Article 1, paragraph 6 defines the period of coverage as: "A period of payment of contributions or a period of earnings from employment or self-employment, as defined or recognized as a period of coverage by the laws under which such period has been completed, or any similar period in so far as it is recognized by such laws is equivalent to period of coverage." By this definition, an individual's period of coverage in Canada is clearly a period of coverage of earnings under the Canada-US Social Security Agreement. Combined with the US earnings period of coverage, the Canadian period of earnings coverage totals well over 30 years of substantial earnings. Any Canadian in this position qualifies for the WEP exemption. "The WEP 30 years of coverage exemption" can be found in the Social Security Act section 215(a)(7)(D) and the definition of what constitutes covered employment or periods of earnings can be found at Section 210(a)(C) which refers to Section 233(b)(2).
- The Canada-US Social Security Agreement Part 1, Article 1, paragraph 7 defines benefit as "any benefit provided for in the laws of either contracting State." Since the 30 years substantial earnings exemption from the Windfall Elimination Provision is clearly a benefit to Canadians and also Americans who have worked at least part of their careers in Canada, they are certainly entitled to it. Based on the Canada-US Social Security Agreement definition of both benefits and period of coverage, this article clearly confirms that the agreement considers periods of coverage in Canada

equivalent to periods of coverage in the US for the purpose of determining whether or not a Canadian is entitled to benefits.

- The Canada-US Social Security Agreement Part 5, Article 19, paragraph 4 states "this agreement shall not result in the reduction of benefit amounts because of its entry into force." By attempting to deny benefits, the Social Security Administration goes against both the spirit and the letter of this article and therefore the agreement in its entirety. The WEP should not result in reduced Social Security benefits, as most Canadians have sufficient earnings to qualify for the 30-year exemption.
- If you have a pension other than OAS that Social Security is attempting to use to reduce your Social Security benefits, you may be able to use some additional support for your petition. This additional defence may be available because the Canadian pension is based on "covered employment," and therefore the WEP does not apply. "Covered employment" is defined in Section 210 (a)(C) of the Social Security Act and clearly states that "employment" includes service rendered abroad for an employer when the service is designated as employment or recognized as equivalent to employment under a totalization agreement such as the Canada-US Social Security Agreement. Although employment is not defined in the Canada-US Social Security Agreement, we would respectfully suggest that working in Canada, particularly when Canadian social security taxes are withheld from the wages, should be considered employment almost anywhere. Because the service underlying the foreign pension is covered employment, the standard benefit formula when calculating the Social Security benefits must be applied without a WEP reduction. A reader of *The Border Guide* who followed this chapter to win his appeal against the WEP provisions that were being used to reduce his Social Security pension has provided other *Border Guide* readers with hope; this win is good news for anybody going through this appeals process. This individual won the WEP appeal from an unexpected angle, but one that must have been considered a logical one by the judge. The judge stated that because the Canada/US Totalization Agreement was used as far as finding periods of covered employment and non-covered employment that his Social Security pension WEP was exempt because of the fact the Totalization Agreement applied. Because of this, we have a new argument to add to the list. As with all Social Security appeals, there is a significant amount of luck involved.

Working with the Social Security Administration on these cross-border issues can be time-consuming and frustrating, and I can guarantee that your patience will be tested. Be prepared to be persistent: appeals can take from one to years. I would not recommend this as a do-it-yourself project. Because there are few people in the US who ever deal with these issues, it is also hard to get legal or other assistance. In addition, people who fight Social Security and win do not necessarily set precedents for other cases because each appeal judge makes his or her own decision. Generally, appeal cases are not even available for public review. The final level of recourse, once your case goes through all Social Security appeals, is to take the Social Security Administration to court. But if you are sure you are correct, persistence will usually make you victorious.

There is both good and bad news with respect to the Social Security Administration applying WEP incorrectly to Canadians covered under the Canada/US Social Security agreement. The bad news is that the legal case we had going before the federal courts to solve this problem once and for all was tossed out on procedural grounds. Fortunately, I was contacted by an attorney looking to help on this WEP problem for Canadians who heard that I had been working on this for a number of years. He has applied to the federal courts to have the case that was dropped reopened based on pretty solid grounds so we feel we have a good chance of reopening and getting it adjudicated soon. In addition, this same attorney has started a class-action lawsuit representing multiple Canadians affected by WEP incorrectly and we have been helping him pull information and people together for this lawsuit. We have a double approach that will take some time to work through the system but feel it will be successful based on this attorney's new research and diligence, building on what we have already accomplished. This attorney is willing to help any Canadian affected by WEP with the appeals process and other advice including adding them to the class-action lawsuit. He offered to do some of this on a pro bono or no-fee basis. If you understand how difficult it is first all find an attorney that knows anything about the US-Canada Social Security Agreement and Social Security Administration WEP rules and then spend an incredible amount of time fighting the government and not getting paid for most of it, then you understand finding this attorney was an incredible stroke of luck. You can contact this attorney directly for all WEP assistance. His name is Jonathan Bruce, phone number 859-905-9678, email Bruce@jonathanbrucelaw.com. Email us if you run into a brick wall or can't get a hold of Jonathan: info@keatsconnelly.com.

Border Guide readers are encouraged to participate in a cross-border Q&A through the new Cross-Border Forum, which is a platform where, after registering, you can easily post questions about the contents of this book. You can also post comments or create discussions with other Border Guide readers to share experiences and swap cross-border financial planning tips. To post a question or comment, go to keatsconnelly.com and click on the Cross-Border Forum tab at the top of the first page.

CROSS-BORDER Q&A

SOCIAL SECURITY SPOUSAL BENEFIT GOOD FOR CROSS-BORDER WORKER

I am a Canadian citizen with a US green card and have been living in Florida since 2013. I commute to work in Canada from Florida, and my wife works in Florida. I pay quarterly taxes to the IRS and have some tax withheld by Canada, which I use as a credit on my US return. To date, I have not paid anything to US Social Security, although my wife pays into the system on her salary, and my Canadian-source income has CPP deductions. I have eleven years to retirement and am wondering what the benefit of paying additional monies to US Social Security would be. I've put this in a nutshell so that you might decide whether or not you can provide advice. Alternatively, perhaps there is someone with whom you are affiliated in Florida to whom you can refer me. I enjoyed reading The Border Guide *when I left Canada in 2005. I have used several sections as reference material, yet I feel my situation might require unique advice.*

— Douglas E., Ft. Lauderdale, Florida

It is difficult to give you a specific answer without knowing all the details, but I can give you some general direction.

If you are looking for the best return on your money, you are better off with only one spouse paying into US Social Security. This is because a non-contributing spouse gets a benefit equal to 50 percent of the contributing spouse's Social Security pension, as well as free Part A Medicare, which would otherwise cost about $500 per month. Consequently, if you started contributing now to Social Security, you would get a very poor return on your contributions, since you have already qualified for major benefits under your wife's plan. Your Social Security pension would be the higher amount of either 50 percent of your wife's pension or 100 percent of your benefits through your own contributions, but you would not get both amounts, and you only need to qualify for Medicare once.

However, if your income were high, and if you were to contribute long enough yourself, your 100 percent could eventually be more than your 50 percent spousal benefit, and the combined pensions between the two of you could be higher than if you contributed nothing. Therefore, it depends whether you are trying to get the best return on your investments in Social Security or the maximum pension possible.

You are likely best off contributing the maximum to CPP and nothing to Social Security while your wife contributes the maximum to Social Security, but have a cross-border financial planning professional run the numbers for you. There are also disability and death benefits attached to contributing to US Social Security that should be carefully looked at to see whether they are beneficial to you and your wife.

IT WORKS: A CANADIAN'S NEW MARRIAGE TO AN AMERICAN DOES MAKE HIM ELIGIBLE FOR US SOCIAL SECURITY BENEFITS

I married a US wife last year and she sponsored me for a green card. We both are age 66. This is my first time I am going to file a US tax return. I understand that I have to also file a tax return in Canada. Do I have to do this every year?

— Jiri K., Kingston, Ontario

Once you do your Canadian return for 2015, put the date you left Canada on the first page of the return and that will be the last return you need to file with Canada. Then in 2016, and future years, you will file only in the US. I would recommend professional help on your exit return from Canada and on your first return in the US, as there are some difficult forms and elections that you do need to incorporate into them.

FIGHTING THE WINDFALL ELIMINATION RULES WITH SOCIAL SECURITY

This letter will be of much interest to you for one of these reasons:

1. *There is a major omission in your book,* The Border Guide. *My explanation will help you correct the oversight for future editions.*
2. *All the [other] information in your book is correct and complete. Therefore, the Social Security Administration is wrong in its handling of my application for a US Social Security pension. In that case, I need your specific advice and request a copy of your fee schedule.*

I am a US citizen who lived and worked in the US until I was 30. I was a USAF officer for four years, from 1964 to 1968. When I was 28, I married a Canadian. Two years later we moved to Winnipeg, where we have since resided. I taught in Winnipeg for 25 years, until my retirement. We bought the 1992 and 1995 editions of The Border Guide *and, acting on its advice, I took a part-time job in North Dakota after retirement from teaching. When*

I moved to Canada in 1971, I had already earned 33 quarters toward my US Social Security pension. By working in North Dakota from 1995 to 1998, I earned 12 more quarters. This, according to the information in your book, meant I qualified for a US Social Security pension and Medicare benefits for my wife and myself. The last statement of benefits I received from the SSA came in 2014, and indicated my pension would be about $403 a month at age 62, and should I predecease my wife, the widow's benefit would be about $513 monthly. My wife and I carefully planned our retirement income, buying your books and visiting US SSA offices for information. Imagine our shock when I had my interview for the Social Security pension recently and was told I will receive only about 40 percent of the earned pension because of the Windfall Elimination Provision! I was told to expect a monthly pension of $190 (and my wife was to receive $95). In addition, I was told my wife would be eligible for Medicare only after five years of US residency. Nobody at the SSA office ever hinted at the Windfall Elimination Provision! Of course, we are desperately hoping the SSA clerk who is processing my application is wrong and you are right! Please advise. Is the SSA clerk correct?

— Kimber H., Winnipeg, Manitoba

The Windfall Elimination Provision is real, and the Social Security Administration has changed the application of the rules in the past few years to try to bring CPP benefits and other foreign pensions into its forms. The application forms for Social Security have been modified to ask questions on foreign benefits (question 8. (a) and (b)) that were never asked before; consequently, more people seem to be getting caught up in these rules. The Windfall Elimination Provision should not apply to you because of the Canada-US Social Security Agreement, Article IV, which states that you must receive treatment equal to that given other US citizens. The Windfall Elimination Provision is not supposed to apply to you if you have 30 or more years of "substantial" earnings in a job where you paid Social Security taxes. Under the agreement, your time in Canada when you were paying into the Canadian social security plan is supposed to be added to the time you paid into the US Social Security system, so you would have more than 30 years of combined contributions. Along with your Social Security application, you should complete Form SSA-2490-BK, Application for Benefits Under a US International Social Security Agreement, to apply for the 30-year exemption from this Windfall Elimination Provision. State that Social Security is using this rule to reduce your benefit inappropriately. If this additional form does not work, you can appeal it to a Social Security judge, and I think you would have a decent chance of success. The situation is complicated. It will be pure luck if you can get someone at the lower levels in the Social Security Administration to remove the Windfall

Elimination Provision, so you may need to go to appeal within 60 days of receiving the incorrect amount of benefits.

With respect to your wife on Medicare, she should immediately be covered under the spousal benefit of a US citizen. Some offices apply this correctly, and others don't, so it is the luck of the draw working against you here. This too can be appealed if necessary.

ELIGIBILITY FOR US MEDICARE PART B

In November of 2014, my wife and I started receiving Social Security Benefits as she worked for a US company for 11 years. We are Canadian but live in our Florida home for five to six months of the year. We seem to be eligible for Medicare A and we were wondering if there were any possibilities that we could also apply for Medicare B if it would be advantageous to our situation. Also, will we have to start filing in both countries again because we have this US income?

— Jim, C., Waterloo, Ontario

If you are eligible for Medicare Part A (which is for major US medical/hospital care), you are eligible for Medicare Part B as well (which is for outpatient type care), at a cost of around $110 per month each. If you are past age 65, you need to apply for Medicare Part A and B during the annual application window of January 1 to March 31. Visit the Social Security website at ssa.gov for information. You will be able to use US Medicare while in the US as a backup to Canadian medicare, in case you happen to get on a waiting list for treatment in Canada. It can also be a backup or substitute for travel insurance for your Florida winter stays. In fact, it is usually much better than travel insurance because you can use it on a non-emergency basis. I would recommend that you get a Medicare supplement from an organization like the AARP. The US Medicare claims processing has been giving Canadians a bit of a hassle because they want you to prove that you entered the country legally. You should ensure that your passport is stamped whenever you enter the US.

You do not have to file US tax returns just because you are receiving US Social Security. Under the Canada/US Tax Treaty, US Social Security is only taxable in Canada at your normal Canadian rates with the first 15 percent of the Social Security pension being tax-free.

SOCIAL SECURITY WEP 30-YEAR EXEMPTION

My question is specific to pensions. I have been a Canadian permanent resident of the US since 1996. I receive a small CPP benefit, and last year I started getting Social Security. Due to being 1 year short of 30 years of "substantial earnings" and the fact that I receive CPP, I am subject to the WEP reduction. After extensive research on the Social Security website, I came to the conclusion that my benefits are probably correct. The research included the totalization agreement with Canada. I also reconfirmed the pension amount using the WEP Online Calculator on the website and came up with the same dollar amount as my official benefit award. In your book, you indicate that the totalization agreement "would still exempt persons from WEP who had a total of 30 years in Canada and/or the US" (which I do) based on "a statement that the WEP doesn't apply to benefits under a Social Security agreement with the US." I am unable to find any such statement other than that WEP definitely does not apply to Canadian Old-Age Security pension. Incidentally, I recently received an increase in my award after protesting when my Social Security award was not recalculated after my 2010 earnings had been posted.

— Dr. Y., San Diego, California

WEP does not apply in your situation. Instead of sending you into a complicated and lengthy appeal, my recommendation, since you are only 1 year short of your 30-year WEP exemption, is to get 1 more year of earnings that are subject to Social Security taxes. To do this you only need someone to pay you about $6,000 before the end of this year for legitimate employment of any kind. It could be something as simple as performing as a director of a corporation or consulting/self employment. This is easier and less costly than anything else I can recommend for you.

SOCIAL SECURITY APPLICATION DENIED: NO 1099 SLIPS

I was a client of yours some nine years ago, and you were a great help in my moving from Canada to the US.

Each year, your office prepared my tax return, and based on your advice, certain self-employment fee income of approximately $6,000 USD was included as business income each year since 2006, with the objective of attaining 40 quarters for Medicare purposes.

This year, I applied for certain benefits and was told that my last three years' earnings did not qualify because I didn't have Form 1099s, the income slip similar to the Canadian T4s. I never had 1099s from the start. Is there any good reason to appeal this ruling?

— John S., Palm Harbor, Florida

I believe someone at the Social Security Administration is just giving you a hard time. Your income is self-employment income, for which no 1099s are normally issued. You have an obligation to report self-employment income and pay Social Security tax, and the IRS rules ensure that you do: you have no choice. I have never heard of this rule, and if one does exist, it is likely only at an administrative level in Social Security. Ask for a copy of the chapter and verse that says this is so. If there is such a procedure, you can ask for reconsideration and/or appeal it once they officially turn you down. The appeals judges normally ignore these internal procedures, as such procedures are not, in fact, the law.

KNOW SOCIAL SECURITY RULES

I worked for three years as a professor in the US. The US Social Security office tells me I have 12 quarters of qualifying time toward a US monthly Social Security pension but I must have a minimum of 40 quarters of employment history before I may receive any benefits. I also have nearly $70,000 USD accumulated in a TIAA-CREF (this is similar to a Canadian Registered Retirement Savings Plan) that I contributed to while I was in the US to take a deduction against my teaching salary. The questions I would like to ask are as follows:

1. *As a Canadian resident, can I continue to pay into Social Security so my wife and I can collect Social Security benefits in our retirement years and, if not, how can I get my money back from them?*
2. *Do you have any other suggestions? What should I do about my TIAA-CREF?*

— Walter J., Saint John, New Brunswick

1. Yes, you can continue to pay into Social Security, but only if you earn $6,000 USD or more per year of qualifying employment-type income sourced and taxable in the US. The $6,000 of earnings will give you four quarters of Social Security credit per year. Once you have your total of 40 quarters of benefits or credits both you and your wife can receive US Social Security and Medicare at age 65 even if you don't wish to become US residents in the future under the Canada-US Social Security Agreement. You will need some form of legal immigration status in the US before you can earn employment-type income in that country. You can get the Social Security money back by applying for a reduced monthly benefit under the Canada-US Social Security Agreement through any US Social Security office once you reach age 62 or older even if you do not contribute any more to the US Social Security system.

3. The tax treatment of the Teachers Insurance and Annuity Association-College Retirement Equities Fund (TIAA-CREF) and other RRSP-type, US-qualified plans in Canada has recently been

changed retroactively. The new Canadian rules, as outlined in Section 243(1), reg S.6803 of the *Income Tax Act*, state that income earned on these US accounts is not taxable until withdrawals are made from the plan. At time of withdrawal, both income and principal are taxed at the current Canadian rates as income. Therefore, withdrawals should be made at times when income is lower, such as retirement, in a similar manner to Canadian RRSPs. You are also subject to US rules and taxes on the withdrawals from your TIAA-CREF. You must commence your withdrawals during or before the year in which you become age 70½. Any tax you may pay to the IRS would be a credit on your Canadian return, so you should not be double-taxed on this income.

WORK FOR US SOCIAL SECURITY

I am in the process of obtaining my green card. I shall be sponsored by my son who is an American citizen and I will work for him for three or more years. My question concerns Medicare and health insurance at the age of 65. Does the agreement on Social Security between the United States and Canada offer any credits toward Medicare coverage?

— F.W., Orillia, Ontario

In order to qualify for US Medicare paid by Social Security at age 65 or later, you need to have 40 quarters or ten years of contributions to Social Security through employment income in the US. You would be eligible for US Medicare after you have had your green card for five years and have reached age 65. If you do not have the required 40 quarters of contributions, you will have to pay approximately $600 in premiums per month for the coverage instead of $100. If you are married, your spouse will qualify for Medicare at age 65 as well as a monthly Social Security payment based on employment contributions to the plan. Making the effort to earn $6,000 each year, the minimum amount to get 4 quarters of qualification during a year, for the total of ten years can give you both a total of more than $14,000 USD of Medicare benefits plus a small pension for each of you per year for life. This is quite a return on your investment, considering that the Social Security tax on $6,000 USD of earnings is only about $450 ($900 if you are self-employed).

You can make contributions to Social Security through your earnings at any age, so the sooner you get started the sooner you will qualify. If you work only three years, the agreement on Social Security between the US and Canada will help you receive a reduced monthly Social Security pension, but since US Medicare is not part of this agreement you will get none of your Medicare premiums paid by the Social Security.

If you are not married and find a US citizen spouse (one who has qualified for Social Security based on earnings), after one year of marriage you will get not only a spouse's Social Security pension equal to about 50 percent of monthly benefit but you will get US Medicare as well.

MEDICARE COMES FASTER THROUGH MARRIAGE

I have read your answer to a question, in which you write: "If you marry a US citizen sponsor, you would get a temporary green card for two years, which would become permanent if you are still married after two years. You may also be eligible for US Social Security and Medicare after one year of marriage, providing your wife had her own employment for ten years or more."

I came to Florida in October 2010, after I got a temporary green card following my marriage to a US citizen. My permanent green card was issued in November 2012 and is valid for ten years. I am 71 years old and my wife retired two years ago, after 40 years of work in the US. She receives Social Security pension and is covered by Medicare. I have had a Social Security card since 2010. I have been covered by my wife's health insurance until now, but the end of that coverage comes in October 2012. I applied for Medicare and the Social Security Administration told me I would not be eligible before I have been a "US resident for five consecutive years."

— G.G., Marco Island, Florida

The Social Security Administration (SSA) is not correct in its assessment of your eligibility for Social Security and Medicare. It appears to be applying the rules for immigrants/green card holders who do not have a US-citizen spouse sponsor who has qualified for Social Security and Medicare. You need to stress that you are applying for a spousal benefit and have been married for more than one year. The spousal benefit does not require a five-year presence in the US. It may be difficult to convince the lower level of SSA to read their own rules, but if you can get an experienced representative you should be able to clear this up without having to appeal your application. If you don't get satisfaction, you can appeal before an administrative judge to review the law as it applies to you. If your case reaches this point, I recommend you get some legal advice.

AGREEMENT BETWEEN US AND CANADA CAN WORK TO SNOWBIRDS' ADVANTAGE

Can work in Canada (as landed immigrants) contribute to US credits for Social Security? We have our US Social Security records and the years 1979–1995 are "non-income" years for my husband and me due to employment in Canada. We have 25 employment years in the US, which we accumulated before and after our time in Canada. As I understand it, the complex formula used in determining US benefits takes an average of earnings over one's working lifetime. The "zero income" years presumably would affect that average in a negative way. If the earnings in Canada are factored in, the benefits should be greater. Please advise if there is a possibility of combining these earning years.

— D.M., Ocala, Florida

The Canada-US Social Security totalization agreement would allow you to use time spent working in Canada (if you need it) to assist you to qualify for Social Security benefits. For example, you need ten years of employment in the United States to qualify for a Social Security pension and Medicare. However, if you had worked only eight years in the United States, but had worked at least two years in Canada, this time in Canada would help you qualify for the Social Security Pension. However, since you already have more than ten years of employment in the United States, you cannot use time in Canada to increase your Social Security benefit. Technically you would not lose benefits since you contributed to the Canada Pension Plan for the time you were in Canada and will receive a pension from the plan as well as a partial OAS based on the number of years you lived in Canada. Since you had less than 20 years in Canada you will need to use the totalization agreement to get an OAS benefit for each of you. Consequently, you will get some benefits from the totalization agreement, but not from the US Social Security as you expected.

PRIVATE INSURANCE FILLS GAP UNTIL MEDICARE COVERAGE STARTS

I am 67 and my wife is 58 and we are both Canadian citizens. We spent more than four years in Georgia some time ago, and I contributed to Social Security for approximately 17 quarters while there. I now receive pensions from both Social Security and the Canada Pension Plan. Our original intention was to spend six months at our home in Tucson and six months in Canada so that we could maintain Canadian medical coverage as both my wife and I have pre-existing conditions. We both received green cards last year and I am aware of the tax complications and costs arising from our present plan. Our family situation in Canada has recently changed and there is no longer any reason for us to return to Canada other than for family vacations. My concerns are (1) When will my wife and I be eligible to purchase Medicare insurance? Do my contributions to Social Security reduce the five years' residence requirement? and (2) Are there insurance carriers you can recommend in addition to Ingle Health?

— P.F.D., Tucson, Arizona

Since you did not obtain 40 quarters of credit from Social Security, you are not eligible for US Medicare until you have had your green card for five years. So until then, you will need private insurance. Your wife will not be eligible for Medicare until she turns 65 and also has five continuous years of residence in the United States on a green card.

Since you are nearly halfway to having your full 40 quarters, you should consider working in the United States for the next six years and earning a minimum of approximately $6,000 USD per year so both you and your wife will get US Medicare Part A for free.

Until you can get Medicare, there are several non-US insurance carriers you will be able to get coverage through under the Affordable Care Act policies available through healthcare.gov. Cross-border tax issues are quite complex and I know of only a handful of CAs who can deal with them adequately, so I still recommend you get some help in this area rather than try to do it yourself.

EXTRA WORK TRIGGERS SOCIAL SECURITY FOR CANADIAN

I am a US citizen and my residence since 1990 has been Ontario, Canada. To receive Social Security I need 40 credits, and at this time I have 39. I can earn the extra credit by going on my ex-employer's payroll for one month (associate for US company), earning $1,000 US, paying tax and Social Security. Would this trigger a US tax return and future returns? Would the Social Security income received be taxed by either government?

— R.H.T., Fort Pierce, Florida

Since you are a US citizen, you are required by the IRS to file US tax returns every year that your income exceeds the personal exemption and standard deduction amount (approximately $10,500 for a single person over age 65). Consequently, earning $1,000 doesn't trigger any new filing requirements since you likely already have an obligation to file. You must file to get the Social Security quarter credited.

Your plan to earn one more credit toward your 40 quarters should enable you to get a Social Security pension and US Medicare at age 65, providing the work is done in the United States. As a US citizen in Canada, you can also complete the work in Canada, but you will need to use the Canada-US Social Security Agreement when you apply for benefits. According to the 1996 amendment to the Canada/US Tax Treaty, Canada would be the only country to tax your Social Security benefit, with 15 percent of it being totally tax-free.

Taking Care of Business 16

How Small-Business Owners Can Reap Huge Rewards

There is no other area of financial planning that a cross-border financial planning professional can recommend that offers owners of small, closely-held businesses more income tax-saving potential than adopting the Settler cross-border lifestyle in the US. A good cross-border financial plan can save a business owner between several thousand and several million dollars, both on the one time sale of the business and on the ongoing annual investment income produced by the cash from the business sale, depending on the size or the nature of the business. Most of these planning opportunities arise solely because of a simple adjustment to the Settler lifestyle. They are not available to business owners not in the process of adjusting their lifestyles from a Vacationer/Snowbird to a Settler or at least willing and able to relocate to the US for a few years.

Unfortunately, a business owner's trusted advisors of many years often become the major deterrents to making these savings happen. Financial advisors may operate under some popular misconceptions or just plain misunderstandings, because very few of them are aware of cross-border financial planning tools available to those business owners that want to move from the Snowbird lifestyle to the Settler lifestyle. Therefore, they tend to discourage the business owner from transitioning as the safe position that they understand is to have the business owner stay put, even though they may not have their ideal cross-border lifestyle and miss some substantial income tax savings. As a result, the business owner is misled or discouraged from taking advantage of great opportunities to realize a much higher net value after taxes on the sale of his or her business; a business that he or she worked hard on for many years and has earned the right to do what he or she wants with. The business owner must look elsewhere for cross-border financial planning opportunities and use his or her trusted advisors as part of the new team that will work in the owner's best interest to make the move successful.

The major considerations that small-business owners and/or entrepreneurs need to be aware of are outlined in the next sections.

A CANADIAN CORPORATION CAN ASSIST WITH US IMMIGRATION

Many successful entrepreneurs have worked long and hard to establish businesses. Later, when they want to retire or sell the businesses to try something new, they apply the same amount of diligence to disposing of their businesses. When the money from the sale is sitting in the bank and all the income taxes are paid, they start thinking about adopting a full cross-border lifestyle in the US, where they may have been wintering for many years. Unfortunately, our hypothetical business owners may have just sold off their simplest and best means of US immigration.

As you may recall, the procedures outlined in Chapter 8 all require some form of business or a family connection for US immigration. So if you have no close family members (parents, children, or a spouse) in the United States and you have sold your principal business, you may need to establish a new business in order to complete your immigration, to be able to create the Settler cross-border lifestyle you desire.

A better route for business owners may be to use a cross-border financial planning professional to complete a comprehensive cross-border plan before the sale of a business. If time and circumstances permit, a sale could either be delayed for a short period of time or structured in such a way as to incorporate the necessary means to acquire a visa or a green card. This forward planning could save the business owner a great deal of time and money. In addition, the failure to complete a cross-border plan before a business is sold could mean that both vendor and purchaser paid thousands or even millions more in income tax on the sale than was necessary.

HOW TO TAKE A CAPITAL GAINS TAX HOLIDAY

Canadian small-business owners are currently limited to a once-in-a-lifetime tax-free capital gains exemption of $826,176 (2016 amount, indexed for inflation) if they meet CRA requirements to qualify for this exemption on the shares of personal business. If the proper planning has been done, then this exemption may be effectively doubled (or better) by including a spouse and/or children as co-owners of the business(es). What happens if you have no exemption remaining, you need to sell the assets of your company rather than shares, your business does not qualify for the exemption, or your capital gains exceed the $826,176 exemption limitations? A tax rate, which is currently 25 percent or more in most provinces, is applied to the amount of capital gains not eligible for the exemption, and when the assets are sold, there is often a recapture of previous depreciation write-offs that attract an even higher rate of tax (around 50 percent depending on your province of residence).

So how much tax can those adopting Settler lifestyles save by making the sale using cross-border financial planning tools? A properly drafted cross-border financial plan can reduce this tax liability to just 5 percent or less, using certain provisions included in the Canada/US Tax Treaty. The 5 percent tax paid to CRA may then be partially or completely recovered in the US through foreign tax credits on income generated by a properly designed investment portfolio or other foreign tax credit planning methods. Contrast this 5 percent Treaty tax with regular Canadian tax noted above between 25 and 50 percent on the sale of a business. It doesn't take a math scholar to figure out the Treaty rate versus the regular Canadian rates can save a business owner becoming a Settler a great deal of money. Between the Canada/US Tax Treaty and the IRS's generous rules concerning foreign tax credits, this tax paid on the sale of the business can normally be recovered over about ten years. The result is that a business owner can sell his or her business and pay very low or even no net tax with a full recovery of all the tax credits.

These potentially enormous tax savings can be obtained based on sound legal precedents, but the rules are complex and need to be so highly customized to each business situation that I won't even attempt to explain them in a general guide such as this book. The key point is that business owners should be aware that major tax savings are possible and available. To use a cross-border plan to maximum advantage, business owners need to seek out the services of a qualified cross-border financial planning specialist early in the process of developing their chosen cross-border lifestyle and/or selling their businesses. If the cross-border financial planning professional is brought in early enough, the planning can actually facilitate the cross-border lifestyle process while simultaneously providing major tax advantages to the purchaser as well as the owner. Invariably, the business owner's current advisors don't have the answers to assist the business owner and the family members in doing what they want to do in the manner they want to do it to take advantage of the cross-border opportunities presented.

A good example of such a situation is a case we dealt with in which two brothers equally owned a multimillion-dollar business in Calgary. The younger of the two brothers wanted to retire to his winter home in

Arizona, but a study the brothers had commissioned from one of four big accounting firms in Calgary (and for which they had paid tens of thousands of dollars) told them there wasn't enough cash flow from the business for the older brother to buy out the younger one and pay all the taxes due at the same time. The accountants and company bankers also told them that if they borrowed the money to complete the sale, the debt load would likely sink the business. For more than two years these brothers sought someone to help them through this dilemma. They were referred to us by another client, and within a year the younger brother was golfing in Arizona, free and easy, the older brother owned the business, and because the tax burden on the sale between the brothers was reduced dramatically, there was more than enough cash flow to pay out the retired brother and allow the business to carry on, unimpeded by debt. Without understanding the benefits of the Settler cross-border lifestyle, none of this business transition would have been possible using their previous accounting firms, bankers, and advisors without the necessary cross-border expertise. Now, nearly 15 years later, the older brother has transitioned this very successful business to a third party and used cross-border planning to save several million dollars in income taxes that he and his family are now using to enjoy their Settler lifestyle.

Another client from Vancouver who owned a $15 million business had long-time advisors who were unable to help him successfully retire and transfer the business to a son who was actively involved in the running of the business. With our assistance, he was able to utilize several cross-border financial planning techniques to transition the business to his son, free from income tax on a net basis, and save himself and his family nearly $500,000 per year in income taxes.

On the flip side, we once helped a business owner who, under the advice of a large Canadian law firm, accounting firm, and company CFO, chose to ignore our cross-border expertise in selling the majority of a business with a large Canadian and US operation. Even though we had outlined a plan for this business sale, the Canadian advisors didn't understand and felt they knew better, following their standard ideas for the sale of the business. This business owner paid nearly $3.5 million more in taxes in Canada and over $600,000 in the US above what was necessary. To top it all off, these Canadian advisors, lacking the proper cross-border skill set, developed an estate plan for this family that was, in my opinion, malpractice, as it disinherited this business owner's wife and children entirely if the business owner died before them and before this error was corrected. It was obviously not this owner's intention nor was he aware that his desired beneficiaries would not inherit the majority of his estate.

It is very disheartening to me when I see businesspeople pay such large amounts of taxes unnecessarily because they are not getting the proper cross-border planning advice. I'm a firm believer in paying all the taxes that are legally necessary but absolutely not a penny more; similarly I believe it is important to pay top dollar to get the right advice instead of a similar amount to get the wrong advice.

We have helped many business owners in all types of corporate situations adopt a Settler lifestyle and actually buy a dream house, yacht, private jet, or travel, literally paid for with the taxes saved in selling their businesses; tax dollars that would have been sent off to Ottawa and never seen again. The key is that cross-border planning can provide business owners with a new set of options to help them keep their hard-earned business assets and achieve their retirement goals. Most advisors who do not have cross-border experience will not be aware of these possibilities or even know what tools are legally available.

Business owners who have adopted a Snowbird lifestyle for many years and have developed their businesses to the extent that they can be operated by "remote control" or have children who are now capable of operating the business without mom and dad's day-to-day assistance can develop marvelous Settler lifestyles. They have the option to run their businesses as Settlers/residents of the US yet still transition the business to the next generation, or to a third party. They may also still remain in control and involved in the business by sitting on the board, or as consultants; whatever fits their cross-border lifestyles. They can also loan the money to their children to buy their business and collect interest, free from Canadian taxes as US residents while the children continue to be able to deduct the interest on Canadian tax returns.

For those business owners who wish to transition the business to family but are not yet ready to pull the trigger, adopting a Settler lifestyle will allow a great deal of flexibility to what kind of transition happens, how long it takes, and allows for virtually any period of observation or transition customized to each family situation. At the same time they will have access to much lower tax rates on the owner's dividends, salaries, or bonuses that they wish to take from the business while they are transitioning. The Settler lifestyle clearly offers very useful tools to the business owner that are not available if the business owner utilizes only the Vacationer or Snowbird cross-border lifestyle with the domestic rules on the Canadian side of the border. As outlined in Chapter 9, Settlers can get access to dividends from their corporations in any amount every year at 5 or 15 percent Treaty rates, versus the regular Canadian tax rate between 30 and 45 percent. The tax on salary, bonuses or consulting income can normally be cut in half or less since the owner can perform the majority of their services to the corporations remotely from the US side of the border. The final beneficial tool available to the Settler business owner operating a company in the Treaty environment between Canada and the US is, as already noted earlier in this chapter, the ability to eventually finalize a sale to the family members or to a third-party or combination of both at Treaty rates of tax versus the regular Canadian rates.

OPERATING A CANADIAN CORPORATION AS A SETTLER/ US RESIDENT

If a Canadian business owner wishes to maintain a Canadian corporation after adopting the Settler lifestyle and becoming a resident taxpayer of the US, he or she has a number of options. The departure tax rules noted in Chapter 11 may require a deemed disposition of the corporation shares on the official tax exit from Canada. By utilizing a number of the planning tools provided by the Canada/US tax Treaty and Canadian/US domestic rules, this potential departure/exit tax can be dealt with in a way that it is either totally deferred, greatly reduced/minimized, or converted to a recoverable 5 percent Treaty tax rate on liquidating dividends.

I am often approached by frustrated Canadian business owners whose advisors and accountants have told them the only option they have as a business owner before they can adopt the Settler cross-border lifestyle is to either pay a huge tax on selling their business and/or a very large exit/departure tax to the CRA. With few exceptions, this is totally the wrong advice or at least extremely misleading. Exit planning with a Canadian business requires a specialist with experience with several Treaty and domestic options that can utilize the many tools to design and implement a legal, workable plan for you to benefit greatly from the tax savings provided by your chosen Settler cross-border lifestyle.

Another consideration that a Canadian business owner operating a Canadian business from the US needs to address is that if the Canadian company is largely a passive one earning income from rentals and investments, it will likely be considered a foreign personal holding company by the IRS and be subject to myriad US reporting requirements. For example, the IRS would normally look through corporate structure and ask that you, as the owner of the Canadian corporation, pay tax in the US as if you earned the income from inside the corporation directly; as if corporate structure did not exist. Since the Canadian corporation would be paying tax in Canada as a corporation and you would be paying tax in the US on your individual return, you would not get foreign tax credits on this income in the US because the corporation is a different taxpayer than you as an individual. Fortunately, there is an effective tool to deal with this type of situation, to eliminate this potential double tax problem. The key planning tool we might normally recommend, before the exit from Canada, is that the company be converted to a BC, Nova Scotia, or Alberta Unlimited Liability Company (BCULC, NSULC, or ABULC). A BCULC/NSULC/ABULC is taxed like a partnership for US purposes, so all income follows the owner, to be taxed only once in the US with full foreign tax credits for taxes paid in Canada by the corporation. This unique structure from the cross-border specialist's toolbox, when used in conjunction with planning noted with respect to the exit/departure tax, can provide substantial one-time tax savings on corporate retained earnings on top of annual tax reductions on income earned by the corporation even though the corporation remains in Canada.

Canadian companies owned by Settlers/US residents or citizens that are reporting active business income are also subject to special rules on reporting income. Active Canadian business income qualifies for the reduced small-business tax rates on the first $500,000 of such active business income. Therefore, any business owner wishing to operate a Canadian business as a Settler paying taxes as a US resident simply needs to develop an integrated plan to ensure that he or she maintains the ability to earn and pay tax at the small-business rates for that critical first $500,000 of active income. The earnings and profits from an active Canadian company that are retained in the company will not flow through to the US shareholder on an accrual basis, and generally, the tax to this shareholder may be deferred until the earnings and profits are withdrawn. However, deferring tax on the accrued income in the corporation does not eliminate the double-tax problem on this income unless the corporation is converted to an unlimited liability company as noted above.

There is usually a current tax liability on the income from the holding company, and the US reporting and filing requirements are the same for most companies. With an active Canadian company, and to a lesser extent a holding company, one very good method to reduce corporate income from the operation is to collect a reasonable management fee, which could zero out the corporate net income. The Canadian corporation would be able to deduct the management fee in full, and under the Canada/US Tax Treaty management fees are subject only to a maximum 15 percent withholding tax, as long as the management services were provided from the US side of the border. Care must be taken in these circumstances to ensure the company does not have a permanent establishment by definition under the Fifth Protocol of the Canada/US Tax

Treaty, as having a permanent establishment in Canada will require that the management fee be taxed for Canadian income tax rates. The 15 percent withholding tax is fully recoverable in the United States, through the foreign tax credits allowed by the IRS.

If the actual management work is done on the US side of the border, the Canadian company can pay a reasonable management fee to the owner, or to a related US company exempt from Canadian withholding. Care must be taken when paying these kinds of fees on a cross-border basis in order not to violate Canada Revenue Agency transfer pricing rules. The net result is that income can be removed from the Canadian company without Canadian tax and taxed at the lower US rates. The final tax rate paid will be determined by the owner's marginal tax rate and his or her state of residence. If Canadian salaries are taken by US resident shareholders for services provided in Canada, the shareholders would have to file non-resident Canadian returns and pay tax on the Canadian salary. The Canada/US Tax Treaty states that if the salary is under $10,000 annually, no Canadian return need be filed or Canadian tax paid.

US ESTATE TAX CONSIDERATIONS FOR BUSINESS OWNERS

One final misconception perpetuated by many Canadian advisors is that nothing can be done to protect business owners from US estate taxes when they choose the Settler lifestyle and immigrate to the US. Just as there are many ways to deal with or avoid the Canadian exit tax, there are many strategies to mitigate or eliminate US estate taxes for successful business owners who wish to enjoy reduced taxes on the sale of their businesses or on their business income.

What are the estate-planning considerations of a Canadian corporation owned by a US resident? As we saw in Chapter 5, US residents are taxed at death on their worldwide assets. Canadians who become residents of the United States without proper planning could subject a portion of their Canadian holdings to the US estate tax.

A proper cross-border plan would use one or more of the tools in the cross-border specialist's planning toolbox to design living and/or spousal trusts to eliminate or greatly reduce both the Canadian deemed disposition tax at death and the US potential estate taxes simultaneously. Again, this kind of planning needs to be completed by a cross-border financial planning professional before a business owner immigrates to the United States. Once you become a US resident, the number of planning choices to avoid unnecessary estate taxes is significantly reduced.

Business advisors who do not have cross-border estate and tax knowledge often caution or emphatically deter business owners against adopting a Settler lifestyle to become tax residents of the US because of the burden of US estate taxes. The real fact, as noted in Chapters 5 and 11, is that proper planning and the larger US estate-tax exemptions make the tax paid at death by a US resident substantially less than that paid by a Canadian resident, particularly for those who have estates less than approximately $15 million CAD (for a married couple). Since less than 1 percent of the Canadian population has estates in excess of this dollar amount, it can safely be said that most Canadians would pay lower death taxes as Settlers in the US than they would in Canada as Snowbirds.

FINAL COMMENTS ON CROSS-BORDER BUSINESSES

In summary, this chapter is designed to show business owners that there are numerous planning tools and options, including income tax and estate benefits, to allow the full benefits of a Settler lifestyle whether or not they want to sell the business, transition it over a period of time to family, or simply run it from the US in a more tax-efficient manner. Through all of the incredible new tools for the business owner available from the Treaty and the US domestic rules, near life-changing benefits can be obtained. Not only can the preferred lifestyle be adopted but these tools can allow substantially more after-tax income to enjoy the much-deserved cross-border lifestyle, and provide for a larger and more flexible estate plan for beneficiaries which exempts them from both US and Canadian deemed disposition or estate taxes at death. This leaves more funds for beneficiaries to enjoy their lifestyles, if that is one of your estate planning objectives. In short, you and your beneficiaries get to keep more of your hard-earned dollars and the taxman gets less.

Business owners should not allow self-serving or misguided advisors on either side of the border stand between them and the cross-border tools that can be used to provide their desired lifestyles. These tools may reduce fees advisors can collect from a Canadian business owner, for example, so they may be unwilling to assist. Regardless of the reason, it is not fair nor is it within their rights for these advisors to keep you from your ideal cross-border lifestyle. In fact, they should be the first ones to help you develop and maintain your chosen lifestyle.

Download Kit

Please enter the URL you see in the box below into your computer web browser to access and download the kit.

www.self-counsel.com/updates/borderguide/16kit.htm

The download kit includes:

- Choosing a cross-border financial planning professional
- List of useful, free publications
- Provincial/Territorial and State Tax Rates
- Canadian Embassies and Consulates in the United States
- US Embassies and Consulates in Canada
- Canadian Tax Services and Publications in the United States
- Immigration Services